MONOPOLIES

7 Ways Big Corporations Rule Your Life
and How to Take Back Control

SALLY HUBBARD

SIMON & SCHUSTER
NEW YORK   LONDON   TORONTO   SYDNEY   NEW DELHI

Simon & Schuster
1230 Avenue of the Americas
New York, NY 10020

First Simon & Schuster hardcover edition October 2020

SIMON & SCHUSTER and colophon are
registered trademarks of Simon & Schuster, Inc.

For information about special discounts for bulk purchases,
please contact Simon & Schuster Special Sales
at 1-866-506-1949 or business@simonandschuster.com.

The Simon & Schuster Speakers Bureau can bring authors to your live event.
For more information or to book an event, contact the
Simon & Schuster Speakers Bureau at 1-866-248-3049 or
visit our website at www.simonspeakers.com.

Interior design by Ruth Lee-Mui

Manufactured in the United States of America

1   3   5   7   9   10   8   6   4   2

Library of Congress Cataloging-in-Publication Data

Names: Hubbard, Sally (Antitrust expert), author.
Title: Monopolies suck : 7 ways big corporations rule your life
and how to take back control / Sally Hubbard.
Description: First Simon & Schuster hardcover edition. | New York, NY :
Simon & Schuster, [2020] | Includes bibliographical references and index.
Identifiers: LCCN 2020032883 (print) | LCCN 2020032884 (ebook) |
ISBN 9781982149703 (hardcover) | ISBN 9781982149727 (ebook)
Subjects: LCSH: Monopolies—United States. | Corporate power—United States.|
Corporations—Moral and ethical aspects—United States.
Classification: LCC HD2757.2 .H83 2020 (print) | LCC HD2757.2 (ebook) |
DDC 338.8/20973—dc23
LC record available at https://lccn.loc.gov/2020032883
LC ebook record available at https://lccn.loc.gov/2020032884

ISBN 978-1-9821-4970-3
ISBN 978-1-9821-4972-7 (ebook)

*To my children. May you learn to speak up,
take action and trust that possibility is infinite.*

CONTENTS

INTRODUCTION

America isn't alright. Our economy is working for a select few. Even before the coronavirus pandemic wreaked its devastation, most Americans could see that our country—the Land of Opportunity—wasn't how it was supposed to be. But COVID-19 spelled it out for us in neon lights.

When the world as we knew it came crashing down, some of the lowest-paid Americans were revealed to be our most essential workers, risking deadly exposure to keep their jobs while supporting everyone else. Communities of color were among the hardest hit by the virus, laying bare the compounding effects of systemic racism. As of this writing, small businesses are fighting to survive, and unemployed Americans face hunger and homelessness, while some of the wealthiest profiteer.

The clear coronavirus victors are monopolies, and we now depend on them even more. But in a winner-take-all economy, their strength has come at the expense of all others, leaving the rest of us to battle the pandemic from a point of weakness. Monopolies will make it out of the crisis just fine, but will we?

Decades of rampant health-care mergers made us sitting ducks for COVID-19, with only a few big companies left to produce critical supplies. Masks, ventilators, gowns, reagents—we couldn't get enough because so few suppliers remain, and they have stopped making things in America. Ever since the 1980s, politicians, antitrust law enforcers, and judges have bought into the myth that bigger is better, which has allowed monopolies to take over with barely any resistance. They sacrificed our resiliency and made America fragile.

The policy choices our government has made amid the COVID-19 crisis will shape power and wealth for years to come, and the most dominant companies have used their political influence to grow even more so. Most of us just have wanted our lives to go back to normal. But normal isn't good enough.

In normal times, if you're like many Americans, no matter how hard you work, you feel like you can't get ahead. You race through your days, but you can't possibly get everything done. You keep trying because you don't know what would happen if you eased up. Maybe you're burnt out, but you don't see a path out of the grind. Nothing feels certain or stable.

Overcoming your daily struggles is up to you—or so you're told. You just need to get better at "self-care" and setting boundaries at work. And if only you meditated every morning, decluttered your home, and stopped eating gluten, you'd have the energy and presence of mind to manage an avalanche of stressors headed your way.

But perhaps you have a nagging sense that your everyday problems go beyond you.

You're living in the New Gilded Age after all, a time of excess wealth reminiscent of the late 1800s, when industrialist tycoons accumulated riches off of workers' backs. Inequality today is stark, like in San Francisco, where 75 billionaires coexist with thousands of homeless people. The American government has failed to ensure its citizens have access to the basics of humanity, from affordable health care to a habitable planet to safe food and water. You may ask yourself: why do taxes keep going up—for everyone except the ultrarich—when government doesn't do the bare minimum its job requires?

People all across America feel the ground is constantly shifting underneath them. Inequality and hopelessness are making some people so angry they have to find others to blame, like immigrants, people of color, LGBTQ+ individuals, and/or women. But those with historically less power in our society are not the source of America's problems.

Beneath all of this pain lies a hidden culprit: pure, unbridled monopoly power. No matter your race, gender, age, sexual orientation or identity, religion, class, or political party, we're all getting screwed on a systemic level by the same menace of monopoly. The most vulnerable among us get hit the hardest.

Monopolies pervade our everyday lives in ways we don't realize. When your expenses keep going up but your income does not, when you're price-gouged buying an EpiPen for your child's life-threatening allergy, when you struggle to parent a child who is addicted to social media, and when you can't find common ground with millions of your fellow Americans, monopoly power is playing a key, destructive role. But you can help stop it. In this book, I will show you how monopoly power rules your life and what must be done to put an end to it.

Monopolists of the past who controlled entire industries like railroads and oil were aptly called robber barons because they built their business models on exploitation. I'll explain how today's global monopolies are no different. They're robbing us of money by charging high prices, skirting taxes, and reducing our pay and economic opportunities. This theft is only the beginning. They're also robbing us of innovation, choice, the ability to take care of our sick, a healthy food supply, a habitable planet, our privacy, fair elections, a robust press, and, ultimately, the American dream.

While Amazon promises low prices, and Facebook and Google offer services for "free," in truth, tech giants' prices are exorbitant, but you have no way of knowing how much you are paying. This book will expose the true costs.

But America's monopoly crisis is not just about Big Tech. It's big health care, big agriculture, Big Pharma, big . . . pick an industry, any industry. Big *everything*. Our economy is ruled by behemoths because, decades ago, our government chose to dismantle anti-monopoly laws and policies.

We blame the economy for our financial struggles, but the economy—apart from the COVID-19 catastrophe—has been doing just fine. The problem is that the ultrarich are hoarding its spoils. What changed from the 1980s to today that made the economy stop working for the middle class? A big piece of that puzzle is monopoly. When Boomers were raising their families, few industries were highly concentrated in the hands of giant companies. Now, few are not. This concentration of power allows corporations to adopt business models that are extractive rather than generative, or more simply, they're focused on *taking* rather than *making*.

If we don't act immediately, corporate giants will control more and more of our lives, and their economic power will buy ever-increasing political power as they spend their monopoly money on lobbying. It's now, or possibly never, as our democracy continues to slip away before our eyes. The will of the people is losing out to the will of the monopolists.

In this book, I'll show you seven ways giant corporations are making your life harder every day by breaking the laws that were designed to protect you. I'll share a positive vision of life without monopoly, an escape route from being stressed out, overworked, underpaid, and underrepresented. A better future can be yours—ours—and I'll show you what must be done to get back the power and control that rightly belong to you.

Defeating monopoly is not a silver bullet that will automatically solve every one of our problems, but *we won't be able to cure America's ills if we don't first weaken corporate giants' power*. Like constructing a house on a faulty foundation, building a better world upon the flawed structure of monopoly is doomed from the outset. If we don't fix the systemic problem of concentrated power, our efforts to gain control of our lives will be like trying to empty an ocean with a slotted spoon.

The first step to loosen monopolies' grip on our lives is to become informed citizens. Active citizenship is even more important than trying to change your consumer habits—your power as a citizen is greater than your power as a consumer.

The onus isn't on the consumer to stop using monopolies when monopolies have become essential infrastructure for our economy; often, you simply have little or no choice but to depend on a monopolist. The onus is on the government to make companies obey the law, to protect consumers from their harms, and to promote an open and competitive marketplace. Pressuring government to do its job is the best way we can make a difference.

In that sense, the onus *is* on us, as citizens, to fight for shared prosperity and power. America has always been "about what can be achieved by us, together, through the hard and slow, and sometimes frustrating, but ultimately enduring work of self-government," said former U.S. president Barack Obama in his 2016 Democratic National Convention speech. And as abolitionist leader Frederick Douglass famously said in 1857: "Power concedes nothing without a demand. It never did and it never will." The Black Lives Matter movement shows this still holds true today.

We must demand our government work for the people instead of big corporations. You *need* to know about monopoly rule because that's how we fight back—learning about it, getting pissed off about it, and not being willing to take it anymore. With the world in upheaval and transition in the wake of COVID-19, this is the time to demand the change we need.

Now for the good news: we've already overcome this exact challenge in our nation's past. We have dismantled monopoly power before! We already have the tools, we just need to use them again. Just as we defeated the original robber barons of yore, we can weaken the power of today's monopolies and take back what they've stolen from us.

It was the outrage of citizens that took down the most notorious monopoly in American history, Standard Oil. Investigative journalist Ida Tarbell exposed the market power abuses and political corruption of the Standard Oil Company in a series of articles for *McClure's Magazine*, which were compiled into a 1904 book, *The History of the Standard Oil Company*. Tarbell sparked a citizen outcry that spurred the government to break up Standard Oil and pass important antitrust reforms.

Your awareness is critical for change to occur. In our battered democracy, where our elected officials are beholden to powerful monopolies and their lobbyists, we the people must still have the final say.

Why I Became an Octopus Hunter

I became a trust-buster, an anti-monopolist, or as Teddy Roosevelt was called, an octopus hunter, partly by accident and partly by fate.

I long aspired to fight for women's equity as a career, and somehow convinced myself that law school was the best way to do it. After trying unsuccessfully to get an unpaid internship at any women's advocacy organization, despite being at one of the best law schools in the nation, I decided to take a job at a big law firm upon graduation to pay down my student loan debt. I remember confessing to my grandpa Andy, who believed in enjoying life and doing what you love, that I was going to work at a big law firm even though I knew I would hate it, assuring him that I only planned to do the job for one year. He shook his head and grumbled disapprovingly, "It's gonna be a long damn year."

Like Google in its early days, I set out to not "be evil" in my new role. But on my first day, a partner assigned me research for the defense of a corporate executive in the Enron scandal, one of the biggest corporate accounting frauds in American history. I saved my pennies, sold my possessions, paid off as much of my student loan debt as I could, and quit after one year and one day.

I went to work at the D.C. Circuit Court of Appeals, where now-chief justice John Roberts was a judge. He was personable and pleasant, the kind of guy who's hard not to like. But I disagreed with most of his decisions. In one case, I was alarmed at what I considered a vote to violate a person's constitutional rights. In another, I was troubled by what, to me, was a vote for the outcome that aligned with Roberts's conservative political views instead of the outcome the law supported. So when Roberts was nominated to the U.S. Supreme Court, I didn't sleep a wink that night, worrying about how his lifetime appointment could impact equity and justice for decades to come. Little did I know that the court would skew so far to the right that Roberts would become viewed as a comparatively moderate swing vote.

After leaving the D.C. Circuit job, I struggled to find my place and was on the verge of giving up law entirely when I landed a job as an assistant attorney general in the Antitrust Bureau of the New York Attorney General's Office. Going into it I believed that I had long ago given up my dream of fighting for equity—but I couldn't have been more wrong. The moment I started fighting companies that were consolidating power, now fifteen years ago, I started fighting inequity. I simply expanded who I was fighting for. I was still fighting for women, but not only women—all Americans. The vast majority of us lose power, wealth, rights, and opportunities when dominant companies control our economy and influence our government. Women and people of color suffer some of the worst consequences, a topic we'll explore in chapter 7.

I've come to realize that the inequality monopolies wreak also threatens democracy. In 1933, Edward Keating, a congressman and confidant of the late Supreme Court justice Louis Brandeis, penned an editorial called "Stop the Concentration of Wealth." He wrote: "Justice Brandeis declared some years ago that America, before long, must make a choice. We can have democracy, or we can have a horde of multi-millionaires. We cannot have both."

Anti-monopoly is a cause that Americans can unite around because concentrated wealth and power hurts us all.

ANTITRUST IS NOT JUST FOR NERDS

If the word "antitrust" makes you yawn and want to shut this book, please don't yet! That's exactly what monopolists want you to do, for they don't want you to understand antitrust law. "It's complicated" is code for "do nothing," which is what those holding all the marbles want us to do—nothing.

When the main U.S. antitrust law, the Sherman Act, was passed way back in 1890, inequality was causing widespread discontent. It was the original Gilded Age, and powerful monopolies, like the oil and railroad trusts, dominated the U.S. economy. As he proposed the law, Senator John Sherman pronounced: "If we will not endure a king as a political power, we should not endure a king over the production, transportation, and sale of any of the necessities of life." One hundred and thirty years later, we are once again ruled by the types of kings Senator Sherman sought to prevent.

If you were king, would you want peasants to know *how* to overthrow you? Of course not! Today's monopolists don't want people to know how antitrust law can be used to weaken their power. But it can! And you can help. Let me break it down for you because it's actually not that complicated.

Senator Sherman's law has two main parts. Section 1 of the Sherman Act prohibits companies from agreeing to restrain trade. This means companies aren't allowed to agree with one another to not compete; for example, by conspiring to charge the same prices or divvying up business among themselves. You may have seen the Sherman Act in action from recent Section 1 cases that have alleged chicken producers conspired to inflate chicken prices and drug manufacturers agreed to fix the prices of generic drugs. Not only do these kinds of illegal agreements cost a company greatly in fines and damages, but they also can land executives in jail.

The next part of the Sherman Act, Section 2, reads, "Every person who shall monopolize, or attempt to monopolize, or combine or conspire with any other person or persons, to monopolize . . . shall be deemed guilty of a felony." This tool allows us to go after big companies that use their muscle to squelch competition.

In 1914, Congress passed another important antitrust law, the Clayton Act, following the breakup of Standard Oil. Section 7 of the Clayton Act prohibits mergers and acquisitions where the effect "may be substantially to lessen competition, or to tend to create a monopoly."

If you think antitrust laws passed more than a century ago couldn't possibly address our problems in the digital age, you're mistaken. The laws were designed for exactly the same challenge we face today—concentrated power. And much like the U.S. Constitution, the antitrust laws were written broadly enough to handle whatever the future might hold.

The Cops on the Beat

Our mighty antitrust enforcers at the federal level are the Federal Trade Commission and the Department of Justice. Or often less mighty than we'd hope. Here's how it should work: The agencies receive notifications from corporations that they plan to merge, or the agencies get a complaint, tip, or news report about anticompetitive behavior. After investigating corporations and finding they've violated the above antitrust laws, enforcers can't just declare that a corporation broke the law or that a merger is illegal. Unlike their counterparts in other parts of the world, America's antitrust enforcers must sue corporations in court (and the FTC can bring administrative charges). If they win, the judge will grant the remedy that enforcers seek, such as blocking a merger, punishing and stopping anticompetitive behavior, or, in the most severe of cases, breaking up corporations.

While sometimes antitrust enforcers lose in court, more often they settle their cases rather than taking the risk of losing and spending a ton of time and money bringing an antitrust case. Merger cases can be done quickly, but cases involving anticompetitive behavior can take years. Here's where one of our main problems shows itself: these government settlements can be too much of a compromise and often don't fix the issues that enforcers sued over in the first place. From airlines to pharmaceuticals, I'll show you how this happens all too often.

When the FTC and DOJ drop the ball or don't do their job, state attorneys general can step in and fill the void that federal agencies leave, without having to take direction from the feds. State AGs can bring their own antitrust cases, having state antitrust laws plus the power to enforce the federal ones. That's the beauty of federalism, with its built-in checks and balances.

Regular people and businesses also have the power to bring cases under the antitrust laws. Antitrust class action lawsuits brought by consumers used to be an effective way to keep monopoly power in check, but in recent decades conservative courts have made it difficult for class actions to see the inside of a courtroom. Corporate defendants in the 1990s and 2000s persuaded courts to erect obstacles to such lawsuits, so that an antitrust class action has to overcome lots of hurdles just to avoid getting dismissed.

Antitrust agencies in other parts of the world can enforce laws against global corporations that do business with their people. The European Commission has made headlines for multibillion-dollar antitrust fines against Google (fines that unfortunately amount to pocket change for the tech giant). Europe's antitrust laws have some differences from U.S. laws, but I'd argue that many of the European Commission's enforcement actions against Big Tech prosecuted behavior that is also illegal in America. What has been lacking until recently in the United States is enforcers' political will to take on America's superstar companies.

Antitrust Off the Rails

In spite of our broad antitrust statutes and the antitrust agencies empowered to enforce them, America faces a monopoly crisis. Between 1997 and 2014, corporate concentration increased in 80 percent of industries by an average of 90 percent, according to economists. The crisis pervades our economy: baby formula, where three companies control 80 percent of the market; washer and dryer manufacturing, where three companies control 100 percent of the market; dialysis centers, where two companies control more than 90 percent of the market; textbooks, where three publishers control 80 percent of the market, and so on. At the time of this writing, two of those textbook publishers are seeking antitrust clearance to merge, even though college textbook prices increased 88 percent between 2006 and 2016.

Our antitrust statutes were designed to protect us from kings of commerce, and yet a few kings dominate nearly every industry. What went wrong?

What's right are our main antitrust statutes—the Sherman Act and the Clayton Act, which prohibit monopolizing, restraints of trade, and mergers that may lessen competition. But the case law interpreting these statutes is broken and has made way for monopolies to take over. Violations of antitrust law are not open-and-shut like, say, exceeding the speed limit. When judges apply the law to the facts before them, they make case-by-case determinations about what's illegal anticompetitive behavior and what's legal aggressive competition. Two judges presented with the same set of facts can each come to a different conclusion on whether the antitrust laws have been violated. I argue throughout this book that big corporations are breaking the antitrust laws, but those companies of course would contend the opposite, and the outcome of any individual case can depend on the judge assigned to it. Judges' case-by-case decisions create a body of case law called legal precedent, which sets standards going forward. In recent decades, legal precedent has strayed far away from the legislative intent of our antitrust statutes.

We can thank a not-so-noble fellow for helping create our current monopoly crisis: Robert Bork, a legal scholar and judge who promoted an ideology called the Chicago School of Economics, originating at the University of Chicago. Bork, incidentally, served as solicitor general under President Nixon and fired the special prosecutor who was investigating the Watergate scandal, after the attorney general and deputy attorney general resigned rather than do so. With Bork's help, the Chicago School of Economics started to fundamentally change the interpretation of antitrust law in the early 1980s, convincing the courts that the laws' goal first and foremost is to promote corporate efficiency. What companies gain in efficiency they would pass on to consumers as lower prices, the ideology claimed, to the benefit of "consumer welfare."

But the Sherman Act says nothing about corporate efficiency! The law is about promoting competition and preventing concentrated power. The craziest part? The Chicago School takeover of antitrust law has actually led to higher prices for consumers by allowing monopolies to rule America, as you'll see in the next chapter, even as it promised the opposite result.

This obsession with corporate efficiency meant antitrust plaintiffs suing to stop big corporations from kicking out rivals could rarely win monopolization cases in court unless they could prove the anticompetitive behavior raised prices. And antitrust enforcers couldn't block mergers unless they could prove to a court that the merger would almost certainly cause prices to go up. Antitrust cases became duels between highly paid economists, with corporate defendants offering complex economic models to convince courts that eliminating competition is, perversely, good for consumers. Corporate efficiency became the excuse to let monopolies take over America.

Several decades of bad court decisions have made it harder for antitrust enforcers to win cases. Partly for this reason, Sherman Act Section 2 is long neglected, and in fact, it's so underenforced that most Americans think illegal monopolization is just the way business is done.

Because the Chicago School takeover of the courts made mergers harder to block, decades of merger mania and a massive consolidation of corporate power ensued. Since the 1980s, mergers and acquisitions have climbed, both in number and value. In 2018 alone, there were 19,757 mergers and acquisitions in the United States. This is a main reason we find ourselves living under the rule of monopoly kings. The Boomers, in contrast, raised their families in an economy that was far less monopolized, benefiting from decades of robust antitrust enforcement up until the early 1980s.

MERGERS & ACQUISITIONS UNITED STATES OF AMERICA

gray bars = number
black line = value

Source: IMAA analysis; imaa-institute.org

The current federal antitrust agencies include decision makers who believe the market will cure almost everything, which only compounds the problem of bad case law. The (wrongly named) "free market" ideology teaches that enforcement of antitrust laws will create more problems than it'll solve. But I disagree, and so do many lawyers working at the antitrust agencies who struggle to get approval from agency heads to bring cases. The way I see it is, the market can't fix problems if the market isn't working. When antitrust enforcers and lawmakers don't ensure that markets are indeed free and functioning, monopolies run amok. Allowing monopolies to rule is in fact the *opposite* of a "free market."

The short history of monopolies in our country is that money and power fought the people, and money and power won. Such is the eternal struggle of all humankind. Whenever the people get lulled into complacency and lose their vigilance, power consolidates.

When I Say Monopolies Suck, I'm Talking About Duopolies and Oligopolies Too

Many markets are ruled by just one king, and many others are ruled by two or three. Markets ruled by two companies are called *duopolies*, and markets ruled by a few are called *oligopolies*. Although more desirable than monopolies, duopolies and oligopolies operate in the same way. To keep things simple, throughout the book when I refer to "monopolies," I'm using it as shorthand for monopolies, duopolies, and oligopolies. A market dominated by a few companies is still *not* a properly functioning market, and it's not enough competition to keep you from getting screwed.

When only a few corporations dominate an industry, companies often just play "follow the leader" on prices or divide up business, carving out their own particular niches without robustly competing against one another. Without competition, they can charge you whatever they like and treat you however they want. Now's the time for that to change.

We must fight back.

7 WAYS MONOPOLIES RULE YOUR LIFE

ONE

MONOPOLIES TAKE YOUR MONEY

"All this extra legroom wasn't cheap, but maybe we should have upgraded to the pressurized cabin."

MONOPOLIES SQUEEZE YOU WITH HIGH PRICES

Wait, what? Your airfare didn't include a single suitcase? Not even a carry-on? Why on earth would you take a five-hour flight and not bring any clothes? You've got no choice but to fork over the extra fifty bucks. Next you'll waste money on overpriced food at the airport because your flight doesn't come with a meal, which used to be a given. You'll be lucky if the airline gives you a bag of pretzels without an extra charge!

Your monthly expenses practically swallow your paycheck whole.

Your broadband bill feels like a rip-off, but what are you going to do? You wouldn't be able to do your job without an internet connection. If you're lucky enough to have a choice of broadband providers, the price of the other option is pretty much the same. You pay up. Next comes your mortgage or rent, your wireless bill, and your food. You're just covering your overhead, and you're already running out of cash.

At least you get a whole bunch of stuff for free in the digital age, right? You can connect with friends, have a GPS in your pocket, and watch unlimited YouTube videos. Maybe there is such a thing as a free lunch! But wait, these tech giants are making billions off of our data (a topic we'll cover in detail in chapter 4). If the price for these "free" services is data, how come you don't know how much you're paying?

Lattes Don't Make You Broke, Monopolies Do

Get your spending under control. So the narrative goes—if only you were more frugal with your spending, you wouldn't feel so stretched. You just need to stop buying lattes! Curb your late-night online shopping! Get some self-discipline! Although we all could benefit from less consumerism in our lives, when we focus only on individual choices we become blind to systemic forces, like the monopolies (and oligopolies and duopolies) that are fleecing us with high prices left and right.

Let's start with airlines. If the Chicago School mentality is that mergers end up benefiting the consumer in the end with lower prices, let's check that theory with this one industry that probably has changed during your travel history. Merger upon merger took away your choices and allowed airlines to start robbing you with fees and abusing us all with terrible treatment, like squeezing in more seats that worsen already-cramped conditions. Airlines have divvied up routes so you have only a few choices on any particular journey. What allowed for this to happen is that the Department of Justice waived through nine large airline mergers starting in 2001.

Remember, Clayton Act Section 7 prohibits mergers and acquisitions that may substantially lessen competition or tend to create a monopoly. In 2013, with the benefit of hindsight, the DOJ started to get a clue that airline mergers were devastating competition. Finally the DOJ had had enough, and it sued to block one of these anticompetitive mergers: the combination of American Airlines and US Airways. Announcing the lawsuit, Bill Baer, the then-head of the DOJ's antitrust division, said, "Increases in the price of airline tickets, checked bags or flight change fees resulting from this merger would result in hundreds of millions of dollars of harm to American consumers." On a press call, Baer said that after investigating the deal for six months, the DOJ had concluded it was "pretty messed up," and "pretty bad for consumers." The airlines "don't want to compete," Baer concluded, adding that reducing the number of "legacy" airlines, those with extensive routes and fleets, from four to three would make it easier for the airlines to coordinate prices with each other.

The DOJ's complaint described how past mergers had allowed the major airlines to raise prices, impose new fees, and reduce service. It even quoted senior executives touting these merger-induced price increases as an achievement! US Airways then-president Scott Kirby said publicly, "Three successful fare increases—[we are] able to pass along to customers because of consolidation." Executives' private emails to their competitors exposed efforts to stick together on prices, and the DOJ presented evidence that airlines had matched each other's fee increases in the past. "By reducing the number of airlines, the merger will likely make it easier for the remaining carriers to coordinate fee increases, resulting in higher fees for consumers," the DOJ argued when announcing its suit to block the deal.

But then, seemingly out of nowhere, the DOJ let the deal go

through despite its harsh allegations in its complaint. It settled the case and accepted merger conditions that couldn't possibly fix the wide-ranging problems the DOJ had identified. The DOJ's settlement required the combined American Airlines/US Airways to sell off a number of airport gates and slots, which represent an airline's right to schedule a takeoff or landing during a certain time period at particular airports. Selling slots couldn't solve the main problem of the merger, that four legacy competitors would be reduced to three, making collusion easier and more likely. The only real solution to that problem would be a full block of the merger.

Some commentators suggested that politics played a role in the DOJ's decision to settle the case, as the airlines engaged in a major pro-deal lobbying effort with pressure from political leaders, advertising campaigns, and even Capitol Hill rallies. Baer denied this claim. We might never know what happened, but we sure know how it turned out for us. We all live with absurd fees on everything from baggage to flight changes. These fees are a form of *monopoly rents*—excess returns above what airlines could bring in if they faced competition. So next time you're packing a week's worth of clothing into a backpack and emptying your wallet for a snack on your flight, you can thank the DOJ for *not* having your back.

Your Disappearing Paycheck

You're not just being squeezed through travel. When it comes to your fixed monthly expenses, monopoly power has caused prices to rapidly rise and put pressure on stagnant wages. Let's look at a few of your expenses, the first being your home. A recent study shows how oligopolies have raised home prices. Economists studied 137 housing markets between New York and Washington, D.C., and found most were controlled by only a few home builders. The study concluded that between 2013 and 2017 the prices of homes increased at more than double the rate they would have gone up if the market hadn't become concentrated.

These housing markets became highly concentrated for two reasons. One, a series of mergers between large home builders between 2009 and 2017. Two, Congress passed a stimulus package in 2009, during the Great Recession, that gave billions of dollars in tax benefits to the largest home builders, while smaller home builders suffered bankruptcy. If the markets had remained competitive, the study estimated 150,000 more housing units would be built each year in these areas, with greater supply keeping prices in check. Stimulus bills shape markets for years to come, and congressional decisions amid the COVID-19 pandemic that favor big companies will similarly have long-lasting effects on competition.

As for internet access, fewer than 20 percent of U.S. census blocks have access to more than two high-speed broadband providers, meaning these companies can charge monopoly prices in most of America. A study by the *Wall Street Journal* found that Comcast offers 25 percent higher discounts in areas where people have at least one other high-speed option. People think broadband companies are "natural monopolies," meaning competition isn't really possible because of the high costs of building out broadband networks. But anticompetitive behavior is a major source of the problem. Consider this typical practice: An upstart network begins to challenge a monopoly broadband provider, and the monopoly lowers its prices just long enough to drive out the challenger. Once the challenger has been decimated, rates go right back up.

Another tactic broadband monopolists use is to lobby state politicians to pass laws prohibiting competition! One way to create broadband competition is through city-run networks, also called municipal broadband networks, but thanks to lobbying, nineteen states have laws discouraging such networks. In 2011, for example, North Carolina's state legislature passed HB 129, a law that prevents communities in the state from investing in broadband infrastructure, after the city of Wilson had decided to invest in its own broadband network. Telecom lobbyists drafted early versions of the bill and handed them off to lawmakers, and community broadband advocates were no match for industry influence over state politicians.

Turning to your wireless bill, only three companies compete for your business, forming yet another oligopoly. In 2019, the DOJ approved a merger between Sprint and T-Mobile, which narrowed your options from four down to three: AT&T, Verizon, and T-Mobile. Several state attorneys general sued to block the deal, in a bid to protect your pocketbook. The states' expert predicted the deal could lead to $8.7 billion in price increases in 2020 alone. Roger Solé, Sprint's former chief marketing officer, even said in a 2017 text message to Sprint's then-CEO that the deal could allow a five-dollar monthly increase in revenue per subscriber. Solé added that Verizon and AT&T would also gain from the deal, texting that this was "the benefit of a consolidated market."

At trial, the states produced evidence of the DOJ's Antitrust Division chief, Makan Delrahim, exchanging text messages with the then-CEO of T-Mobile. As the *New York Times* reported, "The text messages show that he played a crucial role in bringing together top executives of T-Mobile, Sprint and another company, Dish, for negotiations." Delrahim's job is to sue to block illegal mergers on behalf of the American people, but instead he seems to have acted more like a corporate deal lawyer on behalf of the merging companies. The DOJ even advocated for Sprint and T-Mobile in the states' case, filing a brief arguing that the deal should be cleared. The judge ruled in favor of Sprint and T-Mobile in a stunning decision that ignored even today's weak antitrust standards, under which a merger from four to only three competitors with projected price increases should easily be blocked. The judge bizarrely credited "the demeanor" of the T-Mobile execs at trial, whose charisma and hot pink shirts apparently convinced him, despite all evidence to the contrary, that the merged company would slash prices the way T-Mobile had done in the past.

The food industry, like the rest, is highly concentrated, a subject we'll explore in detail in chapter 6. A recent lawsuit alleges the big four poultry companies agreed to rig prices and screw you over for a decade, costing the average American family $330 more a year. And that's just chicken! Imagine how much less you'd pay for food if every food category were competitive. Your monthly overhead creeps higher and higher as competition goes lower and lower.

The Illusion of Choice

Even when you think you can choose among a range of companies competing for your business, such choice is often an illusion. You're looking for a deal on shoes online. Should you choose Amazon or 6pm.com or Zappos? Same company. Renting a car? Eleven rental car brands are really a mere three companies. Mega-corporations create the false appearance of choice, tricking you into believing you're in the driver's seat.

No wonder you can't find a deal! False choice means you don't really have the power to vote with your feet when companies treat you poorly or rip you off.

If Au Bon Pain raises its prices, you could go to Panera or Pret A Manger instead for lunch. But surprise! They're all owned by the same private equity firm, JAB Holding Company. So JAB can charge you more or give you crappier service without risk of losing your business. If you switch to a competitor, odds are high that JAB owns them, too. JAB also owns Keurig Green Mountain, Caribou Coffee, Krispy Kreme, Peet's, Einstein Bros., Stumptown—the list goes on.

Comparing prices between detergent brands Tide, Gain, Bounce, Era, Cheer, and Downy? They're all owned by Procter & Gamble. Even Burger King and Popeyes have the same owner! Thirsty for some beer and deciding between Pilsner Urquell, Blue Moon, and Miller Lite? They're all owned by Molson Coors, which owns 107 brands of beer, cider, and other beverages. AB InBev is even bigger, with over 500 brands and 42 percent of the beer industry as of 2017.

Perhaps you are wary of mega-corporations, and their tendencies to prioritize profits over quality of ingredients or fair trade. You support smaller brands like Burt's Bees, Tom's of Maine, and Ben & Jerry's ice cream. But you might not know that Burt's Bees is owned by Clorox, Tom's of Maine is owned by Colgate-Palmolive, and Ben & Jerry's is owned by Unilever. Even I was taken aback when touring the Ben & Jerry's factory on a family vacation in Vermont and the Wi-Fi network popped up on my phone as Unilever! Talk about killing the small-town Vermont charm. Even if these particular acquisitions of small brands may not individually run afoul of the antitrust laws, the illusion of choice creates the impression that our markets are more competitive than they really are and that you have more power as a consumer than you really do.

Monopolies Tax You Like Governments

More often than not, we as consumers don't even know we're paying inflated prices. Take iPhone apps. In the recent case *Apple v. Pepper*, the U.S. Supreme Court ruled that consumers have the right to sue Apple for charging them a 30 percent commission on every app sale. The plaintiffs are consumers who argued that Apple used its monopoly power to charge them more for their iPhone apps than they would have paid in a competitive market.

Like other tech giants, Apple extracts revenue on its own terms because it lacks competition. In 2019 alone, the 30 percent so-called Apple tax, which is embedded in the app prices users pay, brought in $15 billion of revenue for Apple. Why is Apple's cut called a tax? Just like the IRS, Apple sets the rate and iPhone users pay it. Taxpayers can't bargain with the IRS, nor can they choose a different IRS if they don't like the one they've got. iPhone users similarly don't have the choice to lawfully buy their apps elsewhere. When app prices increase, iPhone users are unlikely to respond by switching to an Android phone, so the Android app store doesn't meaningfully constrain the tax that Apple can charge.

When AT&T had a monopoly over phone networks, before its 1982 breakup, consumers were required to purchase AT&T phones to connect to its network. But the Federal Communications Commission ruled in 1968 that phones and devices made by other companies could connect to the AT&T network, allowing innovation and competition to flourish. Just because Apple makes the iPhone doesn't mean it should face no competition on every feature that connects to or could interoperate with the iPhone. Multiple app stores could compete for iPhone users' business by offering innovation and low prices. Apple can charge whatever it wants in its App Store because it lacks competition, but it doesn't have to be this way, nor should it be.

Data Is the New Monopoly Money

But hey, at least we get a lot of free stuff in the digital age, right? Wrong. What you don't pay for in dollars, you pay for in data. Even though it's not easy to assign a dollar amount to our data, we know it has tremendous value. Only by tracking us and targeting ads to us based on our data, a topic we'll cover in detail later, did Facebook make more than $70 billion in 2019. Brad Smith, the president of Microsoft, reinforced just how valuable our data is, saying in an NPR interview last year, "I worry that if all of the data on which the world relies is in the hands of a small number of tech companies, you're going to see a massive transfer of economic wealth."

Facebook and Google have long evaded antitrust enforcement

because they are purportedly "free." But not only are they not free, economists say the platforms should be paying you because your information is more valuable than the services you're getting. If digital markets were competitive, platforms could even compete against one another to offer you the best price for your data!

Tech companies should be paying us for how rich our data is *and* because we're basically already working for them. Yep, you are actually doing work for big tech companies, helping to train their algorithms. The concept is called "digital labor," and we're all doing it without compensation. As entrepreneur Joe Toscano explains in his TEDx Talk, "Want to Work for Google? You Already Do," Google Maps is only as good as it is because billions of us effectively work for Google, taking pictures of meals, adding ratings and reviews, and pinning locations. "Companies have turned billions of us into unpaid machine trainers," said Toscano, creating "a multi-trillion-dollar stream of unpaid untaxable labor."

HOW MONOPOLIES SUCK
AWAY TAX DOLLARS

A large piece of your paycheck disappears before it even hits your bank account, as the government takes its cut. Meanwhile you hear that some corporations manage to avoid income taxes altogether, despite high profits, and Congress keeps giving them more tax breaks. You're contributing more than your fair share, while big companies aren't paying their part.

If you're a parent, you receive endless requests from your child's school to volunteer at fund-raisers, even to pay for basic supplies like paper towels and pencils. What are your tax dollars paying for anyway?

Too Powerful to Pay Taxes

Ninety-one corporations paid zero federal income tax in 2018, according to a study by the Institute on Taxation and Economic Policy. Several companies paid a negative tax rate, meaning they actually received a check from the IRS. That list was full of companies with monopoly or oligopoly power, including Amazon, Molson Coors, Delta Air Lines, Whirlpool, and Halliburton. Amazon's federal income tax rate in 2018 was negative 1.2 percent, and its income taxes were negative $129 million.

"The tax breaks identified in this report are highly concentrated among a few very large corporations," the study reported, explaining that just "25 companies claimed $37.1 billion in tax breaks in 2018." That figure is about half of the $73.9 billion in tax breaks that all 379 companies in the study received.

Facebook is currently fighting a lawsuit from the IRS, which is seeking up to $9 billion in back taxes. Thank you, Mark Zuckerberg, for donating $25 million for therapeutics research during the COVID-19 pandemic, but $9 billion would help the country a lot more. Whenever you see acts of charity from monopolists, know that they give a little with one hand and take away a lot more with the other.

Monopolies use their political power to influence tax policy, get sweetheart tax breaks, and evade taxes without being held accountable. Of course, the problem of corporate power having undue influence on our government is not a new one; it existed before our economy became so consolidated, and it was exacerbated by the 2010 U.S. Supreme Court case *Citizens United*, which deemed corporate political spending to be protected speech. But a handful of companies having unprecedented wealth means that political power, just like economic power, is highly concentrated among the few. Monopolies and oligopolies are like corporate power on steroids.

Monopoly power and political power create a self-reinforcing feedback loop. As monopolies' economic power grows, they buy up increasing amounts of political power. That political power, in turn, strengthens their monopoly power as they use the government to pursue laws and policies that further tilt the playing field in their favor. And monopolies use their political power to stave off attempts to regulate against their interests or enforce antitrust laws against them.

Buying a Heli-Pad for the Richest Man in the World

New York City public schools commonly display a "Buy On Amazon" button prominently on their home page. When parents click on the link, they are taken to a website that explains Amazon will donate 0.5 percent of eligible purchases to the charity or school of your choice, under the heading, "You Shop. Amazon Gives." Parents feel like they're doing a good deed by shopping on Amazon, and Amazon gets credit for funding schools. Meanwhile, Amazon escapes blame for all that it takes away, the billions of dollars that it has depleted from state and local tax bases—the same tax coffers that fund many of our schools.

On top of not paying income taxes and getting paid by the IRS, Amazon avoided sales taxes altogether for years, amounting to billions of dollars drained from tax bases. Amazon got its start by being an internet company where you could buy books but not pay sales taxes, and a large part of its initial success was due to this discount. Amazon eventually capitulated and began paying taxes for products that it sells itself, the "sold-by-Amazon" products. But until recently Amazon still refused to ensure taxes were collected for products sold by third-party marketplace sellers.

When I was working as an investigative journalist, a source shared an extensive data set with me that showed that third-party sellers on Amazon's marketplace failed to pay an estimated $1.9 billion in state sales tax in 2016 alone. Nearly $2 billion in a single year would buy a lot of pencils, snacks, and books for schools and their students. Under political and legal pressure in 2018, Amazon began to collect taxes on third-party sellers in most but not all states that collect sales tax. Billions of dollars in back taxes still have not been collected.

As consumers, we loved buying stuff without sales tax, and we think we're getting a good deal on Amazon, but we just end up paying in other ways—by our schools not having basic necessities like paper towels, by decrepit public transportation making our commutes slow and miserable, or by higher income taxes to make up for budget shortfalls. After starving public institutions of the tax funds needed to succeed, big corporations then point to government failures and push for privatization, so that profit interests can further overtake the public interest.

When Amazon skirts taxes, small businesses still pay up, distorting the competitive playing field even further. The state of Virginia recently gave Amazon up to $550 million in cash incentives to open headquarters in Crystal City. This taxpayer-funded deal particularly rubbed salt into the wounds of local bookstore owners, who had always contributed to the tax base, while Amazon didn't pay taxes in Virginia until 2013, nearly two decades after it was founded. Kelly Justice, owner of an independent bookstore called Fountain Books, told the *Richmond Times-Dispatch*, "I actually voted for people who are using my tax dollars to put me out of business." Ward Tefft, owner of Chop Suey Books, told the paper, "It's like we're bowing down and kissing the hand of the king just to get some scraps."

Back in the day, Senator Sherman wanted to save us from the rule of kings for exactly this reason. We didn't vote for King Bezos. But Amazon can make the nation's local governments dance for it, in hopes of bringing a second Amazon headquarters to their communities. More than 200 cities submitted bids for HQ2, in major efforts that involved elaborate, detailed presentations and were paid for with taxpayer dollars. In hindsight, the HQ2 city tour seems more like an opportunity for Amazon to gather data about cities and their citizens to use for business intelligence than a legitimate search for a headquarters location.

When New Yorkers got wind of the sweet deal their governor and mayor had offered Amazon—$3 billion of incentives—they rose up and resisted. New York City's public infrastructure, from subways to schools, is greatly underfunded, so taxpayers were not pleased with the notion of funding a helipad for the richest man in the world. Nor were they happy that local residents likely would get priced out of their homes as Amazon employees moved in. After grassroots activists mobilized to defeat the incentive package, Amazon backed away. Months later, Amazon quietly announced it was coming to New York City regardless, without the taxpayer help that the company, valued at nearly a trillion dollars, never needed. New Yorkers revolted, showing the power of citizen outrage, but Amazon has reportedly received close to $3 billion in subsidies from local governments around the country.

A company is nearly four times more likely to receive an economic incentive package in a state where it gives money to state-level political candidates than in states where it doesn't, according to a recent study. The study also shows that incentive packages given to corporations that didn't give money to state politicians generate greater job and economic growth than incentives given to corporations that did. This study quantified what we already knew—corporate bribery is good for politicians but not their constituents. Monopoly money only exacerbates this problem because the concentration of wealth in the hands of fewer corporations translates to inordinate influence over policymakers.

On top of taxes, Amazon has used its political muscle to pass its utility costs on to regular people like you and me. In Virginia, citizens objected to a power line Amazon wanted to lay across a Civil

War battlefield to one of its data centers. The citizens' activism was victorious, or so they thought. Amazon agreed to bury the line underground, but the utility and state legislators simply passed the $172 million cost onto the people, tacking on a monthly fee to Virginians' utility bills. Virginia's House of Delegates did the bidding of the tech giant at a direct cost to voters. Amazon data centers don't even bring a large number of jobs, as data centers industry-wide tend to employ less than fifty people.

You Foot the Bill When Monopolies Exploit Their Workers

Amazon is not alone in converting its monopoly power to political power that extracts wealth from taxpayers. In 2017, Walmart had sixty-two lobbyists working to influence the government. Walmart has spent tens of millions of dollars lobbying against things like minimum wage laws, estate taxes, and corporate taxes and in favor of food stamp funding. Walmart pays its employees so little that they make up the single largest group of food stamp recipients in many states. You pay higher taxes so that Walmart employees can live.

In another sickening twist, Walmart earns about $13 billion in annual revenue from the food stamp program, as an estimated 18 percent of all food stamps are redeemed at Walmart. Amazon, too, is joining in on this double-extraction from taxpayers, participating in a pilot program that allows food stamp recipients to buy food online at the same time that many of Amazon's employees receive food stamps, including one-third of its employees in Arizona. But influencing policy that takes from taxpayers and gives to Walmart is only the beginning. Walmart has allegedly skimped on $2.6 billion tax dollars using a purportedly fake Chinese joint venture and has reportedly sheltered $76 billion in tax havens. To put that nearly $80 billion of unpaid taxes into context, the Centers for Disease Control's public health preparedness and response budget is only a fraction of that amount,

$850 million in fiscal year 2020. We are underprepared in a pandemic while monopolists line their pockets with taxpayer dollars.

Tax breaks for behemoths don't tend to result in those companies investing their gains in employees or innovation. In a monopolized economy, corporate profits are high because of extraction—from customers, employees, taxpayers, and suppliers. The Trump administration rolled out corporate tax cuts in 2017 that led to record levels of companies buying back their own stocks, which then led to inflated stock prices. Big corporations' incentives to invest in research and development vanished along with competition because, among other reasons, they can charge high prices and make a ton of money without improving their products and services, as long as consumers lack alternatives.

The same corporations that bought back their own stocks came begging for taxpayer dollars when COVID-19 hit. Major airlines spent 96 percent of their free cash flow buying back their own stocks in the last decade, more than $47 billion, but they still received a $58 billion bailout in the 2020 Coronavirus Aid, Relief, and Economic Security (CARES) Act. We can see the Senate cares . . . about oligopolies. The rest of us are expected to have saved our money for a rainy day, but the biggest corporations can tap into taxpayer funds like a cash machine.

Your Life, Better

It's time to dethrone America's monopoly kings and put the people in charge. We as citizens must demand campaign finance and tax reform, but our efforts will not succeed if we build them on the faulty foundation of monopoly markets. Reviving antitrust law and enforcement and restoring competitive markets will disperse giant corporations' economic and political power, creating the structural change needed for real reform.

If markets were open across the board and prices were at competitive levels, think of how much more wealth would be in your hands instead of the hands of airlines, private equity firms like JAB, Amazon, your wireless provider, and all of their CEOs, to start.

Your monthly overhead would be lower, with competition driving down prices for the must-haves in your life. If you weren't filling the gaping hole left by corporate giants that don't pay their due, your taxes and utility bills could be lower, too. You'd have a chunk of change that you don't have now. What would you do with it? Would you invest it for a nest egg for more financial security? Would you put it toward your child's college? Would you take your family on a much-needed vacation? Monopolies are standing in the way of you living a more financially abundant life.

We don't have to take it anymore.

TWO

MONOPOLIES GOUGE YOU WHEN YOU'RE SICK

"And these you'll need when
the insurance bill arrives."

MONOPOLIES ENDANGER OUR HEALTH

We pay more for health care in America than citizens of any other country, but when COVID-19 hit, we didn't have enough ventilators, hospital beds, masks, gowns, swabs, or reagents. How could that be?

Our government let big corporations take over medicine and kick smaller companies out of the competition through mergers and monopolistic behavior, making our health care markets highly concentrated. Only two companies make the swabs used for coronavirus testing, for example. Prioritizing profits and efficiency, big medical corporations offshored manufacturing and moved to "just in time" production, a manufacturing model that focuses on keeping costs and inventory low and having the parts arrive at the plant just in time. Or in the case of COVID-19, not nearly in time.

The Chicago School's takeover of antitrust law, with its narrow-minded focus on efficiency, sacrificed our resiliency. Corporate concentration in health care put critical supply chains at risk of collapse in the event of a pandemic or other shock to the system. When antitrust went off the rails, it put lives at risk.

One of the reasons why our health care supply chains are so consolidated is the perverse incentives of group purchasing organizations (GPOs), which hospitals use to buy drugs, medical equipment, and medical supplies. These GPOs are supposed to work for hospitals to keep costs down, giving hospitals bargaining power to negotiate with big suppliers of drugs and equipment. But instead of getting paid by hospitals, GPOs are paid by the suppliers, who kick back to them a percentage of the hospital contracts they negotiate. In 1987, Congress created a legal safe harbor for these kickbacks, meaning GPOs couldn't be criminally prosecuted for them. The law was supposed to benefit hospitals, but it aligned GPOs' financial incentives with those of the biggest medical and drug suppliers.

The bigger the contract that a GPO secures, the bigger the kickback. GPOs designate the biggest corporations as "preferred" vendors for hospitals, and get them the lion's share of the business. Smaller companies don't get a real chance to compete for hospital contracts. The result is less competition, less innovation, drug and medical supply shortages, and a fragile supply chain. Research has shown that GPOs don't even get hospitals lower prices than they would get if they did their own negotiating!

The anticompetitive practices of GPOs have been the subject of scrutiny for decades, including antitrust investigation, multiple congressional hearings, and a months-long *New York Times* investigation in 2002, and yet nothing changes. Why? GPOs and the biggest drug and medical supply manufacturers spend huge sums to lobby Washington, but no such powerful lobby exists for America's patients. That's where our voices come in. We may not have the millions of dollars that lobbyists can spread around, but as voters we have the power to remove politicians who work for GPOs and medical monopolists instead of us.

On top of anticompetitive practices that exclude competitors, health care mergers have dangerously put all our eggs in a few baskets, crippling our medical response to the pandemic. When a company buys a competitor just to eliminate it, antitrust lawyers call it a "killer acquisition." An apparent killer acquisition—taking that term to a grotesque level—contributed to the U.S. ventilator shortage when COVID-19 arrived.

In 2010, the U.S. Department of Health and Human Services awarded a contract to a small company, Newport, to make affordable ventilators for the U.S. stockpile, paying it over $6 million to get started. But in 2012, before Newport finished making those ventilators, it was bought up by a larger company, named—you can't make these things up—Covidien. "Government officials and executives at rival ventilator companies said they suspected that Covidien had acquired Newport to prevent it from building a cheaper product that would undermine Covidien's profits from its existing ventilator business," reports the *New York Times*. The FTC cleared the merger quickly, without conducting a longer, in-depth investigation. Covidien had little interest in building the lower-cost ventilators for the government, and it managed to get out of Newport's contract in 2014. The health agency started over, agreeing in 2014 to pay Philips, a giant in medical equipment, to design ventilators for the stockpile. After FDA approval, the agency placed its ventilator order in September 2019, but the contract didn't require full delivery until 2022. Philips hadn't yet supplied a single ventilator when COVID-19 hit America's shores.

Part of a larger pattern, Newport was only one of 17 companies that Covidien bought between 2008 and 2014, before being bought itself by an even bigger company, Medtronic, in 2015. Medtronic has made almost seventy acquisitions in the last two decades, and the FTC let the Covidien deal go through, resolving its competitive concerns by merely requiring Medtronic to sell a single product line. Buying Covidien made Medtronic's stock value instantly jump, in large part because Medtronic structured the deal as a controversial "corporate inversion," where the acquiring company moves its headquarters to the country where the company it purchases is based. Medtronic switched its Minnesota headquarters to Ireland, where Covidien was based, taking tax dollars away from America.

Medical companies' relentless drive for corporate profits and efficiencies have made shareholders rich, robbed taxpayers and patients of money, and built a fragile system where only a few companies make the things Americans need in a pandemic. And the FTC, beholden to the Chicago School ideology that prioritizes efficiency above all else, let it happen.

Medical Monopoly Money

It's not just you—your health insurance costs more and covers less than just a decade ago.

And the prices Americans pay for medicine can be downright shocking. In a notorious example, millions of parents fill their children's EpiPen prescription diligently upon expiration, with a list price of $600. Allergies can be a life-and-death matter, so these parents have no choice but to pay whatever price is dictated to them. Worse, sometimes the pharmacist says supplies have run out. Parents get on a waiting list for when the shortage ends and hope their child doesn't encounter any life-threatening peanuts in the meantime. Even if you're lucky enough that you don't personally need any high-cost drugs, you're still paying a price for them through your insurance premiums and taxes.

The reasons used to explain these high costs is that insurance companies have gotten too greedy, and that Americans pay more than everyone else for health care because we consume more medical services than people in other countries. Plus, we have the best quality medical care, and you get what you pay for, including funding research, which costs a lot. Under this line of thinking, the solution to our problems is to stop corporations from being greedy and convince Americans to go to the doctor less.

But that's not going to work.

Corporations, under current interpretations of corporate law, are designed to be greedy and are focused on maximizing short-term profits for their shareholders. Lawmakers are the ones who are charged with protecting us from that greed, constraining corporations from pursuing profits in ways that hurt us and ensuring competitive markets that get us the best prices and service. They have failed us.

When your health insurance premiums, copays, and deductibles go up or you get an insane medical bill, you probably don't blame monopoly power. But you should. A lot of things are wrong with America's health care system, but monopoly is a huge root of the problem. Fixing monopoly problems alone would return billions of dollars to hardworking Americans—in 2018, the average cost of health care for a family of four in the United States with a preferred provider organization (PPO) plan through their employer was over $28,000. These families pay on average nearly $12,000 directly out of their pocket in premiums and copays. As for the roughly $16,000 covered by the company, it's considered part of an employee's compensation package, and employers ordinarily just allocate less money to the employee's pay and other benefits. With a median household income in 2018 of $63,179, even families who are lucky enough to have health insurance through an employer spend nearly 20 percent of their income on health care. How are those numbers supposed to work, let alone for families that don't get coverage through an employer?

When Boomers were raising families, it wasn't anything like this. Employees' insurance premiums rose by a whopping 242 percent between 1999 and 2016. On top of premiums, deductibles have increased eight times as fast as wages between 2008 and 2018.

Before assuming that health insurance companies are public enemy number one when it comes to high prices, focus your attention on hospitals. Hospital bills make up the biggest piece of our collective health care costs—a full one-third of total health care spending, to be precise. In a mere seven years, from 2007 to 2014, hospital inpatient prices grew 42 percent.

To explain the skyrocketing of hospital prices, look no further than hospital mergers. Hospitals are merging at a rate of more than 100 per year, becoming local monopolies in many areas. When hospitals merge, they often cut hospital beds, and these mergers are a big reason why America faced a shortage of beds to handle COVID-19. The number of hospital beds declined from 1.5 million in 1975 to approximately 900,000 in 2017.

The most recent hospital merger wave has been driven by private equity firms buying up hospitals. These firms borrow money in order to buy the hospitals but then turn around and saddle them with their debt, while often collecting fees and dividends from the hospitals to enrich the private equity owners. In 2017, for example, the private equity firm Cerberus bought the small rural hospital Easton in Pennsylvania. It loaded up the hospital with debt, making it pay inflated rent on the building it had owned for over 127 years. Cerberus then threatened to close Easton in the midst of the COVID-19 pandemic unless it received a taxpayer bailout. Cerberus received a commitment of millions of dollars in taxpayer funds through the CARES Act, even though Cerberus had financially weakened the hospital as part of its highly lucrative business model.

When hospitals merge to monopolies, prices go up. Insurance companies or employers who want to create health care plans have to negotiate with these hospital monopolies over rates. But insurers don't have the power to walk away from the bargaining table, because local hospital care is a must-have for their insurance plans. Knowing this, hospital monopolies become bullies. They dictate high prices, apply those prices across the board to every hospital in their massive systems, and tell insurers they have to take it or leave it.

A study by a team of economists recently found that hospital prices without competition will cost you 12 percent more than one in a hospital that faces competition. Another report, by the University of California, Berkeley's Petris Center on Health Care Markets and Consumer Welfare, compared hospital rates in Northern California, where the hospital market is highly concentrated, to rates in Southern California, where the hospital market is more competitive. Inpatient prices were 70 percent higher in Northern California, or 32 percent higher after taking into account cost-of-living differences.

Who do these hundreds of hospital mergers mostly benefit? Not patients. One study found a more than 3 percent increase in the mortality rate for heart attack victims after hospitals merge. Not health care workers either. Their wages rose only 8 percent between 2005 and 2015, almost 2 percent less than the national average. Even doctors aren't the biggest winners. When the price of hospital-based outpatient care rose 25 percent between 2007 and 2014, doctors' prices rose only 6 percent. Take a wild guess at who benefits the most from hospital mergers, in the New Gilded Age in which we live. You got it—CEOs! Major nonprofit medical center CEOs' pay has risen by 93 percent between 2005 and 2015. The richest of the rich keep getting richer, at everyone else's expense.

The FTC deserves credit for aggressively trying to block some hospital mergers. On occasion the FTC has succeeded, but often it has lost in court as judges accept the hospitals' arguments that their mergers will increase efficiency and reduce prices. To reiterate, the Clayton Act prohibits mergers that may lessen competition or tend to create a monopoly, and makes no mention of efficiency or prices. The perverse result of antitrust law's modern obsession with prices is that competition among hospitals has been destroyed and patients are getting soaked.

Hospitals are buying each other, and they're buying doctors' groups, more than 8,000 between 2016 and 2018. When hospitals buy doctors' groups, studies show that prices go up, but quality of care doesn't. Doctors charge an average of 14 percent more for the same services after they've been acquired, and even more when they are bought by a monopoly hospital, according to research.

You should remember this power structure when you go to the doctor, being aware of the financial incentives of doctors and hospitals. After I investigated a wide range of anticompetitive health care practices as part of my job as an antitrust enforcer at the New York Attorney General's Office, my eyes were opened to the business nature of medical care. I then used this knowledge as a patient. I remember once when a surgeon was eager to put me through every variation of invasive medical diagnostics without much discussion or in the end, need. When it came to the judgment calls about what procedures were necessary and what weren't, the surgeon's interests in making money ran counter to my interests in minimizing my suffering and avoiding the procedures' risks.

Every patient needs to be their own advocate. A procedure that benefits the hospital's or medical group's profits may not be the best decision for your health, so try to get a second or even third opinion before undergoing anything invasive, miserable, or risky. When I got additional opinions, I learned that less aggressive approaches were available to me and were perhaps far better for my overall health.

Fewer Options, Higher Bills

Although hospital mergers are the largest contributors to health care costs, mergers are rampant throughout every corner of the health care industry. Fresenius Medical Care and DaVita, for example, together control a 92 percent market share in the $24.4 billion dialysis industry. They gained dominance by buying up their competitors. And patients pay the price, with Fresenius recently sending a patient a half-a-million-dollar dialysis bill for fourteen weeks of treatment. Fresenius charged the patient $13,867.74 per dialysis session, which amounts to approximately 59 times the $235 rate that Medicare pays. Fresenius forgave the bill after it was publicly exposed, saying the patient was misclassified as out of network.

Large dialysis companies have raised prices while delivering worse patient care, according to a study out of Duke University's Fuqua School of Business. The study found that as large dialysis chains bought more than 1,200 smaller providers from 1998 to 2010, they cut skilled staff, took on more patients, changed drug regimens, and hurt patient health. Another study found a 19 and 24 percent higher risk of death at two large for-profit dialysis chains than at a nonprofit dialysis chain.

Rampant mergers have occurred in every nook and cranny of the health care business. Everything from medical device makers to syringe manufacturers are monopoly, duopoly, or oligopoly industries. Mergers in one part of the health care industry lead to mergers in another part, as companies bulk up to get greater bargaining power to negotiate against one another. Health insurance companies, too, have merged, in part to get more leverage in negotiating rates with hospitals, medical suppliers, drugmakers, dialysis centers, and other sectors that have merged like mad. Consolidation brings more consolidation in a merger snowball effect.

The Villains of Big Pharma

As drug costs skyrocket, it's easy to point the finger at individual personalities, as some pharmaceutical execs are almost caricatures of evil. Take former Vyera (now Phoenixus) CEO Martin Shkreli, a one-time hedge fund manager with no medical expertise, who bought the rights to a drug called Daraprim, which was developed in the 1950s. Daraprim was relied upon by AIDS patients, and Shkreli increased its price by more than 4,000 percent, from $17.50 to $750 a pill.

The New York Attorney General and the FTC sued Shkreli and his company in early 2020 for blocking lower-cost generic versions of Daraprim from coming on the market. Their lawsuit seeks repayment of illegally obtained profits and a lifetime ban on Shkreli working in pharma. Shkreli will defend the suit from prison because, after gouging AIDS patients to line his own pockets, Shkreli was convicted of securities fraud in an unrelated matter. At first Shkreli was free on bail, but his bail was revoked for making threats against Hillary Clinton. Now he allegedly runs Phoenixus from prison, using a contraband cellphone to strategize about stopping generic drug competition to Daraprim. Shkreli "plans to emerge from jail richer than he entered," reports the *Wall Street Journal.* Focusing on wicked personalities, though, distracts us from the structural problems of market power in the drug industry.

Instead of trying to eliminate evil—good luck with that—a more practical solution is to stop drug company mergers and anticompetitive behavior. My investigations at the New York Attorney General's Office covered a wide range of industries, from oil and gas to Wall Street. But the industry practices that disturbed me the most were Big Pharma's. Their ever-evolving tricks to squelch competition directly endangered human life. With billions of dollars at stake, Big Pharma executives get creative in the anticompetitive tactics they use to attain and preserve monopoly power.

The most basic of those techniques is buying up the competition.

"From 1995–2015, 60 pharma companies morphed into just 10 giants," tweeted FTC commissioner Rohit Chopra in November 2019, announcing his dissent to the FTC's approval of a $74 billion merger between drugmakers Bristol-Meyers Squibb (BMS) and Celgene.

Three Republican FTC commissioners approved the deal, while the two Democratic commissioners, Chopra and Rebecca Slaughter, both dissented. The dissenters took issue with the way the FTC analyzes pharmaceutical mergers, and rightfully so—the method the FTC uses has infuriated me for years. If both companies make or are developing drugs for the same condition, the FTC will require one of the pharma companies to sell off the pertinent division to a competitor, and that's pretty much it. The FTC satisfies itself that it has ensured competition for the drugs that both companies make and gives the merger the go-ahead.

Antitrust enforcers should be thoughtful about competitive consequences and not treat multibillion-dollar mergers with huge impact on public health as robotic exercises. This is another absurd result of the Chicago School takeover of antitrust law, because proving to a court that any single drug company merger will definitely raise prices is difficult. Cumulatively, the FTC's routine approvals of drug company mergers have led to a drastic reduction in the number of pharma companies competing on price and is a major reason we have drug shortages today. Plus these mergers cause innovation to go down because fewer drug companies are left to compete.

In his dissent, Commissioner Chopra noted that the BMS/Celgene merger appeared more motivated by financial engineering and tax considerations than any benefits to patients. Both dissenting commissioners expressed concern about the merging companies' histories of anticompetitive tactics and the merger's potential to exacerbate such behavior going forward.

More than ten years earlier, as an assistant attorney general, I saw what Chopra and Slaughter were referring to. I was working on a case involving BMS that seemed more like a mafia tale than the business dealings of a company dedicated to improving health. In 2003, BMS settled antitrust charges that it blocked the entry of lower-priced generic drugs for three of its top-selling drugs, including two anti-cancer drugs and one anti-anxiety drug. The FTC and several states alleged that BMS's behavior "protected nearly $2 billion in annual sales at a high cost to cancer patients and other consumers, who—being denied access to lower-cost alternatives—were forced to overpay by hundreds of millions of dollars for important and often life-saving medications." That settlement required BMS to submit any future agreements with generic drugmakers to the FTC and state attorneys general for approval.

The government wanted to review BMS's future agreements in part to make sure BMS didn't make any "pay-for-delay" deals with generic drugmakers. "Pay-for-delay" is when branded drug companies pay generic drugmakers millions of dollars to *not* make generic versions, so that the branded drug companies can keep charging high prices. Patents are government-granted monopolies, but when they expire, generic drugmakers can then offer lower-priced alternatives. Branded drugmakers' profits can drop by billions of dollars when generics enter the market, so they try to stop them.

Antitrust enforcers have successfully stopped pay-for-delay practices in court, but that doesn't stop drugmakers from trying a myriad of tactics to keep generic drugs off the market as long as possible. In pursuit of this goal, BMS entered into an agreement with a drugmaker in 2006 that sought to make a generic version of BMS's multibillion-dollar heart drug Plavix. Per its 2003 settlement, BMS was required to submit the agreement to the FTC and state attorneys general for approval. After the government pushed back on the agreement, then-BMS senior vice president Andrew Bodnar instead entered into an oral agreement with the generic drugmaker in order to hide it from enforcers. They say the mafia never puts anything in writing.

For deceiving the government, Bodnar was criminally prosecuted. "The prosecutions of BMS and its former senior executive, Andrew Bodnar, should send a strong message to the pharmaceutical community that attempts to undermine the federal government's critical role of ensuring Americans have access to life-saving drugs, like Plavix, at the most competitive prices will not be tolerated," said Scott D. Hammond, acting assistant attorney general in charge of the DOJ's Antitrust Division, in a press release. But in an absurd example of how rich white male corporate executives face few consequences for their actions, Bodnar pled guilty to a misdemeanor and the federal judge merely ordered him to pay a $5,000 fine, serve probation, and—you won't believe this—to write a book about the Plavix case as a cautionary tale to other executives. I'm writing a book right now, voluntarily, and I'm enjoying it! Bodnar did apparently write a book called *The First Question*, but it seems to exist only in case files, not a place where people will actually read it.

Given BMS's decades-long history of behaving badly, the FTC should have thought hard about how its massive $74 billion acquisition of Celgene could enable and worsen such behavior. The more muscle a monopoly has, the easier it can play puppeteer and prevent competition on the merits. As Commissioner Chopra eloquently stated in his dissent, "The financial crisis and the Great Recession taught our country a tough lesson: when watchdogs wear blindfolds or fail to evolve with the marketplace, millions of American families can suffer the consequences." The likely consequences of the BMS/Celgene merger, like those pharma mergers that came before it, are predictable—higher drug prices and less innovation.

85,000 Percent Shameless

For a stunning example of how buying up the competition lets pharma companies gouge patients, let's take a look at how the pharma company Questcor (now called Mallinckrodt) increased the price of one drug by 85,000 percent. Questcor bought Acthar—the only hormone product used to treat rare but serious infant seizures—from Aventis Pharmaceuticals in 2001 for a mere $100,000. Questcor then raised the price of Acthar from $40 per vial to $34,000 per vial in sixteen years. Imagine being a parent with a baby who is having seizures, and the only available medicine is priced at thirty-four grand per vial and typically requires three vials per treatment.

When a potential alternative emerged, Questcor bought it. The FTC and five states then sued Questcor for monopolization, eventually settling the suit by requiring Questcor to pay a $100 million fine and to license the synthetic drug Synachten to a competitor. "By acquiring Synachten, Questcor eliminated the possibility that another firm would develop it and compete against Acthar," said the government's complaint.

The FTC and the states deserve credit for bringing this case, but in the end a $100 million fine is nothing compared to the more than $1 billion in revenue Questcor made on Acthar in 2015 alone. The fine is a mere cost of doing business for Questcor, their anticompetitive conduct ended up making economic sense, and if given the chance, they'd likely do it all over again despite the fine. The penalties for violating antitrust laws are not high enough to overcome Big Pharma's financial incentives to break the law. Bad actors are not deterred by the threat of enforcement, and enforcers are left playing Whac-A-Mole as Big Pharma's anticompetitive tactics spring up everywhere.

A Monopoly-Made EpiPen Crisis

To understand the full gamut of anticompetitive tactics drug companies use to keep prices high, an antitrust lawsuit filed in 2017 by pharmaceutical company Sanofi against Mylan, maker of the EpiPen, is an illuminating read. Mylan bought the drug company Merck in 2007, thus acquiring the rights to EpiPen when it was priced at $100. A decade later in 2017, Mylan had increased EpiPen's average price to a whopping $600.

In its lawsuit that is ongoing at time of writing, Sanofi alleges that Mylan used a whole bag of tricks to shut out Sanofi's competing product, Auvi-Q. First, Sanofi alleged that Mylan, with 90 percent of the market, was able to jack up EpiPen prices above competitive levels. Mylan then used its monopoly profits to give lucrative rebates to pharmacy benefit managers, the middlemen that negotiate with drugmakers and pharmacies on behalf of insurance companies. But Mylan would only pay the rebates, which are essentially kickbacks, if the pharmacy benefit managers and insurance companies refused to cover Epi-Pen's competitor, Auvi-Q.

Second, Sanofi alleged that Mylan defrauded the federal government to pay for those kickbacks, pointing out that the DOJ had sued Mylan for Medicaid fraud and settled the suit for $465 million. Sanofi also accused Mylan of misleading consumers about the safety and effectiveness of Auvi-Q. Last, Sanofi pointed the court to Mylan's requirement that schools that wanted discounted EpiPens could not purchase any competing products. "No traditional competitor puts 'strings attached' to budget-constrained schools requiring them not to stock a single life-saving Auvi-Q if they also want the cheapest available EpiPen," wrote Sanofi in a court filing. Mylan had previously lobbied to get rules requiring epinephrine injectors in schools in the first place, adding lobbyists in thirty-six states between 2010 and 2014 according to the Center for Public Integrity.

Multiple senators and antitrust enforcers took issue with Mylan's exclusivity requirement for schools, and Mylan withdrew it under pressure. But just think about it: Mylan is a monopoly that deliberately excluded competition for a lifesaving product, but then can't itself meet the demand for that product. To explain shortages, Mylan has cited problems with the factory that makes its injector. But the real problem is that Americans at risk of fatal allergic reactions have all their eggs in one basket. Monopolized markets, as we saw with COVID-19, lead to life-threatening shortages.

New alternatives to EpiPens are finally gaining ground, but Americans should never have been in this dangerous and vulnerable position in the first place. In their quest to kick rivals out of the game, pharma monopolists put us all at the mercy of a limited number of suppliers. The FDA keeps a list of drug shortages, and at the time of writing, the list has more than one hundred and twenty-five entries, including epinephrine injectors like EpiPens.

Often the excuse to justify inaction against high drug prices is that research and development is so expensive that we need to make sure drugmakers are rewarded for the investment and risks they take, or drug innovation will suffer. But in the examples of Daraprim, Acthar, and EpiPen, the drug company that raised prices sky-high didn't even invent the drug. The price hikers bought old drugs, raised prices astronomically, and then used anticompetitive tactics to keep out lower-priced alternatives. Pharma monopolists seem to spend more energy crafting schemes to keep out competition than besting rivals based on superior therapies.

Americans Pay More for Less

Million-dollar hospital bills, crowd-sourced funding for lifesaving medicine, and health-care-induced homelessness happen in America, but not other industrialized nations. Compared to our counterparts around the world, we're getting robbed. The same appendectomy that runs about $3,800 in Australia costs $16,000 or more in the United States. Delivering a baby costs around $2,000 in Spain, but even without complications costs on average $11,000 in the United States, with expensive hospitals charging more than $18,000. Hospital stays in industrialized countries run $10,500 in the middle range, while a hospital stay in the United States costs more than double that at over $21,000, even though hospital stays in America are shorter than in most industrialized nations.

We tell ourselves that the quality of care in America is so much better, but the facts show otherwise. Our life expectancy is lower than Chile, Slovenia, and most of the European Union. "It's not that we're getting more; it's that we're paying much more," said Gerard F. Anderson, a Johns Hopkins professor who coauthored a study showing America spends a lot more money than every other country for less care.

And we pay on average over 50 percent more for the same drugs that other developed nations pay, and 80 percent more for cardiovascular, musculoskeletal, and nervous system drugs, according to global information provider IHS Markit. Even if it were true that the high prices you're paying went primarily to research and development rather than Big Pharma CEOs' bank accounts, how do you feel about funding innovation for the entire world? It's sure generous of you to take on so much financial stress for the French, who pay one-third of what you do for the same drugs. But then again, you really don't have a choice when you're living under monopoly rule!

Monopoly Overlords Make the Rules

When judges get antitrust wrong, as they have when they shut down the FTC's attempts to block anticompetitive hospital mergers, lawmakers have the power to step in and put judges back on track. Legislators could pass laws with clear rules that prohibit such mergers or that overrule wrongheaded cases that are getting in the FTC's way. But hospital monopoly money is flowing to lawmakers, discouraging them from taking steps that would protect patients. The Center for Responsive Politics, an organization that tracks the influence of money on politics and posts it on OpenSecrets.org, estimates that hospitals and nursing homes spent $102 million on lobbying in the 2018 election cycle alone.

Congress could also pass laws ensuring fair competition in pharmaceuticals. Rather than antitrust enforcers having to bring a lawsuit every time a drug company implements a new scheme to exclude competition, laws could prohibit the conduct in the first place and bring automatic fines that are big enough to deter the behavior. But Big Pharma spent $167 million last year on lobbying, and 573 of Pharma's lobbyists are former government insiders, according to Open Secrets.

On top of competition issues, major regulatory problems affect drug prices. Big Pharma lobbying led to a 2003 George W. Bush administration rule that the government can't negotiate with drug companies for Medicare Part D drug prices. Other countries don't just pay Big Pharma whatever they're asking. When it comes to health care, politicians are often beholden to medical monopoly money instead of you. As long as voters are in the dark, elected representatives can get away with it.

Let politicians know you're on to them. Check OpenSecrets.org to see if your representatives accept campaign contributions from Big Health Care. Then demand that your representatives put a stop to hospital mergers and acquisitions, and bar Big Pharma's pay-for-delay agreements and other competition-killing schemes. Fines should amount to double the illegally obtained profits. While you're at it, tell lawmakers to implement "Medicare Prices for All," an idea proposed by Phil Longman in *Washington Monthly*, which would apply the health care prices that the government does negotiate to all Americans, even those with private insurance. This measure alone would lower prices across the board and eliminate out-of-network overcharges.

Medical Monopolies Limit Your Career Opportunities

On top of taking our money, medical monopolies constrain our earning potential by making the leap to entrepreneurship even harder. I don't know about you, but I hate having a boss. No offense to the great bosses I've had in my life, but I just prefer to be the captain of my own ship. I grew up with two parents who ran their own small businesses, and I always thought I'd have the independence they enjoyed.

But whenever I calculate whether I can take the risk of leaving a steady paycheck, the cost of health care always puts me over the edge. Not only do I have to cover my monthly bills, but I've got to make sure I can cover tens of thousands of dollars in health care for my family. And then there's the entrepreneur's cost of paying for employees' health care, too.

I know I'm not alone in this. Imagine how much this obstacle to entrepreneurship drags down our economy. A study by the Kauffman-RAND Institute for Entrepreneurship Public Policy Studies shows that those with access to a spouse's health insurance plan are much more likely to become self-employed, and that self-employment rates rise when Medicare becomes available. Increasing the availability of affordable health insurance for the self-employed is important for entrepreneurship, the study concludes. A key to affordability is eliminating medical monopoly rents by ensuring free and fair competition.

Your Life, Better

The days of fragility and weakness in our medical system must come to an end. Now is the time to stop monopoly rule over health care and restore resilience and strength in our medical supply chains and infrastructure. At the very least, we owe it to our health care workers who risked their lives every day fighting COVID-19 without enough personal protective equipment and essential medical devices. Our health care system is fragile and expensive because of policy choices—it's not inevitable.

Imagine if the cost of health care didn't weigh you down. You would know what your medical procedure would cost before you get it done because the health care provider would post the standard Medicare Prices for All in a handy menu, like you get at a restaurant. When you receive an explanation of benefits, you relax because you know you're covered. You get health care and medicine when you need them, instead of stressing over costs. EpiPens cost $70, like they do in Europe, not $600. Prescription drug prices are down across the board. And the pharmacy doesn't run out! When your fellow Americans experience a medical emergency, they don't also face a financial crisis, compounding the trauma they are already experiencing.

If you spent the same percentage of your income on health insurance, deductibles, premiums, and drugs as Americans did in the 1980s, you'd get back the majority of what you're currently paying. Think of all the ways the cost of health care has stressed you out, constrained your freedom, or caused real hardship, and imagine them lessened, if not entirely gone. Much regulatory reform is needed to fix the morass that is the U.S. health care system, but a competitive health care marketplace alone would lighten the oppressive weight that health care costs are exerting on most Americans. And the travesty of 27.5 million Americans not being covered at all, a figure that predates the massive job losses of COVID-19, could easily be remedied if we reduced health care costs across the board by promoting competition and eliminating monopoly pricing.

We have the solutions. We just need our elected representatives to summon the will to fight the power of medical monopolies, and they need us to build a movement of people behind them. Members of Congress who want to pass needed reforms are up against the monopoly money being thrown at their colleagues and political opponents. Yet we as citizens who cherish our democracy must do the work of self-governance. We have to let policy makers who want to do the right thing know that we've got their backs, and we're not going to take medical monopoly rule anymore.

PEOPLE V. GIANT TECH MONOPOLIES

To understand the legal definition of monopoly, what types of behavior are illegal, and how there's hope that today's monopolies can be reined in by enforcing antitrust laws, it helps to take a look at the case the government brought against Microsoft more than two decades ago.

When the Department of Justice and twenty states sued Microsoft in 1998, Microsoft's Windows operating system had a 95 percent share of the market for "intel-compatible PC operating systems." Microsoft's Windows operating system was so dominant that companies that make personal computers didn't have much of a choice but to use it. Microsoft weaponized this dominance to illegally squash Netscape Navigator, a competitor of its Internet Explorer browser, using a slew of exclusionary tactics.

For example, Microsoft required personal computer makers to preinstall Internet Explorer in every PC that ran on Windows (which was pretty much all of them). Microsoft also technically integrated Internet Explorer into Windows so that using a non-Microsoft browser would be difficult and glitchy.

Messages between senior executives showed Microsoft didn't think it could win against Netscape if it just competed to be the best. A senior Microsoft executive wrote: "Pitting browser against browser is hard since Netscape has 80% market share and we have

20%. . . . I am convinced we have to use Windows—this is the one thing they don't have." He added that competing against Netscape to make a better browser wasn't enough, saying "we need something more—Windows integration." The exec planned to offer an upgrade to Windows that "must be killer" on computer shipments "so that Netscape *never gets a chance* on these systems" (emphasis added).

Even if Netscape offered a browser that was superior to Internet Explorer, Netscape didn't have a shot. Netscape lost market share, was acquired by AOL, and eventually shut down. Microsoft's anticompetitive practices not only allowed it to take over the browser market at that time, but also protected Microsoft's Windows monopoly power by eliminating a potential threat to the operating system. Navigator was emerging as an alternative platform around which to build apps and could in the future serve as a partial substitute for Windows. Microsoft was determined to use its muscle to kill that potential.

Monopolization Requirement #1: Monopoly Power

Being a monopoly on its own is not illegal—Sherman Act Section 2 makes it illegal to *monopolize*. Illegal monopolization has two requirements: 1) monopoly power, and 2) a company has "acquired or maintained" that monopoly power using "exclusionary conduct." Monopoly power is the ability to control prices or exclude competition. In other words, if a company has the power to kick a competitor out of the game or to set prices, it has monopoly power. Here Microsoft had the power to kick Netscape out of the competition.

monopoly power = ability to control prices or kick out rivals

The best way to prove monopoly power is through direct evidence: showing a company actually controlled prices or kicked out rivals. In the Microsoft case, there was direct evidence that Microsoft excluded competition from Netscape.

A second-best option for proving monopoly power is through indirect evidence, using market share and showing that barriers make it hard for competitors to enter the market. Contrary to popular belief, monopoly power doesn't require 100 percent market share or zero competitors. Under court decisions, a market share of 70 percent or more automatically qualifies as monopoly power, while lesser market shares can be enough, too.

Share of What Market?

The definition of the market is important. A market includes only those companies that customers are likely to switch to when prices go up or quality goes down a small amount. With Microsoft, for instance, Windows had a 95 percent share of a market defined as "Intel-compatible PC operating systems." The court didn't define the market as "all software." That's because the options for customers to switch to were quite limited. Operating systems for Macs weren't included in the product market because the customers at issue—the PC makers—could not switch to the operating system that only runs on Macs as a substitute. Without an alternative, PC makers had little choice but to accept Microsoft's requirement that they install Internet Explorer as the default browser.

Corporate defendants in antitrust cases typically argue that courts should define the market as broadly as possible in order to make their market share smaller. If Mac operating systems were included in the market definition, for example, then Windows' market share would be lower.

As a customer, your ability to switch to a substitute is important because having a choice empowers you and helps constrain companies from treating you badly. When you—as a consumer or a businessperson—don't have much of a choice but to deal with a company on terms that it dictates, monopoly power is the likely culprit. Competition gives you options. The ability to vote with your feet by walking away helps protect you from getting screwed.

Monopolization Requirement #2: Kicking Competitors Out of the Game

A thriving economy requires that companies duke it out to be the best, not act like wimps afraid of getting bested. The second requirement of illegal monopolization is called "exclusionary conduct," meaning that a company is trying to kick out rivals in order to get or keep monopoly power, rather than competing on the merits to be the best. The wimpy way out of a challenge is to try to stop opponents from even being able to play the game. People mistakenly think monopolizing behavior is aggressive and strong, but it's actually the chicken-shit, innovation-killing way to go.

Microsoft met this second requirement of illegal monopolization because it drove Netscape out of the game, rather than competing against Netscape to be the best.

One question gets at the heart of identifying illegal monopolization that violates Section 2 of the Sherman Act: *If a challenger puts forth a product or service that is equal to or better than a powerful company's offerings, do they have a shot at success?* If the answer is no, the market is not working and instead a monopolist is pulling strings like a master puppeteer, eliminating competition itself.

To summarize:

illegal monopolization = monopoly power + preventing rivals from competing based on merit

The antitrust case against Microsoft sadly came too late to save Netscape. But if the government never brought the case, Google may not exist because Microsoft could have used the same tactics against Google that it used against Netscape. After taking over the internet browser market, Microsoft could have required computer makers to use its own search engine, too. *U.S. v. Microsoft* made Microsoft curb its monopolistic practices, and competition and innovation flourished as a result.

But fighting monopolies requires constant vigilance. DOJ brought *U.S. v. Microsoft* more than twenty years ago, and it's long past time to bring back Sherman Act Section 2 in full force. Power wants to consolidate, and it's up to us, our elected representatives, and the law enforcers who work for us, to constantly combat the accumulation of excessive private power.

No One's Trying to Punish Companies for Being the Best

Bigness on its own does not violate the antitrust laws. The government did not sue Microsoft for having the best operating system or for having a large market share. If a company is a monopoly just because it's the best, and it stays a monopoly by outcompeting everyone else fair and square, that's cool. But dominant companies often focus more effort on keeping out competitors than on competing to be the best. It turns out that once companies have the power to squash competition, they use it. Especially because in recent years the consequences for breaking the antitrust laws, if any, have been small enough to be a rational cost of doing business.

The Monopoly Power of Today's Giants

U.S. v. Microsoft was my introduction to antitrust law. As a student intern at a law firm, back in the summer of 2001, I was assigned to update the antitrust group's legal manual with the Microsoft ruling. I spent a good chunk of my summer poring over the case. Fifteen years later, I could easily see that each tech giant—just like Microsoft—was leveraging its platform power to make fair competition impossible. In 2016, I began writing about how the Big Tech platforms were monopolizing markets just as Microsoft had done, predicting the tech giants would face antitrust trouble in America soon based on just how many illegal behaviors and mergers had been unchecked.

Now perhaps just like me, you too can begin to see how Google, Apple, Facebook, and Amazon are monopolies—and the potential cases against them for growing and maintaining their monopoly power through buying and kicking out rivals.

The tech giants started on their paths to dominance with innovation, but their monopoly power is not purely the result of competing on the merits or being the best. Though at one point start-ups themselves, they now have grown into entrepreneur-squashing behemoths through hundreds of acquisitions. Together Facebook and Google have bought over 150 companies just since 2013. Google alone has acquired nearly 250 companies since 2006. At last count, Apple has bought over 100 companies and Amazon nearly 90. Many of these acquisitions were illegal under the Clayton Act, Section 7, which, to say it again, prohibits mergers and acquisitions where the effect "may be substantially to lessen competition, or to tend to create a monopoly." Google acquired Android and YouTube; Google also bought up the digital ad market spoke by spoke, including Applied Semantics, AdMob, and DoubleClick, cementing its market power in every aspect of the ecosystem.

Acquisitions of competitive threats have allowed Facebook to amass and maintain market power. Instagram built a thriving social network with 27 million users on iOS alone, centered on sharing images. Then Facebook bought it.

WhatsApp too was a potential competitor before Facebook gobbled it up. Facebook bought an app called Onavo in 2013 that allowed it to detect early competitive threats and buy them or build its own versions. "Facebook used Onavo to conduct global surveys of the usage of mobile apps by customers, and apparently without their knowledge. They used this data to assess not just how many people had downloaded apps, but how often they used them. This knowledge helped them to decide which companies to acquire, and which to treat as a threat." These are the conclusions of a British Parliament committee after reviewing internal Facebook documents it had seized from a plaintiff in a private lawsuit against the tech giant.

In the documents, one executive was explicitly worried about mobile messaging apps as a competitive threat, and Onavo data identified WhatsApp as the top contender. Onavo data revealed that WhatsApp was sending more than twice as many messages per day as Messenger. Facebook even promoted Onavo as a way for users to keep their Web traffic private, yet it surveilled them and analyzed their usage.

Lack of antitrust enforcement against illegal mergers is half of the picture, leaving the other half, lack of enforcement against illegal monopolization. Big Tech has been following Microsoft's playbook, squashing challengers without antitrust enforcers or lawmakers stopping them. In chapter 3 I'll provide multiple examples of the tech giants kicking out rivals, which is direct evidence of monopoly power. The platforms ignore this direct evidence and focus on the indirect method for proving monopoly power, using market share. Direct evidence is stronger than indirect evidence as a legal principle, but the tech platforms want everyone to focus on market share and to believe their bogus definitions of what the relevant market is under antitrust law. Each giant tries to define their market broadly, as in "all e-commerce," "all social media," or "all mobile operating systems," to try to make their market share look small and hide their monopoly power.

Amazon maintains it doesn't have monopoly power because it defines the relevant product market as "all retail," which includes every single type of online and physical store in America. But remember, a relevant market under antitrust law only includes substitutes that consumers readily switch to in response to a price increase or reduction in quality. If Amazon raises prices for beauty supplies, the local hardware store is not a substitute! And what are the substitutes that customers can switch to if Amazon raises its Prime membership fees? Certainly not all retail! We shouldn't even need to define the product market because we have stronger proof of Amazon's monopoly power than the indirect evidence of market share—we have direct evidence that Amazon controls prices and excludes competition.

For example, Amazon doesn't just control the prices you pay on Amazon.com, but it can control the prices you pay on Walmart .com and Target.com and all across the Web. And it can make those prices higher. Amazon has forbidden sellers and brands from offering lower prices anywhere else on the Web than they offer on Amazon. After German and British antitrust enforcers investigated Amazon in 2013, Amazon dropped the requirements in contracts in Europe. Five years later, Connecticut senator Richard Blumenthal wrote a letter to the FTC urging it to investigate Amazon over these pricing requirements. Only in 2019 did Amazon quietly drop the contractual terms in the United States.

But sellers have since reported that Amazon is reaching the same ends through different means. Some sellers recently sued Amazon in a class action over its policies, alleging, "Absent Amazon's anticompetitive price policies, third-party sellers would have set a lower price on a platform with lower fees than Amazon or an even lower price on the seller's own website." This control over prices is just one of countless examples of Amazon's monopoly power.

Like Amazon, direct evidence shows that Facebook has monopoly power—chapter 3 will give examples of how it excludes rivals. But Facebook argues it doesn't have monopoly power, focusing on indirect evidence and wrongly defining the market as "all social media." All social media platforms are not substitutes for Facebook: you can't see baby pictures on LinkedIn, and you probably can't keep in touch with Grandma on Twitter. When Facebook users were mad about how the company had allowed their data to be used for Russian propaganda in the 2016 U.S. presidential election, many switched to Instagram—but Facebook had already bought its top substitute. Disgruntled users, however, did not switch to LinkedIn in any significant number. This means LinkedIn does not apply competitive pressure to Facebook, and LinkedIn should not be included in the market definition that is relevant for antitrust law.

People who question whether Facebook is a monopoly often ask me, "Can't people just stop using Facebook altogether?" Well, sure. It would be harder for some people, like business owners whose potential customers spend a lot of their time on Facebook or Instagram, or members of communities that treat Facebook, Instagram, and WhatsApp as primary means of communication. Personally, whenever I've launched a new venture or idea that I want to reach people, creating a Facebook page seemed a necessity, not an option. But the ability to #DeleteFacebook doesn't make Facebook any less of a monopoly. A company does not have to offer a mandatory product to have monopoly power. Anyone could decide to stop drinking milk, for example, but that doesn't mean there's no such thing as a milk monopoly.

Each tech giant provides useful, high-quality services to some portions of the public. But these benefits do not make monopolization okay, nor do they justify the exploitation of monopoly business models in ways that harm entrepreneurs, innovators, independent business owners, and employees. A factory that expels toxic smoke into the air can make a product that offers benefits to consumers, but that doesn't make pollution legal. Offering some benefits to consumers does not give Google, Amazon, Facebook, and Apple a free pass to break our antitrust laws. That they innovated and created something of value doesn't mean we should let the giants stop others from doing the same.

THREE

MONOPOLIES LOWER YOUR PAY AND CRUSH THE AMERICAN DREAM

"Regarding your compensation,
The Company firmly believes 'less is more'."

MONOPOLIES DEVOUR THE FRUITS OF YOUR LABOR

If you live your daily life like many Americas, you're working your butt off. From dawn until dusk, you barely stop. When your alarm goes off in the morning you roll out of bed and grab your phone in a single swoop. You check your work email and immediately start stressing about everything you need to do. You end your day as you began it, looking at your phone. You remind yourself to do all the things tomorrow that you didn't get to today and vow to do better. At the same time, you beat yourself up for not "living your best life" nor getting the rest and exercise your worn-out body needs.

The work-life balance gurus say you'd work smarter if you slowed down, but you can't seem to take your foot off the pedal. Deep down you're scared. What would happen if you ignored your work email? Would you get fired? Could you support yourself or your family? Life feels like a race you're not winning, but you can't stop running. You might wonder if you'll ever be able to retire.

If you were privileged enough to experience a comfortable middle-class existence when you were growing up, you may long to provide the same comfort for yourself or your family. But covering the bills requires a relentless pace of work, and you feel like the rug could be pulled out from under you at any time. What the hell happened?

Work Got Greedy Because It Could

At the same time that prices have gone up across the board, employee pay has flatlined. No wonder you feel squeezed. Corporate profit margins have doubled from around 20 percent in the 1980s to around 40 percent in 2017, while reduced competition from decades of mergers allowed corporations to extract wealth from consumers through higher prices. But corporations' extra dough has not gone to their employees.

Employee pay has been stagnating for forty years. From 1973 to 2014, most employees' pay went up only 9 percent when adjusted for inflation, a rate of 0.2 percent a year. Yet during that time productivity—the amount of economic output that results from an average hour of work—rose 72 percent, a rate of 1.33 percent a year, according to the Economic Policy Institute. Employees' share of the value of goods and services produced in America's economy (known as the gross domestic product, or GDP) has plummeted since the 1980s. The graph below plots the ratio of employees' pay over the value that was added for all industries, and it isn't pretty. Employees are getting a smaller and smaller cut of the value they help create.

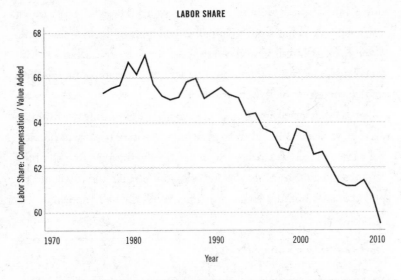

LABOR SHARE

Source: Emmanuel Saez and Gabriel Zucman, 2016. "Wealth Inequality in the United States since 1913: Evidence from Capitalized Income Tax Data," *The Quarterly Journal of Economics* 131(2), pages 519–578.

CEO pay at top firms, in contrast, has grown 940 percent since 1978. In 2018, CEOs were paid an average of $17.2 million, which is 278 times what employees were paid. Compare that to 1965, when CEOs made 20 times more than employees, or even 1989, when they made 58 times employees' pay. With CEOs being compensated predominantly with stock, they share in the monopoly gains that result from higher consumer prices and lower employee pay. As employees have become more productive, the gains have gone straight to corporate shareholders' and CEOs' pockets. This decline in employees' cut of the value they create, combined with rising prices under monopoly rule, is a main reason why your parents' generation probably had it easier than you do—you're not imagining it.

What changed since the 1980s that allowed corporations to share less of their gains with their employees? For one, competition for employees withered, as monopolies, duopolies, and oligopolies took over our economy. In most industries, your employer doesn't have to compete with a lot of other companies to hire or keep you because few companies are left after decades of anticompetitive mergers and behavior. With weak competition, employers can work you to the bone, taking a larger and larger percentage of the value you add. Work is greedy and more demanding because it can be.

Factors like globalization and technological change have also impacted pay, as has corporations' increased focus on short-term shareholder profits at the expense of all else. But the consolidation of our economy under the control of monopolies is a significant contributor to Americans' pay flatlining.

Let's apply the simple economics principle of supply and demand: Your labor is a service in limited supply—the more buyers you have for your labor, the higher the price you can charge for it. When our economy is highly concentrated, the number of buyers for your labor is lower than if each industry included dozens of potential employers (as many did in the past). Fewer buyers means you get paid less.

Companies can pay their employees meagerly without having to worry about losing them to competitors. One economic study found a 17 percent decline in wages when a labor market goes from the 25th percentile to the 75th percentile in concentration. It also found that labor markets across the country are highly concentrated on average. Such concentration "impairs the transmission of productivity growth into wage increases," found another study. In other words, monopoly rule means employees don't get paid more even when they're more productive.

Monopoly means a single seller has all the power, and "monopsony" is the term used for the other side of the coin, buyer power. Employers are the buyers, and monopsony power over labor means one or a few employers have outsized power over employees. Employees get lower pay or worse employment conditions than they'd have if lots of employees were competing to hire and retain them.

Given what we learned in chapter 2 about how monopolies are ruling health care, you won't be surprised to learn that health care employees are getting screwed over in their pay because of monopsony power. Take nurses. Even before COVID-19, nurses were in high demand, as many localities have a shortage of qualified nurses. The pandemic showed nurses are highly valuable, desperately needed, and vastly underpaid. In a competitive labor market, a shortage of nurses would mean higher pay. But most local health care markets have become monopolies or oligopolies, so nurses have seen their wages depressed. Average pay for a nurse is $68,000, but economists estimate that "a true competitive wage for a nurse would be at least $90,000, possibly as much as $200,000."

With high concentration being the nationwide norm, you may be getting robbed, too. Fewer companies in each industry decreases your mobility as an employee, that is, your ability to switch jobs. With less mobility, you have less power to bargain for higher pay. A common way that employees get raises is by receiving a competing offer from another employer and giving their current employer a choice: pay me more or lose me to the competition. But evidence shows employees are getting fewer offers to work at other companies, and this decline has contributed to stagnating pay. The "labor markets where mobility has decreased the most are the ones where earnings have as well," finds a Roosevelt Institute study.

Lower competition for employees is hitting Millennials and Gen-X hardest. The Great Recession of the late 2000s took a toll on Millennials' financial well-being through layoffs and unemployment for those already in the workforce, while drying up job openings for those about to enter it. Yet the worst part of the recession for Millennials may have been that it decreased the number of companies competing for their services. Boomers were less affected, in part because they change jobs less often. The negative consequences for younger generations' earnings are not abating and "appear to be increasing in magnitude over time," wrote Kevin Rinz, author of a 2019 study finding that the Great Recession's effects on competition for employees has led to a sustained loss of earnings for Millennials and Gen-X. This means the reduction of competition caused by the recession may actually be more harmful to younger workers over time than its job losses.

At time of writing, the first rounds of government bailouts in the COVID-19 crisis have repeated the government's mistakes of the Great Recession, sending millions of dollars to companies that are "too big to fail," without extending enough relief to small and midsized companies. Unless the government changes course, the pandemic will further concentrate our economy and have long-lasting damaging effects on Americans' earnings.

Monopolies reduce employees' pay in another way. If you are an employee of a company that supplies a product or a service to a monopolist or an oligopolist, you likely get paid less than you'd make if your employer could sell its offerings to more buyers. Monopolies can pay their suppliers low prices and demand they do business on unfair terms because their suppliers don't have other choices. When monopolies squeeze your employer, your employer squeezes you. The classic example is Walmart, which decimated the profit margins of consumer product brands, driving those brands to cut costs by reducing employees' pay. "Concentration can also affect workers further up the supply chain, as powerful buyers squeeze suppliers who in turn seek to reduce costs by holding down wages," explains Sandeep Vaheesan of the Open Markets Institute.

As monopoly rule squeezes you—charging you higher prices, reducing your pay, and, as we'll discuss below, working you to the bone—our society has become obsessed with "self-care." But this individualistic focus obscures the fact that we are getting screwed systemically. No matter how hard we try to handle stress in our own lives, our monopolized economy is working against us.

Mergers Kill Jobs

Mergers are a main reason we're in this monopoly mess, where few companies in each industry are competing to employ us. Mergers have skyrocketed since the time of the middle-class Boomers' comfortable existence, and mergers eliminate jobs. Take the 2013 merger of Kraft and Heinz, which led to 10,000 workers being laid off; the 2005 merger of Procter & Gamble and Gillette, which was estimated to result in 6,000 job losses; or the 2019 merger of Viacom and CBS, which led to layoffs within a single week and several rounds of ongoing layoffs. The American Airlines merger with US Airways that we talked about in chapter 1 didn't just lead to higher baggage fees for all of us; it also made people lose their jobs.

Under modern antitrust doctrine, firing workers is considered a good thing, and job losses weigh in favor of enforcers approving a merger! The idea is that when two companies merge, they can fire the workers who are doing the same job at each separate company. The merged company will thus save money by eliminating these duplicative workers and will operate more efficiently. The merged company will pass on these cost savings to consumers as lower prices, so says the Chicago School of Economics, making firing employees "efficient" and good for competition. But this promise—that mergers will lead to lower prices for consumers—hasn't panned out, as we saw in chapter 1.

Whether firings are efficient even under Chicago School standards is questionable, since laying off workers leads to loss of institutional knowledge and takes a hit on the morale of employees who remain. The failure rate of mergers and acquisitions ranges from 70 to 90 percent, according to studies. But even if merger-related firings were efficient, they still don't lead to lower prices for consumers.

The Chicago School's gutting of antitrust law has allowed thousands of anticompetitive mergers to go through, and countless anticompetitive acts to go unprosecuted, with the ultimate effect of both higher prices and lower pay for all. "Consumer welfare" has been an effective pretense for neutering the antitrust laws and ensuring that corporate power grows unfettered.

Labor economists suggest that the government's merger reviews should scrutinize whether deals would reduce competition for employees, instead of viewing firings as cost savings that are good for competition. In the past antitrust enforcers have blocked mergers because the deals would decrease the prices paid to suppliers of goods. Enforcers should do the same when mergers would lower the prices paid to suppliers of labor. When mergers kill jobs or lower employees' pay below competitive levels, these effects are bad for competition—not good for it!

Senator Sherman was concerned not only about concentrated power and freedom; he was also concerned about Americans earning competitive pay. In promoting his anti-monopoly law, Sherman explained that monopoly "commands the price of labor without fear of strikes, for in its field it allows no competitors."

Working for the Monopoly Man

Less competition for your labor doesn't just mean lower pay; it also means you'll have worse working conditions and crappier benefits. Just as when consumers lack alternatives and can't vote with their feet, monopolies can screw them over, the same is even more true for employees. Employees already have lower bargaining power than their employers, because they typically need their jobs more than their employers need them, and switching jobs is not easy to do even under the best of circumstances. But when you have fewer options of companies to hire you, you have even less bargaining power. Employers can take, take, take from you, working you to the bone, without fear of losing you to the competition.

Employee bargaining power affects things like health and retirement benefits, working hours, family leave, and even harassment or discrimination at work. Compared to most employees today, workers in the 1980s had a higher number of possible employers. It made business sense for employers to keep their employees happy, with a sane workday, good health benefits (which was also easier to do because monopolies didn't rule health care), and even pensions that allowed for secure retirement.

Labor unions have traditionally been a way for employees to join together to have more bargaining power against employers for better pay and better terms of employment. But as corporations have consolidated power, labor union membership simultaneously has dropped to the lowest it's been since 1964, when the Bureau of Labor began reporting the data. "In contrast to the 1950s when roughly a third of wage and salary workers were unionized, only a small percentage of workers are members of labor unions today—around one in ten among all workers, and one in sixteen among workers in the private sector," wrote Vaheesan.

Anti-labor policy is largely the reason for this decline, but monopolies actively fight unionization as well. "While Amazon has been diligently working to shut down any prospect of its workers unionizing, investigative journalists and activists have uncovered widespread abuses of workers," writes Michael Sainato for the *Guardian*. After Amazon warehouse employee Christian Smalls spoke out about dangerous risks of COVID-19 exposure at work at the start of the pandemic, Amazon fired him. His termination set off worker protests and an investigation from the New York attorney general for potential violation of whistle-blower laws. Meanwhile *VICE News* published leaked notes from an internal meeting of Amazon leadership, in which an executive called Smalls "not smart or articulate" and strategized to make him "the face of the entire union/organizing movement." Amazon workers continued to protest unsafe conditions during the pandemic, as the virus spread to over fifty warehouses, even painting a "Protect Amazon Workers" mural in front of Jeff Bezos's Washington, D.C., residence at the end of April. Just over two weeks earlier, on April 14, Jeff Bezos grew an estimated $6.4 billion richer when Amazon's stocks jumped due to increased demand during the pandemic.

Google, too, has been accused of wrongful termination and fighting unionization. At the end of 2019, five Google engineers filed complaints with the National Labor Relations Board (NLRB) accusing Google of illegally firing them for engaging in union-organizing activity. In a separate ruling in December 2019, the NLRB showed hostility to unions and ruled that employers may prohibit employees from using company email for union-organizing purposes, overruling its own 2014 decision that allowed such email use. Google had urged the NLRB to make this change. With the NLRB siding with Google, employees face an uphill battle in their quest to gain bargaining power against the tech giant. In a labor market that's not competitive, unions are needed now more than ever, for employees of all kinds, to bargain for fair pay and quality of life. But corporate giants' political power is making union organizing even harder.

More Than 35 Million Employees Aren't Allowed to Compete

On top of employees lacking bargaining power, employers are imposing contractual terms that take away what little power employees have left. At least 35 million employees are subject to noncompete clauses that prohibit them from leaving to work for a competitor. A rationale behind noncompetes is to stop employees from handing trade secrets over to a competitor, but noncompete clauses are used for employees who don't even have access to such valuable information, like fast-food workers. Noncompete clauses trap employees in their jobs, and in chapter 7 we'll examine how women and people of color are disparately impacted by these clauses.

FTC commissioner Rohit Chopra has written that the noncompete clause "dries up opportunities for employees to find better jobs using their skills and takes away their bargaining leverage in negotiations for advancement." Chopra added that these noncompete clauses also harm the economy as a whole because they hurt employees' ability to switch to the best-fitting jobs where they'd be most productive.

The Open Markets Institute, joined by a broad coalition of organizations, has petitioned the FTC to prohibit the use of noncompete clauses as an unfair method of competition. After all, the clauses have "noncompete" right in the name! Noncompete clauses lead to lower pay and lower rates of entrepreneurship, as employees are barred from striking out on their own in their industry.

Bosses Collude Against Employees

When Steve Jobs, then the CEO of Apple, learned in 2007 that a Google employee had attempted to recruit an Apple engineer, he emailed the CEO of Google at the time, Eric Schmidt. "I would be very pleased if your recruiting department would stop doing this," Jobs wrote. Schmidt forwarded Jobs's email internally, asking, "Can you get this stopped and let me know why this is happening?" The Google staffing director responded that the employee who contacted the Apple engineer would be fired within the hour, adding, "Please extend my apologies as appropriate to Steve Jobs."

In chapter 1, we talked about how the US Airways and American Airlines merger would reduce the number of airlines competing with each other and make it easier for airlines to collude to charge you higher fees. The same collusion happens in the labor market. The fewer companies in your industry, the easier it is for them to collude to keep your pay down. Such collusion occurs across the professional spectrum. Nurses have sued hospitals across the country for conspiring to keep their pay low, and shepherds have sued ranchers for conspiring to depress their wages. You'd think that tech employees would be guaranteed competitive pay, since demand for their skills far exceeds the trained workers available. Yet even they got screwed by their bosses' anticompetitive tactics.

Beginning around 2005, Apple, Google, Intel, and other major tech companies began agreeing not to recruit each other's employees. The DOJ investigated and concluded in 2010 that the companies had entered into illegal agreements that "interfered with the proper functioning of the price-setting mechanism that otherwise would have prevailed in competition for employees." The penalty that the Obama administration DOJ doled out, however, for this most serious, often criminally prosecuted, type of antitrust offense—collusion in violation of Sherman Act Section 1—was a slap on the wrist: don't do it again. The settlement prohibited the conspirators from breaking the law in the future, which is not a punishment at all. The companies had always been prohibited from breaking the law!

Private attorneys stepped in and brought class-action lawsuits against the colluding tech companies. The plaintiffs were able to overcome the procedural obstacles that courts have erected to antitrust class actions, a feat that defies odds. The court filings discussed a 2007 message from then–Intel CEO Paul Otellini that read: "Let me clarify. We have nothing signed." He added, "We have a handshake 'no recruit' between Eric and myself. I would not like this broadly known." Collusion among employers is often done in secret. On the rare occasions when employers are found out, enforcers need to bring the full weight of antitrust law to bear and dole out penalties that make engaging in such illegal behavior painful and unprofitable. The

DOJ settled its case for zero dollars, while the private class actions settled for $435 million.

Creators and Artists Get Robbed

If tech workers have it bad, the situation for creatives is much worse. "The middle class has been almost obliterated now," Helienne Lindvall, chair of the Songwriter Committee and board director at the Ivors Academy, a professional association for music writers in Europe, told me. These are "really desperate times for songwriters," she said. I have heard this same lament from artists worldwide.

"Starving artists" have always had a tough time making a living, but artists today face challenges they didn't encounter in the past. Artists and creators lack bargaining power against tech platforms that turn a blind eye to theft of their work or pay artists so little they're nearly stealing their work anyway. Google's YouTube pays "$0.0006 per stream to unsigned artists, and a fraction more to those with a record deal," writes competition journalist Ron Knox in *Global Competition Review*. To earn a month's worth of minimum wages, "artists would need their music to be streamed 2.4 million times."

YouTube pays a tiny portion of what other streaming services pay but accounts for nearly half of all digital music streams, so artists have little choice but to deal with YouTube on its terms. That YouTube has the power to set the price it wants to pay is evidence of its monopsony power.

Artists have resorted to using their music to promote their live shows and merchandise, which actually pay, but this option doesn't work for nonperforming songwriters (nor are live shows an option for artists during a pandemic). In Europe, songwriters get a small portion of the amount YouTube pays to recording artists per stream of their song. Songwriters are paid differently in the United States, where there's a statutory rate for songwriters to get paid. The rate was recently raised after years of stagnation, but Google, Spotify, Amazon, and Pandora have appealed the decision.

When Helienne first started out as a songwriter in 2000, she got a small advance from a publisher that was enough to sustain her, even though the publisher had no guarantee she'd make money. "My publisher took a risk in me," Helienne said. Advances are essential for songwriters to make ends meet because they don't get paid until after their songs are made and released. But now artists usually have to be proven to get advances because music publishers are getting squeezed by YouTube, too. Unlike publishers, YouTube takes its cut from musicians and songwriters without investing in their work. Songwriters put in the work and bear the risks, and then tech platforms collect a large part of the pay.

To make a living, songwriters now depend on brand partnerships or placing their songs in commercials or movies, where at least they can negotiate the rate. But this constraint means songwriters have to make music that's palatable for brands. And to make any decent money from monopoly platforms, artists have to make their music palatable to the widest range of people possible. Only hitmakers can survive. A small loyal following can't sustain artists who want to take risks or create interesting art that may not be easily accepted by the masses. Music is losing its political role of social critique.

Internet content of all kinds is molded to maximize its chances of ranking in Google's monopoly search engine, with an entire industry called search engine optimization dedicated to this effort. In music, the streaming business model means songs have to be shorter. In the first five seconds, a song has to grab people with a hook or they skip to the next free song. The album is almost over, with musicians releasing individual songs instead that they hope can gain online attention.

Traditional gatekeepers like record labels have had too much power and have been far from ideal, but writers and artists have even less say when it comes to distribution by platform monopolists.

Musicians can't refuse to be on YouTube because of its dominant share of the market and because musicians' work ends up on YouTube whether they put it there or not. Google has fought copyright laws worldwide in court and through lobbying, as creators—from musicians, to authors, to journalists—seek to have their work protected from being incorporated into products like Google News, Google Books, and Google Search. Copyright protection runs counter to Google's highly lucrative business model of showing people ads and collecting their data while they consume content created by others.

The current legal framework in the United States puts the onus on music artists to vigilantly guard against infringement on their work, not the platforms. But as soon as artists take songs down, the songs often just go right up again.

The digital age is supposedly a great time to be a creator. Anyone can just deliver their art to the world, without having to get through traditional gatekeepers. Kids want to be professional YouTubers when they grow up, and some people have made a great living doing just this. But don't let your kid drop out of school to film themselves playing video games just yet! A 2018 study showed that 96.5 percent of all YouTubers won't make enough money off advertising to crack the U.S. poverty line. In contrast, YouTube's net advertising revenues amounted to $15.1 billion in 2019. Google rakes in billions of dollars generated by the labor of creators of all kinds.

Tech platforms also adjust their user interfaces to steer customers to subscribe to their own unlimited offerings (which allow maximum revenue extraction from artists) rather than to purchase the art from individual artists (which still allows platforms to take a cut). One day I was trying to buy a song from an artist using my iPhone, but I kept finding myself steered to subscribe to Apple Music. Later that same day, I was trying to buy an individual book that was only available on Amazon, but Amazon kept channeling me to their subscription service, Kindle Unlimited. The pushes and nudges that platforms give to manipulate our behavior are called "dark patterns." These particular dark patterns are all about channeling the maximum amount of profits to the platform instead of the artist.

Digitization has helped YouTube frame their ads and surveillance around the work of others, work that used to be tangible, not digital. I'm a child of the 1980s, when buying an album was a big deal. Stores gave us clear visual cues that music wasn't to be stolen—cassette tapes were kept in long plastic anti-theft contraptions. The checkout clerk had a tool to unlock the device and liberate the cassette. I remember saving up my allowance to buy my first album. I headed off to Kmart with my family to buy Olivia Newton John's *Physical*, but my older brother convinced me to get Men at Work's *Business as Usual* instead. I immediately had buyer's remorse, but regardless of which album I chose, I fully expected that a good chunk of my hard-earned allowance money was going to the artist whose music I was buying.

I'm not suggesting we go back to the days of cassette tapes, but I am suggesting that we loosen the power of dominant gatekeepers like YouTube. If competition existed, musicians could say no to You-Tube and platforms would have to compete to list musicians' songs by compensating them appropriately. Weakened monopoly power would translate to weakened political power and less influence over copyright law. Antitrust enforcement is more important than ever to make sure creators and makers of all kinds reap the fruits of their labor.

Musicians' and artists' organizations agree, and they have made antitrust enforcement a top priority. The Future of Music Coalition wrote in 2019, "Musicians have experienced ownership consolidation in nearly every part of our industry and in adjacent industries, and it interferes with our ability to reach audiences and be fairly compensated for their creativity and labor." Thus it's time for "fresh thinking and revitalized anti-trust enforcement at the Federal Trade Commission and Dept of Justice."

If today's robber barons are decimating the earnings of employees and creators, perhaps the best path to financial success is through entrepreneurship, you might think. But even entrepreneurs aren't safe from monopolists' tentacles.

MONOPOLIES CRUSH THE AMERICAN DREAM

Innovation Graveyards

In the early 1990s, Lillian Salerno and her business partner, Thomas Shaw, wanted to help people during the AIDS crisis. Lillian's friend was dying from HIV, and a twenty-four-year-old woman in her and Thomas's office contracted HIV from a boyfriend who was an injection drug user. So Lillian and Thomas called up the National Institutes of Health (NIH) and asked how they could make a difference. In Lillian's words, the NIH told her: "You know, we've got a real problem. The standard disposable syringe is a bad device in an AIDS epidemic because people reuse syringes, and nurses are frightened to treat AIDS patients because they are worried about contracting HIV. And the biggest manufacturer—Becton, Dickinson—they have no one working on this."

Thomas, a civil and structural engineer, bought a bunch of syringes from the local pharmacy and started throwing them at a dartboard to test them out. Lillian and Thomas began working with the county hospital in Dallas, Texas, that at that time had a staggering three full floors of HIV-positive patients. If nurses were scared to treat AIDS patients, Lillian and Thomas then asked them what they wanted from a syringe. Over a four-year period, Thomas invented a retractable syringe that would protect nurses from accidental needle sticks. But as Lillian explains it, their small company, Retractable Technologies Inc. (RTI), couldn't get its syringe into hospitals because a huge corporation,

Becton, Dickinson & Company, controlled more than 80 percent of the syringe market and blocked RTI's lifesaving devices at every turn.

Lillian tried to sell RTI's retractable syringes, which she says nurses overwhelmingly preferred to standard syringes, to hospitals and clinics. But she was dumbfounded that so many facilities were in long-term sole-supply contracts with Becton, Dickinson.

Lillian, an attorney, went to D.C. to ask the antitrust agencies for help. But because of Chicago School thinking, the agencies told her, in Lillian's words: "Lillian, it's about pricing. . . . We need these guys who are real big. They make a lot of stuff and we can get our costs down." Lillian would respond, "At the expense of who? Of the nurses who are treating HIV patients? Or the fourteen-year-old . . . who now has HIV instead of just being a drug addict?"

When antitrust enforcers and lawmakers failed to act, Lillian and Thomas took matters into their own hands. RTI sued Becton, Dickinson in 2001 for unfair competition. Becton settled the case for $100 million in 2004. But Becton continued to use anticompetitive tactics, so RTI sued Becton again in 2007. After a trial, the jury found that Becton had illegally attempted to monopolize the safety syringe market. The jury found that Becton engaged in false advertising that disparaged RTI's syringes and praised its own, including an untruthful claim that Becton's syringes had the "World's Sharpest Needle." An internal document presented at trial showed that Becton viewed this false claim as necessary to avoid losing market share, and to preserve the "10–30% price premium" that Becton enjoyed over the competition.

The jury awarded RTI $113 million in damages. That amount was then tripled—drafters of the Sherman Act thought deterring antitrust violations was so important that all damages must be multiplied by three.

Lillian and Thomas spent the better part of more than twenty years mired in litigation to try to bring their syringe to market, asking for help from their congressional delegations, the FTC, and the DOJ. "We've been denied every time," said Lillian.

The biggest harm of Becton's illegal behavior, however, was not revenue RTI lost because of illegal monopolization. Becton's "attempted monopolization of the safety syringe market injured the public by limiting the marketplace's access to retractable syringes," said the court, noting that Becton's practices limited innovation. "Innovation and market competition go hand-in-hand, and antitrust laws protect both," said the judge.

Health care monopolies, then, are not only gouging you on price. They're also creating innovation graveyards, depriving you and your family of the best medical solutions that the smartest minds, like Lillian and Thomas, have to offer. Allowing giants to rule based on a myth of low pricing—Becton's internal documents showed they charged higher prices—is not good for consumers. What's best for consumers and innovation is merit-based competition.

Like Lillian and Thomas, entrepreneurs across America are getting crushed by monopolies that have the power to shut them out of markets, copy their innovations, and compete unfairly. Investors know this and won't fund new ideas that tread on monopolists' turf. Even if you never aspired to entrepreneurship, all this dream-killing sucks for you, too. On top of making less money because fewer companies can get off the ground and compete to hire you, you miss out on innovation that would make your life better. You don't know it because these innovations never see the light of day.

When I was a journalist, I once investigated a merger of two companies that made cable boxes for TV. I was stunned to learn that cable engineers had been creating highly innovative cable boxes for years, but cable companies refused to roll them out! The high-tech boxes collected dust in innovation graveyards because cable companies knew they'd have to provide the boxes to customers once word got out of the improved version, and the cost of providing new higher-tech boxes to their customers would cut into their profit margins. Cable companies had a gravy train going, charging customers excessive monthly rental fees for cable boxes that looked like they were built in the 1960s. No need to invest in improving the product when there's so little competition!

Consumers only benefited from new innovative cable boxes when Netflix came along and competed against cable. Without competition, new innovations—from syringes that save lives to high-tech cable boxes that make lives just a little bit better—meet untimely deaths.

Dynamism Lost

With giant corporations across the country squashing innovators like Lillian and Thomas, entrepreneurship has plummeted. While our society has heralded the young geniuses who dropped out of college to build in their garages what have since become tech giants, they have in turn shut out opportunities for other aspiring entrepreneurs. Google, Apple, and Amazon are more than twenty years old, Facebook is more than fifteen years old, and all four have dominated their respective arenas for more than a decade.

Big Tech is only the beginning, and entrepreneurship is suffering across the economy. The share of employment accounted for by new companies has dropped by almost 30 percent over the last thirty years. And the share of companies less than a year old has declined by almost a half since 1980. Such a decline hurts both job creation and innovation.

"[T]he great burst of business activity in the 1980s and '90s was to a significant extent the result of actions taken by the federal government during previous decades of anti-trust enforcement," write Barry

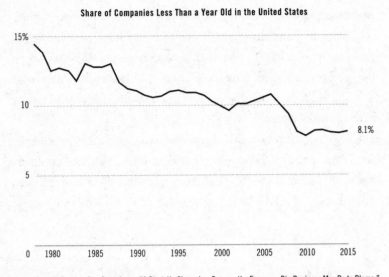

Share of Companies Less Than a Year Old in the United States

Source: Census Bureau; Ben Casselman, "A Start-Up Slump is a Drag on the Economy. Big Business May Be to Blame," *New York Times*, September 20, 2017.

Lynn and Phillip Longman of Open Markets Institute. So when antitrust went off the rails, starting in the early 1980s, the ability for future generations to succeed as entrepreneurs took a hit. A main goal of antitrust law is to stop established companies from shutting out entrepreneurs and smaller companies with new ideas. If entrepreneurs bring their hard work and the best ideas, products, and services forward, an open and freely competitive market should reward them with success and prosperity. This is the American dream.

As late Supreme Court justice Thurgood Marshall once wrote, the antitrust laws "are as important to the preservation of economic freedom and our free-enterprise system as the Bill of Rights is to the protection of our fundamental personal freedoms." He continued, "And the freedom guaranteed each and every business, no matter how small, is the freedom to compete—to assert with vigor, imagination, devotion, and ingenuity whatever economic muscle it can muster."

Squashing entrepreneurs by monopolizing markets is not just a terrible mess we've found ourselves in—it's illegal! We can begin to invigorate the American dream and help restore the engine of our economy if we strongly enforce the antitrust laws again.

Technological change can explain the decline of new businesses in some industries, like manufacturing and physical retail stores, but entrepreneurship in the tech sector has also declined. The number of businesses that are not at the mercy of Big Tech is declining every day, as the giants continue to expand into, or become gatekeepers for, almost all industries—including yours, most likely.

Tech Monopolies Prey on Entrepreneurs

The tech giants are following Microsoft's playbook, leveraging what I call "platform privilege"—the incentive and ability to favor their own goods and services over those of competitors that depend on their platforms. In antitrust speak, this behavior could also be called "monopoly leveraging," which means using monopoly power in an anticompetitive manner to create a dangerous probability of monopolizing a second market, another type of antitrust case that the Chicago School has made harder to win. Platform privilege means that competitors don't get a fair shot because the platform monopolists get to both play the game and control it, too.

Because Google, Amazon, Facebook, and Apple each have monopoly power and engage in exclusionary conduct to acquire or maintain that power, I believe that each platform is illegally monopolizing in violation of Section 2 of the Sherman Act. This is bad for every entrepreneur—bad for those who must rely on their services, and bad for those who create an innovative product or service only to see it stolen from them or choked off in favor of a product owned by the platforms. This distorted playing field strikes at the heart of the American dream, and it deprives consumers of the choice, innovation, and quality that come from real competition. Companies of all sizes can get decimated at the will of the kings of tech, so your livelihood is at risk even if you're an employee.

Google's Don't Be Evil

Google is not a single monopoly, but rather has monopolies in multiple markets. Google Search accounts for approximately 92 percent of internet search globally, and Google Android accounts for more than 85 percent of the world's smartphones. In 2019, Google's ad revenue alone was nearly $135 billion. Google has seven products with more than a billion users each:

1. Search
2. Android
3. Chrome
4. YouTube
5. Maps
6. Gmail
7. Google Play

Just as Microsoft used its monopoly in PC operating systems to kick Netscape out of the competition in internet browsers, Google used its monopoly power in mobile operating systems to kick out entrepreneurial makers of mobile apps. The European Commission fined Google $5 billion in July 2017 for abusing its dominance—the European equivalent of monopolization—by requiring phone makers using Android, with its 80 percent market share in Europe, to pre-install Google's apps, like Google Search, Chrome, Gmail, YouTube, and Maps. The commission ordered Google to stop its anticompetitive contracts in Europe and to offer consumers a choice of what apps are installed on their phones, and Google has appealed.

Just like the PC makers dealing with Microsoft, phone makers

didn't have the power to disobey Google's anticompetitive requirements because they lacked a viable alternative for an operating system.
Google's anticompetitive exclusion of competition allowed Google
to extend its monopoly power in Search and Chrome on computer
desktops into phones as the world went mobile. Entrepreneurs who
wanted to challenge any of a suite of Google apps didn't have a shot
at getting pre-installed in 85 percent of the world's phones.

Android users could still install competing apps after they got
their phones, but users don't tend to do that when they already have
the same type of app on their phone, a phenomenon known as default
bias. Default bias is so powerful that Google paid Apple $12 billion
in 2019, according to Goldman Sachs estimates, to be the default
search engine on Apple devices, like iPhones, iPads, Apple Watches,
and Macs.

Search is what Google is most known for, and its monopoly in
this area has given it control over the internet itself, disadvantaging
entrepreneurs and creators of all stripes.

At a House Judiciary Subcommittee hearing in summer of 2019,
Google was asked if it's true that less than 50 percent of total U.S.
mobile and desktop Google searches result in clicks to non-Google
websites, as research had shown. When Google's representative gave
an unclear answer, the subcommittee followed up with written questions that requested a "yes or no" answer and even provided check
boxes. Google ignored the "yes or no" instruction, and responded by
saying, among other things, that Google has "long sent large amounts
of traffic to other sites." But in the same letter, Google answered a
different follow-up question with a straightforward "no," making its
failure to answer this question with a "no" telling. The subcommittee
is still investigating the issue at time of writing. With over 90 percent
of search market share worldwide, sending such a large percentage of
traffic to its own sites amounts to Google colonizing the internet—
and the flow of information around the globe.

Google's control of internet traffic means nearly any entrepreneur could get crushed if Google decides to enter their market. Husband-and-wife pair Adam and Shivaun Raff, founders of a Britain-based service called Foundem that helps consumers compare products when shopping online, met this exact fate.

In 2017, eight years after the Raffs filed a complaint, the commission fined Google $2.7 billion for abuse of dominance, finding that Google buried its competitors in the comparison shopping market on page four, on average, of Google search results. The commission ordered Google to treat its competitors equally as it treats itself in search.

Google has made changes but the Raffs say Google is still not complying with the European Commission's requirement of equal treatment. Google has also been accused of prioritizing its own reviews, maps, images, and travel booking services in its search results, excluding competition in what are collectively called "vertical search" markets. Google has rejected claims that it uses its muscle to crush competitors, and has appealed the decision.

Google's platform privilege doesn't just destroy the dreams of entrepreneurs; it also means you are getting worse service and less innovation as a consumer. "The Commission is concerned that users do not necessarily see the most relevant results in response to queries—this is to the detriment of consumers and rival comparison shopping services, as well as stifling innovation," read a European Commission press release about the Google comparison shopping case. One study concluded that Google degraded its search quality results in order to prioritize its own services or content that keeps users on Google search pages.

And the requirement that entrepreneurs and businesses of all sizes pay Google to appear at the top of searches for their business name is effectively a tax, which wouldn't be necessary if Google consistently delivered the most relevant results. A small tech company called Basecamp pays upwards of $72,000 a year on Google ads just to be a top result when people search for its trademarked name. One of the few companies outspoken about Google's monopoly power, Basecamp runs the below ad copy:

> **Basecamp.com | We don't want to run this ad.**   ⓘ
> [Ad] www.basecamp.com
>
> We're the #1 result, but this site lets companies advertise against us using our brand. So here we are. A small, independent co. forced to pay ransom to a giant tech company.

Back in the early 2010s, the United States also investigated Google for monopolization, but it did not take action. An FTC staff memo on the investigation that was mistakenly released and then obtained by the *Wall Street Journal* said that Google's "conduct has resulted—and will result—in real harm to consumers and to innovation in the online search and advertising markets." The staff recommended the FTC sue Google, but the FTC's Bureau of Economics, composed of economists trained in Chicago School ideology, had recommended against it. We don't know why the FTC dropped the case. Many also suspect that politics may have played a role, even though the FTC is supposed to be an independent agency.

A 2016 article written by David Dayen for the *Intercept* called "The Android Administration" detailed the close ties between the Obama administration and Google. "Google representatives attended White House meetings more than once a week, on average, from the beginning of Obama's presidency through October 2015," wrote Dayen. "Nearly 250 people have shuttled from government service to Google employment or vice versa over the course of his administration."

Six years after the FTC's initial Google Search investigation, Google's use of platform privilege has not subsided and has grown.

The FTC and DOJ, fifty-one states and territories, and the House Judiciary Antitrust Subcommittee are all investigating Google at the time of this writing.

Digital Advertising Is a Googlopoly

In 2007, Brian O'Kelley founded AppNexus, a software company that helped companies buy ads on the internet. His company was a huge success, valued at $1.2 billion in 2014. Then Google kicked AppNexus out of the game, prohibiting companies from buying ads on YouTube using outside software like theirs. Because of YouTube's monopoly power over video, O'Kelley could no longer offer customers access to the vast majority of online video advertising. "It's not a supply-and-demand problem. It's a 'You just broke our entire business' problem," O'Kelley told *Bloomberg*.

The European Commission has fined Google nearly $1.5 billion for abusing its dominance in the market for the brokering of online search advertising. Like the other two Commission decisions, Google has appealed.

Google has far-reaching monopoly power in digital advertising because it acquired every spoke of the ecosystem, while exercising platform privilege. In 2007, when Google bought DoubleClick, a marketplace for buying and selling digital advertising, the FTC did only a cursory investigation and cleared the deal. But one FTC Commissioner at the time, Pamela Jones Harbour, dissented. Her predictions about how the merger could harm competition and threaten privacy have since come true.

"I am convinced that the combination of Google and Double-Click has the potential to profoundly alter the twenty-first-century internet-based economy—in ways we can imagine, and in ways we cannot," wrote Jones Harbour in her dissenting statement. She argued the FTC should take a closer look and answer several questions, including whether any other companies will have the ability to compete meaningfully in the market after the merger. The deal has potential to "harm competition, and it also threatens privacy," she wrote. "By closing its investigation without imposing any conditions or other safeguards, the Commission is asking consumers to bear too much of the risk of both types of harm."

Twelve years after Jones Harbour's dissent, in 2019, Texas AG Ken Paxton spoke about Google's advertising dominance when he announced the 51 states and territories' investigation into Google. Paxton said, "They dominate the buyer side, the seller side, the auction side, and the video side with YouTube." If Google had not bought DoubleClick, and in 2009, Admob, the leading mobile advertising company, plus a slew of other adtech companies, things could have been different. These acquisitions violated Clayton Act Section 7's prohibition of acquisitions that may substantially lessen competition or tend to create a monopoly. Ignoring Jones Harbour's concerns and allowing Google to amass the monopoly power that lets it squash entrepreneurs was a choice, not an inevitability.

King Bezos and His Ever-Expanding Amazon Empire

Before COVID-19, Amazon accounted for roughly one out of every two dollars spent online. It counted an estimated 112 million Amazon Prime customers in the United States by December 2019. For perspective, America had almost 129 million households in 2019, with an estimated 12 percent of the U.S. population living in poverty. If most households have a single Prime account, then nearly all U.S. households above the poverty line are Prime members. In 2019, Prime members spent on average $1,400 on the platform. During the pandemic, demand for product delivery skyrocketed and undoubtedly drove these numbers even higher.

Amazon, too, is following the monopolist's playbook, picking and choosing which products consumers discover and determining which entrepreneurs and businesses get to compete on its platform. Amazon has become the infrastructure for brands and retailers to reach customers, giving it "the power to dictate the terms by which its competitors and suppliers operate, and to levy a kind of tax on their revenue," reads a 2016 report by the Institute for Local Self-Reliance. Even investors see that Amazon has monopoly power. "We believe there is a multi-trillion dollar monopoly hiding in plain sight," said Chamath Palihapitiya, founder of Social Capital, at the Sohn Investment Conference in May 2016. Palihapitiya also reportedly described Amazon Web Services, Amazon's cloud infrastructure service, as "a tax on the internet." Under monopoly rule, entrepreneurs don't just pay taxes to the government, they pay taxes to Big Tech.

Amazon does not merely control its marketplace. Amazon acts as a retailer, buying products at wholesale and selling them on its platform (those are the products that say "sold by Amazon," also called "first-party" products). It thereby pits itself against those small, mid-sized, and large businesses that sell products on Amazon.com (known as "marketplace sellers"). Amazon also acts as a brand, selling its own private label products, both "AmazonBasics" products and products under more than 400 Amazon house labels.

Every entrepreneur who sells on Amazon is both competing against the giant and dependent on it. Many brands and small- and mid-sized retailers have no choice but to sell on Amazon if they want to stay in business. No entrepreneur or businessperson wants to be dependent on their competitor, who can disadvantage them, take a cut of their profits, knock them out of the competition, or knock them off. That's not how the American dream is supposed to work.

Amazon leverages its platform privilege to pick and choose what markets it wants to dominate, markets like skin care (91 percent share of retail e-commerce as of the first quarter of 2018), batteries (97 percent share), or even golf (92 percent). They are "constantly looking to cut you out," a marketplace seller told me (who asked to remain anonymous, as nearly all do out of fear of retaliation), and "they've been locking the [product] categories down."

Amazon often justifies excluding competition on its platform as needed to police counterfeits. But one marketplace seller told me he was kicked off the platform under the guise of counterfeits, only for Amazon to turn to him for supply of the same supposedly counterfeit items. And David Barnett, the CEO of PopSockets, maker of PopGrips for phones, submitted testimony to Congress saying "on multiple occasions we found that Amazon Retail was itself sourcing counterfeit PopGrips and selling them alongside our authentic products." Amazon would only address the problem of counterfeit PopSockets on its platform in exchange for the company committing to spend nearly $2 million on retail marketing programs, said Barnett.

When Amazon doesn't kick the competition out entirely by prohibiting marketplace sellers from listing certain products and brands, it pulls a number of levers to distort competition in its favor. Amazon has given its own private label products and first-party products advantages over competitors in a number of ways, from elevating its own products to the top of Amazon search results, to giving itself premium advertising placement not available to others, to targeted marketing to Amazon customers based on data collected about them that only Amazon has, to exclusive customer reviews that competitors can't access. Sellers and brands cannot market to their Amazon.com customers, or know much about them, because Amazon controls the relationship with customers.

Whether Google puts its shopping competitor on page four of its search results or Amazon buries its brand or retailer competitors, the result is the same. The giants are taking their monopolies in one market and leveraging them to take over new markets that depend on their platforms, destroying competition itself. They claim monopolies for themselves in the secondary markets, while maintaining and growing their monopoly power in their primary markets. The platforms crush entrepreneurs and businesses of all sizes in the process. Employees of those businesses lose jobs or get paid less. And the platforms degrade the quality of their offerings to consumers, who expect to get the most relevant search results, not results that prioritize Amazon's or Google's profits.

As Amazon rolls out Alexa—in 100 million devices as of January 2019—it's creating an entirely new and extreme version of platform privilege. The problems of Amazon and Google putting themselves first will be way worse when voice search brings only one or a few search results. Forget about being on page four of Google search or the bottom of Amazon's search ranking; if an entrepreneur's product or business is not answer 1, 2, or 3 in voice, it will be as if they don't even exist.

On top of its opaque product ranking algorithm, Amazon also has control over the "buy box," the area to the right of the product description that contains the "Add to Cart" yellow button, which yields an estimated 90 percent of sales. "If you don't have the buy box," meaning the product you are selling isn't the one that will automatically be put in someone's cart when they click buy, "and you're the same price as Amazon, you get zero sales," one marketplace seller explained to me. "You basically have to liquidate your inventory." Amazon is picking the winners and losers of commerce, and the winner is . . . Amazon.

Most Amazon marketplace sellers do not consider other online marketplaces to be viable alternatives to switch to if Amazon imposes prices or terms they don't like, because Amazon accounts for such a large share of online spending. This means marketplace sellers lack bargaining power, and Amazon can dictate the terms of dealing, including the fees it takes, how long Amazon waits to pay them for their sales, and sellers' recourse (or lack thereof) when Amazon decides to prohibit them from selling a particular item.

Amazon has reportedly kicked entrepreneurs out of the competition in yet another way—by knocking off their ideas. Take the laptop stand innovator who one day discovered their sales had plummeted when Amazon knocked them off and then ranked above them in Amazon search results. Or the innovator who is pretty sure Amazon's Echo Show is the video intercom he had invented. Executives of Sonos, the speaker company, say Amazon and Google both stole their technology, but they could only risk suing one of the two. They sued Google in January 2020, alleging theft of intellectual property and antitrust violations. Sonos's lawsuit is bold given Google's tremendous litigation budget and ability to pick the winners and losers of the internet, which is why the giants can usually get away with stealing entrepreneurs' ideas. Google has responded by suing Sonos back.

You may wonder how Amazon making its own copies of products is different from the long-standing practice of stores making their own generic version of a product. When a retailer that is not dominant has its own brands, like a local grocery store, it doesn't violate the antitrust laws because it doesn't have monopoly power. Makers of the knockoff won't get decimated because there are many other stores available to sell their product. The types of conduct that are exclusionary and illegal when a firm has monopoly power are not illegal when a firm does not have monopoly power. (Remember, illegal monopolization = monopoly power + preventing rivals from competing based on merit.)

The tactics that Amazon employs to harm competition on its e-commerce platform are only the half of it. Amazon pulls the same types of anticompetitive levers in its cloud computing arm, Amazon Web Services (AWS), to co-opt innovations of others, a practice some call "strip-mining," reports the *New York Times*. "It has given an edge to its own services by making them more convenient to use, burying rival offerings and bundling discounts to make its products less expensive," writes Daisuke Wakabayashi. Yet just like Amazon's e-commerce marketplace, rivals don't feel like they have a choice to walk away from AWS because of its market power.

Knowledge Is Power

Amazon doesn't merely control the platform, it controls the data and can peek inside entrepreneurs' businesses. At time of writing, the DOJ, FTC, and House Judiciary Antitrust Subcommittee are investigating Amazon, with the European Commission undertaking a years-long investigation into whether Amazon uses data anticompetitively. Curious what the commission was likely to find when I was working as an investigative journalist in 2018, I spoke to former Amazon employees, who asked to remain anonymous due to concerns about their careers.

"Everybody has access to all the seller data," one former midlevel employee told me, which means Amazon employees can "data mine all the bestselling products and go make a private label." He went on to say, "I had access to a data warehouse as an employee at Amazon and could literally pull up any transaction from any seller. I had access to every single sale and was data mining the hell out of it for my job."

He then laid out a hypothetical of what he would do if he were proposing a new private label product at Amazon: "Let's say Amazon wants to get into folders. I would find all of the [listings] that are being sold on the website now. I'd pull up the history. I'd look at the volumes, price points. Regardless of whether it was sold wholesale or third party, I'd pull it all together. I'd look and see what's the hottest product. What's the hottest variation in color? We'd have these folders in these colors at this price point, and we'd go off and make it ourselves."

Another former Amazon manager told me, "If Amazon owns a product, it's almost impossible for anyone to compete. . . . Even if you make a better product, you can't market it to anyone—Amazon owns the customers, pricing, merchandising, marketing, and all the data to know which products to build, to whom, and when."

The most valuable data Amazon collects, according to this second source, is who has searched for a particular product in the past. This "consideration data" allows Amazon to "target their private label products with perfect precision," he explained.

Entrepreneurs and businesses of all sizes that don't have access to comparable data can hardly compete against Amazon. And because keeping their products off Amazon's platform is nearly impossible, these entrepreneurs are defenseless in handing over their proprietary business information to their competitor.

Price-Cutting to Squash Entrepreneurs

Yet another wrinkle Amazon presents is that it can eliminate entrepreneurial rivals easily because it can forgo revenue for as long as it takes. Amazon followed in Walmart's path of monopolization through a low pricing strategy that is not just about competing with rivals but rather aims to drive them from the market entirely, a tactic also used by the original robber barons. This practice is called predatory pricing and is illegal under the antitrust laws, but judges, under the influence of the Chicago School of Economics, have erected standards that made winning a predatory pricing case a losing proposition. Without enforcement, Amazon was able to evade antitrust laws, which antitrust scholar Lina Khan, then a law student, detailed in her influential 2017 paper "Amazon's Antitrust Paradox" for the *Yale Law Journal*.

Predatory pricing is quite effective at eliminating competition and was part of the DOJ's charges against Microsoft. "We are going to cut off their air supply. Everything they're selling, we're going to give away for free." These are the words of Paul Maritz, a former vice president at Microsoft, speaking to executives about Netscape, as quoted in the *New York Times*. "Microsoft invested hundreds of millions of dollars to develop, test, and promote Internet Explorer, a product which it distributes without separate charge," reads the DOJ's complaint.

Amazon has a well-documented track record of pricing below cost to drive out competition. One example of predatory pricing was Amazon's weakening of upstart competitor Diapers.com to force its 2010 sale to Amazon by pricing diapers at a loss. Brad Stone's book *The Everything Store* discusses the chain of events in detail, saying Amazon was on track to lose $100 million in three months on diapers alone before buying Diapers.com. By 2017, Amazon announced it was shutting down the company. Amazon's ability and willingness to sustain temporary losses, paired with lack of enforcement on predatory pricing, allowed it to eliminate an entrepreneurial challenger.

Amazon can use other arms of its business, like its highly profitable AWS cloud computing business, to fund any short-term losses that fortify its long-term dominance. Any company that makes or sells products now has to compete against a giant that can predatory-price them out of existence. We need to fix and enforce predatory pricing laws, otherwise no entrepreneur, brand, or retailer—no matter how efficient, innovative, or high quality—stands a chance at competing against Amazon, or any other monopoly.

Entrepreneurs Get "Sherlocked" by Apple

Relative to Google, Amazon, and Facebook, Apple seems like a warm and fuzzy monopolist. Its business model depends on selling luxury devices, and it has focused less on surveillance or controlling commerce than have its fellow tech giants. But Apple still has monopoly power because there's no real substitute for the App Store for iPhone owners, as we saw in chapter 1 with the 30 percent "Apple tax" on app sales. Apple's ability to control prices through tax-setting is direct evidence of its monopoly power.

As Apple grows into new lines of business, it has the same platform privilege as these other companies, to the detriment of entrepreneurs and businesses. For example, Apple has been accused of discriminating against Spotify and giving favorable treatment to Apple Music. Spotify recently sued Apple in Europe, arguing that Apple leveraged its platform to distort competition with unfair app store terms. The general counsel of Tile, a company that helps people find misplaced items using an app that pairs with physical "tiles," made similar claims when testifying before Congress in January 2020. Apple launched an app called FindMy, which is pre-installed and cannot be deleted, that competes directly with Tile. On top of its own app benefiting from default bias, Apple pulled a number of anticompetitive levers to disadvantage Tile, according to the testimony, including kicking Tile's products out of Apple's physical stores, making Tile harder to find on the iPhone, and making it difficult for iPhone users to activate their Tile devices, among other things. As Apple plans to enter more and more markets, including streaming TV, credit cards, and online gaming, Apple will increasingly play the game and control it, too.

When Apple introduces a new version of its iPhone operating system iOS or its macOS operating system, it often incorporates the features of the most popular apps that other innovators built, usually without paying them for it. Apple has been doing this for so long that developers have named the phenomenon getting "sherlocked." That term dates way back to the early 2000s, when Karelia Software developed a competitor to Apple's Sherlock search tool and named it Watson. Apple simply added Watson's functionality into the next version of Sherlock, killing its rival Watson.

Sherlocking is still alive and well today. In Apple's developer conference in spring of 2019, Matt Ronge, cofounder and CEO of Luna Display, which extends a Mac's display wirelessly to the iPad, learned that his innovation had been sherlocked. "Apple used us for market research," Ronge told *AppleInsider*. He described how Apple invited his company to demonstrate their product to Apple. "They expressed their support and told us to contact them if they could help (we emailed multiple times and never heard back)." Apple then bought dozens of Luna Display units when it launched in 2018. But in 2019 Apple launched its own version of Luna Display, called Sidecar.

Even if Luna Display tries to compete against Sidecar, competing against the platform is never a fair competition. Ronge explained to *AppleInsider* that Apple has access to functionalities that third-party developers don't, including technology that "prioritizes their Sidecar traffic over others." Ronge added, "This is certainly not a level playing field for developers."

Sure sounds a lot like what Microsoft did to Netscape. Monopoly power plus kicking rivals out of the game amounts to illegal monopolization. Just because Apple created the iPhone doesn't mean it should be allowed to take over all markets that depend on its platform without competing fair and square.

Entrepreneurs have no choice but to put up with this abuse, especially since Apple's App Store is the dominant revenue source for apps. Like Amazon for product innovators, Apple's App Store provides a must-have sales volume for entrepreneurs' businesses to survive. The U.S. Supreme Court in *Apple v. Pepper*, the case we talked about in chapter 1 that held consumers could sue Apple for charging them a 30 percent commission on every app purchase, also noted the possibility that "app developers will also sue Apple on a monopsony theory." The Court acknowledged that Apple has market power over app entrepreneurs, who could potentially also bring an antitrust case against Apple. Antitrust enforcers in the United States and Europe have recently opened investigations into Apple as well.

Monopsony, as you've seen, is a huge problem in an economy

where tech giants serve as gatekeepers that set the terms and conditions for suppliers and creators to do business. Ask any Amazon marketplace seller, for instance, if they can negotiate the fees they pay to Amazon—they'll think you're out of your mind. App developers can't negotiate the 30 percent Apple Tax that is charged to buyers of apps, nor do they have the power to stop Sherlocking.

Facebook's Platform Privilege

Like Google, Facebook picks the winners and losers of internet content, as we saw in the 2016 U.S. presidential election and beyond. Because Facebook's platform privilege manipulates us and harms democracy, we'll talk about Facebook's global control over the flow of information—and disinformation—in chapters 4 and 5. So here we'll explore how Facebook squashes new companies that could compete against it and changes entrepreneurs' fortunes just by altering its algorithm.

Facebook has a history of taking entrepreneurs' ideas when they refuse to sell their companies to the platform. As the *Wall Street Journal* explains it, Facebook CEO Mark Zuckerberg met with the founders of Snapchat and Foursquare and gave them two options: either hand over their companies at the price he proposed, or the tech giant would imitate their features and make it harder for them to operate.

When the founders didn't cave, Facebook copied Snapchat and Foursquare's popular features. Instagram's knockoff of Snapchat Stories grew bigger than the original innovation because Facebook applied the feature to its 2.3 billion users, a number that dwarfs Snapchat's 210 million users. Over the years, Snapchat lawyers kept track of tactics by Facebook that they consider anticompetitive in a file called Project Voldemort, named after the villain from Harry Potter. Snapchat reportedly shared the evidence with the

FTC as part of its antitrust investigation into Facebook that began in 2019.

Companies, especially small businesses, can find their fortunes change with the flip of a switch when Facebook makes algorithmic changes that harm their ability to reach their customers. I experienced this firsthand back in 2012, when I cofounded a web start-up called The Parent Maze that helped busy parents find trusted recommendations for parenting services. At the time, Facebook encouraged businesses to create Facebook pages, and then invest in ads to get people to become fans of the pages. Fans would then see content posted by the Facebook business pages, and the investment would pay off as a marketing channel.

But after businesses of all sizes invested in growing their fans, Facebook simply changed the terms. Now businesses would have to pay for their fans to see their content. For my start-up, investment in ads to build our Facebook following had consumed a large part of our shoestring budget because our potential users spent a lot of time there, which, after Facebook's bait and switch, felt like wasted money. Businesses were angry, particularly because Facebook was not forthright about the change, but they lacked bargaining power to do anything about it.

Must Winners Take All?

Pundits say tech markets are "winner take all," or monopolistic by nature, and they point to a principle called network effects. Network effects arise when a user's value from a product increases as others use it. People want to be where their friends are, for example, making a social network without your friends not much use.

But the same was true for the AT&T monopoly since a phone network would serve no purpose if you couldn't call your friends. Government regulators didn't just throw up their hands and say, "Ah well, it's a winner-take-all market with network effects." Instead, the government broke up the AT&T monopoly and required interoperability, making AT&T connect with competing networks in order to open up competition in long-distance calling.

For Big Tech, interoperability would allow users to authorize networks to securely communicate and interface with each other, like how people with different email services can send emails to one another. On top of enforcing the antitrust laws, interoperability is one of several practical, doable solutions that can help revive entrepreneurship, which we'll discuss in the book's final chapter.

Even if it were true that network effects mean there can only be one dominant social network, search engine, video service, mobile operating system, ad tech company, e-commerce platform, mobile app store, and browser, and that Facebook, Google, Apple, and Amazon are natural monopolies, what does the government do to natural monopolies? It labels them utilities and it regulates them. Traditionally, utilities are required to provide equal access to competitors on fair and reasonable terms and prices.

By allowing illegal acquisitions and monopolization, and by abandoning rules and regulations that decentralize communications networks, the government has created monopoly markets—these were policy choices. The government can make the opposite choice and start reviving the American dream. It's up to us to demand government take action.

Your Life, Better

Thomas Philippon, leading economist and author of *The Great Reversal: How America Gave Up on Free Markets,* estimates that bringing competition back would increase employees' income by about $1.25 trillion. Weakening monopoly and oligopoly power could lift that pervasive cloud of financial fear and insecurity that surrounded us even before the COVID-19 pandemic's economic damage. We think life has to be like this, but it doesn't.

In a world free of monopoly rule, you may just be able to pursue that innovative business idea, get it funded, and build a company that doesn't get crushed by powerful companies protecting their turf. Small and big companies could say no to giant corporations' extractive and unfair terms of dealing, stay in business longer, and pay their employees better.

Instead of innovation graveyards, increased antitrust enforcement would create a new burst of innovation, like the one that came after the government took action against AT&T. Imagine what innovation could look like if a handful of companies weren't charting its course.

The defenders of the status quo want us to believe that these problems are too complicated to fix and nothing can be done. But it's not that complicated. We just need to demand that government use the tools it already has to restore a competitive marketplace for employees and entrepreneurs.

FOUR

MONOPOLIES SPY ON AND MANIPULATE YOU

"The house is free, but they own your life."

MONOPOLIES ARE WATCHING YOU RIGHT NOW

You were gifted an Amazon smart speaker for the holidays, and you gave the gadget a go. But then Alexa started talking out of nowhere, when you hadn't even summoned your new "assistant." Exactly what is Alexa listening to, you start to wonder, and what might it be doing with your personal information? You hear on the news that Amazon employees listen to recordings from Alexa, and Apple and Google have people listen to voice audio, too. Maybe you felt better when a robot controlled by a trillion-dollar corporation was listening, but real humans? Did they hear you having sex? Did they eavesdrop on that far-from-perfect parenting moment?

On top of that, online ads are stalking you. Sometimes a shirt you decided against buying follows you wherever you go on the Web, and other times an ad for the exact brand of coconut and chocolate swirl ice cream you bought from the grocery store shows up in your Facebook newsfeed. Last night you offered that ice cream to a guest in your home. Is Facebook listening to you, too?

When you need to get to the bottom of an embarrassing medical condition, you turn to the directory of the world's information, Google. Perhaps you cringe as you hit search, divulging even more personal secrets to the one company that knows the most about you. Google probably doesn't need your search to already know a lot about your health; according to reports, Google has gathered millions of Americans' health records straight from a medical provider without telling patients or their doctors. It feels like nothing is sacred anymore.

Don't Blame Baby Pictures

If you don't want to be tracked, you shouldn't put your whole life online, so goes the typical victim-blaming. All you have to do is stop using social media if you want privacy. This trope is so off base that it exposes deep deception by the companies that track us.

What you knowingly and willingly share, like a post on Facebook, is a tiny fraction of what Facebook knows about you. What you search for on Google is an even smaller percentage of what Google knows about you. Escaping Big Tech's prying eyes is a nearly impossible feat. You're under ubiquitous surveillance, and it's not your fault.

Tech giants have an all-encompassing view of what you read,

think, do, believe, buy, watch, where you go, who you're with, even how many credit lines you have and what you invest in. The companies track you across millions of websites, devices, tech wearables, and offline, and combine the data they collect on you with data from other companies, like data brokers, or your smart TV maker. Seventy-six percent of websites have hidden Google trackers, and Google collects your information through its own services like Search, YouTube, Maps, Android, Chrome, Google Play, Gmail, and Google Home. In one study, an Android phone that was stationary and not in use, but had the Chrome browser open in the background, communicated location data to Google 340 times in twenty-four hours. Google even has trackers on 74 percent of pornography sites.

Facebook tracks you across the Web, including approximately 8.4 million websites with the Facebook "like" button and 16.4 million websites with Facebook login as of 2018, plus any website that uses Facebook analytics or ad tools. Even if you don't use Facebook, Instagram, or WhatsApp, Facebook has created a "shadow profile" of you, tracking your internet browsing history and your social connections by accessing the email contacts of your friends who use Facebook. Facebook uses this data in part to sell targeted ads across thousands of mobile apps and websites through its Facebook Audience Network. Facebook also uses facial recognition technology to identify you in pictures that others take of you, even if they don't tag you in the photo. Amazon, too, is a surveillance giant.

Instead of faulting social media users, we should fault our elected officials who have failed to protect us from a privatized spy net. Life is hard. People have to work all day and feed their families, and they literally couldn't hold down a job if they read every privacy policy that came their way. The task of being endlessly vigilant about our data rights is so daunting and overwhelming that most of us become hopeless and give up altogether.

Award-winning journalist and editor Julia Angwin, author of *Dragnet Nation: A Quest for Privacy, Security, and Freedom in a World of Relentless Surveillance*, tried multiple experiments to protect herself from tracking. Ultimately Angwin concluded, "I'm in an arms race I'm not going to win." The onus to stop surveillance cannot be on the people. The onus must rest on our democratically elected leaders, who can pass strong privacy laws and ensure competitive markets that empower consumers.

Spying Is Social Control

Digital surveillance is relatively new, but surveillance itself is not. Throughout its dark history, surveillance has been used by the powerful to control and persecute innocent people. Take the story of Vera Lengsfeld, who was organizing for peace and human rights in East Germany in the early 1980s. East Germany's communist government, and its secret police force the Stasi, labeled Vera a threat to the state. The Stasi gave her the code name "Virus," tapped her phone, and began recording her meetings. They arrested Vera and threw her in jail when she was carrying a poster that read, "Every citizen has the right to express his opinion freely and openly."

In an act of psychological torture, the prison wardens would play Vera's favorite symphony to remind her of her home and her beloved children, whom she missed dearly. How did the wardens know Vera's music tastes? The Stasi had watched Vera's every move. When the Berlin Wall came down, twenty large files the Stasi had amassed about "Virus" were released. Vera was "quite astonished" to learn that forty-nine regular people—friends, family, and acquaintances—were unofficial Stasi collaborators who kept tabs on her. Among her betrayers was her own husband, with whom she had borne and raised two children. Big Data would be a dream come true for the Stasi.

You're a good, law-abiding person, so you've got nothing to hide, right? Wrong. As we saw with Vera, something as innocuous as your favorite song can be used against you. You may think you don't need to worry because you're not an activist. But someday, if not today, you might become one. These tumultuous times have made clear our democracy and basic human rights are not guaranteed to us. If you're not the type to rise up and resist, you still don't want to live in a world where others cannot. When people know they're being watched, they conform, obey, stay in line, and self-censor.

Yeonmi Park escaped from North Korea's oppressive regime at the young age of thirteen and wrote about her experiences in her book, *In Order to Live*. As a young child, Park's mother taught her that "even when you think you're alone, the birds and mice can hear you whisper." Park learned to not even think critically, and certainly not to speak up. Like the birds and mice Yeonmi's mom warned her about, surveillance giants are watching us even when we think we are alone.

China is giving each citizen a score based on their surveilled obedience, and it's tracking the Uighur Muslim minority with facial recognition technology. A disturbing video surfaced at the end of 2019 that shows Chinese police interrogating a man for apparently criticizing a police officer in a "private" group on WeChat, China's social media network. The man is restrained in a "tiger chair," a torture device that shackles the victim's entire body and is known to bear the slogan: "Truthfully confess and your whole body will feel at ease."

If you don't like being told what to do, having arbitrary rules imposed on you, being controlled in ways you may not even know, or living your life the way other people think you should, then you should guard your privacy with all you've got.

Build It and They Will Come

Big Tech focuses on profits and pays far less attention to the dangers of building an architecture of surveillance that can enable government oppression. In an interview on the *Land of the Giants* podcast, Recode journalist Jason Del Rey asked Amazon executive Daniel Rausch, vice president of Smart Home, whether teams at Amazon look at people's concerns about Alexa. Rausch replied only that Amazon is "deeply optimistic" about what Alexa can do for customers.

In other words, Amazon isn't thinking about the consequences of the surveillance technology it deploys at breakneck pace. The consequences are for the rest of us to bear. The least powerful in our society will suffer the worst consequences of surveillance, as they always have, and Amazon executives safely can get richer knowing deep down they'll be the last ones to pay the price. Amazon's facial recognition technology is already being used by police departments, despite widespread concerns about the technology's discriminatory bias and inaccuracies. A coalition of activists' groups including Fight for the Future and EPIC advocate for a total ban on facial recognition technology, saying it can control and oppress us by enabling "automated and ubiquitous monitoring of an entire population" that "is nearly impossible to avoid." Amazon provides cloud storage for Immigration and Customs Enforcement's deportation operation, ignoring calls by an alliance of 500 Amazon employees and repeated protests about Amazon's government contracts. Amazon has shown it is willing to employ its technologies against the most vulnerable.

Most tracking by tech giants is designed to target us with ads and sell us stuff, which may seem harmless. Whatever data Big Tech collects, however, the government can get. Occasionally we hear a case about a tech platform refusing to cooperate with the government, like when Apple refused to crack open an iPhone from the scene of a 2015 mass shooting in San Bernardino, California. But those examples are in the minority. What we don't hear about are the thousands of secret requests that Big Tech doesn't protest, and that often come hand in hand with a gag order. In fact, between July and December 2018, Apple received nearly 8,500 government requests for customer data and complied with more than 80 percent of those requests. Google received 26,964 government requests for data involving 74,619 customer accounts in a mere six months between January and June 2019, and provided data in response to 82 percent of those requests. In most cases, tech giants would lose in court if they refused to comply. The laws keeping information that tech platforms collect about you out of the hands of the government are incredibly weak. Citizens have no voice in the process and usually don't even know their data is being handed over, all in the name of national security or law enforcement and hidden under the paternalistic umbrella of protection.

Big Tech says that surveillance is good for us because we get relevant ads targeted to us. But never before hypertargeted ads came along did I wish for the convenience of companies spying on me twenty-four hours a day, seven days a week, and then deciding what products I discover. I don't buy that the meager benefits of highly targeted ads outweigh the dangers they bring.

History Repeats Itself

You may think oppression through surveillance can't happen here in America, but it already has—and does. In the late 1940s and early 1950s, Senator Joseph McCarthy used anticommunist hysteria to perpetuate a reign of terror known as McCarthyism or the Second Red Scare. The U.S. government used spying, wiretaps, and infiltration of political groups to accuse anyone with politically left views of being communists and to blacklist them from jobs, or worse.

The FBI director J. Edgar Hoover even labeled Martin Luther

King Jr. a communist and used invasive surveillance to monitor him long after the Second Red Scare had subsided. More recently, the Department of Homeland Security monitored members of the Black Lives Matter movement, continuing America's disturbing and persistent record of surveilling black activists. The surveillance state itself is dangerous to democracy, and Big Tech's spying eyes are making it worse.

If McCarthyism occurred today, it could use the surveillance architecture built by Facebook, Google, and Amazon. Instead of communism, pick any belief you like—feminism, conservatism, anticorruption, or environmentalism. If, for example, the government decided to label people who want to stop the climate crisis as political enemies and blacklist them, it wouldn't need to use spies as it did in the McCarthy era because it could simply use the surveillance Big Tech is already doing.

From search and Web tracking data, the government has the ability to learn who searched for articles and visited websites about climate change. From the purchase data tracked by Amazon, Google, and Facebook, the government can know who purchased energy-efficient products. From Facebook and Google group data, the government is able to identify the members of environmental groups and see their discussions with one another about how to organize for change. Location data tracked by Big Tech can tell the government if you went to a climate march or other activist event, and the government can get your photos from the event, too. Google calendar data reveals plans for future events.

Amazon purchase data and Kindle tracking data can identify people who have bought books about the environment and even what e-book pages they read and what passages they highlighted. People who have written or received Gmail or Facebook messages, watched YouTube videos, or written Google Docs about climate change can all be easily identified thanks to Big Tech's surveillance architecture.

Devices with Alexa, Google Home, or other voice assistants can even offer a live feed into your home to listen to any climate crisis talk.

Big Tech also makes assumptions about you based on the data they collect, known as inferences or correlations. Sometimes these inferences are correct and sometimes they are not. For example, Big Tech could assume you are an environmentalist because you bought Birkenstocks and vegan burgers, and these inferences could land you on our hypothetical government blacklist, too.

Unfortunately, our government has already grown cozy with Big Tech. Amazon has forged partnerships with police departments to use its Ring smart doorbells, which offer surveillance footage surrounding a user's home, to effectively create a spy net in America's neighborhoods. Now not only can your nosy neighbor know all your comings and goings, but so can the police. Ring even created a custom portal for police to easily request Ring footage, touting in a video, "It's like having thousands of eyes and ears on the street."

Google location data is being used to identify everyone in the area of a crime. An innocent man, Jorge Molina, spent nearly a week in jail after his phone was one of many identified by Google data as being in the area of a crime, the *New York Times* reported. Molina was at home at the time of the crime, two miles from the scene.

Our Fourth Amendment right set up to protect us against unreasonable search and seizure is getting weak. The online world has escaped laws intended to protect us in the real world, and these two worlds are melding into one.

Blame Monopoly Power

You may be wondering what smart speakers eavesdropping on you, online ads stalking you, Google knowing your deepest medical secrets, and surveillance-enabled political persecution have to do with monopoly. After all, lots of companies that are not monopolies spy on you and invasively collect your personal information. Yet privacy and monopoly are intricately related, with monopoly power allowing Big Tech to abuse your privacy without losing your business, keeping you in the dark about the ways it abuses your privacy, and buying off lawmakers so they don't pass robust privacy laws.

It works the other way, too. Massive data collection allows giants to strengthen their monopoly power. Big Tech uses that power to shut out privacy-protecting start-ups. Surveillance-based business models are a choice, not an inevitability of the internet, and loosening the giants' monopoly grip could promote competition among business models. Pro-privacy, pro-democracy innovators need the opportunity to break through the monopolists' gates without being crushed by anticompetitive tactics.

Largely, I don't fault tech monopolists as much as I fault the government for failing to act. I'm critical of decisions Facebook CEO Mark Zuckerberg has made, for example, but focusing too much on his character is a distraction. Demonizing individual CEOs confuses the fact that monopoly problems are structural and systemic. We must demand better from our government, and we must not forget that corporations by design are profit-maximizing entities.

Ordinarily, two things constrain corporations from pursuing profits in ways that cause harm: 1) competition and 2) regulation. Tech giants have had neither. Without competition, Big Tech can hurt people without losing profits, and choose dangerous and harmful business models. It is our government leaders who have failed to adequately enforce the antitrust laws, or protect citizens with regulation. This is not a job we can leave to corporations, and putting any faith in Big Tech self-regulation is doomed to fail. Government should not *ask* corporations to do better, it should *make* them do better. Both privacy regulation and competition, created through strong antitrust enforcement and other anti-monopoly polices, must make it unprofitable for corporations to make business model choices that threaten our fundamental rights.

In April 2020, when large corporations sucked hundreds of millions of dollars out of the COVID-19 bailout fund meant for small businesses, comedian and political satirist Trevor Noah said on *The Daily Show* that government should have created rules instead of just letting companies take taxpayers' money in a free-for-all. After all, he said, "companies gonna company." Just the same, government should have created rules instead of letting companies take Americans' data as they pleased. Surveillance giants gonna surveil—unless we make our government stop them.

Monopolies Don't Lose Profits When They Abuse You

Monopoly power allows Big Tech to abuse your privacy without losing your business. Treating customers badly doesn't risk profits when customers don't have anywhere to go. We already talked in chapter 1 about how tech giants are charging you monopoly rents of data, an excessive price rather than the price competition would yield. On top of price-gouging, hidden and invasive surveillance means you're getting a lower quality service. Competition makes companies vie for your business by offering better-quality services. Like the monopoly cable operator that can make you wait eight hours for the set-top-box repair person to show up, monopoly tech platforms can provide poor-quality service, invading your privacy without the risk of losing you to competitors.

At its start, Facebook competed against the then-leading social media platform MySpace on privacy grounds. Former advertising executive Dina Srinivasan has detailed the history of Facebook competing against MySpace as the more privacy-protecting alternative in a paper called "The Antitrust Case Against Facebook," published in

2019 in the *Berkeley Business Law Journal*. For the first ten years of its existence, Facebook promised not to track users for commercial purposes. Facebook even promised users they could remove information Facebook had about them whenever they wanted. Srinivasan details how Facebook's surveillance increased in tandem with decreases in competition over time. With Facebook's competition eliminated, the pressure to protect users' privacy fell away.

When Facebook users learned Facebook had allowed the digital analytics firm Cambridge Analytica to access their personal information, which was used to target users with deceptive propaganda intended to influence the U.S. 2016 presidential election, they were angry. But, as we discussed earlier, this abuse of customer privacy didn't threaten Facebook's profits because disgruntled Facebook users mostly switched to Facebook-owned Instagram.

If Facebook had never bought Instagram, or antitrust enforcers had blocked this, in my opinion, illegal acquisition, Facebook would face competitive pressure. Instead of making only minuscule changes, Facebook would be motivated to stop invading users' privacy.

Facebook's business model must change to fix its privacy problem—small tweaks here and there will not suffice. In 2018 and 2019, Facebook made *more than a billion dollars a week* by collecting data and then targeting ads at individuals based on that data. Risk of profit loss would force Facebook to change its business model more than risk of regulation, which Facebook knows its lobbyists can influence.

Monopolies Can Keep You in the Dark

People need to be able to switch to privacy-protecting alternatives, while also needing to understand how their privacy is being violated. The giants haven't made it easy to know what types of information they are tracking, where and how they are tracking you, and what they are doing with it. Under pressure, both Google and Facebook have unveiled ways to find out what information they've already collected about you, but the tools tell you about all the spying the platforms have already done on you, instead of alerting you to spying in real time. Facebook's and Google's entire business models are built around getting your attention and influencing you with messaging, yet they don't deliver messages clearly announcing, "We are tracking you right now, and here's how."

Big Tech is doing a terrible job informing you because transparency runs directly against their profit motives. Surveillance giants know that if they alerted you in real time, in a way that is understandable, quick, and easy, you might refuse their tracking. Profits lie in their deception, and billions of dollars in revenue depend on a global fraud on the world's citizens. Competition could help shed light on Big Tech's privacy abuses. The privacy-protecting search engine DuckDuckGo, in a bid for your business, provides education through its newsletter on the ways Google and other companies violate your privacy. Just as a sneaker company draws attention to the poorer quality of its competitors' shoes, so could competitors highlight the privacy invasions of Big Tech if markets were free and fair.

Big Tech Uses Their Might to Shut Out Privacy-Protecting Start-ups

Privacy-protecting innovators are waiting in the wings, and they just need a fair opportunity to break through the digital gatekeepers and serve you. But Big Tech controls the infrastructure of business and are the gatekeepers who decide who gets to play the game.

Take the privacy-protecting Brave browser and search engine DuckDuckGo from above. They have been locked out from being the built-in default browser and search engine on Google Android phones, which have a more than 85 percent global market share. This is a huge barrier to privacy-protecting start-ups reaching users because of default bias. Personally, I took the uncommon step of overcoming default bias and installing DuckDuckGo as the primary search engine in my devices, which provided me a calming sense of freedom.

Privacy-protecting start-ups not only have to overcome default bias, but they also have to get through Big Tech's gates to reach users. A company called Candle has set out to create the "privacy-friendly smart home of the future," and has announced a launch of its prototype. But exactly how would such a privacy-protecting voice assistant reach consumers? Amazon, Google, and Facebook each could exert their platform privilege. The giants have the incentive and ability to bury this upstart challenger to their voice assistants, demoting Candle in search listings and newsfeeds by tweaking their algorithms. If enforcers and policy makers unlocked Big Tech's gates and promoted competition, privacy-protecting innovation could flourish.

Data Helps Big Tech Grow and Keep Monopoly Power

While lack of competition allows Big Tech to collect excessive data without losing profits, the data the platforms collect simultaneously shore up their monopoly power. Margrethe Vestager, the European commissioner for competition and the digital age, has explained that "having the right set of data could make it almost impossible for anyone else to keep up." Regulators "need to keep a close eye on whether companies control unique data, which no one else can get hold of, and can use it to shut their rivals out of the market," said Vestager, particularly "data that's been collected through a monopoly."

Facebook, for example, has used its control of data to try to shut out rivals. Leaked internal Facebook documents revealed that Mark Zuckerberg personally kept a list of strategic competitors, who were not permitted to access the Facebook Graph API. (API is short for application programming interface, which allows two applications to talk to each other.) In Facebook's words, the Graph API is "the primary way to get data into and out of the Facebook platform." When Twitter launched its video service Vine, emails show that Zuckerberg approved cutting Twitter off from Facebook's API because Vine was competing with a Facebook "core functionality."

Such behavior is known as a "discriminatory refusal to deal" in antitrust law, which is a type of illegal monopolization under Section 2 of the Sherman Act. Ordinarily, companies do not have obligations to deal with their competitors. But if a monopoly refuses to offer a service to a competitor that it offers to others, or if a monopoly has done business with the competitor and then stops for anticompetitive reasons, such behavior amounts to illegal monopolization.

In another leaked document, a Facebook employee suggested cutting off access to Facebook's API to a competitor and justifying the move as protecting privacy. Although we want Facebook to protect users' privacy, we do not want Facebook to use privacy as a pretense for monopolization. Facebook seems to define privacy as keeping our data out of others' hands, but we also need privacy protection from Facebook itself! Internal documents detail Facebook's aggressive snooping in ways consumers would never expect, including collecting Android users' calls and text records without their knowledge.

Mergers allow dominant companies to acquire data that strengthens or grows their market power. Take Amazon's purchase of Whole Foods. Simplistic antitrust analysis that just looks at the grocery market would conclude the deal doesn't harm competition because Amazon had a small market share in groceries. The FTC quickly approved the deal without doing an in-depth investigation. But antitrust enforcers should try to see the forest for the trees and not undertake such a narrow analysis. I was aghast when I heard from an FTC decision maker that they didn't view the merger as involving data. A former Amazon insider once told me that Amazon is "a data company that happens to sell stuff." To say that any merger involving Amazon doesn't involve data is to fundamentally misunderstand Amazon's business.

If you shop at Whole Foods, have you forked over your data to Amazon yet by logging in as a Prime member? Your data may be more valuable than the Whole Foods discount you receive, but you wouldn't know it. With a tremendous overlap between Whole Foods customers and Amazon Prime members, the merger allowed Amazon to gather even more personal information about its Prime customers. Unlike the Amazon purchases we don't really need, we have to buy food all the time. Acquiring Whole Foods gave Amazon many more opportunities to interact with us and learn about us. What we eat can tell a lot about who we are.

Data that enhances Amazon's ability to precisely target and market to Prime members strengthens its existing online monopoly power. The FTC at the very least should have investigated how the data Amazon would acquire could harm competition and increase barriers for any other company trying to enter Amazon's monopoly markets. The deal also allowed Amazon to terminate Whole Foods' partnerships with delivery company Instacart, an emerging competitive threat to Amazon's core offering of fast delivery. Remember, Clayton Act Section 7 prohibits any merger that may substantially lessen competition or tend to create a monopoly.

Google's acquisition of FitBit causes the same problems, fortifying Google's existing surveillance-based dominance of online advertising. As Amazon and Google expand into health care, our personal data can be used against us in countless ways. Think Amazon expanding into health insurance, and then using your Whole Foods purchase history to decide how much to charge you, or whether to cover you at all. Not enough kale, too much ice cream and beer? Denied! Or picture Google getting into health insurance, and your FitBit showing only one workout a month. High GoogleCare prices for you!

Big Tech Uses Its Monopoly Power to Fight Privacy Laws

Big Tech monopolists are throwing millions of dollars at lawmakers to keep abusing your privacy. As the giants' economic power grows, the companies buy up increasing amounts of political power.

In the years leading up to the 2016 passage of Europe's privacy law, the General Data Protection Regulation (GDPR), Facebook and Google lobbied hard against it. When they lost that battle, the talking heads on Big Tech's payroll, spanning from think tanks to academia, spread a common talking point in unison: Europe's privacy law would strengthen the giants' monopoly power because it would impose burdens on smaller companies.

Huh? If Europe's privacy law was so good for Big Tech, it wouldn't have spent millions of dollars lobbying against it! If the privacy law worked as intended—and why they fought it—it would weaken Big Tech's monopoly power because Facebook and Google's 360-degree view of the user is the source of their dominance in targeted online advertising. But so far the GDPR hasn't really worked, largely because tech monopolies are so powerful they can interpret the law how they choose and wait for government to try to force them to change their practices. Europe is still struggling to get Facebook and Google to comply, with the French data protection commissioner fining Google in 2019 and inquiries into the two companies ongoing.

The United States still lacks a comprehensive consumer privacy law at the federal level. California became the first state to pass such a law in 2018, which went into effect on January 1, 2020. The law puts forth a different legal framework than the GDPR but shares the same goals, giving citizens the right to know what personal information is collected, used, shared or sold, the right to delete personal information held by businesses, and the right to opt out of sale of personal information. Polls show the citizens of California overwhelmingly support the privacy law, but that doesn't stop their elected representatives from putting forth amendments to weaken it on a regular basis. Some of the amendments propose exceptions that would undo the law, like an exemption for digital advertising, the main driver of surveillance.

While relentlessly attacking California's privacy law, Big Tech lobbyists are pushing for a weak federal privacy law, which could override California's law, as well as the laws that any state passes to ensure its citizens' privacy. The monopolists' tentacles extend into government institutions and bend them to their will, away from the will of the people.

The FTC has long been the privacy cop for the American people, primarily using consumer protection laws that prohibit companies from deceiving their customers. But the FTC has failed to stop tech companies from deceiving consumers over and over again. When Big Tech breaks the law, the FTC gives them a slap on the wrist. If the platforms can make tens of billions of dollars a year violating your privacy, and then have to pay a few billions as a fine every decade, it makes economic sense to keep doing it. Paying a fine is just a cost of doing business.

The FTC fined Facebook $5 billion in 2019 for violating a privacy order dating back to 2011, with the two Democratic FTC commissioners dissenting on the ground that stronger measures were needed. Five billion sounds like a lot but consider that Facebook made over $70 billion in 2019 alone by spying on you and then selling advertisers the ability to target you. The FTC's 2011 order was imposed on Facebook for violating users' privacy and required that Facebook "not misrepresent . . . the extent to which it maintains the privacy or security of [personal] information," and establish a comprehensive privacy program that protects the confidentiality of personal information.

For eight years, Facebook basically ignored this order. The only consequence was it had to pay a little over a month's revenue as a penalty. As Commissioner Rohit Chopra stated in his dissenting statement, the settlement will not fix the problem because it did not require Facebook to change its business practices. When the $5 billion fine was announced, Facebook's stock surged.

Our time to demand real privacy laws and enforcement, as well as antitrust action against surveillance monopolists, is short. Federal antitrust enforcers and lawmakers have only begun to exhibit the political will to rein in the powerful and wealthy Silicon Valley giants, and their surveillance-based business models. But as government increasingly grows dependent on Big Tech's surveillance in the name of policing and national security, it will be even less willing to stop it.

Not only can surveillance be used to persecute the innocent, but personal information can be used to screw you over in countless ways, from charging you higher prices than other people pay for the same stuff because your data shows how much you're willing and able to pay, to shutting you out of job opportunities based on personal characteristics, which we'll discuss in chapter 7. And as the following chapters will show, surveillance is also what allows monopolies to hyper target and manipulate you, warp elections, and defund the press.

We can stop the surveillance by demanding our political representatives pass strong privacy laws and enforce the antitrust laws to weaken giant platforms' power and to open up competition to pro-privacy innovators.

MONOPOLIES MAKE YOU SCARED, ANGRY, AND ADDICTED

These are scary times, but some tech monopolies are making them even scarier. For Facebook and Google, your anxiety maximizes profits.

When it comes to harmful content, most people think Facebook and YouTube's main problem is they can't take millions of posts down quickly enough. But both platforms actually *boost* hate and disinformation. Their algorithms prioritize "engagement" (that is, clicks, likes, comments, and shares) to keep users on their platform longer because content that provokes fear and anger—the most incendiary content—"engages" humans the most.

The more time people spend on Facebook's and YouTube's platforms, the more data the platforms collect, the more ads they show, and the more money they make. On Facebook's first quarter 2016 earnings call, CEO Mark Zuckerberg announced that users spend on average more than fifty minutes a day using Facebook, Instagram, and Messenger, up ten minutes from the number reported in 2014. Facebook reports to investors how much of your time and attention it can hoard because that's what fuels Facebook's targeted advertising business model. Advertising accounted for approximately 84 percent of Google's revenue and 98 percent of Facebook's revenue in 2019.

Giving incendiary content top priority best serves Facebook's and YouTube's business models because "engagement" makes them the most money. Their amplification of hateful content is not an inevitability of the internet or human nature—it's a business decision.

In 2017, I interviewed NYU Stern professor and author Scott Galloway, and he said he often gets the question from media about whether it's possible for the platforms to police their content. Galloway said he thought that was such a strange question, given their tremendous cash flow. "We're not talking about the realm of the possible here," said Galloway, "we're talking about the realm of the profitable." He added that "when big tech starts making noises that old media and the government seems to buy into that something would be impossible, that's Latin for we would be less profitable if we did this."

Prioritization of the types of content that rake in the most dough means the platforms' newsfeeds do not neutrally reflect the content people post. Consider the trials and tribulations of Women You Should Know, a pioneering online publisher that has been telling empowering women's stories for years. The site's founders, Jen Jones and Cynthia Hornig, built their small business with Facebook at its core, growing their Facebook fan base to more than 400,000 loyal followers. Their digital ad-supported business thrived, with their Facebook followers regularly clicking to read their articles on WomenYou ShouldKnow.net.

But the site's founders began getting confusing messages from their Facebook fans, messages criticizing Women You Should Know for straying from their positive brand by only sharing negative stories of violence against women. Jen and Cynthia were baffled. Sure, they occasionally shared a story about gender-based violence, an important issue, but the uplifting stories immensely outnumbered those articles. Jen and Cynthia checked their Facebook statistics and realized that Facebook's algorithms—programmed to prioritize engagement—often were not showing followers their positive stories, but rather serving up the stories that provoke fear and anger. Jen and Cynthia wanted to empower women, but Facebook made women afraid instead.

Rather than blaming profit-maximizing algorithms, we tend to blame humanity itself. Humans are the ones who post incendiary content, and humans are terrible for being drawn to this content. But the algorithms prioritize a much bleaker picture than reality reflects, because they bury the middle-of-the-road, reasonable, and even-toned content.

A major reason that humans are drawn to scary content, why it's more "engaging" for us, is our survival instinct. A post reporting a pedophile loose in your neighborhood, whether true or not, will go viral because of humanity's genetic programming to protect our young. We shouldn't feel bad about our survival instinct, but instead fault the giants who profit by setting it off, getting our cortisol pumping, and getting us clicking and sharing. Yes, the current political climate is toxic, but engagement-prioritizing algorithms make it even more so. No wonder we're all so agitated and stressed out!

You may strive to live a calmer life where you are less reactive to the content that barrages you daily, but the richest and most powerful companies in the world have designed their technology to make us do the exact opposite! Clicks, likes, shares, and "being engaged" are reactions that serve Big Tech business models and maximize profits. Facebook and YouTube could prioritize what content is served up to people in countless other ways besides engagement, including simple chronology. Users could even control what types of things are prioritized in their newsfeeds.

Addiction for Profit

When tech companies' profits depend on how much of our time they can hoard, they build addiction into their design. Stanford University even created a program called the Persuasive Technology Lab, where students learned how to build technologies that addict and manipulate.

Tristan Harris, a former Google design ethicist and cofounder of the Center for Humane Technology, explained some of the tricks tech companies employ to addict users in written congressional testimony in January 2020. "'Likes' and 'filters' *exploit teens' need for social validation and approval* from others," wrote Harris, while notifications condition us to expect "frequent rewards." Infinite feeds are "designed to operate like slot machines, offering 'intermittent variable rewards' as you check for notifications, maximizing addiction," he continued. These tricks are rooted in the work of psychologist B. F. Skinner, who learned how to manipulate the behavior of mice back in the 1950s.

Sean Parker, Facebook's founding president, has explained of the social media platform, "It's a social-validation feedback loop . . . exactly the kind of thing that a hacker like myself would come up with, because you're exploiting a vulnerability in human psychology." And

Chamath Palihapitiya, who was Facebook's vice president for user growth, said in an interview that "the short-term, dopamine-driven feedback loops we've created are destroying how society works."

In the same interview, Palihapitiya said he feels "tremendous guilt" for his involvement in building Facebook and noted that his own children "aren't allowed to use that shit." Parents in Silicon Valley reportedly put tight controls on their own kids' use of technology, while many work for companies that profit from addicting other people's kids. Sean Parker has said of Facebook, "God only knows what it's doing to our children's brains."

Harris, too, has sounded the alarm about how addictive technology is affecting our kids. "We are raising a generation of children who are more distracted, less creative, more narcissistic, and more vulnerable to bullying and teen suicides than in the last few decades," wrote Harris. He pointed to a 170 percent increase in high-depressive symptoms for 13–18-year-old girls between 2010 and 2017, which NYU researchers link to social media usage.

Simultaneously, suicide rates in the United States have skyrocketed, doubling for girls aged 15 to 19 between 2007 and 2015. Definitively proving that social media causes increases in depression and suicide is nearly impossible, as causation is notoriously difficult to prove. But it's not a stretch to conclude that social media is harming mental health.

And while forbidding your kids from using social media seems like the solution, it's easier said than done. Teens don't communicate with their friends over email or by calling on the phone. They use platforms like Instagram. Cutting them off from communicating with their friends is a challenge, to say the least, at a developmental stage when peers' opinions mean everything.

As a parent myself, I think about how much easier it was for parents in the 1980s. As a child growing up before call-waiting was even invented, I would call my friend to play and be greeted by a busy signal while her teen sister held up the line for hours. I'd eventually give up, hop on my bike, and fetch my friend in person. Parents in those days merely had to yell "Get off the phone!" without having to battle against billion-dollar corporations who have the exact opposite goal they do.

Extremism Is Engaging

Engagement-maximizing business models don't stop at stressing us out and addicting us—they also foster extremism. As she explained in her TED Talk, "We're building a Dystopia Just to Make People Click on Ads," University of North Carolina associate professor and techno-sociologist Zeynep Tufekci viewed Donald Trump rally videos on YouTube as part of her research. YouTube next served up to her videos of white supremacy through its auto-play feature, which is designed to capture attention. Tufekci watched a video about vegetarianism, and YouTube auto-played her videos about being a vegan. "The algorithm has figured out that if you can entice people into thinking that you can show them something more hardcore, they're more likely to stay on the site watching video after video going down that rabbit hole while Google serves them ads," said Tufekci. Seventy percent of what people watch on YouTube is determined by recommendation algorithms.

YouTube has said it made changes to its algorithm in January 2019 to address concerns about the content it auto-plays. But reporter and producer Emily Gadek tweeted in September 2019 about her experience watching a documentary video produced by *The Atlantic* about rats in New Zealand on YouTube. She left the video running on mute when a meeting began, and within three hops the algorithm had auto-played her a Fox News clip about illegal immigrants entering

America. Was the algorithm drawing a connection between rats and immigrants?

The Mozilla Foundation conducted a campaign to collect You-Tube users' stories about its recommendation engine leading down "sometimes dangerous pathways." Among the stories collected were LGBTQ+ youth watching empowering videos only to be barraged with homophobic content, and a ten-year-old girl's search for "tap dance videos" leading her to body-shaming content that her mother worries has triggered the beginnings of an eating disorder.

Facebook's and YouTube's algorithms take fear-mongering to the extreme by targeting content at individuals based on all the bits of data the platforms have collected about them. The algorithms know exactly how to push your particular buttons because of the platforms' spying on you. Facebook and Google have so much data on you and people who are like you that the algorithms know what content is likely to make you react and know how to target you based on your particular vulnerability.

These giants take all the information they gather on you and crunch it together with the data of billions of other people, so that they can infer things about you that you don't even know about yourself! This means what Facebook and Google know about you is not limited to the tremendous amount of data they've collected about you, but their algorithms draw inferences about you based on the data of billions of other users—that you of course don't have access to. The scale of the data they collect is the problem because they have so much information about so many people that they can know the most personal things about you that you have not in any way disclosed. They can target and manipulate users based on these inferences, knowing what types of messages they are most susceptible to.

Fear, anger, addiction, and extremism are monopoly problems for the same reason privacy is a monopoly problem: monopolies don't lose profits when they abuse you, they can keep you in the dark without the sunlight that competition brings, they buy off lawmakers to stop regulation of harms they cause, and they can shut out innovators with better business models.

Because of their sheer scale, Facebook and Google have outsized control on the flow of information worldwide. If competition existed, purveyors of hate, fear, and disinformation wouldn't have as much of an impact. They wouldn't be able to reach potentially 2.3 billion users on a single platform that boosts their hate. And if digital markets were more competitive, Facebook and Google would have less influence on the worldwide distribution of content.

Just as tech giants can abuse privacy because people can't vote with their feet and switch to alternatives, so too can they push all our buttons and make us angry and fearful without competitive constraint. If competition existed among algorithms and the way content is prioritized and delivered to us, users could choose platforms that don't worsen anxiety and polarization.

Some say an open market would just lead to a race to the bottom as companies competed with one another to addict us. But regulation that incentivizes better business models and makes addictive ones unprofitable or illegal could prevent such an outcome. We can demand our political representatives take action.

Polarizing Media Is Also a Monopoly Problem

Big News also amplifies polarization in America. News companies have always tried to freak us out to get our attention and sell ads. "If it bleeds it leads," was the slogan of newspapers from long ago. But America used to have rules that preserved diversity in the marketplace of ideas and limited how much power one company could have over the flow of information. The rules that remain have been under attack, as the Federal Communications Commission has pursued monopoly-friendly deregulation under its Trump-appointed chairman, Ajit Pai. On top of rubber-stamping the Sprint/T-Mobile merger, the FCC under Pai rolled back long-standing rules that limited the number of stations broadcasters can own. A federal court of appeals invalidated the FCC's rule change, and the FCC has appealed to the Supreme Court.

Pai led the effort to relax broadcast ownership limits after he and his staff had several meetings with executives of Sinclair Broadcast Group, a giant in broadcasting. Sinclair owns and operates 191 broadcast television stations in 89 markets, and has in the past used shell corporations to evade broadcast ownership limits. Sinclair has spread its right-wing viewpoint across the country, including racist and anti-Muslim propaganda. During the 2016 presidential election, Sinclair reportedly ordered its stations to air a video segment that suggested voters should not support Hillary Clinton because the Democratic Party was historically pro-slavery.

In cable, Fox News has a strong grip on the dissemination of information to a large portion of the country. News outlets that reach viewers who are information-poor have greater "media power" and influence, according to researchers. If measured by "attention share," they concluded, "Rupert Murdoch is the most powerful U.S. news owner, both because Fox News has a large viewership and because its viewers are information-poor: they access a smaller number of other sources than users of most other sources." Comcast, which includes NBC, MSNBC, and CNBC, and Time Warner, which includes CNN, each had less than half the attention share of Fox's owner News Corporation.

Such concentrated control of news is not only politically polarizing but can also be dangerous to public health, as we saw at the onset of the COVID-19 pandemic. Fox News has come under fire for minimizing the virus and referring to it as a hoax that was politically motivated to attack Trump. Seventy-four journalism professors wrote a letter to Fox asking the network to urgently "help protect the lives of all Americans—including your elderly viewers—by ensuring that the information you deliver is based on scientific facts." Exposure to different viewpoints is lacking not only on social media, but also in media at large. When media is in the hands of a few owners, information oligopolists can more easily manipulate public opinion.

Your Life, Better

An alternate reality from relentless spying is possible. In that reality, meaningful privacy regulation, not crafted by monopoly lobbyists, curbs surveillance by default. Big Tech is no longer exempt from norms and laws against spying that have long existed in the offline world, like the prohibitions on reading someone else's mail or recording a phone call without consent. Antitrust enforcement brings competition and ensures you have the option of voting with your feet if a company dares abuse your privacy.

You're free to talk to Alexa and control exactly what information Amazon gathers about you and how it's used. Maybe you can even talk to Alex instead—perhaps new competitors don't make all assistants be women by default. Dystopia through surveillance is the stuff of novels like *The Handmaid's Tale* and *1984*, not real life.

When you check social media, you see a range of ideas and outlooks on current affairs that are even-toned and thoroughly researched. Competition and privacy regulation could go a long way to making us feel calmer, safer, more united, and more connected. The needed changes may not be profitable for Big Tech, but they are indeed possible.

For now, a few privacy-protecting alternatives could bring you at least a bit of peace. They include DuckDuckGo for privacy-friendly searching, Brave for private browsing, Protonmail for encrypted email, and Signal for encrypted messaging. DuckDuckGo provides a range of privacy-protecting options on its website spreadprivacy.com. The site also gives tips for adjusting the settings on your devices to maximize privacy and for opting out of online tracking.

FIVE

MONOPOLIES THREATEN DEMOCRACY AND YOUR FREEDOM

"Tonight, Americans find out which candidate
the social media algorithms have selected."

MONOPOLY POWER ENDANGERS OUR ELECTIONS

Facebook's business model is harming political discourse and elections around the world. Ever since the 2016 U.S. presidential election, Facebook has promised to work on its disinformation problem, yet has offered only minor, ineffective Band-Aids. Lies are also spreading on YouTube, Twitter, TikTok, and other platforms, but Facebook likely is the biggest threat because of its massive scale and its micro-targeting features. The problem is not solved—Facebook fueled disinformation in the 2019 British election and the 2020 U.S. Democratic primary.

Drastic, urgent action must be taken against Facebook's surveillance-based, hypertargeted advertising business model, or our democracy risks being subverted to Facebook's financial interests in the 2020 U.S. presidential election and beyond.

Truly fixing Facebook's threat to free and fair elections would require fundamental changes to its business model, but Facebook is not going to upset its gravy train unless it's forced to do so.

By 2016, the digital analytics firm Cambridge Analytica had developed psychological profiles of every American voter, it asserted, using Facebook data. Working hand in hand with Facebook employees, Cambridge Analytica targeted "persuadable" American voters in swing states with propaganda intended to help elect Donald Trump, whose campaign paid the company nearly $6 million. Alexander Nix, Cambridge Analytica's then-CEO, was caught on film pitching the company's disinformation services to reporters, who posed as potential clients interested in changing the outcome of the Sri Lankan elections. "It doesn't have to be true, it just has to be believed," said Nix. Cambridge Analytica has claimed credit for helping to elect far-right leaders around the globe, from Tobago to Kenya to Brazil.

According to congressional testimony by whistle-blower Chris Wylie, Cambridge Analytica cofounder Steve Bannon oversaw the company's campaign to suppress African American voting before leaving the company to become the Trump campaign's CEO. In an interview, Wylie said, "Steve Bannon was looking for ways of fighting a culture war." The weapons are disinformation, and just like a missile or a gun, these weapons need a targeting system, explained Wylie. "So in a culture war, your payload is a narrative, and your targeting system becomes data and algorithms in order to fire at culture, where he needed to literally treat it like a war." Once Steven Bannon and alt-right hedge fund billionaire Robert Mercer learned of the warlike capabilities of the company then called SCL, they bought into it with $10 million to start Cambridge Analytica.

SCL's expertise "was in 'psychological operations—or psyops— changing people's minds not through persuasion but through 'information dominance,' a set of techniques that includes rumour, disinformation and fake news," reports Carole Cadwalladr, the *Guardian* journalist who exposed the Facebook Cambridge Analytica scandal. SCL previously had been hired by the U.S. government's Defense Advanced Research Projects Agency (DARPA) to develop profiling tools. "So all of a sudden," said Wylie, "all of the people who were there when we were looking at research on how to defend Britain, defend America, the tools and the weapons and the things that we were looking at in order to defend the people was now acquired by people who wanted to invert them on those same people and treat an American voter in the same way that we treat a radical Islamist terrorist."

Surveillance done in the name of keeping us safe can easily be turned against us.

Leading up to the 2016 presidential election, Cambridge Analytica harvested the personal data of a reported 87 million Facebook users with a personality quiz that collected users' personal data, and the data of their friends, without their knowledge. This data harvesting operation was led by a Russian-American researcher at the University of Cambridge, Dr. Aleksandr Kogan. Wylie's written testimony said that while Dr. Kogan was working with Cambridge Analytica, he was simultaneously building algorithms using Facebook data for psychological profiling for Russia in St. Petersburg. The Russian project focused on the traits of "narcissism, Machiavellianism and psychopathy," testified Wylie.

Cambridge Analytica, similarly, "sought to identify mental and emotional vulnerabilities in certain subsets of the American population and worked to exploit those vulnerabilities by targeting information designed to activate some of the worst characteristics in people, such as neuroticism, paranoia and racial biases," testified Wylie. He continues, "This was targeted at narrow segments of the population."

What Cambridge Analytica did, however, wasn't a hack on Facebook. Cambridge Analytica played fast and loose with Facebook data, breaking a rule that Facebook failed to enforce. A ton of other apps got access to our personal data, so Facebook hiding behind its meaningless rule is like a bank pointing the finger at robbers when it left its vault open. Overall Cambridge Analytica used Facebook exactly how it is intended to be used—as a manipulation machine.

Through ubiquitous tracking, compiling the data sets of billions of people, and algorithmic inferences, Facebook learns what messages people are susceptible to—whether advertisements, extreme political propaganda, or election meddling. Just as Facebook enables advertisers to influence people's purchasing decisions, it enables propagandists to influence people's political decisions. Facebook made Cambridge Analytica's work easy by spying on us, by programming its algorithms to amplify incendiary content, and by developing micro-targeting that allows propagandists to individually target voters based on highly granular data it has gathered about them. This is still how Facebook's business model works today. In April 2020, *The Markup* reported that Facebook was allowing advertisers to target ads at people it classified as being interested in "pseudoscience," a particularly dangerous proposition amid the rampant disinformation surrounding COVID-19.

In 2017, *The Australian* obtained access to an internal Facebook document that explains how the platform can target "moments when young people need a confidence boost." "By monitoring posts, pictures, interactions and internet activity in real-time, Facebook can work out when young people feel 'stressed,' 'defeated,' 'overwhelmed,' 'anxious,' 'nervous,' 'stupid,' 'silly,' 'useless,' and a 'failure,'" reported the newspaper. Prepared as part of an advertising pitch to one of Australia's big banks, the document stated that detailed information on young people's emotional states is "based on internal Facebook data," according to *The Australian*. The Facebook document includes information on when young people exhibit emotions related to "conquering fear," or moments related to "looking good and body confidence," and "working out & losing weight." When *The Australian*'s report prompted an outcry, Facebook released a statement saying it "does not offer tools to target people based on their emotional state."

But Cambridge Analytica did target users based on emotional vulnerabilities using Facebook data and Facebook micro-targeting. Facebook has even tried to patent psychological profiling, applying for a patent on "determining user personality characteristics from social networking system communications and characteristics."

Facebook rents out its manipulation machine to anyone who will pay, even if their customers are paying for U.S. political ads with rubles. In 2016, the year of the U.S. presidential election and the United Kingdom's Brexit vote, Facebook's ad revenue jumped by nearly $10 billion.

Facebook knew at least as early as 2015 that Cambridge Analytica had harvested users' data, but it didn't warn those users. When the tech giant learned the *Guardian* was going to break the Cambridge Analytica story, Facebook threatened to sue them. Facebook only warned users in 2018, three weeks after the *Guardian*, the *New York Times*, and Channel 4 made the story public. It kicked the whistleblower, Christopher Wylie, off the Facebook, Instagram, and WhatsApp platforms, leading Wylie to ask: "*What happens to our democracy when these companies can delete people at will who dissent, scrutinize, or speak out?*"

Move Fast and Break Democracy

Senator Elizabeth Warren has spoken out against Big Tech and called for the breakup of Facebook, Google, and Amazon. That's a bold thing to do, since Facebook and Google control the flow of information, politicians don't have much of a choice of whether to use them to reach voters, and Facebook is the manipulation tool of choice for elections around the world. In an internal Facebook meeting in July 2019, Mark Zuckerberg predicted that if Warren were to become the next president, "I would bet that we will have a legal challenge. . . ." He vowed to fight such a challenge, saying "at the end of the day, if someone's going to try to threaten something that existential, you go to the mat and you fight."

A few short months later, in the fall of 2019, Mark Zuckerberg had two unannounced meetings with Donald Trump. In mid-October, the week before the second meeting, Zuckerberg gave a speech at Georgetown University stating that although regular ads were not allowed to contain false or deceptive information, "We don't fact-check political ads."

Anyone who speaks out against the monopolist can be punished by the monopolist. Such punishment may come through Facebook business moves that appear neutral on their face. In changing its policies to allow false political ads, which favors Donald Trump, Facebook bought itself protection against getting broken up. Trump probably doesn't want to break up Facebook anyway—he wants to control it. He wants to use the manipulation machine to spread hate-mongering propaganda.

We cannot allow one guy's decisions to influence the election of our nation's leader. I didn't get to vote for Mark Zuckerberg, did you?

Zuckerberg's Georgetown speech justified Facebook's political ad policy as grounded in free expression. But free expression is impossible when one company controls the flow of speech to more than 2.3 billion people, using algorithms that amplify disinformation and surveillance-based ad tools that allow micro-targeting of voters. Facebook picking and choosing what information users see based on how much money the content makes the platform—with "engaging" content being most profitable—is the antithesis of free expression. Deceptive political ads that spread fear and anger, and deceptive content intended to inflame tension and divide Americans on cultural issues, are favored content, boosted by Facebook's business model.

Michelle Obama's slogan, "When they go low, we go high," is not compatible with Facebook's disinformation-amplifying algorithms. Countering hateful propaganda with positive messaging is not possible because Facebook's algorithm will amplify the hate and bury the unifying message. Without Facebook changing its algorithm, being hateful is one of the most effective ways to spread your message and reach voters.

Free expression also requires a public sphere of debate, not individualized feeds of content targeted at people based on information learned about them through surveillance.

In her TED Talk, Zeynep Tufekci talks about how engagement algorithms make the public sphere private: "As a public and as citizens, we no longer know if we're seeing the same information or what anybody else is seeing, and without a common basis of information, little by little, public debate is becoming impossible." This problem of information being siloed and individualized is widely referred to as filter bubbles or echo chambers. When we don't see the same information or if we do, it's presented from the polar opposite perspective, it's no wonder we can't find common ground with each other.

An important principle of First Amendment law is the counter-speech doctrine. Supreme Court justice Louis D. Brandeis established the doctrine in the 1927 case *Whitney v. California*, saying, "If there be time to expose through discussion, the falsehoods and fallacies, to avert the evil by the process of education, the remedy to be applied is more speech, not enforced silence." Brandeis's solution to deceptive or harmful speech is to counter it with speech that sets the record straight or conveys a different message, rather than censoring it. But with targeted social media feeds, users don't see counterspeech. Instead of censorship, one solution is to loosen Facebook's control over the flow of information through competition, as antitrust enforcement could make way for pro-democracy innovators. Another is to prohibit Facebook's surveillance-based, hypertargeted digital advertising business model.

Don't think that Instagram is a disinformation-free alternative to Facebook. A 2018 report by the cybersecurity firm New Knowledge, commissioned by the Senate Intelligence Committee, details the attempts by Russia's Internet Research Agency (IRA) to influence U.S. political discourse. "Instagram was a significant front in the IRA's influence operation, something that Facebook executives appear to have avoided mentioning in Congressional testimony," the report said. "Our assessment is that Instagram is likely to be a key battleground on an ongoing basis."

What's Monopoly Got to Do with It

Facebook is not the only culprit threatening our elections, as a nefarious web of actors are attacking democracy across the globe. But Facebook's scale and lack of accountability make it particularly dangerous, and its political power stands in the way of needed reforms.

Revisiting an earlier point here, what constrains corporations from pursuing profits in ways that cause harm are: 1) competition and 2) regulation. Without either of these, Facebook can choose a business model that endangers our elections, and it doesn't have to worry about losing customers or profits. It can choose to spy on us, program its algorithms to boost incendiary content, and allow propagandists of all kinds—whether advertisers, foreign governments, or lying American politicians—to individually target us based on invasive profiling.

Facebook doesn't have to worry about users defecting to a competitor because Facebook bought its closest substitutes. It can use its monopoly power to shut out potential competitors that would do better, competing by offering different algorithms or business models. Facebook can use its political power to stop lawmakers from making the needed fixes. On that front, the GOP leadership seems to favor Facebook's interests in allowing election interference, believing any interference would be to their advantage, and being willing to trade democracy for political gain.

I've focused on Facebook, but Google's YouTube is also a threat to elections because of its engagement-prioritizing algorithms and 2 billion users. An in-depth report by the *New York Times* looked at YouTube's role in the election in Brazil of far-right president Jair Bolsonaro. "In a country driven to the edge by economic and political crises, YouTube's algorithms may have played a decisive role in Bolsonaro's rise." The sheer scale of Facebook and Google's surveillance, the manipulation they allow, and their massive reach means the dangers they cause are a direct result of lawmakers allowing them to morph into monopoly monsters.

Facebook's and YouTube's power must be checked and their dangerous business models dismantled to save our elections.

Winning this battle will take time, but immediately one simple measure could make a difference in our elections—banning or heavily restricting micro-targeted advertising. As Wylie points out, the weapon in the war against the American voter is disinformation, and disinformation needs a targeting system just like a missile or a gun does. Facebook's own employees have called for restrictions on micro-targeting in a letter to management that included other commonsense measures, like imposing a silence period before elections

nity for content posted on their platforms. News publish-
compete against Facebook and Google while being held
legal standards.

hird-party sellers competing against Amazon on Amazon
pp developers competing against Apple in its App Store,
ishers are in the lose-lose position of competing against the
they must use to reach customers. Facebook and Google
eir gatekeeper positions to divert ad revenue away from
s and into their own pockets. As Jason Kint explains it,
and Facebook have put themselves between news institu-
their readers, often replacing valuable editorial decisions
orithmic decisions." But, says Kint, "They act as absentee
ften missing local context in their understanding of and im-
communities," and "capture outsized profits without the risk
ty for content and programming decisions."
e again, the platform monopolists are controlling the game
ing it, too.

with the Flip of a Switch

e Facebook and Google have concentrated control over the
t, which at its start was wonderfully decentralized, news pub-
became dependent on them to reach users. But over time both
ms have adjusted their product design to keep more and more
t traffic for themselves. Google and Facebook both have busi-
centives to keep users on their platforms to collect more data
ow more ads. More than 70 percent of Google's revenue came
ads on its own properties in 2018. The platforms pull techno-
l levers that keep users within Facebook's and Google's digital
reducing traffic to news publishers' properties and depriving
shers of the ad revenue that funds journalism.

when no political ads can run. Facebook's former chief security officer has also proposed limits to micro-targeting as a solution, as has
Ellen L. Weintraub, a Democratic commissioner of the Federal Election Commission.

Micro-targeting must be banned across the board, not just on
Facebook. Digital strategies also include "geo-fencing," using people's IP addresses to identify whether they attended a Trump rally or
church, for example, and to then target their devices with text messages or app alerts.

The number of tools to spy on and manipulate us is proliferating,
and fixing Facebook won't fix everything. But it'll be a damn good
start. People will say the solutions of ending surveillance and micro-
targeting are too simplistic, unrealistic, naïve, and not possible. Those
are the people who benefit from the status quo and have something
to lose by changing it, who want us all to throw up our hands and say
"it's too complicated" to do anything. But don't listen! Our democracy is worth fighting for, and monopolies' profits are not worth its
sacrifice.

Monopoly power threatens our elections in another way. Russian
hackers targeted voting machines in twenty-one states in 2016 and
breached systems in two states, according to Special Counsel Robert
Mueller's report. Yet a voting machine duopoly stands in the way of
securing our elections from hacking. Two companies, Election Systems & Software (ES&S) and Dominion Voting Systems, together
supply more than 80 percent of America's voting machines. Several of
their lobbyists reportedly made contributions to Mitch McConnell's
campaign and joint fund-raising committee, soon before McConnell
made clear he would not allow any of the bipartisan bills proposing
voting machine reform to reach the Senate floor.

MONOPOLIES RAVAGE THE FREE PRESS ESSENTIAL TO DEMOCRACY

Politicians who are supposed to represent you and your fellow voters are doing the bidding of big business instead. How do they get away with it?

Your local hometown newspaper closed up shop. They'd been around forever and were the only ones keeping tabs on local politicians and writing about what's happening in your community. The local paper just couldn't keep up in the digital age, people say.

Or perhaps your hometown paper still exists but is a shell of its former self. Most of its content is nationally syndicated, with a small local section that's a far cry from hard-hitting news.

Now your favorite online news company is also closing its doors. Tech-savvy Millennials ran that media outlet, and everyone said the founders were so innovative. Innovation apparently wasn't enough to keep their reporting alive, either. Real news is becoming an endangered species, at the same time that "fake news" is booming. Where are the watchdogs that help hold local and federal governments accountable, while helping us know more about our community, by informing, recording, and commenting on what's going on?

The Internet Didn't Kill the News, Monopolies Did

With disinformation running rampant, we desperately need a strong press. But at the same time that Facebook and Google are boosting deceptive propaganda, they're decimating journalism. Facebook and Google are monopolizing ad revenue, while using the content that publishers create as fodder to fuel their platforms. Newspaper employment fell about 47 percent between 2008 and 2018, and more than half of America's counties now don't have a daily local paper. This means thousands fewer reporters and editors are covering the

news. By April 2020, thirty-three th[...] panies were furloughed, had their p[...] COVID-19 pandemic reduced adv[...] the collapse of local news.

Many people think Craigslist is [...] of local newspapers because it pock[...] that had long supported news. Whil[...] a traditionally important source of j[...] cannot be blamed for media outlets'[...] the multibillion-dollar digital ad mar[...] advertising could support journalism j[...] in the past. But Facebook and Google [...] of the growth of the more than $150 [...] European digital advertising market, ac[...] of Digital Content Next, a trade assoc[...] book and Google make a ton of money [...] ers create—without having to pay the c[...] creating the content themselves. Just like [...] wealth from creators like songwriters, Fa[...] the fruits of journalists' labor.

Facebook and Google are publisher[...] user attention, user data, and ad dollars. [...] get through Facebook's and Google's gate[...] the two platforms' concentrated control ov[...] tion globally. More than 68 percent of A[...] news from social media, according to Pew. A[...] second-largest news provider when measur[...] Americans' attention.

Facebook, however, has long maintained [...] and not a publisher, so that it can avoid liabil[...] content under a safe harbor law called Sectio[...] nications Decency Act. Section 230 gives Bi[...]

Facebook has the ability to hoard more user attention, data, and ad revenue simply by tweaking its algorithm. Facebook changed its algorithm in 2018, promising to show more posts from friends and family. This flip of a switch decimated news publishers of all sizes, threatening the survival of outlets like *Mother Jones, Vox,* and *Slate. Slate*'s traffic from Facebook plummeted 87 percent from a peak of 28 million in January 2017 to less than 4 million in May 2018. Even the small media company that I mentioned earlier, Women You Should Know, is still fighting for its survival after the 2018 algorithmic change caused its Web traffic to plummet.

Women You Should Know is a digital native, with almost half a million followers on Facebook, not an old crusty media outlet that couldn't keep up with the digital age. Failure to innovate in the face of disruption is not the problem. Neither are *Vox* or *Slate* old-fashioned dinosaurs. The problem, instead, is Facebook's consolidated gatekeeper power over the internet. Because of Facebook's centralized power, its changes—even purportedly well-intentioned ones—determine the winners and losers of content, including news publishers' very existence.

Publishers never had a fair shot, nor do they have bargaining power against the platforms.

Facebook and Google can pursue profit-maximizing tactics and hurt the profits of real news companies without constraint because the normal checks and balances of a free, competitive market do not exist. Weak antitrust enforcement set the stage for these platforms to extract the fruits of publishers' and journalists' labor, much as monopolies are extracting wealth across most sectors of our economy. If publishers have no choice but to deal with monopolists because they have become the infrastructure of information flow, monopolists can extract wealth and undercut publishers' ability to bring important and diverse viewpoints to the world.

With the ability to control the distribution of information, ad money, and the relationship between the reader and the news outlet, tech platform monopolists now have unprecedented power over reporters and news publishers themselves. In yet another instance of monopolists giving with one hand and taking a whole lot more with the other, Facebook and Google have begun giving grants to news organizations. These grants only increase the platforms' power over journalists and don't fix the real problems.

Spies Like Us

On top of Facebook and Google hoarding internet traffic, a main problem is that Facebook and Google each built an architecture of surveillance—with the help of anticompetitive mergers—that sustains their duopoly power over digital advertising. Publishers and content creators that don't read your email, know your internet searches, track your location, know who your friends are, know every YouTube video you've watched or what you've purchased across the Web, for example, can't really hope to compete with Google and Facebook, who are tracking you in all of these ways and more, for targeted advertising dollars.

Advertising used to be done based on context (you'd see a fishing pole ad next to an article about fishing), rather than by tracking people across the Web and offline to target ads at them (instead you see a fishing pole because a tech platform spied on your fishing trip last weekend). This context-based advertising was a better deal for news publishers and content creators, and for you. Banning hypertargeted advertising would help level the competitive playing field for digital ad dollars, while lessening problems like election interference and user manipulation that we've already discussed.

Monopoly Corruption with No One Watching

A financially frail and smaller press means politicians can cater to monopoly money in the dark. They can represent huge corporations' interests instead of yours, without being held accountable for it.

Kevin Riley, editor of the *Atlanta Journal-Constitution* (*AJC*), testified before Congress about the role his paper has played in protecting the people of Georgia: "At times, the AJC's reporters appear to be among the only journalists covering the bills, the lobbyists and the political developments," wrote Riley. The *AJC* has a reporter who has been covering the state budget for decades, helping to ensure that budgets serve the people instead of powerful corporations. Incidentally, it was the *AJC* that investigated and exposed Georgia's incorrect—some argued misleading—reporting of coronavirus case numbers, while Governor Brian Kemp swiftly reopened the state. Kemp later publicly apologized. When local papers can no longer make ends meet due to monopoly power over digital ad revenue, politicians become unaccountable to the public.

In chapter 4, we discussed how Californians overwhelmingly support privacy legislation, but yet their elected representatives keep proposing amendments to destroy California's new privacy law. In the 2019–20 legislative session, lawmakers proposed more than a dozen amendments to try to weaken the law. Big Tech has limitless funds to throw at local legislators willing to sell out their people in order to fund their next reelection campaign. This reelection strategy only works if voters don't know what their representatives are doing, which is why the destruction of local news is a critical component to the corruption.

As Big Tech exerts political leverage to try to decimate the will of the people, few local journalists are left to expose the politicians acting at Big Tech's behest. And because Big Tech has used its monopoly power to starve journalism, the people of California often don't know their representatives are working for Big Tech instead of them.

Even privacy activists have a hard time keeping up with all the proposed amendments to California's law. They have a limited amount of time to respond, so not knowing about a bill stops them from being able to fight it. The more adept Big Tech is at thwarting privacy regulation, the more it will continue to starve journalism and the more it will be able to influence government under the cloak of secrecy.

Effective privacy laws would go a long way toward opening up competition and leveling the playing field between Facebook and Google on one hand and news publishers on the other. Strong privacy legislation would help save journalism and weaken Facebook's and Google's monopoly power. Yet it risks being thwarted because of that very monopoly power.

Your voice can help make strong privacy laws and antitrust enforcement against platform monopolists happen. Politicians can stand up to corporate power if a movement of people—who refuse to take it anymore—has their back.

Real News Gets Buried

We've talked about how Facebook and YouTube amplify content that makes us fearful and angry, giving a boost to incendiary propaganda and "fake news." This boost means legitimate news that is not incendiary is de-prioritized, pushed to the bottom of newsfeeds or not shown to users at all. Since disinformation that says Hillary Clinton is running a child sex ring out of a pizza place is more "engaging" than a Pulitzer Prize–winning well-researched article, the real article gets buried. As Maria Ressa, CEO and executive editor of the Philippines' *Rappler*, said in a 2019 speech: "Newsrooms are born to compete, but what we're not seeing is that we're no longer competing against each other—we're competing against disinformation networks. We're competing to tell the facts."

If Facebook's algorithms show the content created by legitimate news publishers less often, then Facebook is tipping the competitive playing field against the publishers it competes with for ad revenue and in favor of content that keeps users on its platform. Such exclusionary behavior is not much different than Google sending competing comparison-shopping services to page four of its search results or Microsoft eliminating Netscape as a browser option on computers in favor of its own Internet Explorer. Burying real news is not only terrible for democracy, it's also a form of monopolization.

Your Life, Better

We can no longer tolerate foreign governments, unscrupulous politicians, and alt-right billionaires being able to psychologically profile us and individually target us with deceptive propaganda. We must demand that lawmakers and enforcers dismantle Facebook's manipulation machine, pass tough privacy laws, and ban surveillance-based targeted advertising, particularly micro-targeting around elections. Only we, the people, can save our elections and our democracy.

When the internet is no longer consolidated into the hands of a few gatekeepers, a robust set of open, interoperable platforms can provide consumers varied options for getting their news, and losing referral traffic from Facebook or Google is no longer such a big deal for news publishers. Public discourse is not subject to the whims and profit motives of monopolists, who can no more extract a tax on or silence everyone else's ideas, creations, and whistle-blowers' and watchdogs' important work. We can see what speech others are seeing, and we can respond to any speech we don't like with counterspeech, as the

First Amendment requires. When politicians act on behalf of their monopoly overlords instead of their voters, their betrayals make the front-page news. Knowing they'll face consequences on election day, politicians become more accountable to the people. This reality is less profitable for big tech, but it *is* possible.

SIX

MONOPOLIES DESTROY OUR PLANET AND CONTROL YOUR FOOD

"I don't care what the 'experts' say.
I'm not budging."

MONOPOLIES RUIN HUMANITY'S HABITAT

Perhaps you've given up plastic bags, straws, and bottles. Maybe you stopped eating meat, drive an electric car, or even use a bike as your means of transportation. But you wonder what good it all does when the Environmental Protection Agency has been gutted and the United States has pulled out of the Paris Climate Accord, which most countries weren't complying with anyway.

If you're a parent, you ache to tell your kids that everything is going to be okay and that you will protect them. Your children wonder why you aren't fixing it. Kids are taking matters into their own hands, walking out of school for climate marches and trying to convince the world's political and business leaders to act. Swedish teenage climate activist Greta Thunberg displays the courage that adults lack.

Experts say that if we continue on our current course, the future will be ridden with dangerous weather, a major reduction in global food supply, rampant political conflict, and millions of climate refugees, with entire cities and even countries dropping into the ocean or becoming uninhabitable. It's so terrifying to think about that you probably want to stop reading this right now, but there is reason for hope.

We Know What We Have to Do

We've already caused irreparable damage to our habitat by warming it by one degree Celsius, but if we limit the warming to 1.5 degrees Celsius, we can avert extreme catastrophe. What needs to be done is not a mystery, but rather is a matter of global consensus among scientists (apart from those who are being paid by Big Oil to lie to us). Young Thunberg spelled it out as clear as day at the World Economic Forum at Davos in 2020:

> When we children tell you to panic, we're not telling you to go on like before . . . And let's be clear, we don't need a low carbon economy, we don't need to lower emissions. Our emissions have to stop if we are to have a chance to stay below the 1.5 degree target. And until we have the technologies that at scale can put our emissions to minus, then we must forget about net zero. We need real zero. . . .
>
> We demand that at this year's World Economic Forum, participants from all companies, banks, institutions, and governments immediately hold all investments in fossil fuel exploration and extraction, immediately end all fossil fuel subsidies and immediately

and completely divest from fossil fuels. We don't want these things done by 2050 or 2030 or even 2021; we want this done now. It may seem like we are asking for a lot and you will of course say that we are naive, but this is just the very minimum amount of effort that is needed to start the rapid sustainable transition. So either you do this, or you're going to have to explain to your children why you are giving up on the 1.5 degree target, giving up without even trying. . . . Your inaction is fueling the flames by the hour, and we are telling you to act as if you loved your children above all else.

We have the solutions to the climate crisis. Like so many other problems discussed in this book, we tie ourselves up in knots trying to find solutions that the behemoths in power will accept. We are told the actual solutions are unrealistic and naïve because they won't fly with the monopolies that run our economy and our government. Solutions that won't work are billed as "realistic" because they won't meaningfully impact monopoly profits. But if something doesn't work, it's not a solution at all. What's more naïve than pursuing nonsolutions when trying to avoid global catastrophe? In Thunberg's words, even worse than doing nothing are "empty words and promises which give the impression that sufficient action is being taken."

Just like when Big Tech says change is *not possible* what it really means is change is *not profitable*, the same is true for Big Oil. The people who say that stemming the climate crisis is not possible are the ones who have something to lose. Rex Tillerson, the former CEO of ExxonMobil and former U.S. secretary of state under Donald Trump, feigned ignorance of scientific consensus on the climate impact of cutting emissions in February 2020, saying "whether or not anything we do will ultimately influence [climate change] remains to be seen." He added, "One day we'll know the answer to that, but our ability to predict the answer to that is quite complicated."

There it is again. The old "it's complicated" do-nothing trap again used by those in power who don't want anything to change. It's not that freaking complicated!

As Naomi Klein writes in *On Fire: The (Burning) Case for a Green New Deal*, "If you are part of the economy's winning class and funded by even bigger winners, as so many politicians are, then your attempts to craft climate legislation tend to be guided by the idea that change should be as minimal and as unchallenging to the status quo as possible." Eliminating emissions and meeting the 1.5 degree target is possible. It's just not profitable for the select few who are reaping the spoils of the status quo.

When we let big corporations rule the world instead of people, short-term thinking fixated on maximizing profits for the next quarter determines what is possible and what is not. Michael Mann, one of the world's leading climate scientists, told the *Guardian*, "The great tragedy of the climate crisis is that seven and a half billion people must pay the price—in the form of a degraded planet—so that a couple of dozen polluting interests can continue to make record profits."

Meeting the 1.5 degree target is actually profit-maximizing for most everybody else. From 2017 to 2019, climate disaster events across the United States cost more than $460 billion, according to government reports. Citibank puts the cost of climate inaction at $44 trillion by 2060, while estimating the cost of investing in renewables as lower than the costs of continuing on the current path. Even most of the monopolies in this book see the climate crisis as bad for business. A 2019 report shows that major corporations expect the climate crisis to cost them $1 trillion over the next five years, while estimating opportunities to address climate change could bring in more than $2 trillion.

Greta Thunberg is not the naïve one. What could be more unhinged from reality than flushing trillions of dollars down the toilet while endangering the future of humanity? Governments are planning to produce 120 percent more fossil fuels by 2030 than meeting the 1.5 degree target requires, according to a 2019 report. Talk about being unrealistic.

Opportunity in Crisis

To stem the climate crisis, we must make drastic changes to the way power is structured that will enrich 99 percent of Americans. This gives reason for hope.

This book is all about how concentrated power is ruining our lives. Nowhere is that clearer than in the threat to humanity posed by the climate crisis. Monopolized America is unsustainable, and concentrated power, most literally, will be the end of us unless we act now to break it down and redistribute it. A transition to renewable energy sources would do exactly this. The transition, like all drastic change, will be difficult, but ultimately it will make our lives better, while preserving humanity's habitat. A deconcentrated economy is good for everyone.

And as Naomi Klein explains, "We will not get the job done unless we are willing to embrace systemic economic and social change." For this reason, the Green New Deal doesn't just call for eliminating emissions; it also calls for universal health care, education, and day care and calls for green jobs to be unionized. Some have criticized the Green New Deal approach for focusing on economic and social justice, saying it makes climate action harder to politically achieve. But rather than "weighing it down," the social and economic components of the Green New Deal "are precisely what is lifting it up," writes Klein.

Any plan that passes on the costs of the transition to sustainability to working people is destined to fail, Klein posits, pointing to French president Emmanuel Macron's attempt to increase a fuel tax in 2018. The tax led to protests and riots by workers in yellow safety vests, who were already under intense economic strain. Macron was forced to roll back the tax. "The Green New Deal, however, is already showing that it has the power to mobilize a truly intersectional mass movement behind it—not despite its sweeping ambition, but precisely because of it," writes Klein.

We can't save humanity unless we make people's lives better because, like the yellow vests, Americans already stretched thin, or devastated by COVID-19, cannot withstand greater economic strain. But, as I hope this book has convinced you, attempts to make people's lives better will fail unless we deconcentrate power and stop monopolistic extraction of wealth from us all.

With humanity's future hanging in the balance, then, we have no choice but to fight monopoly power. The Green New Deal recognizes this, including a provision for "ensuring a commercial environment where every business is free from unfair competition and domination by domestic or international monopolies."

The Green New Deal has the potential to democratize power. Open Markets Institute's Sandeep Vaheesan explains how Franklin Delano Roosevelt's New Deal gave loans and support to rural residents who wanted to electrify their communities through cooperation. The program, administered by the Rural Electrification Administration, revolutionized rural America and brought electricity controlled by the people to farms across the country. "Like its 1930s counterpart, the Green New Deal should champion democratic cooperation in electricity," writes Vaheesan. Such a plan "would help put the United States on a path to clean power controlled not by unaccountable and short-termist corporate and financial interests, but by all of us."

The United States Climate Alliance, a bipartisan coalition of twenty-five state governors, announced in November 2019: "we have demonstrated that economic growth and climate action go hand-in-hand. Alliance states have reduced emissions faster than the rest of the country while growing per capita GDP three times as fast. Climate action is a driver of—not a deterrent to—innovation and economic strength."

We're all so accustomed to monopoly rule that we've forgotten what America can achieve when our government works for the people instead of giant corporations.

Oligopolies Brought Us Here

Fossil fuel giants are the epitome of the extractive business model, literally extracting resources from earth while extracting wealth from everyone else—and much worse, extracting the future from humanity.

Chevron, Exxon, BP, and Shell are together behind more than 10 percent of global carbon emissions since 1965, reports the *Guardian*. Together with Total, they invested over $1 billion on misleading climate-related branding and lobbying against climate-motivated policy in the three years following the Paris Agreement, according to the nonprofit InfluenceMap. Five out of the top ten largest global companies by revenue are oil and gas companies. Yet the United States government pays $20 billion in direct fossil fuel subsidies annually, giving a taxpayer handout to the richest companies in the world to destroy humanity's habitat.

Oil and gas giants knew they were endangering humanity long before we did. Exxon actively suppressed research beginning in the 1970s about the effects of fossil fuels on the viability of our habitat. In the early 1990s, Koch Industries joined Exxon in promoting a counter-narrative to climate change. These giants effectively own members of Congress, predominantly in the Republican Party. From 2019 to 2020, sixteen of the top twenty recipients of oil and gas donations were Republican, according to Open Secrets. Mitch McConnell ranked number five and Donald Trump ranked fourth in dollar amount of donations received.

Koch Industries is consistently the top oil and gas donor, donating to Republican politicians and conservative groups. As journalist Christopher Leonard detailed in his book *Kochland*, the Koch brothers built a lobbying powerhouse that included "think tanks, university research institutes, industry trade associations, and a parade of philanthropic institutions to support it financially," known as the "Kochtopus."

To make matters worse, Big Finance and Big Tech are in bed with Big Oil. "The 'big three' asset managers have massive holdings of coal stocks, and the world's largest asset manager, BlackRock, alone holds nearly $61 billion in equity in four of the largest global oil companies," writes Graham Steele for the Great Democracy Initiative, a nonprofit organization developing policy solutions for a rigged economy. Steele proposes that financial regulators use existing legal authority to stop Big Finance's funding of the climate crisis, which poses significant risks to financial stability. Steele notes that the corporations polluting earth are currently being treated as "too big to fail," and concludes, "Instead, it is our planet, not the big banks or Big Oil, that we cannot afford to let fail."

As for Big Tech, they're climate hypocrites. Journalist Brian Merchant exposes the dishonesty in Big Tech's public commitments to sustainability in a piece for *Gizmodo* titled, "How Google, Microsoft, and Big Tech are Automating the Climate Crisis." Google, Merchant writes, is a "veritable innovation arm of the fossil fuel extraction industry," that is "using machine learning to find more oil reserves both above and below the seas, its data services are streamlining and automating extant oilfield operations, and it is helping oil companies find ways to trim costs and compete with clean energy upstarts."

Amazon even has an oil and gas division that pitches its Amazon Web Services to fossil fuel companies! When Amazon employees spoke out against it, Amazon threatened to fire them. "Empowering Oil & Gas with AI," was the theme of Microsoft's November 2018 exhibition at one of the world's largest trade events for oil and gas in Abu Dhabi. Take a minute and contemplate the absurdity of "empowering" companies that are among the most powerful on earth, whose unrelenting quest for profits threaten the future survival of humanity.

On top of Microsoft rolling out its AI to help optimize drilling, Microsoft Azure has a contract with Chevron that is rumored to be worth more than a billion dollars to help it more efficiently destroy planet earth. Microsoft Azure also counts BP, Shell, and an Exxon subsidiary as clients, reports Merchant.

Facebook, for its part, earns tens of millions of dollars on disinformation advertising by Big Oil. InfluenceMap estimated that oil and gas companies and their trade groups spent $17 million on political advertising on Facebook in the United States alone, just between May 2018 and October 2019. This number doesn't include all the deceptive Facebook groups funded by Big Oil, like "Texans for Natural Gas," which has spent up to $750,000 on political social media advertising. InfluenceMap adds that "social media tactics have particularly supported the oil sector and their trade groups' attempts to block or rollback regulation that impacts their sector at the state-level."

Big Oil, Big Finance, and Big Tech are in cahoots, and we must beat them (as well as Big Ag, which we'll talk about in the next section) to save humanity's future. Similar to how monopoly and privacy abuses are intricately related, so too are monopoly power and climate change. Concentrated corporate power allows these companies to destroy earth and hurt us all without losing profits, to choose dangerous business models, to keep us in the dark about the ways they are destroying earth, and to buy off lawmakers to keep them from passing robust environmental laws. Climate-destroying business models are not inevitable. Sustainable, affordable alternatives exist. Big Oil uses their market power to shut out green innovators, and if lawmakers and enforcers would loosen the oligopolists' grip on the rules of the game, it would give green innovations a chance to break through.

But we don't have time to wait for an antitrust case to break up fossil fuel companies. We need to break out everything else in the anti-monopoly toolkit. We need to attack corruption, insist on regulation, and remove financial support for fossil fuels. We need to pass the Green New Deal, or a similar legislative platform. We need to act immediately not just at national and international levels, but also locally.

Consumerism Won't Save Us

The ideological primacy of the consumer over other aspects of humanity has not just destroyed antitrust law (while price-gouging us all in the name of "consumer welfare"), it has endangered humanity itself. We've been operating on a climate-destroying model of economic growth driven by consumption, a model increasingly questioned by economists who fall into two main camps. One camp thinks economic prosperity is possible without growth, by shifting spending from accumulating stuff to services, such as health care and child care. The other camp strives for "green growth"—growth driven by things like sustainable infrastructure investment, without carbon emissions.

Consumerism has been both this country's economic model and our drug. In our monopoly-based system that extracts wealth and power from us and puts us under relentless stress, shopping has been the opiate of the masses. So have the dopamine hits we get from notifications and posts on social media, and quite literally, opioids. These opiates distract us from the robber barons stealing from us and numb the pain of those who suffer the worst consequences of their extraction.

We've been so indoctrinated into the cult of the consumer that we've forgotten how much power we have as citizens. We tend to look for solutions in consumerism but buying metal straws is not the answer. No one can solve this problem individualistically.

Meeting the 1.5 degree target requires collective action. Collective action is daunting when we are all time-starved. But if you reduced your shopping and social media usage, you'd be surprised how much room you actually do have for flexing your citizenship muscle by participating in green groups like Earthjustice, Greenpeace, or local groups in your community. It's not about saying "no" to stuff that makes you happy, it's about saying "yes" to a better life—and a brighter future for our children. Because, let's face it, that stuff never made you happy in the first place. We throw stuff into an unfillable hole left by a life under pressure, a life without enough community and purpose. Civic engagement actually can fill that hole. And whether to be an active citizen is frankly no longer optional.

Humanity will rise to the occasion because it must, and now. The Sunrise Movement championing the Green New Deal is just one example of the type of collective action that, together with movements around the globe, can simultaneously defeat monopolistic extraction, create an economy that works for all, and save humanity's home. The most important obstacle to overcome is the belief—sowed by those who benefit from the status quo—that change is not possible. Don't listen to their nonsense. We will only be able to meet the 1.5 degree target if we believe we can and take action accordingly.

MONOPOLIES CONTROL YOUR FOOD

Only four companies—Bayer-Monsanto, Corteva (formerly part of Dow-Dupont), Syngenta Group, and BASF—control the vast majority of the world's supply of seeds and agricultural chemicals. Among them, Bayer-Monsanto is the world's largest vegetable seed company, cotton seed company, herbicide company, and owner of intellectual property for seed traits. It locks farmers into "platforms" of seeds and herbicides that only work together. If a farmer doesn't use Monsanto's seeds that are formulated to resist its herbicide Dicamba, for example, crops die when Dicamba blows over from a neighboring farm. And Monsanto has sued farmers for patent infringement if it finds Monsanto plants growing in their fields, even though many farmers say their fields were contaminated with Monsanto's seeds without their knowledge, due to wind and rain. Farmers ultimately are left with little choice but to use Monsanto's seeds and Monsanto's herbicides.

Monsanto was already exerting monopoly rule when it merged with the agro-giant Bayer in 2018, yet the world's antitrust enforcers let it happen! Opposing the deal, the National Family Farm Coalition wrote that the combined company's dominance in seeds and pesticides "means that more and more farmers will be compelled to plant these crops and spray more and more toxic herbicides throughout farm country."

Bayer-Monsanto is a dominant tech platform, too, using sensors in farmers' fields and farmers' equipment to track them and using algorithms to manipulate their farming practices. With data-driven agriculture, Bayer-Monsanto tells farmers how many seeds to plant and how much herbicide to use, while also selling farmers the seeds and herbicide. Talk about a conflict of interest.

With four platforms controlling the world's supply of seeds, the consequences of every decision these ag giants make—which are geared toward profit maximizing and shareholder return—are felt worldwide. Merely four companies decide what chemicals and practices farmers use that have tremendous impact on what we eat, on public health, and on the earth.

What could go wrong? Glysophate, the active ingredient in Bayer-Monsanto's Roundup, has ended up in our drinking water and breakfast cereal, for one thing. In June 2020, Bayer-Monsanto agreed to pay $10 billion to settle thousands of people's claims that Roundup caused their cancer but plans to keep selling the product without a warning label. For another thing, our food supply has become increasingly fragile, with every limit to farmers' choices limiting eaters' choices, too.

And it's not just seeds. An in-depth Open Markets Institute report, "Food and Power: Addressing Monopolization in America's Food System," by Claire Kelloway and Sarah Miller, details how every aspect of the food supply has concentrated into a few hands in recent decades: chicken, beef, pork, dairy, seeds, herbicides, farm equipment, grain processing, grocery stores, food brands, cafeteria operators.

By consolidating our food supply, all of our eggs are in a few baskets. Big Ag mergers risk food shortages the way that we've seen Big Pharma mergers lead to drug shortages. Early on in the novel coronavirus pandemic, farmers were dumping up to 3.7 million gallons of milk per day, a single chicken processor was smashing 750,000 eggs each week, and farmers were destroying their produce. Meanwhile, America plunged into a hunger crisis. COVID-19 exposed that a consolidated food supply chain is a fragile one.

"Beginning in the 1980s, the federal government allowed more agribusinesses to merge and grow largely without restraint in the name of efficiency—before, antitrust and other policies helped keep these industries decentralized and competitive," wrote Kelloway for *Washington Monthly*. University of Missouri professor Mary Hendrickson explained in the article, "If you pull out one little thing in that specialized, centralized, consolidated chain, then everything crashes." The consequences have been severe during the pandemic. "Now we have an animal welfare catastrophe, an environmental catastrophe, a farmer catastrophe, and a worker catastrophe altogether, and we can trace a lot of this back to the pursuit of efficiency." When giant plants closed because of COVID-19 outbreaks, farmers began euthanizing their animals by the thousands. Consolidation of the food supply chain leads to massive bottlenecks and locks farmers into contracts for dominant buyers, meaning that farmers can't redirect their products to other plants or purposes.

One of America's biggest COVID clusters occurred at a Smithfield pork processing plant in South Dakota. The workers are mostly immigrants and refugees, and the work is grueling. Union representatives told the BBC that Smithfield had failed to adequately protect its workers, ignoring requests for personal protective equipment, incentivizing sick workers to keep working, and withholding information about the virus's spread. A Chinese conglomerate owns Smithfield, the largest pork producer in the world, which slaughters 1 in every 4 hogs raised in America. Kelloway told me in an interview that Smithfield is "using American land and resources," and "exporting a really dirty form of production to the U.S., growing these hogs, making money on them in the U.S., but also shipping them back to China." An estimated 550 farms send their pigs to this one Smithfield plant in South Dakota. If the industry was less concentrated, these farmers would have more options and flexibility to respond to a single plant closure by sending their pigs elsewhere.

Beef is no better. About 85 percent of beef slaughter is controlled by four companies: Tyson, JBS, Cargill, and National Beef. Consolidation in all aspects of the industry means ranchers cannot get a fair price from monopolist buyers, and an average of nearly 17,000 cattle ranchers have gone out of business every year since 1980. The low prices paid to ranchers have not led to low prices for consumers. The prices of beef and pork went up 41 percent between 2000 and 2010. As of June 2020, DOJ is investigating the beef giants for price-fixing, and has indicted four poultry industry executives for conspiring to set chicken prices. Price-fixing, you'll remember, violates Section 1 of the Sherman Act, and it is easier to do when fewer companies rule an industry.

Merger mania hasn't been good for food quality or safety, either. In 2017, for example, JBS was accused of bribing meat inspectors and exporting rotten meat to the United States. Concentrated control over our food supply leads to massive recalls, like all romaine lettuce, because of the reach monopolies have.

"Food markets are so heavily concentrated today that the big behemoths are eating each other, and what's caught in the middle is the consumer and the farmer, and they're being crushed," said Joe Maxwell, president of Family Farm Action and former Missouri lieutenant governor, at a February 2020 conference hosted by the *Capitol Forum*, noting that Walmart recently opened a beef plant in Georgia. He added that "over a three-year period of time the cattle prices dropped 13 percent and there was an increase to consumers by 4 percent. There was not an increase in cost of production, there was simply more profit made by the largest packers in the world, and they put that money in their pocket."

Big Tech's exploitative relationship with businesses of all sizes looks like a partnership compared to the tyranny of the Monsanto platform over the farmer, or the Perdue platform over the chicken-raiser. Monopoly rule means that three out of every four poultry farmers live below the poverty line, as of a 2001 study. One point eight billion dollars of Americans' tax money was used between 2012 and 2016 to back up loans for poultry farmers from the Small Business Administration, even though poultry farmers are not really small businesses at all but rather operate under near total control of large corporations. Poultry farmers get locked into exploitative contracts with poultry giants that require them to take on debt to build expensive chicken houses, and dictate nearly every aspect of their business operations. According to a 2014 study, poultry farmers who run small operations earn an average hourly wage of $11.50.

Farmers are so powerless that farmer suicides are now a regular occurrence. The nonprofit Farm Aid said in 2018 that increased calls to its hotline "confirm that farmers are under incredible financial, legal, and emotional stress. Bankruptcies, foreclosures, depression, and even suicide are some of the tragic consequences of these pressures." When Brad Pfaff, Wisconsin state agriculture secretary, spoke out about farmer suicides in 2020, the Wisconsin Republican Senate—so controlled by monopoly money—ousted him from office.

Farmers are merely seeking to break even, said Patty Lovera of the Campaign for Family Farms and the Environment at the *Capitol Forum* conference. "The folks I work with are looking for independent family farms to be able to participate in a marketplace where they can get a fair price for what they grow," said Lovera. The reason they don't get a fair price, she said, is "because of the excessive consolidation that we have in literally every step of the food supply from the inputs—from the seeds—all the way to the retailer." Agriculture policy has focused on band-aids, she added, like loans and insurance for farmers, but "the root cause we are not dealing with is that these markets are so consolidated it is not possible for them to work fairly." The groups she works with want to be independent, not locked into working for Big Ag. "They don't want to be gig workers for Smithfield, JBS, or Tyson."

Small farms that want to use better production methods and run diverse, sustainable farms "are entirely cut out from the grocery store in ways that get more and more stark every day," Kelloway explained. "You have big retailers partnering with big food distributors, who are partnering with big food processors, who are partnering with big farms." In order to have a market, farmers are locked into a regime of production methods that is prescribed by the dominant monopoly buyer.

Monopolies even dictate to farmers what hormones and how much feed they have to use, and require them to use highly unnatural techniques. "Because farmers are in such a squeeze, they have no choice," said Kelloway. That means eaters have fewer choices for hormone-free, natural food, too.

In thirty-eight regions across America, Walmart has more than a 70 percent share of the grocery market, reports the Institute for Local Self-Reliance. With fewer and fewer grocery stores, Walmart has the power to demand crazy concessions just for food to get on their shelves. "If you want a prime spot on the shelf, you're going to have to pay Walmart for it, or you're going to have to pay Kroger for it," Kelloway told me. Some oligopoly food processors, like Kraft Heinz, give so much money to these retail chains that they get to be what's called a "category captain." They actually get to decide where their competitors sit on the grocery store shelf! If a small start-up has a great organic product, the category captain will stick them on the very bottom shelf or the very top shelf. Sounds a lot like Google and Amazon being able to make their competitors almost disappear, doesn't it? Speaking of Amazon, Whole Foods is not much better than the big grocery store chains because it has market power in organic grocery.

As a small act of rebellion, and to increase your odds of getting quality food, try shopping the very top and bottom shelves next time you go to the grocery store!

When it comes to food, American taxpayers once again pay the price for monopoly power. For example, U.S. taxpayers pay gigantic corn subsidies—$113.9 billion from 1995 to 2019—which directly benefit Big Ag and indirectly subsidize the meat industry and Coca-Cola and Pepsi. These subsidies make the wrong kinds of food very cheap, and we pay for it in our health care system and in Big Ag pollution, Kelloway said.

Bigger doesn't always mean better when it comes to farms. Farms are expected to be more efficient the bigger they get because they can buy seeds and other inputs for lower prices, but a study of Kansas farms' economic performance showed that once farms reach a certain size, getting bigger doesn't offer advantages. The current system is really only efficient for monopoly profits. As we learned with COVID-19, efficiency is in tension with resiliency, and leads to fragility when pursued above all else.

Big Food Blocks Healthy School Lunches

Imagine if every child got proper nutrition at school, which is far from the current reality with Big Food's control over school lunch, and billions of taxpayer dollars going to food monopolies. For those kids who have no choice but to have school lunch, proper nutrition would go a long way to improving children's ability to learn, improving their health outcomes, and reducing obesity.

The importance of this issue is why Michelle Obama made it a top priority as first lady. Mrs. Obama introduced her campaign as a move to alter policy, requiring changes in food formulations to no longer use excessive sweeteners and fats. But as ThinkProgress pointed out in "How Big Food Corporations Watered Down Michelle Obama's 'Let's Move' Campaign," she ultimately redirected her focus to "exercise and personal fitness—a position favored by processed food companies to divert scrutiny of their products." The article continues, "This avoidance of policy change may have something to do with the food lobby's influence in Obama's White House. According to a 2012 Reuters analysis, 50 food and beverage groups lobbied to a tune of $175 million during the first three years of the Obama administration, dwarfing the $83 million they spent in the last 3 years of the Bush administration.

Journalism professor and author Michael Pollan details every twist and turn of the saga of monopoly power defeating the Obama administration's goals in his *New York Times Magazine* article, "Big Food Strikes Back: Why Did the Obamas Fail to Take on Corporate Agriculture?" "Whenever the Obamas seriously poked at Big Food, they were quickly outlobbied and outgunned," Pollan writes. "Why? Because the food movement still barely exists as a political force in Washington."

No politician can take on monopoly power without the support of a movement of people. You can help defeat Big Food's lobbyists and nourish America's children by adding your voice to the food movement. A list of groups working in this area can be found at MonopoliesSuck .com/action.

The modest gains made by the Obama administration were rolled back by the Trump administration, which claimed the reforms were too burdensome for schools. But Kelloway disagrees: "The number of schools struggling to meet the requirements was actually quite small, and frankly, there's no other way to interpret this but as a handout back to the large processing companies that make so much money off the school lunch program."

People think that providing healthy school lunches would be too expensive and is not realistic. Yet other countries around the world manage to do it just fine. If America cut the billions of dollars of monopoly fat in our budgets, from health care to defense, and stopped subsidizing monopoly profits, the seemingly impossible could be possible.

Big Ag Is Destroying the Planet, Too

The same monopoly power that endangers our health also endangers our habitat. "With the adoption of more regenerative, organic farming practices, for example, today's industrial agriculture could go from being a major source of pollution to a major means of sequestering carbon and achieving other environmental benefits," explains the *Corner* newsletter by the Open Markets Institute. "Yet anyone who wants to reform today's industrial food system must deal with the power of agribusiness giants like chemical maker Bayer-Monsanto and slaughterhouse monopolist JBS, as well as with food retail and processing behemoths like Walmart and Kraft Heinz, who all have a deep interest in maintaining the status quo."

Unlike Big Ag, farmers want to be part of the climate change solution and conversation, said Family Farm Action's Joe Maxwell, speaking on a panel. "Farmers look out their back door; they know something's wrong; they call it different things but something's going on," said Maxwell. "They're in harm's way and on the front line."

In order to "have a meaningful impact on climate change we will have to confront agribusiness, which spends more on lobbying in the United States than even defense lobbyists," writes Timothy Wise, author of *Eating Tomorrow: Agribusiness, Family Farmers, and the Battle for the Future of Food*, in *Wired*. "A good first step in the United States would be to break up agribusiness giants that have virtual monopolies in regional seed, chemical, and meat markets," he writes, including unwinding Monsanto's merger with Bayer.

Instead of being part of the problem, agriculture can actually become part of the solution. "Agriculture is a huge contributor to carbon emissions but it also offers a huge opportunity to reduce carbon emissions and to capture carbon," Anja Geitmann, a professor at McGill University's plant science program, told Canada's CBC News. Farmland can sequester carbon into the soil through the process of photosynthesis, and the earth's existing farmland has the power to absorb all of the world's greenhouse gas emissions for the next 100 years, according to a report by Canada's agriculture department.

A Canadian cattle rancher, Paul Slomp, told CBC news that his farm has already moved away from chemicals and artificial feeds, and his cows graze on grass. He said he's now making more money than before. "Because we're reducing the amount of input that we need to purchase, we're actually able to generate a much better profit margin," said Slomp. "The cows are meant to do this; they thrive in a system like ours, and it can be quite profitable."

Such changes are only achievable for farmers if they are not already hanging on by a thread and beholden to monopoly rule. Just as we need to remove tech gatekeepers so that privacy-protecting pro-democracy innovators can break through, farmers need a way to get to market without having to pass through food giants' gates.

Your Life, Better

Our planet and our food are too important to leave to monopoly rule. Change may not be profitable for Big Oil and Big Ag, but it is possible. "The climate crisis is not only the single greatest challenge facing our country; it is also our single greatest opportunity to build a more just and equitable future," said Bernie Sanders in a written statement. We put people on the moon fifty years ago, and we "can sure as hell transform our energy system away from fossil fuels to 100 percent renewables today and create millions of jobs in the process," reads his website.

We must demand that our government end Big Oil subsidies and investments, divest from fossil fuels, require Big Oil to help fund the transition to sustainability, and open up opportunity to green innovators. The new climate movement is about saying "yes" to shared prosperity and a more equitable distribution of power.

By joining a grassroots movement applying pressure on lawmakers and regulators to do their job or get fired, you would no longer feel helpless.

When the people prevail, your climate anxiety wanes. You enjoy the political stability that comes with your fellow Americans having good green jobs and hope. Most important, you can tell your kids that the world's grown-ups are doing everything they possibly can to protect them.

When you go to the grocery store, you know the food being sold is safe and healthy for you and your family. Children who eat school lunch get the nutrition their young bodies need to learn and to grow into healthy adults. Your food supply is diversified and safer, recalls are smaller in scope, and farming helps save the future of humanity rather than endanger it. This vision of what life could look like may seem unrealistic, but the alternative—staying the course under monopoly rule—is far more so.

SEVEN

MONOPOLIES RAMP UP INEQUALITY

"Shall we play a game?"

The ultrarich are thriving in America, with the rest of us watching their indulgences on social media or bombarded by advertising that idolizes excess. Billionaire Kylie Jenner posted on Instagram a photo of her one-year-old daughter carrying a mini Hermès handbag that retails for over $8,000. The post got more than 4.7 million likes.

With a steady stream of wealth porn around you glorifying the rich, it wouldn't be surprising if you felt a need for more. Whether consciously or unconsciously, some of us are trying to literally "keep up" with the Kardashians, not just "the Joneses" next door. Comparing yourself with those who have more inevitably makes you feel not good enough.

We rarely compare ourselves with those who have less than we do, perhaps because the poor barely exist in our public consciousness, in a world curated by social media. If you're reading this book, you're probably not among the 40 percent of Americans who can't pay an unexpected $400 expense without borrowing money or selling something. When you hear such dire statistics—and that one's from 2018, before COVID-19's financial devastation—you're at a loss for what you can do about it. Like so many other Americans, you're consumed with your own stresses, working long hours to pay high overhead costs, to cover health care monopoly prices, and to save for college or pay off college debts.

You certainly don't *feel* like you have it easy, and the fear of things getting even harder fuels a relentless drive for more. You're not trying to buy designer handbags for your toddler, you just want financial security. But at what dollar figure will you have *enough* to feel secure?

Maybe you are among the few who do feel financially secure. Perhaps you haven't worried much about inequality because you're on the winning side of the equation. No matter how hard you may have worked to get there, don't get too comfortable or expect to stay. Inequality is a conveyor belt, running on an endless loop that will eventually come for you. Unless we do something to stop it, that is.

Inequality hurts even the most fortunate because it destabilizes democracy. If you live in a bubble of privilege, you may be unaware of the hopelessness of large swaths of America. In your head you know the desperation exists, but you may not know what it really feels like. Yet you know what it feels like to be scared. The world feels unbalanced, unstable, and unsafe.

Inequality takes a toll on us all, but our rigged economy deepens existing societal inequities even further. If you're a woman, person of color, LGBTQ+, and/or a member of other marginalized groups, monopoly rule makes your uphill climb even steeper.

The Great Unequalizers

Six heirs to the Walmart fortune have more wealth than 41 percent of all Americans combined. That figure is from 2010, and the Waltons' wealth has grown exponentially ever since. Before Walmart came along, entrepreneurial shopkeepers in towns across America could support their families, pay their workers a living wage, pay their fair share of taxes, and pay companies that make consumer goods a fair price for their wares. Walmart, offering the promise of lower prices for consumers, changed all of this.

As Walmart got bigger and bigger, it used its power as a dominant buyer to squeeze the companies that make and wholesale goods, demanding they sell their products to Walmart for ultra-low prices. Those makers and suppliers earned less money for themselves, had less money to pay their employees, and were often forced to reduce the quality of the goods they offer consumers. Small shopkeepers went out of business when they couldn't compete against Walmart's prices, which were often below cost—amounting to illegal monopolization using predatory pricing, in my opinion. Employees who could otherwise work at those small shops became faced with few employment options, and had little choice but to accept Walmart's pay.

Walmart pays its employees so little, as we discussed in chapter 1, that Walmart employees make up the single largest group of food stamp recipients in many states. Americans pay higher taxes to make up for Walmart's exploitation of its workers and alleged tax evasion.

The end result of Walmart's extraction of wealth from taxpayers, manufacturers, shopkeepers, wholesalers, and employees? In 2019, Walmart had the highest revenue of any company in the world, according to *Fortune*'s Global 500, bringing in a cool $514 billion. (Big Tech companies have less revenue but higher valuations.) The Walton family is reportedly the world's richest, and they get $4 million richer every hour, $100 million richer every day. As a taxpayer, your hard-earned money subsidizes the richest family in the world.

Walmart gets away with monopolizing brick-and-mortar retail because of the Chicago School's twisted interpretation of antitrust law that says low prices are good for consumers, even if it destroys competition. But Walmart's low prices have enabled a host of ills that haven't been good for you at all. Even if you've never shopped at Walmart, you've paid a price.

Walmart may seem like a distant threat in the digital age, but modern monopolies, as I've explained, are following in its footsteps. Today's tech giants may be some of the most powerful extractors our world has ever seen. Amazon is most literally following Walmart's playbook of using below-cost pricing to kick out rivals, squeeze suppliers, skirt taxes, and underpay workers, and Jeff Bezos is Walton Family 2.0. He makes the annual salary of his lowest-paid employee in 11.5 seconds, according to a back-of-the-envelope calculation by Quartz in 2018. His net worth as of May 2020, according to Bloomberg, is 2,327,131 times the median U.S. household income.

I don't begrudge those who find financial success through their ingenuity, innovation, and creation. But when astronomical wealth flows mostly from extraction—illegally kicking competitors out of the game to monopolize markets, stealing the innovations of others, and leveraging monopoly power in one market to take over other markets without competing on merit—that's the American monopoly nightmare.

With monopolies controlling nearly every part of American business, we are all victims of extraction in countless ways every day. Lower wages, higher prices, and the squeezing of suppliers and creators amounts to billions of dollars in wealth transfer to monopolies, duopolies, and oligopolies. Is it really any surprise that we are experiencing economic inequality not seen since the Gilded Age?

C-suite executives and major corporate shareholders are the ones who win when monopolies reign, with the ultrarich capturing the bulk of the wealth that monopolies extract. The richest .1 percent of Americans now own more wealth than the bottom 80 percent, and 400 Americans have more wealth than 150 million Americans do.

We hear a lot about the 1 percent, but the gap between the top 1 percent and top .1 percent is enormous. People between the top 1 percent and the top .1 percent tend to earn their money through wages, and their share of national wealth has made only modest gains for forty years. The people making out like bandits in a monopolized America are the top .1 percent, the approximately 160,000 tax filers with wealth above $20 million. The top .1 percent sharing in the monopoly profits include CEOs and bankers who most benefit from gains in financial markets. They share in the profits monopolies bring in when they can charge consumers more and pay employees less.

Remember, the era of stronger antitrust enforcement spanned from 1913 to 1982, and the years since have been ruled by the Chicago School. From 1978 to 2012, the 0.1 percent of Americans with more wealth than the bottom 99.9 percent of Americans went from owning 7 percent of the country's total wealth to owning 22 percent. The richest Americans have become much richer ever since antitrust enforcement went missing. Here's yet another graph that shows the Boomers had it better than the rest of us! When they were raising their families in the 1970s and the 1980s, the ultrarich were capturing a much lower percentage of America's wealth than they are today. Boomers benefited from the robust antitrust enforcement in the decades before, which deconcentrated the economy and spread the wealth more evenly among Americans.

Although monopolies are far from the only cause of income inequality, trying to achieve equality without weakening monopoly power is a fool's errand. Monopoly is highly concentrated wealth and power in the hands of a few, making it fundamentally incompatible

TOP 0.1% WEALTH SHARE in the United States, 1913–2012

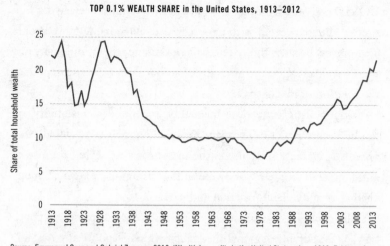

Source: Emmanuel Saez and Gabriel Zucman, 2016. "Wealth Inequality in the United States since 1913: Evidence from Capitalized Income Tax Data," *The Quarterly Journal of Economics* 131(2), pages 519–578.

with equality—the distribution of wealth, opportunity, and power among the many. The two cannot coexist.

As NYU law professor Eleanor Fox has written, the "notion of equality has run through antitrust (or competition) law since the beginning of (antitrust) time." Antitrust law, she said, "focuses particularly on equality of opportunity: keeping open pathways for outsiders to contest markets on the merits."

Inequality Causes Political Instability

Most Americans face steep barriers to financial well-being in our taking economy. That building a wall, the ultimate barrier, has garnered support from millions of Americans is no coincidence. If opportunity is not available to these Americans, they certainly don't want "others" to have it. Xenophobia and anti-immigrant sentiment are nothing new, but scarcity fuels the flames as people look for scapegoats for their suffering.

Don't be mistaken, however; apart from the systemic shock of

COVID-19, ours is not a time of scarcity. We have been living in a time of abundance, but with resources distributed inequitably. People are hopeless because the system isn't working for them, and many just want to burn it all to the ground. An authoritarian leader can pose as the solution to this despair.

Monopolistic extraction, inequality, and political instability are not limited to America's borders; today's monopolies are global. Monopolistic extraction is among the reasons we are seeing the rise of antidemocratic leaders worldwide, aided by monopoly business models that amplify disinformation and hate.

The declining dynamism in America that we discussed in chapter 3 is amplifying regional inequality, which is politically destabilizing. "The rapid retreat of dynamism from all but the largest and fastest-growing metro areas intensifies the geographic inequality being felt across the country—and the most vulnerable areas are falling the furthest behind," reports the Economic Innovation Group. During the economic expansion that occurred between 2010 and 2014, only 5 metro areas accounted for 50 percent of the growth of new companies. Compare that to the expansion from 1983 to 1987, when 50 percent of growth was spread out over 29 metro areas. These days, almost 80 percent of start-up investment goes to just three states. And only 15 percent of all venture capital in 2015 went to the states that voted for Donald Trump for president in 2016.

America the unequal is America the divided. The hyper concentration of wealth and opportunity in a few big cities has led to regional inequality. Such concentration is politically destabilizing in itself but also has rendered the Electoral College an utter disaster to democracy. A more distributed, deconcentrated economy would promote regional equality and the dispersion of wealth and opportunity throughout the country.

Mining Humanity and Knowledge Inequality

We've talked about how access to data distorts the competitive playing field between Big Tech and the companies that must compete against the tech giants on their platforms. We've talked about how data collected about us can be used to target us, manipulate us, and skew elections. We've talked about how data has value, and how massive corporations sucking up our data amounts to tremendous wealth transfer, or outright theft when done without our knowledge or consent. The race to harvest our data is perhaps best understood as a gold rush, with humans as the mines. Or, as privacy advocate Aral Balkan wrote in 2017, "These platform monopolies are factory farms for human beings; farming us for every gram of insight they can extract." Such data extraction worsens inequality.

Shoshana Zuboff, author of *The Age of Surveillance Capitalism* and Harvard Business School professor emerita, describes a new form of social inequality that she calls "epistemic inequality." "Epistemic" means relating to knowledge, so for the sake of simplicity, let's call it "knowledge inequality." Zuboff describes this inequality as "extreme asymmetries of knowledge and the power that accrues to such knowledge, as the tech giants seize control of information and learning itself." Such knowledge inequality extends even beyond the tech giants to other types of platform monopolies, like Monsanto, as it seizes control of the information and learning that used to belong to farmers.

Knowledge inequality is "not based on what we can earn but rather on what we can learn," writes Zuboff, in the form of "unequal access to learning." Knowledge inequality creates a chasm, she explains, between "what we know and what is known about us," and "what we can do and what can be done to us."

Unequal access to learning is a constant in American history, but surveillance capitalism makes it highly automated and targeted with precision, threatening to worsen existing forms of inequality—based on income, gender, race, sexual orientation, sexual identity, class, age, immigration status, disability, and any intersection of these. Using data to learn about ourselves can offer promise, like with personalized medicine, but we the people must demand that safeguards are put in place as new technologies are rolled out.

Knowledge inequality is on track to get worse as the "internet of things" turns everything from our microwave oven to our television into a data mine. This is why we must urgently check monopoly business models.

Rich White Manopoly Is Not a Fun Game

In December 2017, I wrote an article about how monopolies amplify gender inequality, knowing that antitrust lawyers—trained to think antitrust is only about corporate efficiencies and prices—would think I was crazy. I arrived at the connection between antitrust and gender inequality serendipitously.

For the three years prior, I'd been writing about antitrust issues involving the Big Tech platforms and also hosting a podcast called *Women Killing It!*, which focuses on women overcoming barriers to reaching their career potential. Both of my passions—gender equity and antitrust—became hot topics during that time. At the end of 2017, I was exhausted. I told myself, "Sally, you've got to pick just one passion," but I couldn't tear myself away from either one. And that's when it hit me. How could I not have seen it sooner? My passions for antitrust and gender equity were not only related, they were just two dimensions of the very same passion.

That passion is equal opportunity for all, or what we think of as the American dream. I immediately looked up the definition of the American dream, and found this one on Wikipedia:

The American Dream is a national ethos of the United States, the set of ideals—democracy, rights, liberty, opportunity and equality—in which freedom includes the opportunity for prosperity and success, as well as an upward mobility for the family and children, achieved through hard work in a society with few barriers.

I realized that all of these ideals are intertwined. Although the American Dream has never been equally available to all, and the notion that our country is a meritocracy is a myth, I believe that the more we expand opportunities to all Americans, the stronger our democracy will be.

Suddenly it made sense to me why I had been drawn to antitrust enforcement in the first place. After all, our anti-monopoly laws are designed to promote opportunity and upward mobility, keeping markets open so new companies and entrepreneurs can challenge established players on the merits. These laws not only make it illegal for one powerful company to shut out competitors but also prohibit a few powerful players from joining together to control the market and exclude outsiders. Fighting for gender equality also has a lot to do with equal opportunity. The whole point of the American dream is it should apply to all of us, not just those who already have power.

On the flip side, sexism and monopolization both work against the American dream. Sexism wrongfully excludes women and deprives them of equal opportunity to compete on a level playing field, just like monopolies do to start-ups and smaller companies. The glass ceiling is really just a cartel.

Concentrated economic power, unsurprisingly, is bad for women. Discriminatory biases against women's economic participation amount to anticompetitive regulations, writes Chris Pike, a competition expert at the Organisation for Economic Co-operation and Development (OECD). "Competition policy may therefore have a natural role to play in addressing those issues and in building open, fair and efficient markets, levelling the playing field for women and men alike," Pike writes with Estefania Santacreu-Vasut, a French economics professor. Competition policy could result in what they call a "double dividend." That is, "by promoting competition in certain markets, competition authorities may reduce market distortions in a particular market (*first dividend*) and contribute to reduce gender inequality (*second dividend*)."

Another OECD study, "Inequality: A Hidden Cost of Market Power," shows that market power and higher prices increase the wealth of the richest 10 percent of the population while reducing the income of the poorest 20 percent. Women and people of color, then, are particularly hurt by monopolies. Women are 35 percent more likely than men to be poor in America, and 70 percent of the nation's poor are women and children. Poverty rates in America for African Americans are more than twice that of white, non-Hispanic individuals.

And when consumers get screwed by monopolists, we're mostly talking about women, who control 70-80 percent of consumer spending. "If the consumer economy had a sex, it would be female," says a report by Bloomberg. The Chicago School of Economics' "consumer welfare standard," which has been used to justify consolidating the American economy, then, alternatively could be called the "women's welfare standard." But a monopolized America hasn't been good for women's welfare at all!

Monopolies suck for white men too, don't get me wrong, as only a select few reap monopolies' spoils. But the consequences of monopoly power we've talked about in this book are extra bad for women, people of color, and members of marginalized groups, and multiply as these identities intersect. Monopoly amplifies existing inequities in our society, like structural racism and patriarchy.

First, monopolies take even more income from women and

people of color. When concentrated labor markets deprive employees of bargaining power and depress their pay, causing wages to go down or stagnate, female employees and employees of color are even worse off. In the United States, women make 78 cents to a white man's dollar, with black women making 64 cents and Latina women making 54 cents for every dollar a white man makes. Black men earn 73 cents and Hispanic men earn 69 cents to a white man's dollar. As wages by the bottom 99 percent of earners continue to shrink, women and people of color get paid a mere percentage of fewer dollars. The top 1 percent are predominantly white men, and so are the C-suite executives whose pay has skyrocketed while employees' pay has stagnated.

In the 2016 study "Women and the 1%: How Extreme Economic Inequality and Gender Inequality Must Be Tackled Together," Oxfam said that closing gender gaps so that women participate more in paid work and move out of lower-paid sectors could add $12 trillion to the global economy by 2025. Oxfam warns, however, that "[u]nless the causes of extreme economic inequality are urgently addressed, the majority of the benefits of women-driven growth will accrue to those already at the top of the economy."

Second, we discussed in chapter 3 how concentrated markets reduce employees' ability to switch jobs. This lower mobility especially hurts employees who face on-the-job discrimination or harassment. In the wake of the #MeToo movement, the *New York Times* asked women if they've ever felt silenced at work. "Many spoke of the times they had been threatened for requesting equal pay, penalized for taking maternity leave or blacklisted for bringing suit against their attackers." The ability to switch jobs is critical for bargaining power.

Women need to be able to leave hostile work environments and to switch jobs to escape sexual harassment, which we as a society have finally admitted is ubiquitous. A study by three sociology professors found that women who are harassed are 6.5 times more likely to change jobs, and will do so even when it hurts their career and reduces opportunities for advancement. This shows a direct link between sexual harassment and the gender pay gap.

But what if the labor market is so concentrated that women who are harassed don't have anywhere to go? When women make harassment claims, their companies often retaliate against them and even can get them blacklisted from their fields. Companies can easily discredit women to an entire industry when it is ruled by only a few companies, meaning women can lose their careers for speaking up. If many companies competed in each industry for talented employees, blacklisting women would be much harder.

These same considerations apply to racial discrimination at work. Whether experiencing racial harassment or other forms of discrimination—like lower pay, lower recognition, less promotion, or marginalization—employees of color need to be able to easily switch jobs and speak up without losing their careers. Noncompete agreements are especially dangerous because they can trap people of color in hostile work environments.

Who Gets to Innovate, and for Whom?

Monopoly rule also means that women, people of color, and other marginalized groups have fewer opportunities for entrepreneurship than they would have if economic power were more distributed. "If they don't give you a seat at the table, bring a folding chair," Shirley Chisholm, the first black woman elected to Congress, famously said. But if tables today are still not welcoming diversity, entrepreneur Felecia Hatcher told me, "We're now empowered to create our own damn tables."

Hatcher cofounded Code Fever and Black Tech Week to promote inclusive innovation when she noticed Miami's start-up resources were not "crossing the tracks." Hatcher has talked about how she and her husband, Derick, would get invited to start-up events offering great entrepreneurial support and look around and say, "Why isn't there anyone else that looks like us in the room?" They started Code Fever as a way to change that, building their own ecosystem to draw resources, training, and inclusive policies into the black community.

Just as women and people of color have greater needs to be able to switch jobs, they have greater needs for entrepreneurship. Building your own table means being the captain of your own ship and lessening the harm that harassment, discrimination, and bias can cause you. "When a woman runs her own business, she has a reduced chance of being harassed or attacked," writes psychotherapist and author Stephanie Sarkis. "She is able to have more control and influence over what happens in her life."

But building your own table requires money. And the statistics for the share of start-up funding that women and people of color receive are dismal. Less than 3 percent of start-up investment goes to women, and less than 1 percent goes to African Americans and Latinos of both sexes. Since 2009, black women have raised .0006 percent of the $424.7 billion in total tech venture funding.

Now consider how four tech titans are shaping the course of innovation. "What's your exit strategy?" is one of the first questions investors ask entrepreneurs. As Ross Baird, venture capitalist and author of *The Innovation Blind Spot*, explained at the Open Markets America's Monopoly Moment conference, investors are essentially saying, "what are you building that Facebook will want or Google will want or Amazon will want, so they can acquire you one day?" To get funded, then, entrepreneurs need to develop a feature that is interesting enough for Amazon or Facebook to want to buy, said Baird. "That is the incredibly limited design constraint on our innovation economy right now." But start-ups must also avoid direct competition with giants, given their power to squash them.

When the narrow parameters for getting funded are that your creation is not in tech giants' "kill zones" but is a little feature that the tech giants will want to buy, what room does that leave for diversity in innovation? Good luck getting funded unless your innovation conforms to the vision and worldview a few white guys, and one Indian guy now that Sundar Pichai has become the CEO of Alphabet (with the influence of Google cofounders Larry Page and Sergey Brin an open question). With this start-up model, we won't benefit from maximum innovation because the next big thing won't get built. And when a few powerful companies dominate so many markets and prevent new firms and new leaders from competing, women and people of color are particularly shut out.

Baird has explained how the concentration of funding among venture capitalists (VCs) leads to investment in the wrong things. Baird writes that "the resources we're putting into new ideas are concentrated among so few people in so few places" (mostly white men in New York, California, and Massachusetts) and that blind spots prevent "great ideas around the world from having a chance to begin with." Other sources of funding for entrepreneurs have diminished in recent decades, like community banks. The number of banks with assets less than $500 million decreased by about 70 percent between 1990 and 2018, with thousands of institutions lost.

Lynn Perkins, CEO and cofounder of UrbanSitter, shared on my podcast her story of raising funding for her start-up, a popular app for hiring babysitters. Because the predominantly male VCs typically were not the ones in their families hiring babysitters, Perkins said that they did not see the customer problem that UrbanSitter was solving. Perkins got funding only *after* she acquired thousands of active users of her app. Male start-up founders frequently raise funding without any traction at all.

On top of traction, investors want to see strong revenue numbers from start-ups built by entrepreneurs from minority and marginalized groups, said Hatcher. Yet, "you open up *Inc.* magazine and see a company that has zero revenue and you wonder, 'How did they raise

$100 million?'" She noted that entrepreneurs of color face such a bigger ask to validate their start-ups.

In his book, Baird shares the story of entrepreneur Jerry Nemorin, who as a child watched his Haitian immigrant mother take out predatory loans. As an adult, Nemorin came up with a business idea that would help Americans restructure their debt, and he steadily built his business. But when it came time to raise funding to grow to the next level, he hit roadblocks. Nemorin explained that VCs "want to solve my world problems, but forget about real-world problems."

With capital concentrated in the hands of a few, we're not getting the best of the best because there's a whole group of people who are not even getting in the door. Problem-solving through innovation is less effective and impactful because solutions are limited and less diverse. And years of biases and blind spots mean the markets for innovations that serve white male needs are oversaturated, while markets that serve the needs of women and people of color are where the opportunity lies. Investors are missing out and consumers are, too, with their needs left unmet while the twelfth version of Tinder for laundry delivery gets funded.

Move Fast and Break People

When a handful of tech titans decide what innovation looks like, not only do women and people of color get shut out of entrepreneurship, but they also get hurt. The most privileged in our society have been shaping technology in ways that harm women, people of color, and other marginalized communities, without bothering to anticipate consequences. Top leadership of the tech giants is a sea of white men. While they get rich, others bear the consequences of the surveillance and discrimination they automate. Silicon Valley start-ups love to ignore rules designed to protect us, justifying their recklessness in the name of innovation.

Forget about the rules that democracies create to protect their citizens; pesky regulations just get in the way, so the techno-libertarian thinking goes. If innovations hurt people, we'll deal with those problems later, perhaps. This is an ethos that is compatible with the most privileged in society who pay the least consequences for their actions, the same kinds of guys who can be criminally prosecuted and sentenced to write a book. The "precautionary principle," in contrast, requires innovators to anticipate harms before they occur.

Uber, for example, ignored the precautionary principle when it came to protecting its riders. Uber founders probably didn't intend for their innovation to lead to women being raped and murdered, but they also didn't take significant precautionary steps to stop it from happening. After the tragic murder of a University of South Carolina student who got into a car she thought was her Uber, Uber announced it would begin sending a push notification to riders reminding them to check the driver and vehicle and providing the driver's name, photo, license plate number, and vehicle make and model. Why wasn't that feature built before Uber was even launched? Uber execs sure seem to spend a lot of effort strategizing ways to extract wages from their workers. If they had spent a fraction of that time anticipating dangers to users and taking appropriate precautions, that young woman could still be alive today.

Uber reported in 2017 that its tech leadership team was completely white and Asian, and 88.7 percent men. Failing to have women at the decision-making table was not merely a terrible business decision; it was a dangerous one. Perhaps not surprisingly, Uber's own corporate culture was reportedly toxic and hostile. Whistle-blower Susan Fowler, an engineer at Uber at the time, exposed the rampant sexual harassment and discrimination inside of the company in a viral blog post that helped fuel the #MeToo movement, and wrote about it in her book *Whistle Blower*.

While Uber's harms to women may have been accidental oversights, if I'm being generous, exploiting drivers with low pay is integral to Uber's business model. In 2015, Uber's drivers were more than 50 percent people of color. California passed a law to give Uber drivers rights, and Uber is fighting it tooth and nail. Extraction of wealth from its workers *is* Uber's business model.

We Didn't Discriminate, the Algorithm Did It

In *Race After Technology*, Princeton professor Ruha Benjamin argues that "tech fixes often hide, speed up, and even deepen discrimination, while appearing to be neutral or benevolent when compared to the racism of a previous era." She calls the set of practices with discriminatory designs "The New Jim Code." "The power of the New Jim Code," writes Benjamin, "is that it allows racist habits and logics to enter through the backdoor of tech design, in which the humans who create the algorithms are hidden from view."

We often assume that tech and data are neutral, but the data and the way technology is deployed reflects and reinforces society's biases. Cathy O'Neil, author of *Weapons of Math Destruction: How Big Data Increases Inequality and Threatens Democracy*, explains in an interview that "people like to think of algorithms as outside the landscape of morals," but an algorithmic model is a "moral projection." "A model is no more than a formal opinion embedded in code," she said, explaining that people who build algorithmic models decide matters of opinion like what success looks like, what's important, and how to get to success. But the morals projected are often "default morals" that are "thoughtlessly introduced by the ecosystem in which they're built" or "the data that's collected," says O'Neil. The result is they mirror and deepen the biases that exist in society.

That the algorithms are opaque compounds the problems of monopolies being unaccountable for their harmful business models. Each of the four tech giants has been accused of algorithmic bias.

Facebook, in an egregious example, has reportedly allowed housing, credit, and employment ads to discriminate by age and gender, which is prohibited by civil rights law. Facebook's business model, based on hypertargeting and personalization, creates huge risks of discrimination.

Discrimination through purportedly neutral tech is particularly dangerous when it comes to the criminal justice system. At every stage of the U.S. penal process, Benjamin explains, "from policing, sentencing, and imprisonment to parole—automated risk assessments are employed to determine people's likelihood of committing a crime." This predictive policing software will recommend surveillance of predominantly black neighborhoods "because the data that this software is drawing from reflect ongoing surveillance priorities that target predominantly black neighborhoods." Such predictions, then, become self-fulfilling prophecies with "the allure of accuracy." Unequal surveillance perpetuates and amplifies existing inequities, and algorithms identifying patterns from surveillance data make the problem even worse.

LGTBQ+ individuals, the disabled, and any group that does not fit the mold of those shaping new technologies also are at risk of disparate treatment. An organization called Queer in AI focuses on the impact artificial intelligence and machine-learning algorithms have on people, "and the potential for these powerful learning and classification technologies to out queer people." AI also disproportionately harms the disabled, with ableism baked into assumptions. Thinkers and advocates are highlighting the need for inclusively designed AI and rejecting forms that are discriminatory and harmful.

Not all the companies rolling out biased technologies are monopolies. But tech giants use their monopoly-power-turned-political-power to fight efforts to regulate tech and AI. Those fighting for equity in tech should work together with the anti-monopoly movement in order for their efforts to have maximum success.

Your Life, Better

The famous Monopoly board game was originally created and patented by a feminist named Lizzie Magie in 1903 to teach about the harms of monopoly. She didn't get credit for her invention (shocker) but a guy named Charles Darrow did instead. The book *The Monopolists,* by Mary Pilon, tells Magie's story, describing also how the anti-monopoly movement served as a staging ground for women's rights advocates and abolitions at the turn of the century. Today, anti-monopoly activists and advocates for gender and racial justice should join together to maximize their impact. All who advocate on behalf of marginalized groups should incorporate anti-monopoly into their policy agendas.

By overthrowing monopoly power, the New Gilded Age, like the original one, can become a thing of the history books. Polar opposite extremes of wealth and poverty begin to dissipate as the middle class is revived and broadened. People still want more, but sometimes they feel like they have enough. A more equitable distribution of America's abundance restores opportunity and hope, and lessens the despair and anger that embolden authoritarian-style politicians.

Anti-monopoly policy alone won't make this vision of America a reality, but it's an essential part of changing the status quo and sharing prosperity among all.

HOW TO STOP
MONOPOLIES

EIGHT

HOW TO TAKE BACK CONTROL

To simply know a thing is not enough. . . . We must do something about it on a large scale if we are to make headway. These are critical times, and drastic action is needed.

—Lizzie Magie, creator of the original Monopoly board game

Only by ending monopoly rule can we begin to make our lives better: lower prices, more affordable health care, lower taxes, higher pay, better benefits and working conditions, less financial stress and work overwhelm, greater opportunities for entrepreneurship, innovation that improves quality of life rather than degrades it, less corporate spying on your private life, a less agitated state of mind, reduced political polarization, reduced tech addiction, fairer elections, a stronger democracy, more accountable politicians, safer food, a healthier planet, and greater equality.

You deserve all of this.

Our problems are systemic, and we must attack them on a structural level. Keep meditating and doing yoga, or coping on a personal level in whatever way works best for you. But we also need to attack the structures of power if we are to lead better, less stressful lives. Like I said at the beginning, anti-monopoly won't magically solve everything, but we won't be able to cure America's ills if we don't first disperse monopolies' concentrated power.

I often hear the argument that antitrust enforcement isn't going to fix our problems and that a different solution is "the" answer. We don't need antitrust, we need privacy law, people say. Or the solution to tech monopolies isn't antitrust, it's blockchain. But America is in a crisis of concentrated power—no single answer is going to cut it. This isn't an either/or situation! It's a both/and situation. We need *both* antitrust enforcement *and* privacy law. We need *both* antitrust enforcement *and* new technologies that have the potential to decentralize power (as long as we don't let the giants take over these innovations, like Facebook is trying to do with its Libra digital currency). Antitrust law is the tool specifically crafted to combat corporate power, but antimonopoly advocates like myself don't limit our toolbox and consider a range of solutions. We must attack monopoly rule from every angle.

The only reason to discard anti-monopoly weapons in our arsenal would be if they contradicted one another. For this reason, Big Tech presses the narrative that privacy and competition are incompatible, opportunistically cutting off competitors under the guise of protecting privacy. But this is a false dichotomy: competition can be promoted by giving users real control over their data, which competitors might use it, and how. Both privacy and competition are possible, and, as we've discussed, competition will open up the gates of opportunity for pro-privacy innovators.

We've Done It Before, We Can Do It Again

What monopolies have done to our world is depressing, but don't despair! We have been here before. We stood up to powerful monopolists when we broke up Standard Oil and AT&T, and when we stopped Microsoft's anticompetitive practices, among other monopolies in our history. Each time, we were better for it. We unleashed new waves of innovation. We dispersed opportunity. We restored our markets and removed gatekeepers.

The result of the golden age of antitrust enforcement from 1913 to 1982 was an economy with distributed opportunity. The Boomers benefited from this deconcentration, among other economic factors, but Generation X and Millennials are navigating their careers and raising families during a time when economic opportunity is highly concentrated. The gutting of anti-monopoly policy got us here, but life doesn't have to be this way.

As I mentioned at the start, citizens' outrage after *The History of the Standard Oil Company* was published spurred the government to break up Standard Oil. The Federal Trade Commission was established, and the Clayton Act was passed after the outcry. Standard Oil had tremendous political power and was extracting unprecedented wealth, but angered average Americans helped to break it up.

Anti-monopolists at the turn of the century used political cartoons to capture the menace of monopoly and bring their message to the American people. This rich history of art as protest inspired the cartoons in this book. In the digital age we have endless options to use creativity to inspire political action, from memes, to short videos, to documentary films, but cartoons can still bring to life the dangers of modern monopolies. Published in 1904, a famous cartoon shows Standard Oil as an octopus with its tentacles wrapped around the steel, copper, and shipping industries, the U.S. Capitol, a state legislature, and with a tentacle reaching toward the White House. Just like today's monopolies, Standard Oil had tremendous economic and political power, but the people, undaunted, decided they weren't going to take it anymore.

The fight against monopoly requires constant vigilance, to protect us from the undemocratic concentration of private power. Just like now, many saw monopolies as more powerful than government at the turn of the century. But like the Americans who came before us, we have to fight for our democracy, not just cede it to monopolists. We must hold our elected representatives accountable to the people instead of corporate overlords. The 1889 *Bosses of the Senate* cartoon portrays corporate interests as giant money bags towering over the

senators below, under the motto, "This is the Senate of the Monopolists by the Monopolists and for the Monopolists!" The popular perception of monopolies' undue influence on politics contributed to the passing of the Sherman Act the following year, in 1890.

Monopolies at the turn of the century cheated Americans out of their pay, subjected them to poor working conditions, and ripped them off with high prices. The caption to this 1901 cartoon reads, "The little boy [Common People] and the big boys [Trusts] prepare for the baseball season." Monopolies of old were called "trusts," hence the term "antitrust." The monopolies are pelting balls at "the common people" that say "low wages," "high prices," and "oppression." Sound familiar?

For at least 137 years it's been obvious that monopoly is at war with workers getting fairly compensated for the fruits of their labor, which the 1883 cartoon titled "The tournament of today—a set-to between labor and monopoly," illustrates. Shared economic prosperity and monopoly are incompatible, and we must join together to fight for the more just and equitable future we deserve.

THE TOURNAMENT OF TODAY.—A SET-TO BETWEEN LABOR AND MONOPOLY.

America overcame the rule of monopoly kings before, and we can do it again. The 1904 cartoon titled "Our Uncrowned Kings" asks, "Where is the spirit of '76? This is what your forefathers did to King George." More than a century later, we again find ourselves under the rule of kings—kings of commerce, information, health care, agriculture, energy, and more. It's time we harness America's revolutionary spirit and dethrone our uncrowned kings, using democratic institutions and laws we already have.

All but one of the above cartoons were published by *Puck*, a magazine that created political satire from 1871 to 1918, which was housed in downtown New York City's famous Puck Building. In a sign of the second Gilded Age, Jared Kushner now owns the building and converted the top floors to penthouse apartments, one of which was listed for sale in March 2019 for $42.5 million.

The problems we are facing today are not new, nor are they surprising. When it comes to dominant platforms, the mystique of high tech doesn't justify monopolies' exploitative nature. At the turn of the

OUR UNCROWNED KINGS.

century, railroads were high-tech! When we broke up AT&T, it too was high-tech, as was Microsoft when the United States sued it for violating antitrust laws, and antitrust enforcement caused innovation to flourish. We have the tools to fix our monopoly problems, and we just need to use them again.

Replacing Monopoly Rule with People Rule

We know what we need to do. In our battered democracy, where members of Congress are beholden to monopoly money, voters still have the final say. With monopolies spending tens of millions of dollars per year to get their way with our elected representatives, the only way to overcome their power is through the voice of the people. We need to rise up.

It's time to start "flexing your citizenship muscle," in the words of Stacy Mitchell, codirector of the Institute for Local Self-Reliance. When it comes to fighting monopoly, you have more power as a citizen than as a consumer. If everyone who reads this book stopped using Amazon Prime tomorrow, would it make a difference? Probably not. But if everyone who reads this book becomes part of the anti-monopoly movement, which as of now consists of a small cadre of think tanks, scholars, and grassroots organizers, well, that would be a game changer.

Becoming part of the anti-monopoly movement isn't as hard as it might seem. If you start thinking about anti-monopoly, talking about anti-monopoly, supporting anti-monopoly political candidates, joining or supporting organizations that mobilize against monopoly, demanding enforcement of antitrust laws, or pressuring your political representatives to act against monopoly, you could help make your life—and indeed all Americans' lives—better.

Anti-monopoly citizen groups are in the process of forming. If you'd like to know about opportunities to get involved when they arise, sign up at monopoliessuck.com. In the meantime, organizations doing anti-monopoly policy work include the Open Markets Institute, the American Economic Liberties Project, the Institute for Local Self-Reliance, the Roosevelt Institute, and Demos, to name a few. Coalitions of organizations have already formed, like Athena mobilizing against Amazon. Social justice organizations like Demand Progress, Public Citizen, and Artist Rights Alliance frequently join together to take action on particular issues, like the Freedom from Facebook and Google Coalition. Grassroots climate and farming groups are also joining anti-monopoly efforts. Signing up for the newsletters of organizations like these, compiled at the above web address, will keep you in the know and give opportunities to play a part.

Beware false prophets, or organizations that are actually funded by monopolists. An army of supposed experts are on the payroll of corporate giants that are scared of Americans waking up and taking some of their power—including lawyers, economists, professors, and academic centers that pretend to be neutral, conservative think tanks, think tanks that pretend to be progressive, and politicians who accept monopolists' donations.

These include groups that have names designed to trick you into thinking they're on the side of the people, a well-established practice known as "astro-turfing." Money flows to those who buttress monopolists' talking points, creating a loud chorus of individuals whose livelihood depends on hiding the truth—that antitrust law has always been about fighting concentrated power.

When you hear criticism of the ideas presented in this book, ask the speaker: Does a corporation with market power fund you, your employer, or your academic center? For example, Google maintains a list of "politically-engaged trade associations, independent third-party organizations and other tax-exempt groups that receive the most substantial contributions from Google's U.S. Government Affairs and Public Policy team." At the time of writing, the most recent iteration includes more than 350 entries. Facebook has even hired "a Republican opposition-research firm to discredit activist protesters," reported the *New York Times* in an exposé of Facebook's cutthroat tactics against critics, including the Freedom from Facebook Coalition of progressive organizations.

If in addition to flexing your citizenship muscle you also want to boycott corporate giants, to the extent you have other choices, go for it. If you quit Amazon Prime, you may find you have more money and less clutter. That's what happened to me. I thought everything I was buying on Amazon was something I needed, but I was wrong. Habit experts will tell you a simple strategy—you should aim to create friction for bad habits and eliminate friction for good habits. Putting the cookie jar on the top shelf or not keeping sweets in the home are examples of creating friction to discourage a bad habit. Placing your sneakers next to your bedside is an example of reducing friction to encourage the good habit of working out in the morning. Frictionless "one-click" purchases is not what we need when we are stressed about money and drowning in stuff.

If you adopt privacy-protecting substitutes for Google like the DuckDuckGo search engine, you may feel freer like I did. If you stop using Facebook and Instagram, you may be happier and have more free time. That's what happened to me. (My accounts still technically exist, but I have been on a long, relaxing hiatus from them.) Some people can't quit these platforms because they are essential communication networks in their communities, or they need to use the networks to reach their customers, families, or more. Avoiding monopolies in things like health care and agriculture can be incredibly difficult, if not impossible, as a consumer.

Just Say No to Pro-Monopoly Excuses

If fixing our monopoly mess feels too complicated, it's understandable. But! If we give in to complication paralysis, we won't make the world—or our lives—better. "Corruption is everywhere" is another excuse, and it's true, and overwhelming. But if we throw up our hands and accept corruption, rather than trying to change the system, then we are shirking our responsibilities to do "the hard and slow" work of self-governance. With concentrated corporate power posing an existential threat with climate change and endangering democracy itself, using complication or corruption as cover for doing nothing is not an option.

Neither can we depend on monopolies to self-regulate. Corporations have fiduciary duties to maximize profits under current understandings of corporate law, which experts tell me has also been distorted by moneyed interests. For lawmakers to expect corporations to regulate in a way that risks reducing their profits is so misguided that it amounts to an abdication of their responsibility to represent the American people.

Nor can we accept the pro-monopoly talking point that America needs "national champions" to compete against China. What, is there an arms race to show citizens more creepy targeted advertising that no one told me about? In all seriousness, promoting national champions is not the American way. As we have seen through this book, competition makes companies do better. Keeping markets open so that challengers can disrupt powerful companies is what has historically made America the most innovative country in the world.

Columbia law professor Tim Wu has compared the American approach to the Japanese national champion approach in the 1970s and '80s, when Japan was seen as the biggest innovative threat. AT&T and IBM, said Wu in an interview with *Wired*'s Nicholas Thompson, asked the government to support them in their fight against Japan. Instead, the U.S. government broke up AT&T. "Out of that came a new telecom industry, a new internet industry, the ISP industry, and all the industries we're worrying about today," said Wu. Europe and Japan, however, stuck with the national champions approach. "I haven't heard from either of them in a long time in the tech markets," Wu added.

UC Berkeley professor Robert Reich has put forth another strong counterpoint against the national champions argument—America's monopoly companies are becoming less American all the time. American corporations are obligated not to Americans, but rather to their shareholders, writes Reich in the *Guardian*. "About 30% of the shareholders of large American corporations aren't even American," says Reich, and of the 500 largest corporations with U.S. headquarters, a "full 40% of their employees live and work outside the United States." American companies have also been pouring millions of dollars into research and development in China, a condition imposed by the Chinese government to gain access to China's huge market. This practice is a drain on American innovation known as "technology transfer." The ability to compete in a global economy depends, instead, says Reich, on Americans' creativity and productivity, which in turn depends on quality of education, health, and infrastructure.

The monopolization of America, however, works directly against these purposes. As we've seen, corporate behemoths drain resources from our schools by avoiding taxes, raise health care costs, and—with weak competition—reduce investment in research and development. The best way to build America's competitiveness in a global economy is to reduce concentrated corporate power and revitalize competitive markets that allow disruption and enable the American dream.

Tools to Fix Our Monopoly Mess

Policies that need citizen support fall into a few categories. Starting with Big Tech, I use the acronym PAIN to describe a set of solutions for weakening its monopoly grip: Privacy rules; Antitrust enforcement; Interoperability, which gives potential competitors access to monopoly networks; and Nondiscrimination rules, which require platforms to treat everyone equally. I use this acronym not because I'm a sadist, but because interventions that don't put the giants in pain—like the FTC's $5 billion settlement with Facebook—don't fix things.

Fines alone are not enough because they don't change destructive business models and anticompetitive practices. Google has handed over more than $9 billion to the European Commission since 2017 for antitrust violations, without skipping a beat. When it comes to fixing Big Tech, and monopolies in general, if it doesn't hurt, it doesn't work. Tech giants' pain in the short term would bring gains for competition, innovation, and democracy in the longer term.

The solutions to our problems are all possible. What makes them feel hard to achieve is that our democratically elected representatives are beholden to monopoly overlords. So there's a temptation to only propose solutions that are viewed as "realistic" because they sit well with the monopolists running our country. But such half measures are not solutions at all. They're more dangerous than doing nothing because they allow politicians to be off the hook and create the false appearance of solving problems. When we stop operating within the narrow confines of what changes will be palatable to big corporations, the solutions are simple and obvious.

Getting Antitrust Back on Track

The goals of reinvigorated antitrust enforcement should be to open the gates of competition to new and diverse innovators, decrease market concentration, and restore dynamism by halting illegal monopolization that kicks competitors out of the game. When it comes to Big Tech, antitrust enforcement should reduce choke points so that pro-democracy innovation can occur. Entrepreneurs with better business models are waiting in the wings, and antitrust enforcement should aim to enable these new start-ups to bring their innovations to users. Competition among business models is needed to help curb the massive surveillance and manipulation that today's tech monopolies allow.

Getting antitrust back on the rails requires two main approaches: 1) enforcers like DOJ, FTC, and state AGs bringing more aggressive cases under existing legal standards and 2) federal and state lawmakers passing laws that correct bad court decisions and strengthen rules. Big corporations have successfully used the Chicago School ideology to narrow the antitrust laws, throwing money at top lawyers and convincing judges time and again that their bad behavior is legal. Court victory upon victory weakened antitrust standards so that the rules created through case law bear little resemblance to the statutes

Congress enacted. "Nothing can be done," antitrust enforcers often say when faced with complaints of anticompetitive conduct, as they point to this pathetic legal precedent. The main way antitrust enforcers let the wrongheaded interpretation of antitrust statutes prevail is by not bringing enough cases they think they might lose.

Given the state of the law, being an antitrust expert these days often means being able to skillfully articulate exactly why there's no antitrust case—even when the average person plainly can see the merger or behavior is anticompetitive. I know how it happens because in some respects it happened to me when I worked at the New York Attorney General's Office. I took the complicated framework I had learned (that is, the misguided Chicago School version of antitrust law), applied it to the facts presented to me to determine whether we had a case, and in most instances—as was designed by the Chicago School—the answer was no. I did try to push the envelope with some creative case theories, and the New York AG is among the most aggressive of antitrust enforcers.

All of us AAGs were simultaneously drinking from a fire hose on a large number of merger reviews, given merger mania. There was plenty of work to go around a leanly staffed office, so I kept busy on cases that had a stronger shot at winning in court. Sherman Act Section 2 monopolization cases are much harder to win in court than are Sherman Act Section 1 cases, like price-fixing, due to legal precedent that applies a tougher standard. Potential Sherman Act Section 2 cases, then, tend to get lower priority, with the consequence that illegal monopolization runs rampant. The DOJ filed sixty-two Sherman Act Section 2 monopoly lawsuits in federal district court between 1970 and 1979, but only one such case between 2009 and 2018.

Only after I left the New York AG to become a journalist writing about antitrust did I have the luxury of stepping back from the minutiae of trying to build winnable cases and get to study the big picture. I got to see the forest, instead of just the trees. And what I saw was more like a cleared Amazon rain forest than a healthy competitive playing field.

Antitrust enforcers can no longer accept the status quo. They must be more willing to risk losing and bring the strongest cases possible, as court victories can help correct antitrust precedent. Losses can only do so much damage to already-neutered law. Even under existing law, federal antitrust enforcers are not fully using the tools available to combat illegal conduct. The FTC has a powerful law that it seldom uses for promoting competition, Section 5 of the FTC Act. Section 5 declares unfair methods of competition to be unlawful. The law is broader than the Sherman and Clayton Acts, even banning acts "that contravene the spirit of the antitrust laws," explains an FTC statement. The FTC also has the power to make rules, just like other administrative agencies do (think the Federal Communications Commission or the Environmental Protection Agency), but so far it chooses not to use that power to promulgate anti-monopoly rules.

Enforcers need to bring more monopolization cases, like *United States v. Microsoft Corp.* One remedy in monopolization cases is breaking up the corporation, like in the case of AT&T, but that's not the only fix. The Microsoft case did not ultimately result in a breakup, but it did stop Microsoft from extending its tentacles into every market that touched its operating system monopoly, allowing innovation to thrive. Breaking up Big Tech is warranted, but it doesn't solve all of the problems. Even with a breakup, privacy rules, interoperability, and nondiscrimination would be necessary to ensure fair competition.

On top of more aggressive enforcement, Congress should step in and fix bad court decisions so that the antitrust laws can work for all of us again. Legislators, until very recently, have been asleep at the wheel at best, or beholden to their corporate donors at worst. This is changing, under the leadership of lawmakers like Representative David Cicilline and Senator Elizabeth Warren, with members of Congress from both parties becoming active on antitrust issues.

Congress could fix legal precedent that imposes high bars for prevailing on monopolization and attempted monopolization cases (trying to monopolize is also illegal, by the way). Standards that particularly need fixing pertain to monopoly leveraging (using monopoly power in one market to take over other markets), predatory pricing (pricing below cost), and bundling (putting a monopoly product in a bundle with other products, often eliminating competitors in those other product markets). These are all super-effective tactics for monopolies to crush competition without competing to be the best, and they must be stopped. Congress should overrule those cases and put monopolization law back on track.

Procedural obstacles that courts have erected to limit who can sue under the antitrust laws should also be overruled. Barriers to private-class actions should be removed, including the widespread use of clauses that require people to go to arbitration instead of being able to sue in court. A real threat of class actions suing for hundreds of millions of dollars would help deter companies from monopolizing, and would supplement government enforcement.

Congress should also ban certain kinds of monopolizing practices, like the dirty tricks of Big Pharma. Enforcers' endless Whac-A-Mole could be stopped if Congress did its job. Pay-for-delay, where branded companies pay to keep generic drugs off the market, should be outright banned with an automatic fine of double the ill-gotten profits from the conduct. Wimpy fines don't work when billions of dollars of profits make breaking the law a smart business decision.

Legislators should aim to remove complexity and make antitrust cases easier, faster, and cheaper. The Chicago School's mucking up of antitrust law with misguided complexity stole from the people their weapon against concentrated power. Anyone seeking to claim their right to a competitive marketplace has to spend millions of dollars to hire economic experts, thanks to the Chicago School. In 2018, the FTC spent nearly $16 million on fees for testifying expert economists when it already employs about eighty PhD-holding economists! Monopolists' victims can rarely afford to sue them, and this enormous expense also affects enforcers' calculus of whether or not to bring cases.

State and federal legislators should allocate more resources to state antitrust enforcers, who have proven to be more aggressive in enforcement than the FTC or DOJ but are inadequately staffed. While the New York AG has a dozen or so antitrust lawyers, lots of states only have one, or even one-half of an antitrust enforcer, who spends the other half of their time doing consumer protection enforcement.

Ending Platform Privilege

I support a solution that has been advanced by Senator Elizabeth Warren and antitrust scholar Lina Khan: prohibit platforms from competing against companies that depend on them altogether. This would eliminate the problem of platform privilege—if Big Tech umpires the game, it doesn't get to play it, too.

This fix also would address a lot of the conflicts of interest that have driven Big Tech to illegally monopolize by kicking competitors out of the game. And it's not a novel concept. As Lina Khan writes in *Separations of Platforms and Commerce*, this structural solution has been done before, in industries spanning from railroads to banking to TV. Such a separation could be the remedy for a monopolization case or it could be required through new laws passed by legislators.

That platforms shouldn't be allowed to compete against businesses that depend on them is obvious when you think about it. On my *Women Killing It!* podcast I once interviewed a woman named Jillian Wright, an entrepreneur who started out as a skin care aesthetician and then developed her own skin care line. She noticed a need for a service that connects beauty entrepreneurs with buyers and consumers. She launched the Indie Beauty Expo, which provides a platform to showcase independent beauty brands and support the entrepreneurs behind them. Wright spoke to me about her decision to shut down her own beauty brand after the Indie Beauty Expo was a smashing success. She told me, "I can't compete with the brands; I have an extremely unfair advantage." She knows all the buyers and the press, she said, adding, "It's just unethical to me." Although it was not easy to bid farewell to the product she worked so hard to create, Wright said, "it was the right decision to make."

The right answer is not so complicated after all.

Putting a Stop to Harmful Mergers

Antitrust enforcers need to be more aggressive about suing to block mergers of all kinds, but particularly acquisitions of competitive threats. Tech platforms, for instance, are using their control of infrastructure to identify competitive threats when they are new and small. The deals barely even register on antitrust enforcers' radars. Enforcers also need to evaluate every merger's acquisition of data and machine learning, which can lessen competition or fortify monopoly power.

Enforcers should also unwind illegal mergers they didn't catch.

Enforcers, for example, should undo Facebook's acquisitions of WhatsApp and Instagram as violating the Clayton Act's prohibition of acquisitions where the effect "may be substantially to lessen competition, or to tend to create a monopoly." Internal Facebook documents published by the British Parliament show Facebook had identified WhatsApp as a competitive threat before the deal, as mentioned earlier. And the European Commission has already fined Facebook for telling them during the merger review that it would not merge WhatsApp's data with Facebook's data, and then doing it anyway. Since then WhatsApp cofounder Brian Acton admitted to being coached to tell European regulators that merging data would be difficult. It's likely that bad-faith representations were similarly made to the FTC, because the FTC and the European Commission coordinate with each other on global merger investigations.

Antitrust enforcers should also sue to block more mergers that involve one company buying another company that is not a direct competitor but is rather involved in a different stage of production. These types of mergers are called "vertical mergers," and an example would be Pepsi buying the company that bottles its soda. The Chicago School says such a merger is "efficient" and will help Pepsi save money and in turn reduce prices for consumers. In reality, such a merger can help Pepsi drive out competitors that depended on that bottling company by denying them access to it or raising their competitors' costs, and there's no guarantee of lower prices. To the contrary, a recent study found that such mergers drive up prices anywhere from 15 to 50 percent. The Chicago School assumption, still reflected in court decisions, that vertical mergers invariably promote competition has been proven wrong.

Enforcers also should stop putting in meaningless merger fixes that don't work, and are often violated and expire. For example, the DOJ allowed Google to buy a company called ITA, which made software that many travel booking websites depend on. But first, the DOJ filed a complaint against the deal that alleged the merger "will give Google the means and incentive" to "foreclose or disadvantage" its travel search competitors by degrading their access to ITA's software or denying them access altogether. "The proposed merger," said the DOJ's complaint, "is likely to result in reduced quality, variety, and innovation for consumers of comparative flight search services."

The DOJ then gave the deal the A-OK when Google agreed to make ITA's software available to competitors for five years. What happened about six years later? Google pulled the plug on the software, and it was no longer available to competitors, without any consequences from the DOJ. Enforcers have a bad habit of waving through deals with temporary fixes that allow monopoly power to take hold as soon as the merger conditions expire. Enforcers should more often sue to block anticompetitive deals outright, or impose fixes that are structural and permanent.

Congress should impose a moratorium on further acquisitions by mega-monopolies. Facebook, for example, already built something too big for it to control and has shown itself to be a repeat offender of consumer protection law and an FTC privacy order. If behemoths have effectively become unregulatable, lacking accountability to democratically elected governments, then putting a hold on acquisitions is entirely reasonable.

Congress should also reform the law governing mergers. It should shift the burden of proof to the merging companies—instead of the government having to prove a merger is anticompetitive, the companies have to prove a merger is good for competition. Senator Amy Klobuchar has proposed a bill that comes close, shifting the burden to the merging companies to prove their deal doesn't harm competition. Our economy is so concentrated that mergers are more likely than not to be anticompetitive, and a major course correction is needed.

From Consumer Welfare to Human Welfare

Consumers are humans, too—employees, employers, makers, entrepreneurs, creators, taxpayers, and citizens—and antitrust law should reflect this fact. When antitrust enforcers find themselves up against a defendant that insists "consumer welfare" is limited to low prices, they should push for a broader definition of what consumer welfare includes. Harm to innovation or reduced competition in the labor market, for example, should be included in what it means to harm consumers. Antitrust law should still be focused on stopping anticompetitive mergers and behavior, but prices can't be the only way to measure harm to competition.

Lawmakers could scrap the consumer welfare standard altogether as a poor indicator of whether competition itself is reduced, especially since the standard has failed to actually benefit consumers, as this book has shown. One idea that was presented by a committee of academics led by Professor Guy Rolnick was that enforcers should take "citizen welfare" into account in merger reviews that involve media and speech. In a world where the silos of different kinds of media have broken down, enforcers could evaluate "attention shares" instead of market shares to ensure that no company acquires too much control over information flow and the dissemination of news. This concept could be used not only to block mergers but also to sue tech giants when they exclude rivals from disseminating news and content and monopolize attention. Or the concept of attention shares could be used in regulation. The Federal Communications Commission has long had rules prohibiting concentrated control over television, radio, and newspapers, and the attention shares model is a creative way to apply these same types of limits in the digital age.

Because employee welfare also matters, lawmakers should outright ban noncompete clauses that trap workers in jobs and should mandate that merger reviews take into account harm to competition for employees.

Anti-Corruption Is Anti-Monopoly

You might be wondering how the heck lawmakers are going to make any of these changes when they're under the rule of monopoly overlords. Open and competitive markets protect us from highly concentrated economic and political power, so the monopolization of America means we've lost this critical check on corruption. Apple, Facebook, Amazon, and Google/Alphabet have spent more than $330 million on federal lobbying since 2008, and that doesn't include the money poured into the pro-monopoly chorus previously mentioned.

Concentrated corporate power's influence over regulators is not just dangerous to democracy, it's dangerous to human life. Boeing and Airbus together have 99 percent of the global market for large plane orders. Boeing is consistently a top spender on lobbying, greasing the wheels with $285 million in lobbying since 1998, according to the Center for Responsive Politics. Boeing used its political influence to loosen regulatory oversight of its planes, ultimately leading to a staggering loss of human life on its 737 Max. Boeing spent more than $43 billion buying back its stocks over the last decade, rather than investing the funds in research, development, and safety.

America desperately needs anti-corruption reform, including campaign finance reform to get money out of politics. We need rules to combat the "revolving door" of antitrust enforcers between jobs in government and jobs in big corporations or corporate law firms. How tough will an enforcer be on corporate abuse if they plan to later rake in cash working for the abusers? We need similar rules for lawmakers and regulators.

Your voice, and the voices of your fellow Americans, if raised loudly enough, still have the power to overcome the influence of monopoly money. Your support is needed for anti-corruption measures like campaign finance reform.

And your vote is needed for candidates who fund their campaigns with large numbers of small donations and without accepting corporate money, when you have that option. Candidates who collect cash from monopolies on the campaign trail will be beholden to them, not the people. Such candidates are unlikey to make the big structural changes that are needed to improve people's lives.

Spying Must Be Stopped

Your voice is also needed in support of privacy regulation. Strong privacy rules, not crafted by Big Tech lobbyists, would not only protect

Americans from ubiquitous surveillance, but would also level the competitive playing field.

Privacy is considered a fundamental human right in Europe, and the GDPR aims to curb the extensive tracking by Facebook, Google, and others in the digital advertising ecosystem. Although some people—including representatives from institutions funded by Facebook and Google—have argued that the GDPR is a bad idea because it will entrench the tech platforms, privacy reforms, if crafted effectively, will actually undercut Facebook's and Google's dominance. Comprehensive tracking of users is required to support the platforms' hypertargeted digital advertising business models. Unfortunately, the GDPR hasn't yet achieved its goals. As mentioned earlier, the tech giants have interpreted the law to mean what they want it to mean, and enforcement for violations has been slow.

Another step in the right direction is California's Consumer Privacy Act (CCPA), which went into effect in January 2020. Alastair Mactaggart, founder and chair of Californians for Consumer Privacy, has proposed an updated version for the November 2020 ballot. He explained two reasons why: "First, some of the world's largest companies have actively and explicitly prioritized weakening CCPA." And second, "technological tools have evolved in ways that exploit a consumer's data with potentially dangerous consequences."

Still, I worry that privacy laws based primarily on getting consent from consumers don't go far enough. People don't have time to be hypervigilant about their privacy rights, and tech platforms use this fact to their advantage. Opting in to Google's data collection takes one click, for example, while opting out takes seventeen clicks. Forty percent of people abandon a website that takes more than three seconds to load. Do we really expect a consumer to endure seventeen clicks? It's not realistic for how people use the internet.

People are under constant time pressure, in part due to monopoly rule. No one has time to individually assess every companies' tracking policies.

Cambridge Analytica whistle-blower Christopher Wylie shared this same concern in his written testimony to Congress. "Data protection is a consumer safety issue," he wrote, "and we cannot continue putting the burden on consumers by using this false narrative of choice." "We do not allow automotive companies to build unsafe cars as long as they include warning labels," Wylie added, noting that we empower regulators to create safety standards in every other sector. Concerns about regulations hampering innovation are overblown, wrote Wylie, pointing out that "car safety standards have not inhibited innovation or demand, nor have they unreasonably inhibited profit."

In my view, the most invasive forms of surveillance should be outright banned. I second journalist David Dayen, who wrote in *New Republic* that "the U.S. can take one simple, legal step to roll back this dystopian nightmare: ban targeted advertising." This could be done by the FTC through its rule-making function, without needing Congress to pass a law.

In written testimony to Congress, David Heinemeier Hansson, cofounder of Basecamp, also called for Congress to "ban the practice of targeting ads based on personal information, unless each piece of personal information used in the ads was specifically obtained with the voluntary, optional, and informed consent that it be used for marketing purposes." He gave as an example, "Yes, I give permission to Facebook to sell the fact that I'm pregnant to companies that want to advertise to pregnant women." Incidentally, voluntary, specific, and informed consent is required by the GDPR, but I have yet to see these requirements fully satisfied. And I still question whether the consent framework imposes too many burdens on busy people.

Author Shoshana Zuboff wrote in a *New York Times* op-ed that data collected about us "empty into surveillance capitalists' computational factories, called 'artificial intelligence,' where they are manufactured into behavioral predictions that are about us, but they are not *for us*." Rather, "they are sold to business customers in a new kind of market that trades exclusively in human futures," she writes. The ban Zuboff proposes is broader than just targeted advertising, but rather outlaws all human futures markets and eliminates the financial incentives to spy on us. "[S]ocieties outlaw markets that trade in human organs, babies and slaves," as morally repugnant, writes Zuboff, noting human futures markets "challenge human freedom and undermine democracy." Zuboff points out that surveillance capitalism is young but democracy is old, and "Anything made by humans can be unmade by humans."

Interoperability Promotes Competition

Interoperability is an anti-monopoly tool that has been used successfully time and again to promote innovation by reducing barriers to entering markets. Regulators and antitrust enforcers have imposed interoperability requirements against AT&T and Microsoft, opening up competition in long-distance calling, telephones, and internet browsers.

For Big Tech, interoperability would allow users to authorize networks to securely communicate with each other. It would help overcome the "network effects" barrier to entry we discussed earlier, when we talked about how a social network without your friends on it isn't much use. Interoperability could allow new platforms to communicate with Facebook's platform, for example.

Mark Zuckerberg offered up his own set of solutions that no lawmaker should listen to, and one of his proposals was data portability. This means you could take your Facebook data and port it to another platform. But data portability doesn't overcome the network effects barrier for new companies to compete with Facebook, because porting your data to a platform that doesn't allow you to communicate with your friends has little value.

Nondiscrimination and Neutrality

Dominant tech platforms should be subject to rules that prohibit discrimination in price or terms, which we have repeatedly applied to network monopolies in our history. From the post office to the telegraph to cable TV, American government has required nondiscrimination policies to protect the free press and democracy. Nondiscrimination is the principle behind net neutrality, holding that those internet service providers who control the infrastructure don't get to pick the winners and the losers of the internet.

Google being able to pick the winners and losers of internet search, for example, is the same problem we tried to address with net neutrality. We didn't want broadband companies to be able to control what content we see just because they control the pipes. We didn't want companies like Comcast to be able to prioritize their own content or let companies pay to get in fast lanes and interfere with those who don't pay, like a troll demanding a toll to cross the bridge. We have the same problem with a single search engine being the portal to the internet for the world. And with Amazon picking the winners and losers of commerce, with Facebook picking the winners and losers of internet content, and with Apple picking the winners and losers of the App Store.

Nondiscrimination and neutrality will be increasingly important as algorithms that discriminate by design continue to be rolled out, and will require algorithmic transparency to ensure compliance. The separation of platforms from commerce will partly decrease the incentives to discriminate, but not entirely, so neutrality principles would still be required in the event of such separation or a monopoly breakup of any kind. Nondiscrimination can be implemented through legislation, and it can also be a remedy in monopolization cases.

Taming the Wild, Wild West

The online and offline worlds are no longer separate, so giving carte blanche to internet actors to violate offline laws just means we live in a lawless society. Broadcasters and journalists are held to legal standards for political ads, and Facebook, too, should be held to those standards. Wiretapping and reading someone's mail is illegal, and so is recording someone without their consent in twelve states. Shouldn't spying on us through different technologies also be illegal? Fair housing laws prohibit unlawful discrimination in advertising, yet even after Facebook promised to stop this practice, a ProPublica investigation found the discrimination persisted. Discrimination by algorithm should be just as illegal as discrimination by any other means.

Fraud is illegal, but online ad fraud is estimated to cost advertisers billions of dollars per year. Yet it persists. Election tampering is illegal, but Facebook and Google are enabling voter manipulation with hypertargeted propaganda. Violating copyright law is illegal, but YouTube is rife with copyright violations. The list goes on and on.

Tristan Harris of the Center for Humane Technology has pointed out that we used to have protections for Saturday morning cartoons, but attempts at protecting kids online have fallen short. He suggests tech companies be required to report quarterly to the U.S. Department of Health and Human Services how many young users are addicted to their technology and what they are doing to stop it. Cigarettes are regulated; why shouldn't online addiction be too?

Section 230 of the Communications Decency Act has become an unruly monster, extended far beyond its intended purposes, and has allowed lawlessness as it eliminates responsibility for a wide range of illegal behavior. As the online world gobbles up the offline world and the two become one, Section 230 has helped throw our society's law and order out the window.

While the Wild West may sound fun and free, at least in the movies, laws exist for a reason. Laws protect us from abuse at the hands of private corporations that lack competitive constraint. Now there's a different set of laws, those created by the monopolists. Ask any Amazon marketplace seller and they'll tell you they're subject to an intricate web of rules and regulations; the laws are just imposed by the kingdom of Amazon.

Your Life, Better

The challenges you're dealing with in the age of monopoly are not easy. But just like those who came before you, you have the power to join with your fellow Americans and rise up in outrage against monopoly.

Anti-monopoly is one of the few issues people on both the left and the right can agree on. Attorneys general from fifty-one states and territories, for example, have joined together to investigate Google's monopoly abuses. Dethroning America's monopoly kings could begin to heal the deep divides in our country.

Now is not the time to say "it's too complicated," or "it's just the way it is," or "nothing can be done because everybody's corrupt." Now is the time to take action because, truthfully, so much is at stake that we don't have a choice. If we let a few powerful companies control each sector of our economy, then the American dream, democracy, liberty, opportunity, and equality—and worse, the future of humanity itself—are in danger. Now is our chance to build a world that's resilient, sustainable, and just, with shared power and prosperity.

The people who tell you that change is not possible are the ones who are reaping the spoils of the status quo. Don't listen to them.

Change may not be profitable for the monopolies ruling our lives, but that ain't the same thing as impossible.

Beliefs about impossibility are not facts. I learned from guests on my podcast that you can kill it in your career and create your ideal life if you don't limit yourself by false beliefs of impossibility. I talked to Christyl Johnson, the first female African American deputy center director at NASA who invented the first chromium LiSAF laser oscillator to achieve 33 millijoules. She told me, "When someone comes to me and says, 'That's really not possible,' that's when I get excited," because she thinks, "now it's my time to prove to you that that's not true."

Megan Mukuria, the founder of a nonprofit organization called ZanaAfrica, also didn't let beliefs about possibility stand in her way. She was working at a nonprofit, and she had an idea to provide sanitary pads and reproductive education for girls and women in Africa. The board of directors told her it was too big of an idea, too hard to do and not possible. Mukuria went ahead and did it on her own, without them. She recalled, "I was really interested in scale and impact, and I felt this urgency, that we can't just diddle around on the planet and not really do anything of significance. We need to do something that could affect tens of millions of girls and women." Most people on earth would think that's not possible, but Mukuria is on her way. Mukuria exposed the mirage of impossibility.

Another guest, scientist Liz Alter, didn't let beliefs about possibility stop her. She said, "I didn't think that I could be a scientist, as crazy as that might sound today, but neither of my parents were scientists. I didn't have any female role models growing up. . . . It wasn't until I was out of college that I really thought to myself, 'I need to give this a try since this is really what I'm passionate about.'" Now Alter heads up her own science lab and even discovered a new species of fish in the Congo River—the *Teleogramma obamaorum*. Can you guess who she named it after? She told me that families in the region where she discovered the fish commonly had a picture of Michelle and Barack Obama hanging on their wall.

One last example is someone we all know, Olympic swimmer Michael Phelps. No, he wasn't a guest on my *Women Killing It!* podcast, but I'll never forget a TV interview I saw of him after he had won an astonishing number of gold medals. A reporter asked him if he ever believed in his wildest dreams that it was possible for him to win that many gold medals. He looked at her like, "duh," and said that, yes, he did believe it was possible to win that many medals and that's precisely why he did it. "Nothing is impossible," Phelps said after gold medal number eight, which was just the beginning. "With so many people saying it couldn't be done, all it takes is an imagination."

Ending monopoly rule is possible. We've done it before, we can do it again, and we must.

ACKNOWLEDGMENTS

I would like to thank my brilliant editor, Stephanie Frerich, and talented assistant editor, Emily Simonson, for their hard work in bringing this book to life and for patiently shepherding me through the book process as a first-time author. Thanks also to my agent, Mollie Glick, for her unwavering advocacy and confidence in me, and Lola Bellier, for making it all happen. Deepest gratitude to Jonathan Karp, for believing in this project and for time and again publishing books on topics core to our democracy. Each member of the team at Simon & Schuster has made an invaluable contribution to this book's journey, including Cat Boyd, Stephen Bedford, Ruth Lee-Mui, Phil Metcalf, Beth Maglione, Kimberly Goldstein, Alison Forner, and Richard Rhorer.

How lucky I am to know a clever cartoonist, Christian Lowe, who helped bring levity to the heavy topic of monopoly rule and provided much-needed encouragement as the book's first reader. I'm also fortunate to count as a friend Francesca Richer, whose impeccable design sense has come to my aid in so many endeavors, including for this book's cover design.

Thank you to the wise advisors who gave me their time and thoughtful criticism, including Casey Cornelius, Phela Townsend, and Jaret Vadera.

This book is built upon the relentless efforts of the small but mighty—and growing—anti-monopoly movement. The Open Markets Institute has worked tirelessly against concentrated power for more than a decade, and contained within these pages is the expertise of Barry Lynn, Sandeep Vaheesan, Phil Longman, and Claire Kelloway, who also dedicated time to give feedback on drafts. The OMI Team, including Nidhi Hegde, Jody Brannon, Gina Salerno, Michael Bluhm, Katherine Dill, Udit Thakur, Daniel Hanley, Garphil Julien, and Jackie Filson, never ceases to impress me with creativity, energy, and dedication to the cause. Eddie Vale and Carli Kientzle play an essential communications role, as the anti-monopoly message can only have impact if it's heard.

Others whose anti-monopoly work continues to inspire me to fight for a more just economy include Sarah Miller and the team at the American Economic Liberties Project, Matt Stoller, Zephyr Teachout, Lina Khan, Stacy Mitchell, Ron Knox, the full Institute for Local Self-Reliance team, Frank Pasquale, Marshall Steinbaum, Felicia Wong and the thinkers at the Roosevelt Institute, Sanjukta Paul, David Dayen, Tim Wu, Maurice Stucke, and many more who challenge the antitrust establishment. This book includes the ideas of countless smart people whose thinking has informed my own, especially Jason Kint, Roger McNamee, Zeynep Tufecki, Shoshana Zuboff, Lillian Salerno, and Ross Baird. Warm welcome to the young guard of the anti-monopoly movement, who give me hope for the future. I remain in awe of the progressive activists who fight every day for social, economic, and environmental justice, as well as the journalists who give sunlight to monopoly abuses, with extra thanks to those whose work is cited in this book.

Teddy Downey at *The Capitol Forum* gave me the opportunity to see a broader competition picture as a journalist than I had known as an antitrust litigator. Trevor Baine, Jake Williams, and the bright minds at the one-of-a-kind startup publication taught me how to uncover the truth (or rather threw me in and gave me the choice to sink or swim—and learn a ton in the process). Special thanks to Macrui Dostourian, for being my partner in tech monopoly reporting, and Anne MacGregor, for jump-starting my international speaking tour.

The Antitrust Bureau of the New York Attorney General's Office is a rare, noble place with dedicated civil servants fighting for a fair economy for New York citizens and businesses. My former colleagues each taught me so much not only about antitrust law but also about keeping at the hard and slow, but not often glamorous, work of ensuring a just society.

I am thankful for the local, federal, and international lawmakers and antitrust enforcers who bravely hold monopoly to account, like many state AGs and FTC Commissioners Rohit Chopra and Rebecca Slaughter. The list of members of Congress serving their constituents in the fight against monopoly is thankfully getting longer every day, but Representative David Cicilline, the members of the House Antitrust Caucus, and their dedicated staff and counsel, particularly Slade Bond, deserve recognition for their leadership. Senator Elizabeth Warren has long played a lead role in the Senate, and Senator Amy Klobuchar has proposed numerous antitrust reforms, both supported by their hard-working staff.

The guests on my *Women Killing It!* podcast inspired me to look beyond limiting beliefs about what is and isn't possible, and I am indebted to them for sharing their life lessons with me. My dear friends who have provided boundless support over the years and encouraged me to keep going—you know who you are, and I couldn't have made it here without you. Jill Richburg has also provided integral guidance on my path.

Thank you to Ben, Madhu, Sarita, Samar, Sunil, Leena, Aden, Amita, and Rajesh Khurana, and Jill Robinson, for their love and support.

I would never have written this book if not for my mother, a lifelong activist who doesn't accept injustice or buy the lie of "that's just the way it is," who fearlessly speaks truth to power, and feels the pain of others as if it were her own. My father has been a willing wingman in protest, who taught me, in his midwestern, Eagle Scout way, just to do my best, for that's all I can do. My brother gave me the thick skin to handle attacks by monopolists and their shills. I may not have appreciated it as a child, but it comes in handy now! My husband gives his absolute all as a father to our children and an equal partner, and for that I will be forever grateful. I love you all.

NOTES

Introduction

1 *unemployed Americans face hunger and homelessness*: Clodagh McGowan, "Hundreds Line Up for Blocks in Queens for Free Food Distribution," *Spectrum News*, May 4, 2020, https://www.ny1.com/nyc/all-boroughs/news/2020/05/02/hundreds-line-up-for-blocks-in-queens-for-free-food-distribution.

1 *the wealthiest profiteer*: "The Rich Are Having Themselves a Fine Coronavirus," *HuffPost*, April 17, 2020, https://www.huffpost.com/entry/rich-coronavirus-bailout-stimulus-banks_n_5e9762acc5b686ec1570cb44?, and "What You Need to Know about the CARES Act Bailouts," American Economic Liberties Project, April 2020, https://static1.squarespace.com/static/5df44e0792ff6a63789b5c02/t/5e973cdcb00b992d1ceb9b50/1586969820773/Corporate+Power+Quick+Takes_1_CARES+Act+Explainer.pdf.

2 *75 billionaires coexist with thousands of homeless people*: Katelyn Newman, "San Francisco Is Home to the Highest Density of Billionaires," *U.S. News & World Report*, May 10, 2019, https://www.usnews.com/news/cities/articles/2019-05-10/san-francisco-is-home-to-the-worlds-most-billionaires-per-capita, and Kevin Fagan, "Bay Area Homelessness: 89 Answers to Your Questions," *San Francisco Chronicle*, July 28, 2019, https://projects.sfchronicle.com/sf-homeless/homeless-questions/, and "Homeless Population," *City of San Francisco*, https://sfgov.org/scorecards/safety-net/homeless-population.

5 *"about what can be achieved"*: "Transcript: President Obama's Democratic National Convention speech," *Los Angeles Times*, July 27, 2016.

5 *"Power concedes nothing without a demand"*: Frederick Douglass, "West India Emancipation" speech, August 3, 1857, available at https://www.blackpast.org/african-american-history/1857-frederick-douglass-if-there-no-struggle-there-no-progress/.

6 *Ida Tarbell exposed*: Ida Tarbell, *The History of the Standard Oil Company* (New York: McClure, Phillips, 1904).

6 *sparked a citizen outcry that spurred*: U.S. Capitol Visitor Center, "Ida M. Tarbell: Exposing Standard Oil" ("Journalist Ida M. Tarbell brought the company's shady dealings to light, and the federal government sued Standard Oil. The Supreme Court ordered Standard Oil's breakup in 1911. . . . Congress strengthened antitrust laws with the Federal Trade Commission Act and the Clayton Act"), https://www.visitthecapitol.gov/exhibitions/artifact/senate-amendment-hr-15613-act-create-federal-trade-commission-federal-trade.

6 *as Teddy Roosevelt was called*: Tim Wu, *The Curse of Bigness* (New York: Columbia Global Reports, 2018).

7 *"Justice Brandeis declared"*: Peter Scott Campbell, "Democracy v. Concentrated Wealth: In Search of a Louis D. Brandeis Quote," 16 Green Bag 2D 251, Spring 2013, http://www.greenbag.org/v16n3/v16n3_articles_campbell.pdf.

Mini-Lesson: Antitrust Is Not Just for Nerds

8 *"If we will not endure"*: 21 Cong. Rec. 2461 (1890) (statement of Senator Sherman).

8 *Section 1 of the Sherman Act*: 15 U.S.C. § 1.

9 *"Every person who shall monopolize"*: 15 U.S.C. § 2

9 *"may be substantially to lessen competition, or to tend to create a monopoly"*: Clayton Antitrust Act of 1914, Section 7, 15 U.S. Code § 18.

10 *Antitrust class actions lawsuits*: Rathod, Jason and Vaheesan, Sandeep, "The Arc and Architecture of Private Enforcement Regimes in the United States and Europe: A View Across the Atlantic," 14 University of New Hampshire Law Review 303, October 31, 2015, https://ssrn.com/abstract=2684559.

11 *increased in 80 percent of industries*: Gustavo Grullon, Yelena Larkin, and Roni Michaely, "Are US Industries Becoming More Concentrated?" *Review of Finance*, 23, no. 4 (July 2019): 697–743, https://academic.oup.com/rof/article/23/4/697/5477414, and David Autor et al., "The Fall of the Labor Share and the Rise of Superstar Firms," NBER Working Paper, 1981–2012, average industry concentration across all economic sectors increased.

11 *crisis pervades our economy*: "America's Concentration Crisis: An Open Markets Institute Report," Open Markets, https://concentrationcrisis.openmarketsinstitute.org.

11 *textbook prices increased 88 percent between 2006 and 2016*: "Textbooks Are Pricey. So Students Are Getting Creative," *Washington Post*, https://www.washingtonpost.com/local/education/textbooks-keep-getting-pricier-so-students-are-getting-creative/2020/01/17/4e1306b8-30b9-11ea-91fd-82d4e04a3fac_story.html, and "College Tuition and Fees Increase 63 Percent since

January 2006," *U.S. Bureau of Labor Statistics: The Economics Daily*, Aug. 30, 2016, https://www.bls.gov/opub/ted/2016/college-tuition-and-fees-increase-63 -percent-since-january-2006.htm.

12 *Robert Bork:* Robert H. Bork, *The Antitrust Paradox: A Policy at War with Itself* (1978), 405. ("The only goal that should guide interpretation of the antitrust laws is the welfare of consumers. . . . In judging consumer welfare, productive efficiency, the single most important factor contributing to that welfare, must be given due weight along with allocative efficiency.")

12 *could rarely win monopolization cases in court:* Michael A. Carrier, "The Four-Step Rule of Reason," *Antitrust* 33, no. 2 (Spring 2019): 50–55, https://www .antitrustinstitute.org/wp-content/uploads/2019/04/ANTITRUST-4-step -RoR.pdf. Ninety-seven percent dismissal rate in rule of reason cases brought between 1999 and 2009.

13 *mergers and acquisitions have climbed:* "M&A in the United States," IMAA, https://imaa-institute.org/m-and-a-us-united-states/#m-and-a-history.

13 *In 2018 alone, there were 19,757 mergers and acquisitions:* M. Szmigiera, "Number of M&A Deals in the U.S. 2005–2018," *Statista*, June 24, 2019, https:// www.statista.com/statistics/914665/number-of-ma-deals-usa/.

13 *decades of robust antitrust enforcement:* Barry C. Lynn and Phillip Longman, "Who Broke America's Jobs Machine?" *Washington Monthly*, March/April 2010, https://washingtonmonthly.com/magazine/marchapril-2010/who-broke -americas-jobs-machine-3/.

14 *money and power fought the people, and money and power won:* See Matt Stoller, *Goliath: The 100-Year War Between Monopoly Power and Populism* (New York: Simon & Schuster, 2019).

7 WAYS MONOPOLIES RULE YOUR LIFE

One: Monopolies Take Your Money

19 *"Increases in the price of airline tickets":* "Remarks Prepared for Delivery by Assistant Attorney General Bill Baer at the Conference Call Regarding the Justice Department's Lawsuit Challenging US Airways' Proposed Merger with American Airlines," United States Department of Justice, *Justice News*, Aug. 13, 2013, https://www.justice.gov/opa/speech/remarks-prepared-delivery-as sistant-attorney-general-bill-baer-conference-call-regarding.

19 *On a press call, Baer said:* "US Airways/American Airlines: DOJ Sues to Block Airlines Deal; Mitigation Agreement Very Unlikely," *Capitol Forum*, Aug. 13, 2013.

19 *The DOJ's complaint:* "Justice Department Files Antitrust Lawsuit Challenging Proposed Merger between US Airways and American Airlines," United States Department of Justice, *Justice News*, Aug. 13, 2013, https://www.justice

.gov/opa/pr/justice-department-files-antitrust-lawsuit-challenging-proposed
-merger-between-us-airways-and.

20 *Some commentators*: "US Airways/American Airlines: With Settlement, DOJ
Abandons Vision of Competitive Harm Outlined in Complaint; Did PR, Lobbying Influence DOJ Front Office?" *Capitol Forum*, Nov. 15, 2013.

20 *Economists studied*: "Economists Identify an Unseen Force Holding Back Affordable Housing," *Washington Post*, Oct. 17, 2019, https://www.washington
post.com/business/2019/10/17/economists-identify-an-unseen-force-hold
ing-back-affordable-housing/.

21 *fewer than 20 percent of U.S. census blocks*: "But according to Federal Communications Commission data, at a download speed of 100 Mbps, 11% of U.S.
census blocks had no access to broadband, more than one-third had only one
choice of a fixed broadband provider, and 37% had access to only two." "Three
Important Points on Broadband Competition," Benton Institute for Broadband
& Society, March 20, 2019, https://www.benton.org/blog/three-important
-points-broadband-competition.

21 *Comcast offers 25 percent higher discounts*: Inti Pacheco, and Shalini Rama-
chandran, "Do You Pay Too Much for Internet Service? See How Your Bill
Compares," *Wall Street Journal*, Dec. 24, 2019,https://www.wsj.com/articles
/do-you-pay-too-much-for-internet-service-see-how-your-bill-compares-11
577199600.

21 *Consider this typical practice*: Christopher Mitchell, "Fleeced by the Telecoms
and Your State Is Blessing It," *American Conservative*, Oct. 21, 2019, https://
www.theamericanconservative.com/articles/is-your-state-allowing-the-cable
-company-to-rook-you/.

21 *nineteen states have laws discouraging such networks*: Katie Kienbaum, "19 States
Restrict Local Broadband Solutions," Institute for Local Self-Reliance, Aug. 8,
2019,https://ilsr.org/preemption-detente-municipal-broadband-networks-face
-barriers-in-19-states/.

21 *HB 129*: Katie Kienbaum, "How Telecom Monopolies Killed Competition in
North Carolina with HB 129," *Community Broadband Bits*, Episode 412, May
26, 2020, https://muninetworks.org/content/how-telecom-monopolies-killed
-competition-north-carolina-hb-129-community-broadband-bits.

22 *In 2019, the DOJ approved a merger between Sprint and T-Mobile*: "Justice Department Settles with T-Mobile and Sprint in Their Proposed Merger by
Requiring a Package of Divestitures to Dish," *The United States Department
of Justice*, July 26, 2019, https://www.justice.gov/opa/pr/justice-department
-settles-t-mobile-and-sprint-their-proposed-merger-requiring-package.

22 *Several state attorneys general sued to block the deal*: "State Attorneys General
Sue to Block Merger between Sprint and T-Mobile," *Washington Post*, June 11,

2019, https://www.washingtonpost.com/technology/2019/06/11/state-attorneys
-general-sue-block-merger-between-sprint-t-mobile/.

22 *Roger Solé*: David McLaughlin, and Scott Moritz. "Sprint Executive Saw Future Price Hike from T-Mobile Deal," Bloomberg, Dec. 9, 2019, https://www
.bloomberg.com/news/articles/2019-12-09/top-sprint-executive-saw-future
-price-hike-from-t-mobile-deal.

22 *"The text messages show"*: "How a Top Antitrust Official Helped T-Mobile
and Sprint Merge," *New York Times*, Dec. 19, 2019, https://www.nytimes
.com/2019/12/19/technology/sprint-t-mobile-merger-antitrust-official.html,
and "Open Markets Respond to Report That DOJ Antitrust Chief Helped
T-Mobile and Sprint Merge," *Open Markets*, Dec. 20, 2019, https://openmarket
sinstitute.org/releases/open-markets-responds-report-doj-antitrust-chief
-helped-t-mobile-sprint-merge/.

22 *filing a brief arguing that the deal should be cleared*: "Justice Department Wel-
comes Decision in New York v. Deutsche Telecom, the T-Mobile/Sprint
Merger," United States Department of Justice, *Justice News*, Feb. 11, 2020,
https://www.justice.gov/opa/pr/justice-department-welcomes-decision-new
-york-v-deutsche-telecom-t-mobilesprint-merger.

22 *The judge bizarrely credited "the demeanor"*: Steve Goldstein, "The Judge Who
Cleared the T-Mobile-Sprint Merger Says He Relied on Witness Demeanor
and Not Numbers to Make His Decision," *MarketWatch*, Feb. 11, 2020, https://
www.marketwatch.com/story/the-judge-who-cleared-the-t-mobile-sprint
-merger-says-he-relied-on-witness-demeanor-and-not-numbers-to-make
-his-decision-2020-02-11.

23 *A recent lawsuit alleges*: Ben Popken, "You're Getting Skinned on Chicken
Prices, Suit Says," NBC News, Feb. 17, 2017, https://www.nbcnews.com/busi
ness/consumer/you-re-getting-skinned-chicken-prices-suit-says-n721821.

23 *Your monthly overhead creeps higher and higher*: See study by Manhattan Institute
about rising cost of living: Oren Cass, "The Cost-of-Thriving Index: Reevalu-
ating the Prosperity of the American Family," Manhattan Institute, Feb. 20,
2020, https://www.manhattan-institute.org/reevaluating-prosperity-of-ameri
can-family.

23 *Eleven rental car brands are really a mere three companies*: "Car Rental Industry,"
Open Markets, https://concentrationcrisis.openmarketsinstitute.org/industry
/car-rental/.

23 *If Au Bon Pain*: Leah Douglas, "Private Equity Firms Are Buying Up Your
Favorite Food Brands," *Fern's AG Insider*, June 18, 2018, https://thefern.org
/ag_insider/private-equity-firms-are-buying-up-your-favorite-food-brands/.

23 *Burger King and Popeyes have the same owner!*: Sarah Whitten, "Restaurant
Brands in Deal to Acquire Popeyes Louisiana Kitchen for $1.8 Billion,"

CNBC, Feb. 21, 2017, https://www.cnbc.com/2017/02/21/restaurant-brands -in-deal-to-acquire-popeyes-louisiana-kitchen.html.

24   *which owns 107 brands of*: Molson Coors Beverage Company, http://www.mol soncoors.com/en/brands.

24   *with over 500 brands and 42 percent of the beer industry as of 2017*: "Beer Industry Revenue 2017," Open Markets, https://concentrationcrisis.openmarketsinsti tute.org/industry/beer/, and https://www.ab-inbev.com/our-brands.html.

24   *In the recent case* Apple v. Pepper: *Apple, Inc. v. Pepper et al.*, Certiorari to the United States Court of Appeals for the Ninth Circuit, 587 U.S. __ (2019), https://www.supremecourt.gov/opinions/18pdf/17-204_bq7d.pdf.

25   *the Android app store doesn't meaningfully constrain*: European Commission, "Antitrust: Commission Fines Google €4.34 Billion for Illegal Practices Regarding Android Mobile Devices to Strengthen Dominance of Google's Search Engine," July 18, 2018, https://ec.europa.eu/commission/presscorner/detail/en /IP_18_4581.

25   *Federal Communications Commission ruled in 1968*: *Carterfone* (13 F.C.C. 2d 420), 1968.

25   *Only by tracking us*: J. Clement, "Facebook: Annual Revenue 2009–2019," *Statista*, Feb. 3, 2020, https://www.statista.com/statistics/268604/annual -revenue-of-facebook/, and Davey Alba, "Google and Facebook Still Reign over Digital Advertising," *Wired*, July 29, 2017, https://www.wired.com/story /google-facebook-online-ad-kings/.

25   *it has tremendous value*: Andrea M. Matwyshyn, "Privacy, the Hacker Way," *Southern California Law Review* 87, no. 1 (August 1, 2013), available at SSRN: https://ssrn.com/abstract=3004803.

25   *"I worry that if all of the data"*: Aarti Shahani, "Microsoft President: Democracy Is at Stake. Regulate Big Tech," NPR, Sept. 13, 2019, https://www.npr org/2019/09/13/760478177/microsoft-president-democracy-is-at-stake-regu late-big-tech 11/9/19.

26   *economists say the platforms should be paying you*: "Stigler Committee on Digital Platforms: Final Report," Stigler Center for the Study of the Economy and the State, https://research.chicagobooth.edu/stigler/media/news/committee -on-digital-platforms-final-report. "([T]he information is more valuable than the cost of the services. The economics literature has modeled this setting and is able to define a data markup. . . . While the low price can be a blessing for consumers, it has drawbacks for competition and market structure in a world where institutions have not arisen to manage negative prices . . . platforms are able to mark up the competitive price all the way to zero.")

26   *The concept is called "digital labor"*: "What Is Digital Labor?" *I'MTech: IMT*

Science and Technology News, July 25, 2017, https://blogrecherche.wp.imt.fr /en/2017/07/25/what-is-digital-labor/.

26   *"Companies have turned"*: "Joe Toscano," Tedx Lincoln, https://www.tedxlin coln.com/speakers/2019/joe-toscano.html.

27   *Ninety-one corporations paid zero federal income tax in 2018*: "Corporate Tax Avoidance in the First Year of the Trump Tax Law," Institute on Taxation & Economic Policy, December 2019, https://itep.org/wp-content/up loads/121619-ITEP-Corporate-Tax-Avoidance-in-the-First-Year-of-the -Trump-Tax-Law.pdf.

27   *Facebook is currently fighting*: Paul Kiel, "Who's Afraid of the IRS? Not Facebook," ProPublica, https://www.propublica.org/article/whos-afraid-of-the -irs-not-facebook, and Colleen Murphy, "Facebook, IRS Summer Tax Trial Canceled Due to Pandemic," *Bloomberg Tax*, March 27, 2020, https://news bloombergtax.com/daily-tax-report/facebook-irs-summer-tax-trial-canceled -due-to-pandemic.

27   *donating $25 million for therapeutics research*: Theodore Schleifer, "Mark Zuckerberg Is Teaming Up with Bill Gates to Try to Find a Drug to Treat Coronavirus," *Vox*, March 27, 2020, https://www.vox.com/recode/2020/3/27/21196421 /coronavirus-mark-zuckerberg-priscilla-chan-drug-treatment-bill-gates-zuck erberg-initiative.

27   *2010 U.S. Supreme Court case Citizens United*: Tim Lau, "Citizens United Explained," Brennan Center for Justice, Dec. 12, 2019, https://www.brennancen ter.org/our-work/research-reports/citizens-united-explained.

28   *third-party sellers on Amazon's marketplace failed*: "Amazon: Data Analysis Reveals an Estimated $1.9B in Unpaid State Sales Tax from FBA Sales in 2016 Alone; States Targeting Amazon and Sellers in Mounting Legislative and Enforcement Efforts," *Capitol Forum* 5, no. 96 (March 21, 2017), http://create send.com/t/j-2649D429940A23FE.

29   *Under political and legal pressure in 2018, Amazon*: Tae Kim, "Here's the Controversial Tax Practice by Amazon That's Got Trump So Upset," CNBC, March 29, 2018, https://www.cnbc.com/2018/03/29/heres-the-controversial -tax-practice-by-amazon-thats-got-trump-so-upset.html.

29   *Amazon didn't pay taxes in Virginia until 2013*: Graham Moomaw, "Virginia Got Amazon. But Small Bookstores Aren't Cheering," *Richmond Times-Dispatch*, Nov. 30, 2018, https://www.richmond.com/news/virginia/virginia -got-amazon-but-small-bookstores-aren-t-cheering/article_bba9e4cf -778f-5102-9073-dec7e1fe3e13.html.

29   *told the* Richmond Times-Dispatch: Ibid.

30   *an opportunity for Amazon to gather data about cities and their citizens*: Nick Tabor,

"Amazon Is an Infrastructure Company. The HQ2 Bids Were Reconnaissance," *Intelligencer*, Dec. 3, 2018, https://nymag.com/intelligencer/2018/12/amazons -hq2-bids-gave-it-a-blueprint-for-expansion.html.

30   *$3 billion of incentives*: Jimmy Vielkind, "New York Dangled Extra Incentives in Initial Bid to Lure Amazon HQ2," *Wall Street Journal*, Jan. 5, 2020, https:// www.wsj.com/articles/new-york-dangled-extra-incentives-in-initial-bid-to -lure-amazon-hq2-11578153600.

30   *taxpayers were not pleased with the notion of funding a helipad*: Peter Page, "New York Is Giving Amazon a Helipad and New Yorkers Are Furious," *Entrepreneur*, Nov. 14, 2018, https://www.entrepreneur.com/article/323281.

30   *coming to New York City regardless*: Keiko Morris, "Amazon Leases New Manhattan Office Space, Less Than a Year after HQ2 Pullout," *Wall Street Journal*, Dec. 6, 2019, https://www.wsj.com/articles/amazon-leases-new-manhattan -office-space-less-than-a-year-after-hq2-pullout-11575671243?mod=article _inline.

30   *Amazon has reportedly received close to $3 billion*: "Tracking Amazon's Rapidly Expanding Footprint," *Business Journals*, Oct. 19, 2017, https://www.bizjour nals.com/bizjournals/maps/the-amazon-effect, and Good Jobs First, "Amazon Tracker," https://www.goodjobsfirst.org/amazon-tracker, updated June 2020.

30   *company is nearly four times more likely to receive an economic incentive package*: Daniel Aobdia, Allison Koester, and Reining Petacchi, "Who Benefits When State Governments Award Incentives to Politically-Connected Companies?" Chicago Booth Stigler Center, Jan. 7, 2020, https://promarket.org/who-benefits -when-state-governments-award-incentives-to-politically-connected-companies/.

31   *tacking on a monthly fee to Virginians' utility bills*: Mya Frazier, "Amazon Isn't Paying Its Electric Bills. You Might Be," *Bloomberg Businessweek*, Aug. 20, 2018, https://www.bloomberg.com/news/articles/2018-08-20/amazon-isn-t -paying-its-electric-bills-you-might-be.

31   *data centers industry-wide*: Quentin Hardy, "Cloud Computing Brings Sprawling Centers, but Few Jobs, to Small Towns," *New York Times*, Aug. 26, 2016, https://www.nytimes.com/2016/08/27/technology/cloud-computing-brings -sprawling-centers-but-few-jobs-to-small-towns.html.

31   *In 2017, Walmart had sixty-two lobbyists*: "Wal-Mart Says It's 'Neutral' on a Minimum Wage Hike. Lobbying Disclosures Suggest Otherwise," *Washington Post*, Feb. 21, 2014, https://www.washingtonpost.com/news/wonk/wp/2014/02/21 /wal-mart-says-its-neutral-on-a-minimum-wage-hike-lobbying-disclosures -suggest-otherwise/.

31   *the single largest group of food stamp recipients*: Peter Van Buren, "Walmart Wages Are the Main Reason People Depend on Food Stamps," *Nation*,

Feb. 16, 2016, https://www.thenation.com/article/walmart-wages-are-the-main-reason-people-depend-on-food-stamps/.

31 *an estimated 18 percent of all food stamps are redeemed at Walmart*: H. Claire Brown, "Amazon Gets Tax Breaks While Its Employees Rely on Food Stamps, New Data Shows," *Intercept*, April 19, 2018, https://theintercept.com/2018/04/19/amazon-snap-subsidies-warehousing-wages/.

31 *participating in a pilot program*: "Attention, Walmart Executives: Amazon's Coming after Your Low-Income Shoppers," *Washington Post*, June 18, 2019, https://www.washingtonpost.com/technology/2019/06/18/amazons-growing-prime-focus-americas-poor/.

31 *one-third of its employees in Arizona*: Chavie Lieber, "Amazon and Walmart Are Testing a Program to Accept Food Stamps Online," *Vox*, April 19, 2019, https://www.vox.com/the-goods/2019/4/19/18507813/amazon-walmart-snap-usda-pilot-food-stamps, and H. Claire Brown, "Amazon Gets Tax Breaks While Its Employees Rely on Food Stamps, New Data Shows," *Intercept*, April 19, 2018, https://theintercept.com/2018/04/19/amazon-snap-subsidies-warehousing-wages/.

31 *skimped on $2.6 billion tax dollars using a purportedly fake Chinese joint venture*: Max de Haldevang, "Walmart Dodged Up to $2.6 Billion in US Tax through a 'Fictitious' Chinese Entity, Former Executive Says," *Quartz*, Sept. 5, 2019, https://qz.com/1701404/walmart-allegedly-created-fictitious-chinese-jv-to-avoid-us-tax/.

31 *sheltered $76 billion in tax havens*: Jesse Drucker and Renee Dudley, "Wal-Mart Has $76 Billion in Undisclosed Overseas Tax Havens," Bloomberg, June 16, 2015, https://www.bloomberg.com/news/articles/2015-06-17/wal-mart-has-76-billion-in-overseas-tax-havens-report-says.

31 *the Centers for Disease Control's public*: Katelyn Newman, "Chronic Underfunding Crippled America's COVID-19 Response," *U.S. News & World Report*, April 16, 2020, https://www.usnews.com/news/healthiest-communities/articles/2020-04-16/crippled-coronavirus-response-tied-to-chronic-underfunding-report-says.

32 *record levels of companies buying back their own stocks*: Ben Popken, "What Did Corporate America Do with That Tax Break? Buy Record Amounts of Its Own Stock," NBC News, June 26, 2018, https://www.nbcnews.com/business/economy/what-did-corporate-america-do-tax-break-buy-record-amounts-n886621.

32 *Major airlines spent 96 percent*: David Slotnick, "Airlines Will Get the $60 Billion Bailout They Asked for in the $2 Trillion Coronavirus Stimulus Bill That Trump Signed into Law. It Also Prohibits Layoffs, Stock Buybacks, and Dividends," *Business Insider*, March 27, 2020, https://www

.businessinsider.com/airlines-coronavirus-bailout-senate-stock-buybacks 2020-3?op=1, and "U.S. Airlines Spent 96% of Free Cash Flow on Buybacks: Chart," *Bloomberg*, March 16, 2020, https://www.bloomberg.com/news /articles/2020-03-16/u-s-airlines-spent-96-of-free-cash-flow-on-buybacks -chart, and Phillip van Doorn, "Airlines and Boeing Want a Bailout—but Look How Much They've Spent on Stock Buybacks," *MarketWatch*, March 22, 2020, https://www.marketwatch.com/story/airlines-and-boeing-want-a-bailout -but-look-how-much-theyve-spent-on-stock-buybacks-2020-03-18,andhttps:// www.nytimes.com/interactive/2020/03/27/opinion/coronavirus-bailout.html.

Two: Monopolies Gouge You When You're Sick

34   *two companies make the swabs used for coronavirus testing*: Dina Shanker, "Swabs, Stat! Inside the Maine Factory Racing to Supply America with Virus Test Swabs," *Bloomberg*, March 25, 2020, https://www.bloomberg.com /features/2020-coronavirus-puritan-medical-test-swab/

35   *Corporate concentration in health care put*: Barry Lynn, *End of the Line*, (New York: Doubleday, 2005). In a 2005 *Financial Times* op-ed, Open Markets Institute president Barry Lynn wrote that the production of medical masks was particularly at risk of collapse, building on the argument in his book *End of the Line* about how corporate concentration put critical supply chains at risk of catastrophic collapse in the event of a pandemic or other systemic shock.

35   *created a legal safe harbor for these kickbacks*: "AAPS News April 2018: Safe Kickbacks," AAPS, April 1, 2018, https://aapsonline.org/aaps-news-april-2018-safe -kickbacks/; Brian Klepper, "Connecting the Dots: How Anticompetitive Contracting Practices, Kickbacks, and Self-dealing by Hospital Group Purchasing Organizations (GPOs) Caused the U.S. Drug Shortage," *Care and Cost*, Feb. 14, 2012, https://careandcost.com/2012/02/14/connecting-the-dots-how-anticom petitive-contracting-practices-kickbacks-and-self-dealing-by-hospital-group -purchasing-organizations-gpos-caused-the-u-s-drug-shortage/.

35   *GPOs designate the biggest corporations*: Diana L. Moss, "Healthcare Intermediaries: Competition and Healthcare Policy at Loggerheads?" AAI, May 7, 2012, https://www.antitrustinstitute.org/wp-content/uploads/2012/05/AAI -White-Paper-Healthcare-Intermediaries.pdf; Mary William Walsh, "Healthcare Intermediaries: Competition and Healthcare Policy at Loggerheads?" *New York Times*, Aug. 13, 2009, https://www.nytimes.com/2009/08/14/health /policy/14purchasing.html; "What the Experts Say About GPOs," *Puncture*, http://www.puncturemovie.com/what-the-experts-say-about-gpos/.

35   *GPOs don't even get hospitals lower prices than they would get if they did their own negotiating*: "Purchasing Organizations (GPOs) Often Fail to Deliver Best Prices for Hospitals," *Business Wire*, Oct. 6, 2010, https://www.businesswire

.com/news/home/20101006005130/en/Empirical-Study-Competitive
-Bidding-Data-Shows-Group.

36   *spend huge sums to lobby Washington*: Mariah Blake, "Dirty Medicine," *Washington Monthly*, July/Aug. 2010, https://washingtonmonthly.com/magazine /julyaugust-2010/dirty-medicine-2/.

36   *"Government officials"*: Nicholas Kulish, Sarah Kliff, and Jessica Silver-Greenberg, "The U.S. Tried to Build a New Fleet of Ventilators. The Mission Failed," *New York Times*, updated April 20, 2020, https://www.nytimes .com/2020/03/29/business/coronavirus-us-ventilator-shortage.html; Diana L. Moss, "Can Competition Save Lives? The Intersection of COVID-19, Ventilators, and Antitrust Enforcement," AAI, March 31, 2020, https://www .antitrustinstitute.org/can-competition-save-lives-the-intersection-of-covid -19-ventilators-and-antitrust-enforcement/.

36   *The FTC cleared the merger quickly*: "Medtronic, Inc. and Covidien plc, In the Matter of," FTC, Jan. 21, 2015, https://www.ftc.gov/enforcement/cases-pro ceedings/141-0187/medtronic-inc-covidien-plc-matter.

36   *Philips hadn't yet supplied*: Nicholas Kulish, Sarah Kliff and Jessica Silver-Greenberg, "The U.S. Tried to Build a New Fleet of Ventilators. The Mission Failed," *New York Times*, updated April 20, 2020, https://www.nytimes .com/2020/03/29/business/coronavirus-us-ventilator-shortage.html, and Patricia Callahan, Sebastian Rotella and Tim Golden, "Taxpayers Paid Millions to Design a Low-Cost Ventilator for a Pandemic. Instead, the Company Is Selling Versions of It Overseas," *ProPublica*, March 30, 2020, https://www.pro publica.org/article/taxpayers-paid-millions-to-design-a-low-cost-ventilator -for-a-pandemic-instead-the-company-is-selling-versions-of-it-overseas-.

37   *Newport was only one of 17 companies that Covidien bought*: Diana L. Moss, "Can Competition Save Lives? The Intersection of COVID-19, Ventilators, and Antitrust Enforcement," AAI, March 31, 2020, https://www.antitrustinsti tute.org/can-competition-save-lives-the-intersection-of-covid-19-ventilators -and-antitrust-enforcement/.

37   *the FTC let the Covidien deal go through*: "Medtronic, Inc. and Covidien plc, In the Matter of," FTC, Jan. 21, 2015, https://www.ftc.gov/enforcement/cases -proceedings/141-0187/medtronic-inc-covidien-plc-matter.

37   *Buying Covidien made Medtronic's stock value instantly jump*: Joe Carlson, "5 Years Later, a Lawsuit Challenging a $49.9B Medtronic Acquisition Churns On," *Star Tribune*, Feb. 15, 2020, https://www.startribune.com/5-years-later -a-lawsuit-challenging-a-49-9b-medtronic-acquisition-churns-on/56788 5432/.

38   *you're still paying a price for them through your insurance premiums*: Orphan drug monopolies: For example, one patient's annual bill for the drug Strensiq, which

treats a debilitating genetic disorder, totaled close to $2 million last year. The impact on the patient's health plan, available through her husband's labor union, is sobering. As described in one account, 35 cents of every hour of pay for each of the union's 16,000 workers went to pay for that single patient's prescriptions for this one drug. See Katie Thomas and Reed Abelson, "The $6 Million Drug Claim," *New York Times*, Aug. 25, 2019, https://www.nytimes.com/2019/08/25 /health/drug-prices-rare-diseases.html.

38 *in 2018, the average cost of health care*: Christopher S. Girod, Susan K. Hart, David M. Liner, Thomas D. Snook, and Scott A. Weltz, "2019 Milliman Medical Index," Milliman, July 25, 2019, https://www.milliman.com/en/insight /-/media/Milliman/importedfiles/ektron/2019-milliman-medical-index.ashx.

38 *median household income in 2018 of $63,179*: https://www.census.gov/content /dam/Census/library/publications/2019/demo/p60-266.pdf.

39 *insurance premiums rose by a whopping 242 percent*: Martin Gayor, "Examining the Impact of Health Care Consolidation, Statement before the Committee on Energy and Commerce Oversight and Investigation Subcommittee, U.S. House of Representatives," docs.house.gov, Feb. 14, 2018, https://docs.house.gov /meetings/IF/IF02/20180214/106855/HHRG-115-IF02-Wstate-GaynorM -20180214.pdf.

39 *deductibles have increased eight times as fast as wages*: "Average Annual Real Wages in the United States from 2000 to 2018 (in 2018 U.S. dollars)," Statista, https://www.statista.com/statistics/612519/average-annual-real-wages-united -states/; Phillip Longman, "How to End the Democrats' Health Care Demolition Derby," *Washington Monthly*, January/February/March 2020, https:// washingtonmonthly.com/magazine/january-february-march-2020/how-to -end-the-democrats-health-care-demolition-derby/; "Premiums for Employer-Sponsored Family Health Coverage Rise 5% to Average $19,616; Single Premiums Rise 3% to $6,896," KFF, https://www.kff.org/health-costs/press-release /employer-sponsored-family-coverage-premiums-rise-5-percent-in-2018/.

39 *a full one-third of total health care spending*: Caitlin Owens, "Health Care's Big Spending Mismatch," *Axios*, May 6, 2019, https://www.axios.com/health -cares-spending-out-of-pocket-most-expensive-83ace437-b84e-4379-b348 -dd2edf6a50fc.html; Martin Gayor, "Examining the Impact of Health Care Consolidation, Statement before the Committee on Energy and Commerce Oversight and Investigation Subcommittee, U.S. House of Representatives," docs.house.gov, Feb. 14, 2018, https://docs.house.gov/meetings/IF /IF02/20180214/106855/HHRG-115-IF02-Wstate-GaynorM-201802 14.pdf.

39 *hospital inpatient prices grew 42 percent*: "Paper 2: Hospital Prices Grew Substantially Faster than Physician Prices for Hospital-Based Care in 2007–14,"

Health Care Pricing Project, Feb. 2019, https://healthcarepricingproject.org
/paper/paper-2-hospital-prices-grew-substantially-faster-physician-prices
-hospital-based-care-2007,Äi14.

39 *more than 100 per year*: Stefano Feltri, "Hospital Mergers: The Forgotten Problem of American Health Care," ProMarket, Sept. 23, 2019, https://promarket
.org/hospital-mergers-the-forgotten-problem-of-american-health-care/.

39 *to approximately 900,000 in 2017*: Andrea Flynn and Ron Knox, "We're Short on Hospital Beds Because Washington Let Too Many Hospitals Merge," *Washington Post*, April 8, 2020, https://www.washingtonpost.com/outlook/2020/04/08/were-short-hospital-beds-because-washington-let-too-many-hospitals-merge.

39 *Cerberus had financially weakened the hospital*: Eileen Applebaum, "How Private Equity Makes You Sicker," *Prospect*, Oct. 7, 2019, https://prospect.org
/health/how-private-equity-makes-you-sicker/; Rosemary Batt and Eileen Appelbaum, "Profiteers Plunder Hospitals, Then Line Up for Federal Subsidies," *Waco Tribune*, April 7, 2020, https://www.wacotrib.com/opinion/columns/rosemary-batt-eileen-appelbaum-profiteers-plunder-hospitals-then-line-up-for-federal-subsidies/article_d848ffcc-f5fe-5d9b-8b0b-db26eb40c011.html.

40 *They dictate high prices*: See, for example, Catherine Ho, "Major Antitrust Case Against Sutter Over Health Prices Nears Trial," *San Francisco Chronicle*, Aug. 24, 2019, https://www.sfchronicle.com/business/article/Landmark-antitrust-case-against-Sutter-over-14374893.php?psid=l0yeZ.

40 *will cost you 12 percent more*: "Paper 1: The Price Ain't Right? Hospital Prices and Health Spending on the Privately Insured," Health Care Pricing Project, May 2015, https://healthcarepricingproject.org/papers/paper-1.

40 *Inpatient prices were 70 percent higher in Northern California*: Catherine Ho, "Health Care Costs 30% More in Northern California Than in the Rest of the State," *San Francisco Chronicle*, March 26, 2018, www.sfchronicle.com/business/article/Healthcare-costs-30-more-in-Northern-than-in-12782446.php.

40 *Not patients*: Melanie Evans, "Hospitals Merged. Quality Didn't Improve," *Wall Street Journal*, Jan. 1, 2020, https://www.wsj.com/articles/hospitals-merged-quality-didnt-improve-11577916000?mod=hp_lista_pos3.

40 *a more than 3 percent increase in the mortality rate*: Stefano Feltri, "Hospital Mergers: The Forgotten Problem of American Health Care," ProMarket, Sept. 23, 2019, https://promarket.org/hospital-mergers-the-forgotten-problem-of-american-health-care/.

40 *their wages rose only 8 percent*: "Average Annual Real Wages in the United States from 2000 to 2018 (in 2018 U.S. dollars)," *Statista*, https://www.statista.com/statistics/612519/average-annual-real-wages-united-states/.

40 *the price of hospital-based outpatient care*: "Paper 2: Hospital Prices Grew Substantially Faster than Physician Prices for Hospital-Based Care in 2007–14,"

Health Care Pricing Project, Feb. 2019, https://healthcarepricingproject.org
/paper/paper-2-hospital-prices-grew-substantially-faster-physician-prices
-hospital-based-care-2007-14.

40   *CEOs' pay has risen by 93 percent*: Jerry Y. Du, MD, Alexander S. Rascoe, MD,
MBA, and Randall E. Marcus, "The Growing Executive-Physician Wage Gap
in Major US Nonprofit Hospitals and Burden of Nonclinical Workers on the US
Healthcare System," *Clinical Orthopaedics and Related Research*, October 2018,
https://journals.lww.com/clinorthop/Fulltext/2018/10000/The_Growing
_Executive_Physician_Wage_Gap_in_Major.4.aspx.

41   *more than 8,000 between 2016 and 2018*: Andrea Flynn and Ron Knox,
"We're Short on Hospital Beds Because Washington Let Too Many Hospitals Merge," *Washington Post*, Apr. 8, 2020, https://www.washingtonpost.com
/outlook/2020/04/08/were-short-hospital-beds-because-washington-let-too
-many-hospitals-merge.

41   *quality of care doesn't*: Lawrence C. Baker, M. Kate Bundorf, and Daniel P. Kes-
sler, "Vertical Integration: Hospital Ownership of Physician Practices Is Associated with Higher Prices and Spending," *HealthAffairs*, May 2014, https://
www.healthaffairs.org/doi/full/10.1377/hlthaff.2013.1279; Martin Gayor, "Examining the Impact of Health Care Consolidation, Statement before the Committee on Energy and Commerce Oversight and Investigation Subcommittee,
U.S. House of Representatives," docs.house.gov, Feb. 14, 2018, https://docs
.house.gov/meetings/IF/IF02/20180214/106855/HHRG-115-IF02-Wstate
-GaynorM-20180214.pdf.

41   *charge an average of 14 percent more*: Cory Capps, David Dranove, and Christopher Ody, "The Effect of Hospital Acquisitions of Physician Practices on Prices
and Spending," MIT, Jan 12, 2017, http://economics.mit.edu/files/12747.

42   *control a 92 percent market share*: "Dialysis Center," Open Markets Institute,
2018, https://concentrationcrisis.openmarketsinstitute.org/industry/dialysis
-centers/.

42   *misclassified as out of network*: Jenny Gold, "They May Owe Nothing—Half-
Million-Dollar Dialysis Bill Canceled," *Kaiser Health News*, July 26, 2019,
https://khn.org/news/bill-of-the-month-half-million-dollar-kidney-dialysis
-bill-fresenius-now-zero/.

42   *hurt patient health*: James Ives, "Acquisitions by Large, For-profit Dialysis Chains Hurt Patient Health," *News-Medical*, Oct. 24, 2019, https://www
.news-medical.net/news/20191024/Acquisitions-by-large-for-profit-dialysis
-chains-hurt-patient-health.aspx.

42   *19 and 24 percent higher risk of death*: Yi Zhang, Dennis J. Cotter, and Mae
Thamer, "The Effect of Dialysis Chains on Mortality Among Patients

Receiving Hemodialysis," *Wiley Online Library*, Dec. 9, 2010, https://online
library.wiley.com/doi/full/10.1111/j.1475-6773.2010.01219.x.

42   *from medical device makers to syringe manufacturers*: Angie Stewart, "5 Major
      Developments in the US Medical Device Industry," beckersasc, June 15, 2018,
      http://www.beckersasc.com/supply-chain/5-major-developments-in-the-u-s
      -medical-device-industry.html; "America's Concentration Crisis," Open Mar-
      kets Institute, https://concentrationcrisis.openmarketsinstitute.org.

42   *Health insurance companies, too, have merged*: "Health Insurance and Monop-
      oly," Open Markets Institute, http://www.openmarketsinstitute.org/explainer
      /health-insurance-and-monopoly/.

43   *increased its price by more than 4,000 percent*: "Case 1:20-cv-00706-DLC Docu-
      ment 86 Filed 04/14/20," FTC, April 14, 2020, https://www.ftc.gov/system
      /files/documents/cases/161_0001_vyera_amended_complaint.pdf.

43   *on Shkreli working in pharma*: Ibid.; "Attorney General James Sues 'Pharma Bro'
      Martin Shkreli and Vyera Pharmaceuticals for Illegally Monopolizing Life-
      Saving Drug," ag.ny.gov, Jan. 27, 2020, https://ag.ny.gov/press-release/2020
      /attorney-general-james-sues-pharma-bro-martin-shkreli-and-vyera-pharma
      ceuticals.

43   *convicted of securities fraud*: Adam Smith and Julia Horowitz, "Martin Shkreli
      Convicted of Securities Fraud, Conspiracy," *Money*, Aug. 4, 2017, https://
      money.cnn.com/2017/08/04/news/martin-shkreli-verdict/index.html.

43   *making threats against Hillary Clinton*: "Case 1:20-cv-00706-DLC Document
      86 Filed 04/14/20," FTC, April 14, 2020, https://www.ftc.gov/system/files
      /documents/cases/161_0001_vyera_amended_complaint.pdf.

43   *allegedly runs Phoenixus from prison*: Rod Copeland and Bradley Hope, "Mar-
      tin Shkreli Steers His Old Company from Prison—with Contraband Cell-
      phone," *Wall Street Journal*, March 7, 2019, https://www.wsj.com/articles
      /martin-shkreli-steers-his-company-from-prisonwith-contraband-cellphone
      -11551973574.

43   *"plans to emerge from jail richer than he entered"*: Ibid.

44   *"From 1995–2015, 60 pharma companies"*: Rohit Chopra, "Dissenting Statement
      of Commissioner Rohit Chopra," Twitter, Nov. 18, 2019, https://twitter.com
      /chopraftc/status/1196514076400214018?s=20.

44   *both dissented*: "Dissenting Statement of Commissioner Rebecca Kelly Slaugh-
      ter," FTC, Nov. 15, 2019, https://www.ftc.gov/system/files/documents/pub
      lic_statements/1554283/17_-_final_rks_bms-celgene_statement.pdf.

44   *fewer drug companies are left to compete*: Justus Haucap and Joel Stiebale, *How
      Mergers Affect Innovation: Theory and Evidence from the Pharmaceutical Indus-
      try* (Düsseldorf Inst. for Competition Economics, Discussion Paper No. 218,

2016), http://www.dice hhu.de/fileadmin/redaktion/Fakultaeten/Wirtschafts wissenschaftliche Fakultaet/DICE/Discussion Paper/218 Hauca p Stiebale .pdf.; Justus Haucap and Joel Stiebale, "Research: Innovation Suffers When Drug Companies Merge," *Harvard Business Review* (Aug. 3, 2016).

45 *"protected nearly $2 billion . . . and often life-saving medications"*: "FTC Charges Bristol-Myers Squibb with Pattern of Abusing Government Processes to Stifle Generic Drug Competition," FTC, March 7, 2003, https://www.ftc.gov /news-events/press-releases/2003/03/ftc-charges-bristol-myers-squibb-pattern -abusing-government.

46 *"The prosecutions of BMS"*: "Former Bristol-Myers Squibb Senior Executive Pleads Guilty for Role in Dishonest Dealings with the Federal Government," Justice.gov, April 6, 2009, https://www.justice.gov/sites/default/files/atr/legacy /2009/04/09/244479.pdf.

46 *a book called* The First Question: Ed Silverman, "Writing with Conviction: BMS Fraudster Pens His Penalty," Contract Pharma, May 30, 2012, https:// www.contractpharma.com/issues/2012-06/view_pharma-beat/writing-with -conviction/.

46 *"The financial crisis"*: "Dissenting Statement of Commissioner Rebecca Kelly Slaughter," FTC, Nov. 15, 2019, https://www.ftc.gov/system/files/documents /public_statements/1554283/17_-_final_rks_bms-celgene_statement.pdf.

47 *by 85,000 percent*: "Case 1:17-cv-00120 Document 10-1 Filed 01/25/17," FTC, Jan. 25, 2017, https://www.ftc.gov/system/files/documents/cases/170118 mallinckrodt_complaint_public.pdf

48 *acquiring the rights to EpiPen when it was priced at $100*: Carolyn Y. Johnson and Catherine Ho, "How Mylan, the Maker of EpiPen, Became a Virtual Monopoly," *Washington Post*, Aug. 25, 2016, https://www.washingtonpost.com /business/economy/2016/08/25/7f83728a-6aee-11e6-ba32-5a4bf5aad4fa _story.html.

48 *refused to cover Epi-Pen's competitor, Auvi-Q*: Robert B. Barnett Jr., "EpiPen Antitrust Suit Against Mylan for Sherman Act Violations Mostly Survives Dismissal," Wolters Kluwer, Dec. 28, 2017, https://lrus.wolterskluwer.com/news /antitrust-law-daily/epipen-antitrust-suit-against-mylan-for-sherman-act -violations-mostly-survives-dismissal/43716; "Case 2:17-md-02785-DDC -TJJ Document 98 Filed 12/21/17," business.cch, Dec. 21, 2017, http://business .cch.com/ald/inreepipen12282017.pdf.

48 *adding lobbyists in thirty-six states between 2010 and 2014*: Yue Qiu, Ben Wieder, and Chris Zubak-Skees, "Here Are the Interests Lobbying in Every State-house," Center for Public Integrity, Feb. 11, 2016, https://publicintegrity.org /federal-politics/state-politics/here-are-the-interests-lobbying-in-every-state house/.

48   *Multiple senators and antitrust enforcers*: Ed Silverman, "Lawmakers call for
      FTC probe into potential antitrust violations in EpiPen school program," *Stat-
      News*, November 8, 2016, https://www.statnews.com/pharmalot/2016/11/08
      /ftc-mylan-epipen-antitrust/, and "Blumenthal and Klobuchar Call for Imme-
      diate Federal Investigation into Possible Antitrust Violations by EpiPen Man-
      ufacturer," Press Release, September 6, 2016, https://www.blumenthal.senate
      .gov/newsroom/press/release/blumenthal-and-klobuchar-call-for-immediate
      -federal-investigation-into-possible-antitrust-violations-by-epipen-manufac
      trurer, and "A.G. Schneiderman Launches Antitrust Investigation into Mylan
      Pharmaceuticals Inc., Maker of Epipen," September 6, 2016: https://ag.ny.gov
      /press-release/2016/ag-schneiderman-launches-antitrust-investigation
      -mylan-pharmaceuticals-inc-maker.

49   *more than one hundred and twenty-five entries*: "Current and Resolved Drug
      Shortages and Discontinuations Reported to FDA, US Food & Drug Admin-
      istration," FDA, https://www.accessdata.fda.gov/scripts/drugshortages/default
      .cfm.

49   *costs $16,000 or more in the United States*: Paul S. Hewitt and Phillip Longman,
      "The Case for Single Price Health Care," *Washington Monthly*, April/May/June
      2018, https://washingtonmonthly.com/magazine/april-may-june-2018/the
      -case-for-single-price-health-care/

49   *more than $18,000*: Ibid.

50   *a hospital stay in the U.S. costs more than double that*: Dana Sarnak, "Multinational
      Comparisons of Health Systems Data, 2016," The Commonwealth Fund,
      https://www.commonwealthfund.org/sites/default/files/documents/___media
      _files_publications_chartbook_2016_att_fsarnak2016_oecd_data_chartpack
      _final_pdf.pdf.

50   *hospital stays in America are shorter*: "Length of Hospital Stay," OECD, https://
      data.oecd.org/healthcare/length-of-hospital-stay.htm.

50   *Our life expectancy is lower*: "Life Expectancy at Birth," OECD, https://data
      .oecd.org/healthstat/life-expectancy-at-birth.htm#indicator-chart.

50   *"It's not that we're getting more"*: Gerard F. Anderson, "U.S. Health Care Spend-
      ing Highest Among Developed Countries," Johns Hopkins, Jan. 7, 2019,
      https://www.jhsph.edu/news/news-releases/2019/us-health-care-spending
      -highest-among-developed-countries.html.

50   *50 percent more for the same drugs*: IHS Markit, "US Price Gouging in the Phar-
      maceutical Industry," International Drug Price Database, https://ihsmarkit
      .com/solutions/us-price-gouging-pharmaceutical-industry.html.

51   *$102 million on lobbying in the 2018 election cycle alone*: "Hospitals & Nursing
      Homes: Long-Term Contribution Trends," OpenSecrets, https://www.open
      secrets.org/industries/totals.php?cycle=2020&ind=H02, Visited May 14, 2020.

51   *laws could prohibit the conduct in the first place*: For example, the California state legislature passed a law in October 2019 that makes pay-for-delay arrangements between branded drugmakers and generic drugmakers automatically illegal. See "AB-824 Business: Preserving Access to Affordable Drugs," California Legislative Information, https://leginfo.legislature.ca.gov/faces/billNav Client.xhtml?bill_id=201920200AB824

51   *$167 million last year on lobbying, and 573*: "Industry Profile: Pharmaceutical Manufacturing," Open Secrets, https://www.opensecrets.org/federal-lobbying /industries/summary?cycle=2019&id=h4300, Visited May 14, 2020.

51   *for Medicare Part D drug prices*: Ibid.

51   *"Medicare Prices for All"*: Phillip Longman, "How to End the Democrats' Health Care Demolition Derby," *Washington Monthly,* January/February/March 2020, https://washingtonmonthly.com/magazine/january-february-march-2020 /how-to-end-the-democrats-health-care-demolition-derby/.

52   *drags down our economy*: "Does Employer-Based Health Insurance Discourage Entrepreneurship and New Business Creation?" Rand Corporation, https://www .rand.org/pubs/research_briefs/RB9579/index1.html; Noah Smith, "National Health Insurance Might Be Good for Capitalism," Bloomberg, Sept. 23, 2019, https://www.bloomberg.com/opinion/articles/2019-09-23/employer-based -health-insurance-holds-back-u-s-economy.

52   *the study concludes*: Ibid.

53   *know what your medical procedure would cost*: Austin Frakt, "Medical Mystery: Something Happened to U.S. Health Spending After 1980," *New York Times,* May 14, 2018, https://www.nytimes.com/2018/05/14/upshot/medical-mystery -health-spending-1980.html.

53   *27.5 million Americans not being covered at all*: "Health Insurance Coverage Eight Years After the ACA," Commonwealth Fund, https://www.commonwealth fund.org/sites/default/files/2019-02/Collins_hlt_ins_coverage_8_years_after _ACA_2018_biennial_survey_tables.pdf#page=1.

Mini Lesson: People V. Giant Tech Monopolies

55   *"Pitting browser against browser"*: U.S. District Court Findings of Fact, "U.S. v. Microsoft," paragraph 166, justice.gov, Nov. 5, 1999, https://www.justice.gov /atr/us-v-microsoft-courts-findings-fact#iva.

56   *"never gets a chance on these systems"*: Ibid.

56   *the ability to control prices or exclude competition*: United States v. E. I. du Pont de Nemours & Co. (*Cellophane*), 351 U.S. 377, 391 (1956).

57   *lesser market shares can be enough, too*: Image Technical Services, 125 F.3d at 1207 ("50% [market share] . . . would suffice to support a jury finding of market

power for the purposes of ISO's attempted monopolization claim)"; *Weyerhauser*, 411 F.3d at 1044-45 (65 percent monopsony power was enough).

57   *market defined as "Intel-compatible PC operating systems"*: "Microsoft Conclusions of Law: *U.S. v. Microsoft Corporation; State of New York, et al. v. Microsoft Corporation; Microsoft Corporation v. Eliot Spitzer*," justice.gov., https://www.justice.gov/atr/microsoft-conclusions-law-us-v-microsoft-corporation-state-new-york-et-al-v-microsoft.

59   *long past time to bring back Sherman Act Section 2*: "The State of Antitrust Enforcement and Competition Policy in the U.S., Antitrust Institute, April 14, 2020, https://www.antitrustinstitute.org/wp-content/uploads/2020/04/AAI_StateofAntitrust2019_ FINAL.pdf (stating "[S]ince the [*U.S. v. Microsoft*] case some 20 years ago and the handful of other cases litigated at that same time, the DOJ has actually brought only one comparatively insignificant Section 2 case").

60   *bought over 150 companies just since 2013*: Rani Molla, "Amazon's Ring Buy Gives It the Same Number of Acquisitions This Year as Facebook and Google," *ReCode*, March 4, 2018, https://www.vox.com/2018/3/4/17062538/amazon-ring-acquisitions-2018-apple-google-cbinsights.

60   *nearly 250 companies since 2006*: "Infographic: Google's Biggest Acquisitions," CB Insights, Nov. 1, 2019, https://www.cbinsights.com/research/google-biggest-acquisitions-infographic/.

60   *over 100 companies*: "Infographic: Apple's Biggest Acquisitions," CB Insights, May 29, 2019, https://www.cbinsights.com/research/apple-biggest-acquisitions-infographic/.

60   *Amazon nearly 90*: "Amazon Acquisitions," *Crunchbase*, retrieved February 1, 2020, https://www.crunchbase.com/organization/amazon/acquisitions/acquisitions_list#section-acquisitions.

60   *Facebook bought it*: "Facebook Buys Instagram for $1 Billion; Turns Budding Rival Into Its Standalone Photo App," techcrunch, April 2012, https://techcrunch.com/2012/04/09/facebook-to-acquire-instagram-for-1-billion/.

60   *buy them or build its own versions*: Elizabeth Dwoskin, "Facebook's Willingness to Copy Rivals' Apps Seen as Hurting Innovation," *Washington Post*, August 10, 2017, https://www.washingtonpost.com/business/economy/facebooks-willingness-to-copy-rivals-apps-seen-as-hurting-innovation/2017/08/10/ea7188ea-7df6-11e7-a669-b400c5c7e1cc_story.html; Betsy Morris and Deepa Seetharaman, "The New Copycats: How Facebook Squashes Competition from Startups," *Wall Street Journal*, Aug. 9, 2017, https://www.wsj.com/articles/the-new-copycats-how-facebook-squashes-competition-from-startups-1502293444.

61   *"Facebook used Onavo"*: Damian Collins MP, Chair of the UK Parliament Digital, Culture, Media and Sport Committee, "Summary of Key Issues from

Six4Three Files," December 2018, British Parliament, www.parliament.uk /documents/commons-committees/culture-media-and-sport/Note-by-Chair -and-selected-documents-ordered-from-Six4Three.pdf.

61   *identified WhatsApp as the top contender*: Charlie Warzel and Ryan Mac, "These Confidential Charts Show Why Facebook Bought WhatsApp," *BuzzFeed News*, Dec. 5, 2018, https://www.buzzfeednews.com/article/charliewarzel /why-facebook-bought-whatsapp; Parmy Olson, "Exclusive: WhatsApp Co-founder Brian Acton Gives the Inside Story on #DeleteFacebook and Why He Left $850 Million Behind," *Forbes*, Sept. 26, 2018, https://www.forbes .com/sites/parmyolson/2018/09/26/exclusive-whatsapp-cofounder-brian-ac ton-gives-the-inside-story-on-deletefacebook-and-why-he-left-850-million -behind/#2165dc6d3f20.

61   *surveilled them and analyzed their usage*: Lily Hay Newman, "Don't Trust the VPN Facebook Wants You to Use," *Wired*, Feb. 14, 2017, http://www.wired .com/story/facebook-onavo-protect-vpn-privacy/; Josh Constine, "Facebook Will Shut Down Its Spyware VPN App Onavo," Feb. 21, 2019, techcrunch, https://techcrunch.com/2019/02/21/facebook-removes-onavo/.

62   *Certainly not all retail*: Renee Dudley, "The Amazon Lockdown: How an Unforgiving Algorithm Drives Suppliers to Favor the E-Commerce Giant Over Other Retailers," ProPublica, April 26, 2020, https://www.propublica.org/ar ticle/the-amazon-lockdown-how-an-unforgiving-algorithm-drives-suppliers -to-favor-the-e-commerce-giant-over-other-retailers.

62   *urging it to investigate Amazon*: Richard Blumenthal, "Letter to Joseph Simons," Blumenthal.senate.gov, Dec. 19, 2018, https://www.blumenthal.senate.gov /imo/media/doc/12.19.18%20-%20FTC%20-%20Price%20Parity.pdf.

62   *drop the contractual terms in the United States*: Makena Kelly, "Amazon Silently Ends Controversial Pricing Agreements with Sellers," *Verge*, March 11, 2019, https://www.theverge.com/2019/3/11/18260700/amazon-anti-competitive -pricing-agreements-3rd-party-sellers-end.

62   *"Absent Amazon's"*: Western District of Washington at Seattle, *Frame-Wilson v. Amazon*, Case 2:20-cv-00424-RAJ, para. 63, March 19, 2020.

Three: Monopolies Lower Your Pay and Crush the American Dream

65   *from around 20 percent in the 1980s to around 40 percent in 2017*: Tommaso Valletti, "Concentration Trends," European Commission, June 18-20, 2018, https://www.ecb.europa.eu/pub/conferences/shared/pdf/20180618_ecb _forum_on_central_banking/Valletti_Tommaso_Presentation.pdf.

65   *stagnating for forty years*: Nathan Wilmers, "Wage Stagnation and Buyer Power: How Buyer-Supplier Relations Affect U.S. Workers' Wages, 1978–2014,"

Sage Journals, March 27, 2018, journals.sagepub.com/doi/full/10.1177 /0003122418762441; Drew Desilver, "For Most U.S. Workers, Real Wages Have Barely Budged in Decades," Pew Research Center, Aug. 7, 2018, https:// www.pewresearch.org/fact-tank/2018/08/07/for-most-us-workers-real -wages-have-barely-budged-for-decades/.

65 *productivity . . . rose 72 percent, a rate of 1.33 percent*: Josh Bivens and Lawrence Mishel, "Understanding the Historic Divergence Between Productivity and a Typical Worker's Pay," Economic Policy Institute, Sept. 2, 2015, https://www .epi.org/publication/understanding-the-historic-divergence-between-produc tivity-and-a-typical-workers-pay-why-it-matters-and-why-its-real/.

66 *58 times employees' pay*: Lawrence Mishel and Julia Wolfe, "CEO Compensa-tion Has Grown 940% Since 1978," Economic Policy Institute, Aug. 14, 2019, https://www.epi.org/publication/ceo-compensation-2018.

66 *What changed since the 1980s*: David Autor, David Dorn, Lawrence F. Katz, Christina Patterson, and John Van Reenen, "The Fall of the Labor Share and the Rise of Superstar Firms," Harvard University, May 1, 2017, https://scholar .harvard.edu/files/lkatz/files/labshare-superstars-may1-2017.pdf.

67 *each industry included dozens of potential employers*: See, for example, "Defense Contracting Chart," Myth of Capitalism, https://www.mythofcapitalism.com /merger-chart (100 to 6 potential employers in defense contracting from 1980 until now).

67 *17 percent decline in wages*: J. Azar, I. Marinescu, and M. I. Steinbaum, "Labor Market Concentration," NBER Working Paper No. 24147, NBER, 2017, https://www.nber.org/papers/w24147.pdf.

67 *"impairs the transmission"*: E. Benmelech, N. Bergman, and H. Kim, "Strong Employers and Weak Employees: How Does Employer Concentration Affect Wages?" NBER Working Paper No. 24307, NBER, 2018. https://www.nber .org/papers/w24307.

68 *nurses have seen their wages depressed*: Elena Prager and Matt Schmitt, "When an Industry Consolidates, What Happens to Wages?" *Kellogg Insight*, April 4, 2019, insight.kellogg.northwestern.edu/article/merger-consolidation-wages -effect.

68 *"a true competitive wage"*: Suresh Naidu, Eric Posner, and Glen Weyl, "More and More Companies Have Monopoly Power Over Workers' Wages. That's Killing the Economy," *Vox*, April 6, 2018, https://www.vox.com/the-big -idea/2018/4/6/17204808/wages-employers-workers-monopsony-growth -stagnation-inequality.

68 *"labor markets where mobility has decreased"*: Michael Konczal and Marshall Steinbaum, "Declining Entrepreneurship, Labor Mobility, and Business Dyna-mism: A Demand-Side Approach," Roosevelt Institute, July 21, 2016, https://

rooseveltinstitute.org/declining-entrepreneurship-labor-mobility-and-busi
ness-dynamism/.

69 *"appear to be increasing in magnitude over time"*: Kevin Rinz, "Did Timing Matter? Life Cycle Differences in Effects of Exposure to the Great Recession,"
Center for Economic Studies, US Census Bureau, Sept. 8, 2019, https://kevin
rinz.github.io/recession.pdf.

69 *cut costs by reducing employees' pay*: Nelson Lichtenstein, "The Return of Merchant Capitalism," *International Labor and Working-Class History* 81 (2012):
8–27.

69 *"Concentration can also affect"*: Sandeep Vaheesan, "Antitrust Law: A Current Foe,
but Potential Friend, of Workers," Harvard University, https://lwp.law.harvard
.edu/files/lwp/files/webpage_materials_papers_vaheesan_june_13_2018.pdf;
Nathan Wilmers, "Wage Stagnation and Buyer Power: How Buyer-Supplier
Relations Affect U.S. Workers' Wages, 1978 to 2014," *Sage Journals*, March 27,
2018, https://journals.sagepub.com/doi/full/10.1177/0003122418762441.

70 *10,000 workers being laid off*: Leah Douglas, "Private Equity Firms Are Buying
up Your Favorite Food Brands," *Fern*, June 18, 2018, https://thefern.org/ag_in
sider/private-equity-firms-are-buying-up-your-favorite-food-brands/.

70 *estimated to result in 6,000 job losses*: "Boy Meets Girl: Gillette and P&G Hook
Up Their Brands," Wharton School, March 20, 2005, https://knowledge.whar
ton.upenn.edu/article/boy-meets-girl-gillette-and-pg-hook-up-their-brands/.

70 *several rounds of ongoing layoffs*: Nellie Andreeva, "ViacomCBS Layoffs Un-
derway As Re-Merged Company Continues to Cut Costs," *Deadline*, Feb. 27,
2020, https://deadline.com/2020/02/viacomcbs-layoffs-underway-re-merged
-company-continues-to-cut-costs-1202870391/; Lisette Voytko, "Coronavirus
Layoffs: Lyft, Boeing Latest to Cut Workers Amid Pandemic," *Forbes*, April
29, 2020, https://www.forbes.com/sites/lisettevoytko/2020/04/29/coronavirus
-layoffs-boeing-cuts-10-of-workforce-amid-pandemic/#6d09d2c33487.

70 *made people lose their jobs*: Leslie Josephs, "American Airlines Plans Manager
Layoffs, Buyouts to Slim Down 5 Years after US Airways Merger," CNBC,
June 29, 2018, https://www.cnbc.com/2018/06/19/american-airlines-plans-for
-layoffs-buyouts-due-to-us-airways-merger.html.

70 *leads to loss of institutional knowledge*: "The Human Side of Mergers: Those Laid
Off and Those Left Aboard," Wharton School, March 30, 2005, https://knowl
edge.wharton.upenn.edu/article/the-human-side-of-mergers-those-laid-off
-and-those-left-aboard/.

70 *ranges from 70 to 90 percent*: Clayton M. Christensen, Richard Alton, Curtis
Rising, and Andrew Waldeck, "The Big Idea: The New M&A Playbook," *Harvard Business Review*, March 2011, https://hbr.org/2011/03/the-big-idea-the
-new-ma-playbook; see also Bruce Blonigen and Justin R. Pierce, "Evidence for

the Effects of Mergers on Market Power and Efficiency," NBER, Oct. 2016, https://www.nber.org/papers/w22750.

71 *should scrutinize whether the merger would reduce competition for employees*: J. Azar, I. Marinescu and M. I. Steinbaum, "Labor market concentration. NBER Working Paper No. 24147," *NBER*, 2017, https://www.nber.org/papers/w24147.pdf.

71 *because the deals would decrease the prices paid to suppliers of goods*: "Justice Department and State Attorneys General Sue to Block Anthem's Acquisition of Cigna, Aetna's Acquisition of Humana," justice.gov, July 21, 2016, https://www.justice.gov/opa/pr/justice-department-and-state-attorneys-general-sue-block-anthem-s-acquisition-cigna-aetna-s; "Department of Justice Statement on the Abandonment of the JBS/National Beef Transaction," justice.gov, Feb. 20, 2009, https://www.justice.gov/opa/pr/department-justice-statement-abandonment-jbsnational-beef-transaction.

71 *"commands the price of labor"*: Senator Sherman (Congressional Record 2457, 1890).

72 *labor union membership . . . the lowest it's been since 1964*: Doug Henwood, "Unions Still Haven't Rebounded," *Jacobin*, Jan. 25, 2019, https://www.jacobinmag.com/2019/01/union-density-united-states-2018-bls.

72 *"only a small percentage of workers"*: Sandeep Vaheesan, "How Contemporary Antitrust Robs Workers of Power," *Law and Political Economy*, July 18, 2018, https://lpeblog.org/2018/07/19/how-contemporary-antitrust-robs-workers-of-power/.

72 *actively fight unionization*: Verne Kopytoff, "How Amazon Crushed the Union Movement," *Time*, Jan. 16, 2014, https://time.com/956/how-amazon-crushed-the-union-movement/.

72 *"While Amazon has"*: Michael Sainato, "Exploited Amazon Workers Need a Union. When Will They Get One?" *Guardian*, July 8, 2018, https://www.theguardian.com/commentisfree/2018/jul/08/amazon-jeff-bezos-unionize-working-conditions.

72 *an investigation from the New York attorney general*: Alina Selyukh, "Amazon Warehouse Safety 'Inadequate,' N.Y. Attorney General's Office Says," NPR, April 28, 2020, https://www.npr.org/2020/04/27/846438983/amazon-warehouse-safety-inadequate-n-y-attorney-general-s-office-says.

73 *"the face of the entire union/organizing movement"*: Paul Blest, "Leaked Amazon Memo Details Plan to Smear Fired Warehouse Organizer: 'He's Not Smart or Articulate,'" *Vice*, April 2, 2020, https://www.vice.com/en_us/article/5dm8bx/leaked-amazon-memo-details-plan-to-smear-fired-warehouse-organizer-hes-not-smart-or-articulate.

73 *Amazon workers continued to protest unsafe conditions*: https://jewishcurrents.org/amazon-workers-say-warehouse-health-precautions-are-insufficient/;

Karen Weise and Kate Conger, "Gaps in Amazon's Response as Virus Spreads to More Than 50 Warehouses," *New York Times,* updated April 6, 2020, https:// www.nytimes.com/2020/04/05/technology/coronavirus-amazon-workers .html; "athenaforall," Twitter, April 29, 2020, https://twitter.com/athenaforall /status/1255571329912320000?s=20.

73 *Jeff Bezos grew an estimated $6.4 billion richer*: Sergei Klebnikov, "Jeff Bezos Gets $6.4 Billion Richer as Amazon Stock Hits a New Record High," *Forbes,* April 14, 2020, https://www.forbes.com/sites/sergeiklebnikov/2020/04/14 /jeff-bezos-gets-63-billion-richer-as-amazon-stock-hits-a-new-record-high /#4fc4bb6e53b0.

73 *accusing Google of illegally firing them*: "Another Fired Google Engineer Alleges Retaliation for Union Activity," *Washington Post,* Dec. 17, 2019, https://www .washingtonpost.com/technology/2019/12/17/google-fires-fifth-engineer -who-alleges-retaliation-union-activity/.

73 *Google had urged the NLRB*: Josh Eidelson, Hassan Kanu, and Mark Bergen, "Google Urged the U.S. to Limit Protection for Activist Workers," Bloomberg, Jan. 24, 2019, ttps://www.bloomberg.com/news/articles/2019-01-24/google -urged-the-u-s-to-limit-protection-for-activist-workers.

73 *At least 35 million employees*: Alexander J.S. Colvin and Heidi Shierholz, "Non-compete Agreements," Economic Policy Institute, December 10, 2019, https:// www.epi.org/publication/noncompete-agreements/, and FTC, "Re: Petition for Rulemaking to Prohibit Worker Non-Compete Clauses," Open Markets Institute, https://openmarketsinstitute.org/wp-content/uploads/2019/03/Peti tion-for-Rulemaking-to-Prohibit-Worker-Non-Compete-Clauses.pdf.

74 *like fast-food workers*: "Why Aren't Paychecks Growing? A Burger-Joint Clause Offers a Clue," *New York Times,* Sept. 27, 2017, https://www.nytimes .com/2017/09/27/business/pay-growth-fast-food-hiring.html.

74 *"dries up opportunities for employees"*: FTC, Letter to the Honorable Makan Del-rahim "RE: Department of Justice Initiative on Competition in Labor Markets," FTC, Sept. 18, 2019, https://www.ftc.gov/system/files/documents/public_state ments/1544564/chopra_-_letter_to_doj_on_labor_market_competition.pdf.

74 *has petitioned the FTC*: FTC, "Re: Petition for Rulemaking to Prohibit Worker Non-Compete Clauses," Open Markets Institute, https://openmarketsinsti tute.org/wp-content/uploads/2019/03/Petition-for-Rulemaking-to-Prohibit -Worker-Non-Compete-Clauses.pdf.

74 *"Please extend my apologies as appropriate to Steve Jobs"*: Dan Levine, "High-Tech Employee Antitrust Litigation: Apple's Steve Jobs to Google's Eric Schmidt to Stop Poaching Workers," *Huffington Post,* Jan. 27, 2012, https://www.huffpost .com/entry/high-tech-employee-antitrust-litigation_n_1237692.

75 *for conspiring to depress their wages*: FTC, "How the Federal Trade Commission Can Help—Instead of Hurt—Workers," FTC, https://www.ftc.gov/system /files/documents/public_comments/2018/08/ftc-2018-0054-d-0014-154953 .pdf; "No. 17-1113 in The United States Court of Appeals for the Tenth Circuit," Open Market Institute, https://openmarketsinstitute.org/wp-content /uploads/2019/09/OMI-Brief-in-Llacua-v.-WRA-FINAL.pdf.

75 *"interfered with"*: "Justice Department Requires Six High Tech Companies to Stop Entering into Anticompetitive Employee Solicitation Agreements," justice.gov, Sept. 24, 2010, https://www.justice.gov/opa/pr/justice-department -requires-six-high-tech-companies-stop-entering-anticompetitive-employee.

75 *this most serious*: Sandeep Vaheesan and Matt Buck, "Antitrust's Monopsony Problem," *ProMarket*, February 3, 2020, https://promarket.org/2020/02/03 /antitrusts-monopsony-problem/.

75 *"Let me clarify"*: Dan Levine, "Steve Jobs Told Google to Stop Poaching Workers," *Reuters*, January 27, 2012, https://www.reuters.com/article/us-apple-law suit-idUSTRE80Q27420120127, and *In Re: High-Tech Employee Antitrust Litigation*, No. 11 CV 2509 (N.D. Cal.).

76 *private class actions settled for $435 million*: "In re High Tech Employees Antitrust Litigation," Berger Montague, https://bergermontague.com/cases/re-high -tech-employee-antitrust-litigation/.

76 *"artists would need their music to be streamed 2.4 million times"*: Ron Knox, "The Copyright Killer," *Global Competition Review*, Jan. 11, 2019, https://globalcom petitionreview.com/insight/gcr-q1-2019/1179029/the-copyright-killer.

77 *have appealed the decision*: Dani Deahl, "Here's Why Apple Is Saying Spotify Is Suing Songwriters," *Verge*, March 15, 2019, https://www.theverge .com/2019/3/15/18267288/apple-music-spotify-suing-songwriters-eu-anti trust.

78 *Google has fought copyright laws worldwide*: Richard Smirke, "Music Chiefs Slam Google Lobbying Spend Ahead of EU Copyright Vote," *Billboard*, July 3, 2018, https://www.billboard.com/articles/business/8463917/google -lobbying-dollars-eu-copyright-vote-uk-music; Tom Hamburger and Matea Gold, "Google, Once Disdainful of Lobbying, Is Now a Master of Washington," *Washington Post*, April 12, 2014, https://www.washingtonpost.com /politics/how-google-is-transforming-power-and-politicsgoogle-once-dis dainful-of-lobbying-now-a-master-of-washington-influence/2014/04/12/516 48b92-b4d3-11e3-8cb6-284052554d74_story.html; Julia Horowitz, "Google Will Remove News Previews Rather Than Pay Publishers in Europe," CNN, Sept. 25, 2019, https://www.cnn.com/2019/09/25/tech/google-france-copy right-news/index.html.

78 *songs often just go right up again*: "New Survey Documents Independent Labels' Experience with Notice & Takedown," *Future of Music*, Jan. 8, 2019, https://futureofmusic.org/filing/new-survey-documents-independent-labels-experience-notice-takedown (68 percent of the respondents reported that an infringing copy of their music reappeared on the same service even after that music had previously been taken down—the so-called "whack-a-mole" problem); Todd C. Frankel, "Why Musicians Are So Angry at the World's Most Popular Music Streaming Service," *Washington Post*, July 14, 2017, https://www.washingtonpost.com/business/economy/why-musicians-are-so-angry-at-the-worlds-most-popular-music-streaming-service/2017/07/14/bf1a6db0-67ee-11e7-8eb5-cbccc2e7bfbf_story.html.

78 *96.5 percent of all YouTubers*: Chris Stokel-Walker, "'Success' on YouTube Still Means a Life of Poverty," Bloomberg, Feb. 26, 2018, https://www.bloomberg.com/news/articles/2018-02-27/-success-on-youtube-still-means-a-life-of-poverty.

78 *$15.1 billion in 2019I*: "Worldwide Advertising Revenues of YouTube from 2017 to 2019," *Statista*, https://www.statista.com/statistics/289658/youtube-global-net-advertising-revenues/.

79 *"fresh thinking and revitalized anti-trust enforcement"*: "Policy Priorities for 2018," Future of Music Coalition, Jan. 8, 2019, https://www.futureofmusic.org/blog/2019/01/08/policy-priorities-2019.

80 *"You know"*: Panel, "Innovation and Entrepreneurship in an Age of Concentrated Power," Open Markets Institute, Dec. 6, 2017, https://www.youtube.com/watch?list=PLl7VSnPfVKIjDjjK9yw6bQK4964lbJ_Go&time_continue=8&v=bmYBv4Zbn2Y&feature=emb_logo, and author's interview of Lillian Salerno.

81 *Becton settled the case for $100 million in 2004*: Mary Williams Walsh and Salt Bogdanich, "Business Syringe Manufacturer Settles Claim of Market Manipulation," *New York Times*, July 3, 2004, https://www.nytimes.com/2004/07/03/business/syringe-manufacturer-settles-claim-of-market-manipulation.html.

81 *an untruthful claim that Becton's syringes*: "District Court Issues Final Judgment—Retractable Technologies, Inc., et. al. v. Becton, Dickinson and Co.," Retractable Technologies, https://retractable.com/profiles/investor/ResLibraryView.asp?ResLibraryID=74829&GoTopage=6&Category=35&BzID=577&G=984.

81 *to preserve the "10–30% price premium" that Becton enjoyed*: "Retractable Technologies, Inc. v. Becton Dickinson and Company," *Pacer Monitor*, https://www.pacermonitor.com/public/case/5539052/Retractable_Technologies,_Inc_v_Becton_Dickinson_and_Company.

82 *"We've been denied every time"*: Panel, "Innovation and Entrepreneurship in an Age of Concentrated Power," Open Markets Institute, Dec. 6, 2017.

83 *charging customers monthly rental fees for cable boxes*: Herb Weisbaum, "Consumers

Have Scant Choices When It Comes to Set-Top Pay TV Boxes," NBC News, June 11, 2015, https://www.nbcnews.com/business/consumer/consumers -have-scant-choices-when-it-comes-set-top-pay-n407261.

83 *entrepreneurship has plummeted*: Economic Innovation Group, "Dynamism in Retreat: Consequences for Regions, Markets, and Workers," EIG, February 2017, https://eig.org/wp-content/uploads/2017/07/Dynamism-in-Retreat -A.pdf.

83 *all four have dominated their respective arenas*: Mark A. Lemley and Andrew McCreary, "Exit Strategy," Stanford Law and Economics Working Paper #542, SSRN, Dec. 19, 2019, https://ssrn.com/abstract=3506919.

83 *entrepreneurship is suffering across the economy*: Ben Casselman, "A Start-Up Slump Is a Drag on the Economy. Big Business May Be to Blame," *New York Times*, Sept. 20, 2017, https://www.nytimes.com/2017/09/20/business /economy/startup-business.html; Jason Furman and Peter Orszag, "Slower Productivity and Higher Inequality: Are They Related?" Working Paper, Peterson Institute for International Economics, 2018, https://piie.com/system/files /documents/wp18-4.pdf.

83 *hurts both job creation and innovation*: Ryan Decker, John Haltiwanger, Ron Jarmin, and Javier Miranda, "The Role of Entrepreneurship in US Job Creation and Economic Dynamism," *Journal of Economic Perspectives* 28, no. 3 (2014): 3–24, https://www.aeaweb.org/articles?id=10.1257/jep.28.3.3.

83 *"[T]he great burst of business activity"*: Barry C. Lynn and Phillip Longman, "Who Broke America's Jobs Machine?" *Washington Monthly*, March/April 2010, https://washingtonmonthly.com/magazine/marchapril-2010/who-broke -americas-jobs-machine-3/.

84 *"are as important to the preservation of economic freedom"*: "United States v. Topco Associates, Inc., 405 U.S. 596, 610," Justia, 1972, https://supreme.justia.com /cases/federal/us/405/596/.

86 *92 percent of internet search*: "Search Engine Market Share Worldwide Feb. 2019–Feb. 2020," Statcounter, retrieved March 1, 2020, https://gs.statcounter .com/search-engine-market-share.

86 *more than 85 percent of the world's smartphones*: "Smartphone Market Share," IDC, retrieved March 1, 2020, https://www.idc.com/promo/smartphone -market-share/os.

86 *was nearly $135 billion*: "Advertising Revenue of Google from 2001 to 2019," *Statista*, retrieved March 7, 2020, https://www.statista.com/statistics/266249 /advertising-revenue-of-google/.

86 *fined Google $5 billion*: "Statement by Commissioner Vestager on Commission Decision to Fine Google €4.34 Billion for Illegal Practices Regarding Android Mobile Devices to Strengthen Dominance of Google's Search Engine,"

European Commission, July 18, 2018, https://ec.europa.eu/commission/press corner/detail/en/STATEMENT_18_4584.

87 *didn't have a shot at getting pre-installed*: "Google EC Antitrust Enforcement: Expected Android EC Remedies Likely to Make Google Vulnerable to Competitive Threats in Mobile Advertising," *Capitol Forum*, Sept. 30, 2016, http://createsend.com/t/j-189AEA75109E1FA5.

87 *Google paid Apple more than $12 billion in 2019*: Kif Leswing, "Apple Quietly Makes Billions from Google Search Each Year, and It's a Bigger Business than Apple Music," *Business Insider*, February 13, 2019, https://www.businessinsider.com/aapl-share-price-google-pays-apple-9-billion-annually-tac-goldman-2018-9.

87 *requested a "yes or no" answer*: Letter to Kent Walker, Chief Legal Officer of Google, from Representative David N. Cicilline, Chairman of the Subcommittee on Antitrust, Commercial and Administrative Law, Committee on the Judiciary, cicilline.house.gov, July 23, 2019, https://cicilline.house.gov/sites/cicilline.house.gov/files/7.23.2019_ACAL%20Company%20Clarification%20Requests.pdf.

87 *"long sent large amounts of traffic to other sites"*: Letter to Chairman Cicilline from Kent Walker, Google Chief Legal Officer, cicilline.house.gov, July 26, 2019, https://judiciary.house.gov/sites/democrats.judiciary.house.gov/files/documents/07.26.19%20-%20google%20response.pdf.

88 *met this exact fate*: Tom Fairless, "The British Couple Who Began Google's Antitrust Battle," *Wall Street Journal*, April 15, 2015, https://www.wsj.com/articles/foundem-the-unlikely-instigator-of-googles-antitrust-battle-with-the-eu-1429094448.

88 *fined Google $2.7 billion for abuse of dominance*: "Antitrust: Commission Fines Google €2.42 Billion for Abusing Dominance as Search Engine by Giving Illegal Advantage to Own Comparison Shopping Service," European Commission, June 27, 2017, https://ec.europa.eu/commission/presscorner/detail/en/IP_17_1784.

88 *the Raffs say Google is still not complying*: "Google's CSS Auction: Different Name, Same Illegal Conduct," Search Neutrality, Nov. 2, 2019, http://www.searchneutrality.org/google/google-css-auction-different-name-same-illegal-conduct; "Google's Blatantly Non-Compliant 'Remedy' Part III," Foundem, April 18, 2018, http://www.foundem.co.uk/fmedia/Foundem_Apr_2018_Final_Debunking_of_Google_Auction_Remedy/.

88 *"The Commission is concerned"*: "Antitrust: Commission Sends Statement of Objections to Google on Comparison Shopping Service," European Commission, April 15, 2015, https://ec.europa.eu/commission/presscorner/detail/en/MEMO_15_4781.

88 *degraded its search quality results*: See Luca, Wu, Couvidat, Frank, and Seltzer, "Does Google Content Degrade Google Search? Experimental Evidence," Harvard Business School Working Paper, No. 16-035, September 2015 (revised August 2016); Jack Nicas, "Google Has Picked an Answer for You—Too Bad It's Often Wrong," *Wall Street Journal*, Nov. 16, 2017, https://www.wsj.com /articles/googles-featured-answers-aim-to-distill-truthbut-often-get-it -wrong-1510847867.

88 *pays upwards of $72,000 a year*: "Written Testimony of David Heinemeier Hansson CTO & Cofounder, Basecamp," house.gov, Jan. 17, 2020, https:// docs.house.gov/meetings/JU/JU05/20200117/110386/HHRG-116-JU05 -Wstate-HanssonD-20200117.pdf.

89 *but it did not take action*: "Statement of the Federal Trade Commission Regarding Google's Search Practices in the Matter of Google Inc. FTC File Number 111-0163," FTC, Jan. 3, 2013, https://www.ftc.gov/system/files/documents /public_statements/295971/130103googlesearchstmtofcomm.pdf.

89 *"conduct has resulted"*: Brody Mullins et al., "Inside the U.S. Antitrust Probe of Google," *Wall Street Journal*, March 19, 2015, https://www.wsj.com/articles /inside-the-u-s-antitrust-probe-of-google-1426793274.

89 *"Google representatives"*: David Dayen, "The Android Administration, *Intercept*, April 22, 2016, https://theintercept.com/2016/04/22/googles-remarkably -close-relationship-with-the-obama-white-house-in-two-charts/.

90 *fifty-one states and territories*: Tony Romm, "50 U.S. States and Territories Announce Broad Antitrust Investigation of Google," *Washington Post*, Sept. 9, 2019, https://www.washingtonpost.com/technology/2019/09/09/states-usterri tories-announce-broad-antitrust-investigation-google/.

90 *"It's not a supply-and-demand"*: Lucas Shaw and Mark Bergen, "YouTube's Trampled Foes Plot Antitrust Revenge," *Bloomberg*, July 15, 2019, https://www .bloomberg.com/news/articles/2019-07-15/youtube-s-trampled-foes-plot -antitrust-revenge.

90 *fined Google*: "Antitrust: Commission fines Google €1,49 billion for abusive practices in online advertising," European Commission, March 20, 2019, https://ec.europa.eu/commission/presscorner/detail/en/IP_19_1770

90 *acquired every spoke*: "Infographic: Google's Biggest Acquisitions," CB Insights, May 2019, https://www.cbinsights.com/research/google-biggest-acquisitions -infographic/

91 *"By closing its investigation"*: Dissenting Statement of Commissioner Pamela Jones Harbour, *In the matter of Google/DoubleClick, F.T.C. File No. 071-0170*, Dec. 20, 2007, https://www.ftc.gov/sites/default/files/documents/public_state ments/statement-matter-google/doubleclick/071220harbour_0.pdf

91 *one out of every two dollars spent online*: Jay Greene, "Attention Walmart

Executives: Amazon's Coming After Your Low-Income Shoppers," *Washington Post*, June 18, 2019, https://www.washingtonpost.com/technology/2019/06/18 /amazons-growing-prime-focus-americas-poor/.

91   *112 million Prime customers*: "Number of Amazon Prime Members in the United States as of December 2019," *Statista*, https://www.statista.com/statis tics/546894/number-of-amazon-prime-paying-members/.

91   *129 million households in 2019*: "US World and Population Clock," US Census Bureau, https://www.census.gov/popclock/.

91   *an estimated 12 percent of the U.S. population living in poverty*: "Number of Households in the U.S. from 1960 to 2019," *Statista*, https://www.statista.com /statistics/183635/number-of-households-in-the-us/.

91   *spent on average $1,400*: J. Clement, "Projected Retail E-Commerce GMV Share of Amazon in the United States from 2016 to 2021," *Statista*, Aug. 9, 2019, https://www.statista.com/statistics/788109/amazon-retail-market-share -usa/.

92   *"We believe there is"*: Antoine Gara, "Why One Amazon Bull Thinks Jeff Bezos Is Building a $3 Trillion Company," *Forbes*, May 4, 2016, https://www.forbes .com/sites/antoinegara/2016/05/04/why-one-amazon-bull-thinks-jeff-bezos -can-build-a-3-trillion-company/#4c3983315d27.

92   *more than 400 Amazon house labels*: "Share of Amazon's Private-Label Products, by Product Category, March 2019," eMarketer, March 18, 2019, https://www .emarketer.com/chart/227300/share-of-amazons-private-label-products-by -product-category-march-2019-of-total-number-of-brands.

92   *dominate, markets*: Amy Gresenhues, "Amazon Owns More Than 90% Mar- ket Share Across 5 Different Product Categories [Report]," Marketing Land, May 31, 2018, https://marketingland.com/amazon-owns-more-than-90-mar ket-share-across-5-different-product-categories-report-241135.

92   *"constantly looking to cut you out"*: "Amazon Ousted Marketplace Sellers in Order to Be Only Seller of Certain Products; A Closer Look at Monopolization En- forcement Risk," *Capitol Forum*, June 14, 2018, http://thecapitolforum.cmail19 .com/t/ViewEmail/j/96AD55196B0C02DE2540EF23F30FEDED/690A88 7987F4ABF13FEC1D8A50AFD3BD.

93   *"on multiple occasions"*: "Statement of David Barnett, CEO and Founder of PopSockets LLC, Online Platforms and Market Power, Part 5: Competi- tors in the Digital Economy," house.gov, Jan. 15, 2020, https://docs.house.gov /meetings/JU/JU05/20200117/110386/HHRG-116-JU05-Wstate-BarnettD -20200117.pdf. "It was not until December of 2017, in exchange for our com- mitment to spend nearly two million dollars on retail marketing programs (which our team expected to be ineffective and would otherwise not have pledged), that Amazon Retail agreed to work with Brand Registry to require

sellers of alleged PopGrips to provide evidence, in the form of an invoice, of authenticity. As a result, in early 2018, our problem of counterfeits largely dissolved. (Soon thereafter Brand Registry agreed to enforce our utility patent, resulting in the disappearance of most knockoffs.)"

93 *prohibiting marketplace sellers from listing*: "Amazon Ousted Marketplace Sellers in Order to Be Only Seller of Certain Products; a Closer Look at Monopolization Enforcement Risk," *Capitol Forum*, June 14, 2018, http://thecapitolforum.cmail19.com/t/ViewEmail/j/96AD55196B0C02DE2540EF23F30FEDED/690A887987F4ABF13FEC1D8A50AFD3BD; Stacy Mitchell and Olivia Lavecchia, "Report: Amazon's Monopoly," Institute for Local Self-Reliance, November 29, 2016, https://ilsr.org/amazons-monopoly/; "Standards for Brands Selling in the Amazon Store," Amazon, https://sellercentral.amazon.com/gp/help/external/G201797950; Jason Del Rey, "An Amazon Revolt Could Be Brewing as the Tech Giant Exerts More Control over Brands," *Vox*, Nov. 29 2018, https://www.vox.com/2018/11/29/18023132/amazon-brand-policy-changes-marketplace-control-one-vendor.

93 *elevating its own products to the top*: Julie Creswell, "How Amazon Steers Shoppers to Its Own Products," *New York Times*, June 23, 2018, https://www.nytimes.com/2018/06/23/business/amazon-the-brand-buster.html; "Amazon: EC Investigation to Focus on Whether Amazon Uses Data to Develop and Favor Private Label Products; Former Employees Say Data Key to Private Label Strategy," *Capitol Forum*, Nov. 5, 2018, https://thecapitolforum.com/wp-content/uploads/2018/11/Amazon-2018.11.05.pdf.

94 *"You basically have to liquidate your inventory"*: "Amazon: Amazon at Risk of Antitrust Investigation for Working with Manufacturers to Control Prices, Foreclose Competing Sellers, and Ultimately Monopolize Direct Sales of their Products on its Platform," *Capitol Forum*, March 7, 2017, http://createsend.com/t/j-60990BCFC736F15D.

94 *do not consider other online marketplaces to be viable alternatives*: Spencer Soper, "Amazon Squeezes Sellers That Offer Better Prices on Walmart," Bloomberg, updated Aug. 5, 2019, https://www.bloomberg.com/news/articles/2019-08-05/amazon-is-squeezing-sellers-that-offer-better-prices-on-walmart.

94 *marketplace sellers lack bargaining power*: Karen Weise, "Prime Power: How Amazon Squeezes the Businesses Behind Its Store," *New York Times*, Dec. 19, 2019, https://www.nytimes.com/2019/12/19/technology/amazon-sellers.html.

95 *knocking off their ideas*: Spencer Soper, "Got a Hot Seller on Amazon? Prepare for E-Tailer to Make One Too," Bloomberg, April 20, 2016, https://www.bloomberg.com/news/articles/2016-04-20/got-a-hot-seller-on-amazon-prepare-for-e-tailer-to-make-one-too; Ben Fox Rubin, "Amazon 'Probably Copied Us' on Echo Show, Start Up CEO Says," CNET, May 10, 2017, https://

www.cnet.com/news/amazon-echo-show-alexa-probably-copied-us-nucleus
-intercom-startup-ceo-says/.

95   *"It has given an edge"*: Daisuke Wakabayashi, "Prime Leverage: How Amazon Wields Power in the Technology World," *New York Times*, Dec. 15, 2019, https://www.nytimes.com/2019/12/15/technology/amazon-aws-cloud-competition.html.

96   *I spoke to former Amazon employees*: "Amazon: EC Investigation to Focus on Whether Amazon Uses Data to Develop and Favor Private Label Products; Former Employees Say Data Key to Private Label Strategy," *Capitol Forum*, Nov. 5. 2018, https://thecapitolforum.com/wp-content/uploads/2018/11/Amazon-2018.11.05.pdf

97   *handing over their proprietary business information*: See also Dana Mattioli, "Amazon Scooped Up Data from Its Own Sellers to Launch Competing Products," *Wall Street Journal*, updated April 23, 2020, https://www.wsj.com/articles/amazon-scooped-up-data-from-its-own-sellers-to-launch-competing-products-11587650015.

97   *Walmart's path of monopolization through a low pricing strategy*: Stacy Mitchell, "Wal-Mart Charged with Predatory Pricing," ILSR, Nov. 1, 2000, https://ilsr.org/walmart-charged-predatory-pricing/

97   *original robber barons*: Justice Louis Brandeis, "Competition That Kills," *Harper's Weekly*, November 15, 1913. Neither Amazon nor Walmart invented predatory pricing. Late Justice Brandeis wrote about monopolies using low-pricing to eliminate rivals, noting that the consumer unwittingly cooperates in the anti-competitve scheme. He wrote, "Thoughtless or weak, he yields to the temptation of trifling immediate gain, and, selling his birthright for a mess of pottage, becomes himself an instrument of monopoly."

97   *Amazon was able to evade antitrust laws*: Lina M. Khan, "Amazon's Antitrust Paradox," *Yale Law Journal* 126 (2017): 710, 754, https://www.yalelawjournal.org/pdf/e.710.Khan.805_zuvfyyeh.pdf.

97   *"We are going to cut off their air supply"*: "U.S. v. Microsoft complaint" (par ¶¶ 16-17), https://www.justice.gov/atr/complaint-us-v-microsoft-corp; Steve Lohr with John Marshall, "Why Microsoft Is Taking a Hard Line with the Government," *New York Times*, Jan. 12, 1998, https://www.nytimes.com/1998/01/12/business/why-microsoft-is-taking-a-hard-line-with-the-government.html.

98   *well-documented track record of pricing below cost*: Eric Savitz, "Amazon Selling Kindle Fire Below Cost, Analyst Contends," *Forbes*, Sept. 30, 2011, https://www.forbes.com/sites/ericsavitz/2011/09/30/amazon-selling-kindle-fire-be
low-cost-analyst-contends/#3521f2326534.

98   *lose $100 million in three months on diapers alone*: Will Oremus, "The Time Jeff

Bezos Went Thermonuclear on Diapers.com," *Slate*, Oct. 10, 2013, https://slate.com/technology/2013/10/amazon-book-how-jeff-bezos-went-thermo nuclear-on-diapers-com.html; Jason Del Rey, "Amazon Is Shutting Down Diapers.com—Whose Founder Is Now at War with Amazon," *Vox*, March 29, 2017, https://www.vox.com/2017/3/29/15112314/amazon-shutting-down -diapers-com-quidsi-soap-com.

99 *accused of discriminating against Spotify*: Daniel Ek, "Consumers and Innovators Win on a Level Playing Field," Newsroom, March 13, 2019, https://newsroom .spotify.com/2019-03-13/consumers-and-innovators-win-on-a-level-playing -field/.

99 *general counsel of Tile*: "Testimony of Kirsten Daru, Chief Privacy Officer and General Counsel for Tile, Inc, on Online Platforms and Market Power Part 5: Competitors in the Digital Economy, Before the House Committee on the Judiciary, Subcommittee on Antitrust, Commercial and Administrative Law," house.gov, Jan. 17, 2020, https://docs.house.gov/meetings/JU/JU 05/20200117/110386/HHRG-116-JU05-Wstate-DaruK-20200117.pdf.

99 *incorporates the features of the most popular apps*: Buster Hein, "8 Apps Apple Killed Today at WWDC," Cult of Mac, June 10, 2013, https://www.cultofmac .com/231121/seven-apps-apple-killed/.

99 *killing its rival Watson*: Mikey Campbell, "F.lux Says It Is 'Original Innovator' of Nighttime Display Colortech, Asks Apple to Open Night Shift API," *Apple Insider*, Jan. 14, 2016, https://appleinsider.com/articles/16/01/14/flux-says-it -is-original-innovator-of-nighttime-display-color-tech-asks-apple-to-open -night-shift-api.

100 *"Apple used us for market research"*: William Gallagher, "Developers Talk About Being 'Sherlocked' as Apple Uses Them 'for Market Research,'" *Apple Insider*, June 6, 2019, https://appleinsider.com/articles/19/06/06/developers-talk-about -being-sherlocked-as-apple-uses-them-for-market-research.

100 *is the dominant revenue source*: Killian Bell, "App Store Made Almost Twice as Much as Google Play in 2018," *Cult of Mac*, January 18, 2019, https://www .cultofmac.com/601492/app-store-google-play-revenue-2018/.

101 *copied Snapchat and Foursquare's popular features*: Georgia Wells and Deepa Seetharaman, "Snap Detailed Facebook's Aggressive Tactics in 'Project Voldemort' Dossier," *Wall Street Journal*, Sept. 24, 2019, https://www.wsj.com /articles/snap-detailed-facebooks-aggressive-tactics-in-project-voldemort -dossier-11569236404.

101 *210 million users*: "Number of Daily Active Snapchat Users from 1st Quarter 2014 to 1st Quarter 2020," *Statista*, https://www.statista.com/statistics/545967 /snapchat-app-dau/

101 *Project Voldemort*: Georgia Wells and Deepa Seetharaman, "Snap Detailed

Facebook's Aggressive Tactics in 'Project Voldemort' Dossier," *Wall Street Journal*, Sept. 24, 2019, https://www.wsj.com/articles/snap-detailed-facebooks-aggressive-tactics-in-project-voldemort-dossier-11569236404.

102 *businesses would have to pay for their fans to see their content*: Cotton Delo, "Facebook Admits Organic Reach Is Falling Short, Urges Marketers to Buy Ads," *AdAge*, Dec. 5, 2013, https://adage.com/article/digital/facebook-admits-organic-reach-brand-posts-dipping/245530?; Julia Campbell, "Facebook Finally Admits That You Do Have to Pay for Ads to Reach Your Fans," business2 community, Dec. 11, 2013, https://www.business2community.com/facebook/facebook-finally-admits-pay-ads-reach-fans-0711525.

103 *by about $1.25 trillion*: Thomas Philippon, Twitter, Oct. 29, 2019, https://twitter.com/thomasphi2/status/1189172544718462976?s=11; "Innovation and Entrepreneurship in an Age of Concentrated Power," Open Markets Institute, Dec. 12, 2017, https://www.youtube.com/watch?list=PLl7VSnPfVKIjDjjK9yw6bQK4964lbJ_Go&time_continue=8&v=bmYBv4Zbn2Y&feature=emb_logo.

Four: Monopolies Spy on and Manipulate You

105 *employees listen to recordings*: Matt Day, Giles Turner, and Natalia Drozdiak, "Amazon Workers Are Listening to What You Tell Alexa," Bloomberg, April 10, 2019, https://www.bloomberg.com/news/articles/2019-04-10/is-anyone-listening-to-you-on-alexa-a-global-team-reviews-audio, and Joshua Bote, "Google Workers Are Eavesdropping on Your Private Conversations via Its Smart Speakers," *USA Today*, July 11, 2019, https://www.usatoday.com/story/tech/2019/07/11/google-home-smart-speakers-employees-listen-conversations/1702205001/.

106 *gathered millions of Americans' health records*: Rob Copeland, "Google's 'Project Nightingale' Gathers Personal Health Data on Millions of Americans," *Wall Street Journal*, Nov. 11, 2019, https://www.wsj.com/articles/google-s-secret-project-nightingale-gathers-personal-health-data-on-millions-of-americans-11573496790.

106 *an all-encompassing view*: Michael Nunez, "All of the Creepy Things Facebook Knows about You," *Gizmodo*, Aug. 19, 2016, https://gizmodo.com/all-of-the-creepy-things-facebook-knows-about-you-1785510980, and "What Google and Facebook Know about You," Al Jazeera, March 29, 2018, https://www.aljazeera.com/news/2018/03/google-facebook-180329092252320.html.

107 *340 times in twenty-four hours*: Douglas C. Schmidt, "Google Data Collection," DigitalContentNext.org, Aug. 2018, https://www.ftc.gov/system/files/documents/public_comments/2018/08/ftc-2018-0074-d-0018-155525.pdf.

107 *trackers on 74 percent of pornography sites*: Elena Maris, Timothy Libert, and

Jennifer Henrichsen, "Tracking Sex: The Implications of Widespread Sexual Data Leakage and Tracking on Porn Websites," arXiv Cornell University, July 15, 2019, https://arxiv.org/abs/1907.06520.

107 *8.4 million websites with the Facebook "like" button and 16.4 million*: David Baser, "Hard Questions: What Data Does Facebook Collect when I'm Not Using Facebook, and Why?" Facebook, April 16, 2018, https://about.fb.com /news/2018/04/data-off-facebook/, and Rebecca Stimson, "Letter to Damian Collins," Facebook, June 8, 2018, https://www.parliament.uk/documents /commons-committees/culture-media-and-sport/180608-Rebecca-Stimson -Facebook-to-Chair-re-oral-ev-follow-up.pdf.

107 *"shadow profiles"*: Kurt Wagner, "This Is How Facebook Collects Data on You Even If You Don't Have an Account," *Vox*, April 20, 2018, https://www.vox .com/2018/4/20/17254312/facebook-shadow-profiles-data-collection-non -users-mark-zuckerberg, and Salvador Rodriguez and Mike Isaac, "New York Attorney General to Investigate Facebook Email Collection," *New York Times*, April 25, 2019, https://www.nytimes.com/2019/04/25/technology/facebook -new-york-attorney-general-investigation.html.

107 *through its Facebook Audience Network*: David Baser, "Hard Questions: What Data Does Facebook Collect when I'm Not Using Facebook, and Why?" Facebook, April 16, 2018, https://about.fb.com/news/2018/04/data-off-face book/, and Kurt Wagner, "This Is How Facebook Collects Data on You Even If You Don't Have an Account," *Vox*, April 20, 2018, https://www.vox .com/2018/4/20/17254312/facebook-shadow-profiles-data-collection-non -users-mark-zuckerberg, and https://www.facebook.com/business/marketing /audience-networkm.

107 *uses facial recognition technology to identify you in pictures*: David Nield, "You Probably Don't Know All the Ways Facebook Tracks You," *Gizmodo*, June 8, 2017, https://gizmodo.com/all-the-ways-facebook-tracks-you-that-you-might -not-kno-1795604150.

108 *"I'm in an arms race I'm not going to win"*: Marian Berelowitz, "Everybody Has Information about Everybody," Wunderman Thompson, Feb. 26, 2014, https:// www.jwtintelligence.com/2014/02/qa-with-julia-angwin-wall-street-journal -reporter-and-author-of-dragnet-nation/.

109 *"even when you think you're alone, the birds and mice can hear you whisper"*: Tom Huddleston Jr., "This Woman Escaped North Korea at 13—These Are Her Lessons on Perseverance," Make It, Aug. 20, 2018, https://www.cnbc .com/2018/08/20/north-korean-defector-yeonmi-parks-lessons-on-persever ance.html.

109 *shows Chinese police interrogating a man*: Gerry Shih (tweet), https://twitter .com/gerryshih/status/1199525930156216320.

109 *"Truthfully confess and your whole body will feel at ease"*: Gary Feuerberg, "China's Systemic Use of Torture Put under Congressional Scrutiny," *Epoch Times*, April 18, 2016, https://www.theepochtimes.com/chinas-systemic-use-of-torture-put -under-congressional-scrutiny_2026675.html.

110 *building an architecture of surveillance*: Zeynep Tufecki, "We're Building a Dystopia Just to Make People Click on Ads," TedTalks, https://www.ted.com/talks /zeynep_tufekci_we_re_building_a_dystopia_just_to_make_people_click_on _ads/transcript.

110 *"deeply optimistic" about what Alexa can do*: Jason Del Rey, "Land of the Giants," VoxMedia Podcast Network, https://podcasts.voxmedia.com/show/land-of -the-giants.

110 *"automated and ubiquitous monitoring"*: "Ban Facial Recognition," BanFacialRecognition.com, https://www.banfacialrecognition.com.

110 *protests about Amazon's government contracts*: Caroline O'Donovan, "Amazon Employees Demand It Stop Working with ICE. The Company Said It's Up to the Government," *BuzzFeed News*, July 12, 2019, https://www.buzzfeednews .com/article/carolineodonovan/amazon-says-the-government-should-decide -whether-it-can, and Kari Paul, "Protesters Demand Amazon Break Ties with ICE and Homeland Security," *Guardian*, July 11, 2019, https://www.theguard ian.com/us-news/2019/jul/11/amazon-ice-protest-immigrant-tech.

110 *against the most vulnerable*: Nick Statt, "Amazon Told Employees It Would Continue to Sell Facial Recognition Software to Law Enforcement," *Verge*, Nov. 8, 2018, https://www.theverge.com/2018/11/8/18077292/amazon-rekog nition-jeff-bezos-andrew-jassy-facial-recognition-ice-rights-violations, https://mijente.net/notechforice/, and Kate Conger, "Amazon Workers Demand Jeff Bezos Cancel Face Recognition Contracts with Law Enforcement," *Gizmodo*, June 21, 2018, https://gizmodo.com/amazon-workers-demand-jeff-bezos -cancel-face-recognitio-1827037509.

110 *nearly 8,500 government requests*: "United States of America: Transparency Report," *Apple.com*, January–June 2019, https://www.apple.com/legal/transpar ency/us.html.

111 *Google received 26,964 government requests*: "Global Requests for User Information," Google Transparency Report, https://transparencyreport.google.com/ user-data/overview?hl=en&user_requests_report_period=series:requests,accou nts;authority:US;time:&lu=user_requests_report_period.

111 *even labeled Martin Luther King Jr. a communist*: "In the Latest JFK Files: The FBI's Ugly Analysis on Martin Luther King Jr., Filled with Falsehoods," *Washington Post*, Nov. 4, 2017, https://www.washingtonpost.com/news/retropolis /wp/2017/11/04/in-the-latest-jfk-files-the-fbis-ugly-analysis-on-martin-lu ther-king-jr-filled-with-falsehoods/.

112 *monitored members of the Black Lives Matter movement*: George Joseph, "Exclusive: Feds Regularly Monitored Black Lives Matter since Ferguson," *Intercept*, July 24, 2015, https://theintercept.com/2015/07/24/documents-show-department-homeland-security-monitoring-black-lives-matter-since-ferguson/.

113 *a live feed into your home*: "If These Walls Could Talk: The Smart Home and the Fourth Amendment Limits of the Third Party Doctrine," *Harvard Law Review*, 130, 7 (May 9, 2017), https://harvardlawreview.org/2017/05/if-these-walls-could-talk-the-smart-home-and-the-fourth-amendment-limits-of-the-third-party-doctrine/.

113 *"It's like having thousands of eyes and ears on the street"*: Sam Biddle, "Amazon's Home Surveillance Chief Declared War on 'Dirtbag Criminals' as Company Got Closer to Police," *Intercept*, Feb. 14, 2019, https://theintercept.com/2019/02/14/amazon-ring-police-surveillance/.

113 *identified by Google data as being in the area of a crime*: Jennifer Valentino-DeVries, "Tracking Phones, Google Is a Dragnet for the Police," *New York Times*, April 13, 2019, https://www.nytimes.com/interactive/2019/04/13/us/google-location-tracking-police.html.

115 *"companies gonna company"*: *The Daily Show with Trevor Noah*, April 28, 2020 (broadcast).

115 *competing against MySpace as the more privacy-protecting alternative*: Dina Srinivasan, "The Antitrust Case against Facebook: A Monopolist's Journey towards Pervasive Surveillance in Spite of Consumers' Preference for Privacy," *Berkeley Business Law Journal* 16, 1 (Feb. 9, 2019).

117 *tell you about all the spying the platforms have already done on you*: Nicole Nguyen and Ryan Mac, "You Can Finally See All of the Info Facebook Collected about You from Other Websites," *BuzzFeed News*, Aug. 20, 2019, https://www.buzzfeednews.com/article/nicolenguyen/off-facebook-activity-feature-clear-history.

118 *"privacy-friendly smart home of the future"*: "About Candle," Candle Smarthome, https://www.candlesmarthome.com/about.

118 *"data that's been collected through a monopoly"*: "The Commissioners: The European Commission's Political Leadership," Commissioners, speech delivered September 9, 2016, https://ec.europa.eu/commission/commissioners/2014-2019/vestager/announcements/making-data-work-us_en.

118 *allows two applications to talk to each other*: Shana Pearlman, "What Are APIs and How Do APIs Work?" MuleSoft, Sept. 7, 2016, https://blogs.mulesoft.com/biz/tech-ramblings-biz/what-are-apis-how-do-apis-work/.

119 *"the primary way to get data into and out of the Facebook platform"*: "Overview," Facebook for Developers, https://developers.facebook.com/docs/graph-api/overview.

119 *competing with a Facebook "core functionality"*: House of Commons Digital,

Culture, Media and Sport Committee, UK Parliament, "Disinformation and 'Fake News': Final Report," Feb. 14, 2019, https://publications.parliament.uk /pa/cm201719/cmselect/cmcumeds/1791/1791.pdf, and Donie O'Sullivan and Hadas Gold, "Facebook Internal Emails Show Zuckerberg Targeting Competitor Vine," CNN Business, https://www.cnn.com/2018/12/05/media/face book-six4three-internal-documents-emails/index.html.

119   *"discriminatory refusal to deal"*: "Refusal to Deal," Federal Trade Commission, https://www.ftc.gov/tips-advice/competition-guidance/guide-antitrust-laws /single-firm-conduct/refusal-deal.

119   *use privacy as a pretense for monopolization*: House of Commons Digital, Culture, Media and Sport Committee, UK Parliament, "Disinformation and 'Fake News': Final Report," Feb. 14, 2019, https://publications.parliament.uk/pa /cm201719/cmselect/cmcumeds/1791/1791.pdf, and Katie Paul and Mark Hosenball, "Newly Released Court Documents Reveal Facebook Executives Quietly Planned a Data Policy 'Switcharoo,'" *Business Insider*, Nov. 6, 2019, https://www.businessinsider.com/facebook-executives-planned-switcharoo-on -data-policy-change-court-filings-2019-11?op=1.

121   *still struggling to get Facebook and Google to comply*: Johnny Ryan, "New Data on GDPR Enforcement Agencies Reveal Why the GDPR Is Failing," Brave Insights, April 27, 2020, https://brave.com/dpa-report-2020/.

121   *inquiries into the two companies ongoing*: Data Protection Commission, "Annual Report, 1 January—31 December 2019," https://www.dataprotection.ie/sites /default/files/uploads/2020-02/DPC%20Annual%20Report%202019.pdf

121   *The law puts forth a different*: "California Consumer Privacy Act (CCPA) Fact Sheet," California Department of Justice, https://www.oag.ca.gov/sys tem/files/attachments/press_releases/CCPA%20Fact%20Sheet%20%280 0000002%29.pdf.

122   *FTC fined Facebook $5 billion*: "FTC Imposes $5 Billion Penalty and Sweeping New Privacy Restrictions on Facebook," Federal Trade Commission, July 24, 2019,   https://www.ftc.gov/news-events/press-releases/2019/07/ftc-imposes -5-billion-penalty-sweeping-new-privacy-restrictions, and Rohit Chopra, "Dissenting Statement of Commissioner Rohit Chopra Regarding the Matter of Facebook, Inc.," Federal Trade Commission, July 24, 2019, https://www .ftc.gov/public-statements/2019/07/dissenting-statement-commissioner-rohit -chopra-regarding-matter-facebook, and Rebecca Kelly Slaughter, "Dissenting Statement of Commissioner Rebecca Kelly Slaughter Regarding the Matter of FTC vs. Facebook," Federal Trade Commission, July 24, 2019, https://www.ftc .gov/public-statements/2019/07/dissenting-statement-commissioner-rebecca -kelly-slaughter-regarding-matter.

122   *consider that Facebook made over $70 billion in 2019 alone*: J. Clement, "Facebook:

Annual Revenue 2009–2019," *Statista*, Feb. 3, 2020, https://www.statista.com /statistics/268604/annual-revenue-of-facebook/.

122 *"not misrepresent"*: "Agreement Containing Consent Order," *In the Matter of Facebook, Inc., a corporation*, https://www.ftc.gov/sites/default/files/documents /cases/2011/11/111129facebookagree.pdf.

123 *Facebook's stock surged*: Jon Swartz, "Facebook Stock Hits Highest Price in Nearly a Year after Reports of $5 Billion FTC Fine," *MarketWatch*, July 14, 2019, https://www.marketwatch.com/story/facebook-stock-hits-highest-price-in -nearly-a-year-after-reports-of-5-billion-ftc-fine-2019-07-12.

123 *personal information can be used to screw you over*: Arwa Mahdawi, "Cookie Monsters: Why Your Browsing History Could Mean Rip-Off Prices," *Guardian*, Dec. 6, 2016, https://www.theguardian.com/commentisfree/2016/dec/06 /cookie-monsters-why-your-browsing-history-could-mean-rip-off-prices.

124 *"engages" humans the most*: Tobias Rose-Stockwell, "This Is How Your Fear and Outrage Are Being Sold for Profit," *Quartz*, July 28, 2017, https:// qz.com/1039910/how-facebooks-news-feed-algorithm-sells-our-fear-and -outrage-for-profit/, and Marcia Stepanek, "The Algorithms of Fear," *Stanford Social Innovation Review*, June 14, 2016, https://ssir.org/articles/entry/the_al gorithms_of_fear.

124 *up ten minutes from the number reported in 2014*: James B. Stewart, "Facebook Has 50 Minutes of Your Time Each Day. It Wants More," *New York Times*, May 5, 2016, https://www.nytimes.com/2016/05/06/business/facebook-bends-the -rules-of-audience-engagement-to-its-advantage.html.

124 *84 percent of Google's revenue and 98 percent of Facebook's revenue*: "Advertising Revenue of Google from 2001 to 2019," *Statista*, retrieved March 7, 2020, https://www.statista.com/statistics/266249/advertising-revenue-of-google/; J. Clement, "Facebook's Advertising Revenue Worldwide from 2009 to 2019," *Statista*, Feb. 28, 2020; https://www.statista.com/statistics/271258/facebooks -advertising-revenue-worldwide/.

124 *"We're not talking about the realm of the possible here"*: "Transcript of Tech Conference with Scott Galloway," http://thecapitolforum.cmail20.com/t/View Email/j/A39DA2A85002EAE22540EF23F30FEDED/647939D224BDE7F 5C06B463AA70A4F2C.

125 *getting our cortisol pumping*: Nina Godlewski, "Deleting Facebook Could Lower Stress Hormone Levels, Study Finds," *Newsweek*, April 4, 2018, https://www .newsweek.com/facebook-stress-cortisol-social-media-health-break-quit -871521.

126 *some of the tricks tech companies employ to addict users*: Tristan Harris, "Unregulated Tech Mediation, Inevitable Online Deception, Societal Harm," Center for Humane Technology, Jan. 8, 2020, https://energycommerce.house.gov/sites

/democrats.energycommerce.house.gov/files/documents/010820%20CPC%20 Hearing%20Testimony_Harris.pdf.

126   *psychologist B. F. Skinner*: "Variable Rewards: Want to Hook Users? Drive Them Crazy," Nir & Far, https://www.nirandfar.com/want-to-hook-your-users -drive-them-crazy/.

126   *"It's a social-validation feedback loop"*: Olivia Solon, "Ex-Facebook President Sean Parker: Site Made to Exploit Human 'Vulnerability,'" *Guardian*, Nov. 9, 2017, https://www.theguardian.com/technology/2017/nov/09/facebook-sean -parker-vulnerability-brain-psychology.

126   *"aren't allowed to use that shit"*: James Vincent, "Former Facebook Exec Says Social Media Is Ripping Apart Society," *Verge*, Dec. 11, 2017, https://www .theverge.com/2017/12/11/16761016/former-facebook-exec-ripping-apart -society.

127   *put tight controls on their own kids' use of technology*: Nellie Bowles, "A Dark Consensus about Screens and Kids Begins to Emerge," *New York Times*, Oct. 26, 2018, https://www.nytimes.com/2018/10/26/style/phones-children-silicon-valley .html.

127   *"God only knows what it's doing to our children's brains"*: Olivia Solon, "Ex-Facebook President Sean Parker: Site Made to Exploit Human 'Vulnerability,'" *Guardian*, Nov. 9, 2017, https://www.theguardian.com/technology/2017 /nov/09/facebook-sean-parker-vulnerability-brain-psychology.

127   *170 percent increase in high-depressive symptoms*: Tristan Harris, "Unregulated Tech Mediation, Inevitable Online Deception, Societal Harm," Center for Humane Technology, January 8, 2020, https://energycommerce.house.gov/sites /democrats.energycommerce.house.gov/files/documents/010820%20CPC% 20Hearing%20Testimony_Harris.pdf.

127   *NYU researchers link to social media usage*: J. M. Twenge, T. E. Joiner, M. L. Rogers, and G. N. Martin, "Corrigendum: Increases in Depressive Symptoms, Suicide-Related Outcomes, and Suicide Rates among U.S. Adolescents after 2010 and Links to Increased New Media Screen Time," Association for Psychological Science, https://journals.sagepub.com/doi/pdf/10.1177/2167702617723376.

127   *doubling for girls aged 15 to 19 between 2007 and 2015*: Susan Scutti, "Suicide Rate Hit 40-Year Peak among Older Teen Girls in 2015," CNN Health, Aug. 3, 2017, https://www.cnn.com/2017/08/03/health/teen-suicide-cdc-study-bn/index.html.

128   *determined by recommendation algorithms*: "23 YouTube Statistics That Matter to Marketers in 2020," Hootsuite, Dec. 17, 2019, https://blog.hootsuite.com /youtube-stats-marketers/.

128   *Emily Gadek tweeted in September 2019*: "Emily Gadek" (tweet), https://twitter .com/emilygadabout/status/1176517141400440834?s=11.

129		*Among the stories collected were*: "01: A Deadly Fall," Mozilla, https://foundation
.mozilla.org/en/campaigns/youtube-regrets/.

129		*target you based on your particular vulnerability*: Zeynep Tufekci, "#78–
Persuasion and Control," Sam Harris, samharris.org/podcasts/persuasion-and
-control/, and Jeremy B. Merrill and Olivia Goldhill, "These Are the Political Ads Cambridge Analytica Designed for You," Quartz Daily Brief, https://
qz.com/1782348/cambridge-analytica-used-these-5-political-ads-to-target
-voters/.

129		*their algorithms draw inferences about you*: Sandra Wachter and Brent Mittel-
stadt, "A Right to Reasonable Inferences: Re-Thinking Data Protection Law
in the Age of Big Data and AI," *Columbia Business Law Review* 2 (April 2019),
https://ssrn.com/abstract=3248829.

131		*rolled back long-standing rules*: Cecilia Kang, Eric Lipton, and Sydney Ember,
"How a Conservative TV Giant Is Ridding Itself of Regulation," *New York
Times*, Aug. 14, 2017, https://www.nytimes.com/2017/08/14/us/politics/how-a
-conservative-tv-giant-is-ridding-itself-of-regulation.html, and Cecilia Kang,
"F.C.C. Watchdog Looks into Changes That Benefited Sinclair," *New York
Times*, Feb. 15, 2018, https://www.nytimes.com/2018/02/15/technology/fcc
-sinclair-ajit-pai.html?partner=IFTTT.

131		*has appealed*: Michael Balderston, "FCC Eyes Supreme Court for Media Own-
ership Dereg Case," TV Technology, https://www.tvtechnology.com/news/fcc
-eyes-supreme-court-for-media-ownership-dereg-case.

131		*he and his staff had several meetings with executives*: Cecilia Kang, Eric Lipton,
and Sydney Ember, "How a Conservative TV Giant Is Ridding Itself of Regulation," *New York Times*, Aug. 14, 2017, https://www.nytimes.com/2017/08/14
/us/politics/how-a-conservative-tv-giant-is-ridding-itself-of-regulation.html,
and Cecilia Kang, "F.C.C. Watchdog Looks into Changes That Benefited Sinclair," *New York Times*, Feb. 15, 2018, https://www.nytimes.com/2018/02/15
/technology/fcc-sinclair-ajit-pai.html?partner=IFTTT.

131		*used shell corporations to evade broadcast ownership limits*: https://www.fcc
.gov/document/broadcast-radio-ownership-47-cfr-section-733555 47 C.F.R.
§ 73.3555(e), and Timothy Karr, "Sinclair's Defense Is as Bogus as the Shell
Companies It Uses to Evade the FCC Rules," *Free Press*, Oct. 24, 2013, https://
www.freepress.net/news/press-releases/sinclairs-defense-bogus-shell-compa
nies-it-uses-evade-fcc-rules.

131		*racist and anti-Muslim propaganda*: Dana Floberg, "Free Press to FCC: Viral
Vid Shows We Must Stop Sinclair," *Free Press*, April 19, 2018, https://www
.freepress.net/news/updates/free-press-fcc-viral-vid-shows-we-must-stop
-sinclair.

131 *reportedly ordered its stations to air a video segment*: Sydney Ember, "Sinclair Requires TV Stations to Air Segments That Tilt to the Right," *New York Times*, May 14, 2017, https://www.nytimes.com/2017/05/12/business/media/sinclair -broadcast-komo-conservative-media.html?_r=0.

131 *has a strong grip on the dissemination of information*: "Who Controls the Votes?" Columbia Business School, Ideas and Insights, https://www8.gsb.columbia .edu/articles/ideas-work/who-controls-votes.

131 *"Rupert Murdoch is the most powerful"*: Patrick Kennedy and Andrea Prat, "Information Inequality" *Vox CEPR Policy Portal*, November 25, 2017, https:// voxeu.org/article/information-inequality.

131 *referring to it as a hoax*: Bryan Sullivan, "Fox News Faces Lawsuit for Calling COVID-19 a 'Hoax,'" *Forbes*, April 10, 2020, https://www.forbes .com/sites/legalentertainment/2020/04/10/covid-19-lawsuit-against-fox -news/#586e45885739, and Luke Darby, "Fox News Staffers Got Coronavirus after Anchors Downplayed the Pandemic," *GQ*, March 23, 2020, https:// www.gq.com/story/fox-news-coronavirus, and Ken Stone, "Washington State Group Is 1st to Sue Fox News for Calling Coronavirus a 'Hoax,'" *Times of San Diego*, April 2, 2020, https://timesofsandiego.com/business/2020/04/02 /washington-state-group-is-1st-to-sue-fox-news-for-calling-coronavirus -a-hoax/, and "A Beloved Bar Owner Was Skeptical about the Virus. Then He Took a Cruise," *New York Times*, April 18, 2020, https://www.nytimes .com/2020/04/18/nyregion/coronavirus-jjbubbles-joe-joyce.html.

132 *"help protect the lives of all Americans"*: James Walker, "Journalism Professors Call for an End to Fox News Coronavirus 'Misinformation' in Open Letter to Rupert Murdoch," *Newsweek*, April 2, 2020, https://www.newsweek.com/journalism -professors-fox-news-end-coronavirus-misinformation-open-letter-1495688.

Five: Monopolies Threaten Democracy and Your Freedom

135 *Cambridge Analytica had developed psychological profiles*: See Karim Amer and Jehane Noujaim (producers and directors), *The Great Hack*, Netflix, 2019.

135 *targeted "persuadable" American voters*: Sabrina Siddiqui, "Cambridge Analytica's US Election Work May Violate Law, Legal Complaint Argues," *Guardian*, March 26, 2018, https://www.theguardian.com/uk-news/2018/mar/26/cam bridge-analytica-trump-campaign-us-election-laws; Eric Auchard and David Ingram, "Cambridge Analytica CEO Claims Influence on U.S. Election, Facebook Questioned," Reuters, March 20, 2018, https://www.reuters.com/article /us-facebook-cambridge-analytica-idUSKBN1GW1SG; Alex Hern, "Cambridge Analytica: How Did it Turn Clicks into Votes?" *Guardian*, May 6, 2018, https://www.theguardian.com/news/2018/may/06/cambridge-analytica-how -turn-clicks-into-votes-christopher-wylie.

135 *"It doesn't have to be true, it just has to be believed"*: Ben Popken and Anna Schecter, "Hidden Camera Shows Cambridge Analytica Pitching Deceptive Tactics," NBC News, March 18, 2018, https://www.nbcnews.com/news/all/hidden-camera-shows-cambridge-analytica-pitching-tricky-tactics-n857936.

135 *helping to elect far-right leaders*: Larry Madowo, "How Cambridge Analytica Poisoned Kenya's Democracy," *Washington Post*, March 20, 2018, https://www.washingtonpost.com/news/global-opinions/wp/2018/03/20/how-cambridge-analytica-poisoned-kenyas-democracy/.

135 *to suppress African American voting*: "Part," *Listen Notes*, April 29, 2019, https://www.listennotes.com/podcasts/deepak-chopras/part-two-minds-and-ma chines-Li02qCOt81l/.

136 *"was in 'psychological operations'"*: Carole Cadwalladr, "'I Made Steve Bannon's Psychological Warfare Tool': Meet the Data War Whistleblower," *The Guardian*, March 18, 2018, https://www.theguardian.com/news/2018/mar/17/data-war-whistleblower-christopher-wylie-faceook-nix-bannon-trump.

136 *"insurgency that was catalyzed by targeted disinformation"*: Ibid.

137 *"This was targeted at narrow segments of the population"*: Chris Wylie, "Written Statement to the United States Senate Committee on the Judiciary In the Matter of Cambridge Analytica and Other Related Issues," para. 42, https://www.judiciary.senate.gov/imo/media/doc/05-16-18%20Wylie%20Testi mony.pdf.

137 *breaking a rule*: UK Information Commissioner's Office, "Investigation Into the Use of Data Analytics in Political Campaigns, Investigation Update," July 11, 2018, https://ico.org.uk/media/action-weve-taken/2259371/investiga tion-into-data-analytics-for-political-purposes-update.pdf, "Facebook's policies permitted third-party apps to obtain personal data about users who installed the app. . . . Facebook's default settings also allowed user's friends' data to be collected by the app unless the friends themselves had specifically changed their privacy settings to prevent this from occurring. There were, however, limitations in what this data could be used for . . ."

137 *classified as being interested in "pseudoscience"*: Aaron Sankin, "Want to Find a Misinformed Public? Facebook's Already Done it," Markup, April 23, 2020, https://themarkup.org/coronavirus/2020/04/23/want-to-find-a-misinformed-public-facebooks-already-done-it.

137 *"By monitoring"*: Darren Davidson, "Facebook Targets 'Insecure' Young People," *Australian*, May 1, 2017, https://www.theaustralian.com.au/business/media/digital/facebook-targets-insecure-young-people-to-sell-ads/news-story/a89949ad016eee7d7a61c3c30c909fa6.

138 *"does not offer tools to target people"*: Facebook, "Comments on Research and

Ad Targeting," April 30, 2017, https://about.fb.com/news/h/comments-on
-research-and-ad-targeting/.

138   *using Facebook data and Facebook micro-targeting*: Sophia Porotsky, "Cambridge
Analytica: The Darker Side of Big Data," *Global Security Review*, June 10, 2019,
https://globalsecurityreview.com/cambridge-analytica-darker-side-big-data/.

138   *"determining user personality characteristics,"* Patent #9,740,752, June 3, 2016,
available at https://patents.justia.com/patent/9740752.

138   *U.S. political ads with rubles*: Harper Neidig, "Franken Blasts Facebook for
Accepting Rubles for U.S. Election Ads," *Hill*, October 31, 2017, https://the
hill.com/policy/technology/358102-franken-blasts-facebook-for-accepting
-rubles-for-us-election-ads.

138   *ad revenue jumped*: J. Clement, "Facebook: Annual Revenue 2009–2019,"
Statista, Feb. 3, 2020, https://www.statista.com/statistics/268604/annual-reve
nue-of-facebook/.

138   *Facebook threatened to sue them*: Justin Carissimo, "Facebook Knew of Illicit User
Profile Harvesting for 2 Years, Never Acted," CBS News, March 17, 2018,
https://www.cbsnews.com/news/cambridge-analytica-facebook-knew-for
-two-years-no-action-taken/, and Jamie Grierson, "Facebook Says Warning
to Guardian Group 'Not Our Wisest Move,'" *The Guardian*, March 23, 2018,
https://www.theguardian.com/news/2018/mar/23/facebook-says-warning-to
-guardian-group-not-our-wisest-move.

138   *"What happens"*: Chris Wylie, "Written Statement to the United States Senate
Committee on the Judiciary In the Matter of Cambridge Analytica and Other
Related Issues," para. 48, https://www.judiciary.senate.gov/imo/media/doc/05
-16-18%20Wylie%20Testimony.pdf.

139   *"I would bet"*: Casey Newton, "Read the Full Transcript of Mark Zuckerberg's
Leaked Internal Facebook Meetings," *Verge*, October 1, 2019, https://www
.theverge.com/2019/10/1/20892354/mark-zuckerberg-full-transcript-leaked
-facebook-meetings.

139   *two unannounced meetings*: Dylan Byers and Ben Collins, "Trump Hosted
Zuckerberg for Undisclosed Dinner at the White House in October," NBC
News, November 20, 2019, https://www.nbcnews.com/tech/tech-news/trump
-hosted-zuckerberg-undisclosed-dinner-white-house-october-n1087986.

139   *"We don't fact-check political ads"*: Salvador Rodriguez, "Mark Zuckerberg:
I thought about banning political ads from Facebook, but decided not to,"
CNBC, October 17, 2019, https://www.cnbc.com/2019/10/17/mark-zucker
berg-says-he-wont-ban-political-ads-on-facebook.html.

139   *grounded in free expression*: Ben Gilbert, "Facebook refuses to fact-check political ads and it's infuriating employees and lawmakers. Here's why the issue

continues to dog the company," *Business Insider*, December 14, 2019, https://
www.businessinsider.com/facebook-political-ads-fact-check-policy-explained
-2019-11?op=1#so-what-is-it-about-according-to-zuckerberg-its-about-free
-speech-3.

140 *"As a public"*: Zeynep Tufekci, "We're Building a Dystopia Just to Make People Click on Ads," Ted, September 2017, https://www.ted.com/talks/zeynep
_tufekci_we_re_building_a_dystopia_just_to_make_people_click_on_ads.

140 *"If there be"*: "Whitney v. California, 274 U.S. 357 (1927)," Justia, https://su
preme.justia.com/cases/federal/us/274/357/.

141 *"Our assessment"*: Renee DiResta et al., "The Tactics and Tropes of the Internet Research Agency," int.nyt, https://int.nyt.com/data/documenthelper/533
-read-report-internet-research-agency/7871ea6d5b7bedafbf19/optimized/full
.pdf#page=1.

142 *"in Bolsonaro's rise"*: Max Fisher and Amanda Taub, "What Is YouTube Pushing You to Watch Next?" *New York Times, The Weekly*, August 9, 2019, https://www
.nytimes.com/2019/08/09/the-weekly/youtube-brazil-far-right.html.

142 *own employees have called for restrictions*: "Read the Letter Facebook Employees Sent to Mark Zuckerberg About Political Ads," *New York Times*, October 28, 2019, https://www.nytimes.com/2019/10/28/technology/facebook-mark
-zuckerberg-letter.html.

143 *proposed limits to micro-targeting as a solution*: Peter Kafka, "Facebook's Political Ad Problem, Explained by an Expert," *Vox*, December 10, 2019, https://
www.vox.com/recode/2019/12/10/20996869/facebook-political-ads-targeting
-alex-stamos-interview-open-sourced.

143 *Ellen L. Weintraub, a Democratic commissioner*: Ellen L. Weintraub, "Don't Abolish Political Ads on Social Media. Stop Microtargeting," *Washington Post*, Nov. 1, 2019, https://www.washingtonpost.com/opinions/2019/11/01/dont
-abolish-political-ads-social-media-stop-microtargeting/.

143 *target their devices with text messages or app alerts*: Thomas Edsall, "Opinion: Trump's Digital Advantage Is Freaking Out Democratic Strategists," *New York Times*, January 29, 2020, https://www.nytimes.com/2020/01/29/opinion
/trump-digital-campaign-2020.html.

143 *more than 80 percent of America's voting machines*: Penn Wharton Public Policy Initiative Report, "The Business of Voting," March 2017, https://trustthevote
.org/wp-content/uploads/2017/03/2017-whartonoset_industryreport.pdf; Jordan Wilkie, " 'They Think They Are above the Law': The Firms That Own America's Voting System," *Guardian*, April 23, 2019, https://www.theguard
ian.com/us-news/2019/apr/22/us-voting-machine-private-companies-voter
-registration; Sue Halpern, "How Voting-Machine Lobbyists Undermine the

Democratic Process," *New Yorker*, January 22, 2019, https://www.newyorker
.com/tech/annals-of-technology/how-voting-machine-lobbyists-undermine
-the-democratic-process?.

143 *lobbyists reportedly made contributions to Mitch McConnell's campaign*: Donald Shaw, "As He Blocks Election Security Bills, McConnell Takes Checks
from Voting Machine Lobbyists," Sludge, June 10, 2019, https://readsludge
.com/2019/06/10/as-he-blocks-election-security-bills-mcconnell-takes
-checks-from-voting-machine-lobbyists/, and Nicole Goodkind, "Mitch
McConnell Received Donations from Voting Machine Lobbyists Before
Blocking Election Security Bills," *Newsweek*, July 26, 2019, https://www.news
week.com/mitch-mcconnell-robert-mueller-election-security-russia-1451361.

144 *they're decimating journalism*: See *Online Platforms and Market Power, Part 1: The
Free and Diverse Press: Before the Subcomm. on Regulatory Reform, Commercial
and Antitrust Law of the H. Comm. on the Judiciary*, 116th Cong. (2019) (submitted testimony of Sally Hubbard, Director of Enforcement Strategy, Open Markets Institute), https://docs.house.gov/meetings/JU/JU05/20190611/109616
/HHRG-116-JU05-Wstate-HubbardS-20190611.pdf.

144 *newspaper employment fell about 47 percent*: Jonathan O'Connell and Rachel
Siegel, "America's Two Largest Newspaper Chains Are Joining Forces. Will
It Save Either?" *Washington Post*, August 5, 2019 https://www.washingtonpost
.com/business/2019/08/05/gannett-merge-with-gatehouse-media/.

145 *thirty-three thousand employees*: Victor Pickard, "Coronavirus Is Hammering the
News Industry. Here's How to Save It," Jacobin, April 20, 2020, https://jacobin
mag.com/2020/04/coronavirus-news-industry-newspapers-journalists-layoffs.

145 *85 to 90 percent of the growth of the more than $150 billion*: Testimony of Jason
Kint, CEO of Digital Content Next, House of Commons Standing Committee on Access to Information, Privacy and Ethics, May 27, 2019, https://
www.ourcommons.ca/DocumentViewer/en/42-1/ETHI/meeting-151
/evidence#Int-10649964.

145 *More than 68 percent of American adults*: Media Subcommittee, Digital Platforms
Project, "How to Protect the News Media in the Age of Digital Platforms,"
Pro Market, May 10, 2019, https://promarket.org/how-to-protect-the-news
-media-in-the-age-of-digital-platforms/.

145 *share of Americans' attention*: Ibid.

145 *has long maintained it is a neutral platform and not a publisher*: Sam Levin, "Is
Facebook a Publisher? In Public It Says No, but in Court It Says Yes," *Guardian*, July 2, 2018, https://www.theguardian.com/technology/2018/jul/02/face
book-mark-zuckerberg-platform-publisher-lawsuit.

145 *wide-reaching legal immunity*: "Artist Rights Alliance Opposes Exporting Safe
Harbors in Trade Deals," medium, Oct. 29, 2019, https://medium.com/@art

istrightsnow/artist-rights-alliance-opposes-exporting-safe-harbors-in-trade
-deals-befc5fa3976d.

146 *More than 70 percent of Google's revenue*: J. Clement, "Distribution of Google's Revenues From 2001 to 2018, By Source," *Statista*, Feb. 5, 2020, https://www .statista.com/statistics/266471/distribution-of-googles-revenues-by-source/.

146 *depriving publishers of the ad revenue that funds journalism*: Sally Hubbard, "Fake News Is a Real Antitrust Problem," *Competition Policy International Antitrust Chronicle*, December 2017, https://www.competitionpolicyinternational.com /wp-content/uploads/2017/12/CPI-Hubbard.pdf.

147 *from friends and family*: Mark Zuckerberg's Facebook page, January 11, 2018.

147 *like* Mother Jones, Vox, *and* Slate: Monika Bauerlein and Clara Jeffery, "How Facebook Screwed Us All," *Mother Jones*, March 2019, https://www.mother jones.com/politics/2019/02/how-facebook-screwed-us-all/; Jeremy Barr. "Post-Facebook News Feed Tweaks, Vox Media Lays off 50 Employees," *Hollywood Reporter*, February 21, 2018, https://www.hollywoodreporter.com/news /vox-media-laying-around-50-people-1086869; Will Oremus, "The Great Facebook Crash," *Slate*, June 27, 2018, https://slate.com/technology/2018/06 /facebooks-retreat-from-the-news-has-painful-for-publishers-including-slate .html.

149 *"At times, the AJC's reporters"*: Congressional testimony of Kevin Riley, editor, *Atlanta Journal-Constitution, Online Platforms and Market Power, Part 1: The Free and Diverse Press*, June 11, 2019, https://www.congress.gov/event/116th -congress/house-event/109616

149 *reporting of coronavirus case numbers*: Alan Judd and Carrie Teegardin, "Faulty Data Obscures Virus' Impact on Georgia," *AJC*, April 14, 2020, https://www .ajc.com/news/faulty-data-obscures-virus-impact-georgia/LhCiI0bVKXO QW9VuEF9OrN/.

149 *publicly apologized*: Willoughby Mariano and J. Scott Trubey, "'It's Just Cuckoo': State's Latest Data Mishap Causes Critics to Cry Foul," *AJC*, May 13, 2020, https://www.ajc.com/news/state—regional-govt—politics/just-cuckoo -state-latest-data-mishap-causes-critics-cry-foul/182PpUvUX9XEF8v O11NVGO/.

149 *try to weaken the law*: Kartikay Mehrotra, Laura Mahoney, and Daniel Stoller, "Google and Other Tech Firms Seek to Weaken Landmark California Data-Privacy Law," *Los Angeles Times*, September 4, 2019, https://www .latimes.com/business/story/2019-09-04/google-and-other-tech-companies -attempt-to-water-down-privacy-law; amendments tracked in the text of the California Privacy Rights and Enforcement Act here: https://uploads-ssl .webflow.com/5aa18a452485b60001c301de/5d8bc3342a72fc8145920a32 _CPREA_2020_092519_Annotated_.pdf.

150   *"Newsrooms"*: Gaelle Faure, "Maria Ressa on the Battle for Truth, the Role of America's Social Media Platforms, and What Comes Next," Global Investigative Journalism Conference, September 29, 2019, https://gijc2019 .org/2019/09/29/maria-ressa-on-the-battle-for-truth-the-role-of-americas -social-media-platforms-and-what-comes-next/.

Six: Monopolies Destroy Our Planet and Control Your Food

154   *by warming it by one degree Celsius*: Umair Irfan, "A Major New Climate Report Slams the Door on Wishful Thinking," *Vox*, Oct. 7, 2018, https://www.vox .com/2018/10/5/17934174/climate-change-global-warming-un-ipcc-report -1-5-degrees.

154   *catastrophe*: "Special Report: Global Warming of 1.5 degrees C," IPCC, https:// www.ipcc.ch/sr15/.

154   *Young Thunberg spelled it out*: 2020 World Economic Forum, "Greta Thunberg: Our house is still on fire and you're fueling the flames," https://www.weforum .org/agenda/2020/01/greta-speech-our-house-is-still-on-fire-davos-2020/.

155   *"One day we'll know"*: Rachel Adams-Heard and Akshat Rathi, "Tillerson Questions Human Role in Halting Climate Change," Bloomberg, Feb. 04, 2020, https://www.bloomberg.com/news/articles/2020-02-04/rex-tillerson -questions-human-role-in-battling-climate-change; "Rex Tillerson to Oil Industry: Not Sure Humans Can Do Anything to Battle Climate Change," *Dallas Morning News*, Feb. 4, 2020, https://www.dallasnews.com/business /energy/2020/02/04/rex-tillerson-to-oil-industry-not-sure-humans-can-do -anything-to-battle-climate-change/.

156   *"If you are part"*: Naomi Klein, *On Fire: The (Burning) Case for a Green New Deal* (New York: Simon & Schuster, 2019), 289.

156   *"The great"*: Matthew Taylor and Jonathan Watts, "Revealed: The 20 Firms Behind a Third of All Carbon Emission," *Guardian*, October 9, 2019, https:// www.theguardian.com/environment/2019/oct/09/revealed-20-firms-third -carbon-emissions.

156   *cost more than $460 billion*: NOAA National Centers for Environmental Information, "U.S. Billion-Dollar Weather and Climate Disasters," 2020, https:// www.ncdc.noaa.gov/billions/time-series.

156   *on the current path*: Citi GPS: Global Perspectives & Solutions, "Energy Darwinism II: Why a Low Carbon Future Doesn't Have to Cost the Earth," August 2015, https://ir.citi.com/hsq32Jl1m4aIzicMqH8sBkPnbsqfnwy4Jgb1J2kI PYWIw5eM8yD3FY9VbGpK%2Baax.

156   *could bring in more than $2 trillion*: Sara Harrison, "Companies Expect Climate Change to Cost Them $1 Trillion in 5 Years," *Wired*, June 4, 2019, https://

www.wired.com/story/companies-expect-climate-change-to-cost-them-one
-trillion-dollars-in-5-years/.

156   *120 percent more*: Report by UN et al., "The Production Gap: The discrepancy
between countries' planned fossil fuel production and global production levels
consistent with limiting warming to 1.5 or 2 degrees Celsius," 2019, http://
productiongap.org/2019report/.

157   *"We will not get the job"*: Klein, *On Fire*, 33

158   *"Like its 1930s"*: Sandeep Vaheesan, "A Charter for a Clean, Democratic Future,"
The Trouble, May 12, 2019, https://www.the-trouble.com/content/2019/5/12/a
-charter-for-a-clean-democratic-future.

158   *"we have demonstrated"*: United States Climate Alliance, "U.S. Climate Alliance
Governors Oppose Administration's Withdrawal from the Paris Agreement,"
November 4, 2019, https://www.usclimatealliance.org/publications/pariswith
drawal.

159   *more than 10 percent of global carbon emissions*: Matthew Taylor and Jonathan
Watts, "Revealed: The 20 Firms Behind a Third of All Carbon Emission,"
Guardian, October 9, 2019, https://www.theguardian.com/environment/2019
/oct/09/revealed-20-firms-third-carbon-emissions.

159   *invested over $1 billion*: InfluenceMap Report, "Big Oil's Real Agenda on Cli-
mate Change," 2019, https://influencemap.org/report/How-Big-Oil-Contin
ues-to-Oppose-the-Paris-Agreement-38212275958aa21196dae3b76220bddc.

159   *Five out of the top ten largest global companies*: "Global 500," *Fortune*, 2019, http://
fortune.com/global500/list/.

159   *$20 billion in direct fossil fuel subsidies annually*: Klein, *On Fire*, 283.

159   *actively suppressed research*: Christopher Leonard, *Kochland: The Secret History of
Koch Industries and Corporate Power in America* (New York: Simon & Schuster,
2019), 400.

159   *own members of Congress*: Public Citizen, "Corporations United," January 15,
2020, https://www.citizen.org/article/corporations-united-citizens-united-10
-years-report/.

159   *sixteen of the top twenty recipients*: OpenSecrets.org, Center for Responsive
Politics, "Oil & Gas: Top Recipients," 2020, https://www.opensecrets.org
/industries/recips.php?ind=E01&recipdetail=A&sortorder=U&mem=Y&cy
cle=2020, visited March 22, 2020.

160   *the "Kochtopus"*: Leonard, *Kochland*, 395.

160   *"The 'big three'"*: Graham Steele, "A Regulatory Green Light: How Dodd-
Frank Can Address Wall Street's Role in the Climate Crisis," Great Democracy Initiative, January 2020, https://greatdemocracyinitiative.org/document/
dodd-frank-and-the-climate-crisis/.

160   *"veritable innovation arm of the fossil fuel extraction industry"*: Brian Merchant, "How Google, Microsoft, and Big Tech Are Automating the Climate Crisis," Gizmodo, February 21, 2019, https://gizmodo.com/how-google-microsoft -and-big-tech-are-automating-the-1832790799.

160   *threatened to fire them*: Jay Greene, "Amazon Threatens to Fire Critics Who Are Outspoken on Its Environmental Policies," *Washington Post*, January 2, 2020, https://www.washingtonpost.com/technology/2020/01/02/amazon-threatens -fire-outspoken-employee-critics-its-environmental-policies/.

160   *"Empowering Oil and Gas with AI"*: Microsoft: "Microsoft Demonstrates the Power of AI and Cloud to Oil and Gas Players, at ADIPEC 2018," November 12, 2018, https://news.microsoft.com/en-xm/2018/11/12/micro soft-demonstrates-the-power-of-ai-and-cloud-to-oil-and-gas-players-at -adipec-2018/.

161   *spent $17 million*: InfluenceMap Report, "Big Oil's Real Agenda on Climate Change," 2019, https://influencemap.org/report/How-Big-Oil-Continues-to -Oppose-the-Paris-Agreement-38212275958aa21196dae3b76220bddc.

162   *"green growth"*: John Cassidy, "Can We Have Prosperity Without Growth?" *New Yorker*, February 3, 2020.

162   *quite literally, opioids*: Trevor Haynes, "Dopamine, Smartphones, & You: A Battle For Your Time," *Harvard*, May 1, 2018, http://sitn.hms.harvard.edu /flash/2018/dopamine-smartphones-battle-time/; Susan Weinschenk, "Why We're All Addicted to Texts, Twitter and Google," *Psychology Today*, Sept. 11, 2012, https://www.psychologytoday.com/us/blog/brain-wise/201209/why -were-all-addicted-texts-twitter-and-google.

163   *crops die when Dicamba blows over*: Boyce Uphold, "A Killing Season" *The New Republic*, December 10, 2018, https://newrepublic.com/article/152304 /murder-monsanto-chemical-herbicide-arkansas, and also see Dan Mitchell, "Why Monsanto Always Wins," *Fortune*, June 26, 2014, https://fortune .com/2014/06/26/monsanto-gmo-crops/.

163   *Monsanto has sued farmers*: "Farmers vs Monsanto," Food Democracy Now, https://www.fooddemocracynow.org/farmers-vs-monsanto.

164   *antitrust enforcers let it happen!*: "Justice Department Secures Largest Negoti-ated Merger Divestiture Ever to Preserve Competition Threatened by Bayer's Acquisition of Monsanto," justice.gov, May 29, 2018, https://www.justice.gov /opa/pr/justice-department-secures-largest-merger-divestiture-ever-preserve -competition-threatened.

164   *the National Family Farm coalition wrote*: "NFFC Requests DOJ Consider Monsanto-Bayer Approval," National Family Farm Coalition, August 15, 2018, https://nffc.net/nffc-requests-doj-reconsider-monsanto-bayer-approval/.

164   *algorithms to manipulate their farming*: Jason Davidson, "Bayer, Monsanto and

Big Data: Who Will Control Our Food System in the Era of Digital Agriculture and Mega-mergers?" *Medium*, March 20, 2018, https://medium.com/@
foe_us/bayer-monsanto-and-big-data-who-will-control-our-food-system-in
-the-era-of-digital-agriculture-aae80d991e4d.

164 *RoundUp, has ended up*: Mike Barrett, "3 Studies Proving Toxic Glyphosate
Found in Urine, Blood, and Even Breast Milk," Natural Society, May 4, 2014,
https://naturalsociety.com/3-studies-proving-toxic-glyphosate-found-urine
-blood-even-breast-milk/.

164 *Bayer-Monsanto agreed to pay*: Patricia Cohen, "Roundup Maker to Pay $10
Billion to Settle Cancer Suits," *New York Times*, June 24, 2020, https://www
.nytimes.com/2020/06/24/business/roundup-settlement-lawsuits.html.

165 *every aspect of food supply has concentrated*: Claire Kelloway and Sarah Miller,
"Food and Power: Addressing Monopolization in America's Food System,"
Open Markets Institute, https://openmarketsinstitute.org/wp-content/uploads
/2019/05/190322_MonopolyFoodReport-v7.pdf.

165 *"Beginning in the 1980s"*: Claire Kelloway "Why Are Farmers Destroying
Food While Grocery Stores Are Empty?" *Washington Monthly*, April 28, 2020,
https://washingtonmonthly.com/2020/04/28/why-are-farmers-destroying
-food-while-grocery-stores-are-empty/.

165 *"If you pull"*: Ibid.

165 *euthanizing their animals*: Tom Polansek and P. J. Huffstutter, "Piglets Aborted,
Chickens Gassed as Pandemic Slams Meat Sector," Reuters, April 27, 2020,
https://www.reuters.com/article/us-health-coronavirus-livestock-insight
/piglets-aborted-chickens-gassed-as-pandemic-slams-meat-sector-idUSKC
N2292YS.

166 *Union representatives told the BBC*: Jessica Lussenhop, "Coronavirus at Smithfield Pork Plant: The Untold Story of America's Biggest Outbreak," BBC News,
April 17, 2020, https://www.bbc.com/news/world-us-canada-52311877.

166 *550 farms*: Ibid.

166 *nearly 17,000 cattle ranchers*: Claire Kelloway and Sarah Miller, "Food and Power:
Addressing Monopolization in America's Food System," Open Markets Insti-
tute, https://openmarketsinstitute.org/wp-content/uploads/2019/05/190322
_MonopolyFoodReport-v7.pdf.

166 *As of June 2020*: Leah Nylen and Liz Crampton, "'Something Isn't Right':
U.S. Probes Soaring Beef Prices," *Politico*, May 25, 2020, https://www.politico
.com/news/2020/05/25/meatpackers-prices-coronavirus-antitrust-275093,
and Brent Kendall and Jacob Bunge, "Chicken Industry Executives, Including
Pilgrim's Pride CEO, Indicted on Price-Fixing Charges," *Wall Street Journal*,
June 3, 2020, https://www.wsj.com/articles/chicken-industry-executives-in
cluding-pilgrim-s-pride-ceo-indicted-for-price-fixing-11591202113.

166 *exporting rotten meat*: Kelloway and Miller, "Food and Power," and Drovers, "Billionaire Co-owner of JBS Gives Himself Up to Police in Brazil," September 11, 2017, https://www.drovers.com/article/billionaire-co-owner-jbs-gives -himself-police-brazil, and Tom Polsanek, "U.S. Bans Fresh Brazil Beef Imports Over Safety Concerns," *Reuters*, June 22, 2017, https://www.reuters.com /article/us-usa-brazil-beef-idUSKBN19D2VE.

166 *"Food markets"*: Joe Maxwell, panel, "Populism and Political Economy: Science and Regulations," *Capitol Forum*, Feb. 5, 2020, https://youtu.be/cclDU4SnPV4.

167 *out of every four poultry farmers*: Tom Philpott, "The Government's Own Watchdog Says Massive Poultry Companies Are Exploiting Small Business Loans," *Mother Jones*, March 16, 2018, https://www.motherjones.com /food/2018/03/government-watchdog-audit-poultry-small-business-loans -booker-trump-inspector-general-contract-chicken-farmer/.

167 *One point eight billion dollars*: James M. MacDonald, "Technology, Organization, and Financial Performance in U.S. Broiler Production," USDA, June 2014, https://www.ers.usda.gov/webdocs/publications/43869/48159_eib126.pdf ?v=41809.

167 *"confirm that farmers"*: "Farm Aid Statement on CDC Retraction of Farmer Suicide Statistics," Farm Aid, June 28, 2018, https://www.farmaid.org/press -release/farm-aid-statement-cdc-retracton-farmer-suicide-statistics/.

167 *ousted him from office*: Kaitlyn Riley, "Wisconsin State Senate Votes against Pfaff," *WIZM News*, November 5, 2019, https://www.wizmnews.com/2019/11/05 /wisconsin-state-senate-votes-against-pfaff/; Associated Press, "Senate Majority Leader Derides Wisconsin Agricultural Head," *U.S. News & World Report*, July 24, 2019, https://www.usnews.com/news/best-states/wisconsin/ar ticles/2019-07-24/senate-majority-leader-derides-wisconsin-agriculture-head.

168 *"The folks I"*: Patty Lovera, panel, "Populism and Political Economy: Science and Regulations," *Capitol Forum*, February 5, 2020, https://youtu.be/cclDU4SnPV4.

168 *Walmart has more than a 70 percent share*: Stacy Mitchell, "Report: Walmart's Monopolization of Local Grocery Markets," ILSR, June 26, 2019, https://ilsr .org/walmarts-monopolization-of-local-grocery-markets/.

169 *$113.9 billion from 1995 to 2019*: "Corn Subsidies," EWG, https://farm.ewg .org/progdetail.php?fips=00000&progcode=corn.

169 *bigger doesn't always mean better*: "K-State Ag Economists Rank State's Farms Based on 10 Years of KFMA Data," K-State, Oct. 10, 2019, https://www .ksre.k-state.edu/news/stories/2019/10/successful-kansas-farm-rankings.html.

170 *"exercise and"*: Avivia Shen, "How Big Food Corporations Watered Down Michelle Obama's 'Let's Move' Campaign," ThinkProgress, Feb. 28, 2013, https://thinkprogress.org/how-big-food-corporations-watered-down-michelle -obamas-let-s-move-campaign-85d09b60607b/.

170 *lobbied to a tune of $175 million*: Duff Wilson and Janet Robert, "Special Report: How Washington Went Soft on Childhood Obesity," Reuters, April 27, 2012, www.reuters.com/article/2012/04/27/us-usa-foodlobby-idUSBRE83Q0E D20120427.

170 *"a political force in Washington"*: Michael Pollen, "Big Food Strikes Back," *New York Times*, Oct, 5, 2016, https://www.nytimes.com/interactive/2016/10/09 /magazine/obama-administration-big-food-policy.html.

171 *"With the adoption"*: 'The Green New Deal's Key to Success—FTC Commissioner Warns of Monopolists' Harm to Democracy, Civil Rights," *Corner Newsletter*, Open Markets Institute, Feb. 21, 2019, https://openmarketsinstitute .org/newsletters/corner-newsletter-february-21-2019-green-new-deals-key -success-ftc-commissioner-warns-monopolists-harm-democracy-civil-rights/.

172 *"Farmers"*: Joe Maxwell, panel, "Populism and Political Economy: Science and Regulations," *Capitol Forum*, Feb. 5, 2020, https://youtu.be/cclDU4SnPV4.

172 *"have a meaningful"*: Timothy A. Wise, "Big Ag Is Sabotaging Progress on Climate Change," *Wired*, Aug. 28, 2019, https://www.wired.com/story/big-ag-is -sabotaging-progress-on-climate-change/.

172 *"Agriculture"*: Nick Boisvert, "How Canadian Farmers Can Go from Climate Change Polluters to a Key Part of the Solution," CBC, Feb. 11, 2020, https://www.cbc.ca/news/canada/toronto/farmers-for-climate-solutions -launch-1.5458676.

172 *emissions for the next 100 years*: "Greenhouse Gasses and Agriculture," Government of Canada, http://www.agr.gc.ca/eng/agriculture-and-climate/agricul tural-practices/climate-change-and-agriculture/greenhouse-gases-and -agriculture/?id=1329321969842.

172 *"Because we're reducing"*: Boisvert, "How Canadian Farmers Can Go from Climate Change Polluters to a Key Part of the Solution."

173 *"The climate crisis"*: "Issues: The Green New Deal," https://berniesanders.com /en/issues/green-new-deal/.

Seven: Monopolies Ramp Up Inequality

174 *more than 4.7 million likes*: Erica Gonzales, "Kylie Jenner Shares a Video of One-Year-Old Stormi Carrying a Mini Hermès Bag with Travis Scott," *Harper's Bazaar*, April 1, 2019, https://www.harpersbazaar.com/celebrity/latest /a27007208/kylie-jenner-stormi-webster-hermes-purse/.

175 *can't pay an unexpected $400 expense*: "Report on the Economic Well-Being of Households in 2018," Federal Reserve, May 2019, https://www.federalre serve.gov/publications/files/2018-report-economic-well-being-us-households -201905.pdf.

176 *more wealth than 41 percent of all Americans*: "Inequality, Exhibit A: Walmart and

the Wealth of American Families," *Economic Policy Institute*, July 17, 2012, https://www.epi.org/blog/inequality-exhibit-wal-mart-wealth-american/; see also Barry Lynn, America's Monopoly Problem," Open Markets Institute, June 29, 2016, https://www.youtube.com/watch?time_continue=25&v=cabTM kyTDDU&feature=emb_logo.

176 *which were often below cost*: Stacy Mitchell, "Wal-Mart Charged with Predatory Pricing," ILSR, Nov. 1, 2000, https://ilsr.org/walmart-charged-predatory -pricing/.

176 *bringing in a cool $514 billion*: "Global 500," *Fortune*, 2018, https://fortune.com /global500/.

176 *$4 million richer every hour, $100 million richer every day*: Tom Metcalf, Andrew Heathcote, Pei Yi Mak, Sophie Alexander, Tom Maloney, Devon Pendleton, Venus Feng, Yoojung Lee, Blake Schmidt, Jack Witzig, and Steven Crabill, "The World's Richest Families Get $4 Million Richer Every Hour," Bloomberg, August 10, 2019, https://www.bloomberg.com/features/richest-families -in-the-world/.

177 *annual salary of his lowest-paid employee in 11.5 seconds*: Simone Stolzoff, "Jeff Bezos Will Still Make the Annual Salary of His Lowest-Paid Employees Every 11.5 Seconds," Quartz, Oct. 2, 2018, https://qz.com/work/1410621/jeff-bezos -makes-more-than-his-least-amazon-paid-worker-in-11-5-seconds/.

177 *2,327,131 times the median U.S. household income*: "#1 – Jeff Bezos," Bloomberg, https://www.bloomberg.com/billionaires/profiles/jeffrey-p-bezos/.

177 *billions of dollars in wealth transfer*: Lina Kahn and Sandeep Vaheesan, "Market Power and Inequality: The Antitrust Counterrevolution and Its Discontents," *Harvard Law & Policy Review* 235 (2017), SSRN, April 22, 2016 (revised Feb. 22, 2017), papers.ssrn.com/sol3/papers.cfm?abstract_id=2769132.

178 *C-suite executives and major corporate shareholders*: Ibid.

178 *400 Americans have more wealth than 150 million Americans do*: Christopher Ingraham, "Wealth Concentration Returning to Levels Last Seen During the Roaring Twenties According to New Research," *Washington Post*, Feb. 12, 2019, https://www.washingtonpost.com/us-policy/2019/02/08/wealth-con centration-returning-levels-last-seen-during-roaring-twenties-according-new -research/.

178 *the gap between the top 1 percent and top .1 percent is enormous*: Emmanuel Saez and Gabriel Zucman, "Wealth Inequality in the United States Since 1913: Evidence from Capitalized Income Tax Data," *Quarterly Journal of Economics* 131, no. 2 (May 2016): 519–78, http://gabriel-zucman.eu/files/SaezZucman 2016QJE.pdf.

178 *from owning 7 percent of the country's total wealth to owning 22 percent*: Ibid.

179 *"focuses particularly on equality"*: Eleanor M. Fox, "Antitrust: Tracing Inequality—from the United States to South Africa," Competition Policy International, October 14, 2017, https://www.competitionpolicyinternational.com/antitrust-tracing-inequality-from-the-united-states-to-south-africa/.

180 *rise of antidemocratic leaders worldwide*: Staffan Lindberg, "Are Increasing Inequalities Threatening Democracy in Europe?" Carnegie Europe, Feb. 4, 2019, https://carnegieeurope.eu/2019/02/04/are-increasing-inequalities-threatening-democracy-in-europe-pub-78270.

180 *"The rapid retreat of dynamism"*: Economic Innovation Group, "Dynamism in Retreat: Consequences for Regions, Markets, and Workers," EIG, February 2017, https://eig.org/wp-content/uploads/2017/07/Dynamism-in-Retreat-A.pdf.

180 *almost 80 percent of start-up investment*: Ross Baird, *The Innovation Blind Spot: Why We Back the Wrong Ideas—and What to Do About It* (Dallas: BenBella Books, 2017), 10.

180 *only 15 percent of all venture capital*: Ibid., p. 15.

181 *"These platform monopolies"*: Aral Balkan, "We Didn't Lose Control—It Was Stolen," ar.al, March 12, 2017, https://ar.al/notes/we-didnt-lose-control-it-was-stolen/.

181 *"extreme asymmetries of knowledge"*: Shoshana Zuboff, "You Are Now Remotely Controlled," *New York Times*, Jan. 24, 2020, https://www.nytimes.com/2020/01/24/opinion/sunday/surveillance-capitalism.html.

183 *The American Dream is*: "The American Dream," *Wikipedia,* https://en.wikipedia.org/wiki/American_Dream.

183 *amount to anticompetitive regulations*: Chris Pike, "What's Gender Got to Do with Competition Policy?" SSRN, Dec. 1, 2019, https://papers.ssrn.com/sol3/papers.cfm?abstract_id=3487588.

183 *"Competition policy"*: Estefania Santacreu-Vasut and Chris Pike, "Competition Policy and Gender," OECD, Nov. 29, 2018, https://one.oecd.org/document/DAF/COMP/GF(2018)4/en/pdf.

184 *reducing the income of the poorest 20 percent*: Sean Ennis, Pedro Gonzaga, and Chris Pike, "Inequality: A Hidden Cost of Market Power," OECD, 2017, https://www.oecd.org/daf/competition/ Inequality-hidden-cost-market-power-2017.pdf.

184 *35 percent more likely*: "Women and Poverty in America," Legal Momentum, https://www.legalmomentum.org/women-and-poverty-america.

184 *twice that of white, non-Hispanic individuals*: "Unemployment and Poverty Disproportionately Affect African Americans—Making Combatting Hunger Even Harder," Feeding America, https://www.feedingamerica.org/hunger-in-america/african-american.

184 *"If the consumer economy had a sex, it would be female"*: Top 10 Things Everyone

Should Know about Women Consumers," Bloomberg, Jan. 11, 2018, https://www.bloomberg.com/company/stories/top-10-things-everyone-know-women-consumers/.

185 *78 cents to a white man's dollar*: Carmen Rios, "Here's What That '78 Cents to a Man's Dollar' Wage Gap Statistic Really Means," Everyday Feminism, July 12, 2015, https://everydayfeminism.com/2015/07/what-78-cents-wage-gap-means.

185 *Black men*: Eileen Patten, "Racial, Gender Wage Gaps Persist in U.S. Despite Some Progress," Pew Research Center, July 1, 2016, https://www.pewresearch.org/fact-tank/2016/07/01/racial-gender-wage-gaps-persist-in-u-s-despite-some-progress/.

185 *C-suite executives whose pay has skyrocketed*: Lina Kahn and Sandeep Vaheesan, "Market Power and Inequality: The Antitrust Counterrevolution and Its Discontents," *Harvard Law & Policy Review* 235 (2017), SSRN, April 22, 2016 (revised Feb. 22, 2017), https://papers.ssrn.com/sol3/papers.cfm?abstract_id=2769132.

185 *"Unless the causes"*: Francesca Rhodes, "Women and the 1%," Oxfam, April 11, 2016, https://www.oxfam.org/en/research/women-and-1.

185 *"Many spoke of"*: Marie Tae McDermott, "'I Was Blacklisted from Employment': Speaking Up in the Workplace," *New York Times*, https://www.nytimes.com/2017/10/11/business/i-was-blacklisted-from-employment-speaking-up-in-the-workplace.html.

185 *women who are harassed are 6.5 times*: Heather McLoughlin, Christopher Uggen, and Amy Blackstone, "The Economic and Career Effects of Sexual Harassment on Working Women," Sage Journals, May 10, 2007, https://journals.sagepub.com/doi/abs/10.1177/0891243217704631?journalCode=gasa.

186 *in hostile work environments*: Sally Hubbard and Sandeep Vaheesan, "Noncompete Clauses Trap #MeToo Victims in Abusive Workplaces. The FTC Should Ban Them," *USA Today*, May 14, 2018, https://www.usatoday.com/story/opinion/2019/05/14/sexually-harassed-women-trapped-noncompetes-abusive-work-places-column/1184622001/.

186 *"We're now empowered to create our own damn tables"*: Sally Hubbard, "Felecia Hatcher, Co-Founder of Code Fever and BlackTech Week, Works to Make Startup Communities More Inclusive," Women Killing It, Feb 28, 2017, https://womenkillingit.libsyn.com/ep-46-felecia-hatcher-co-founder-of-code-fever-and-blacktech-week-works-to-make-startup-communities-more-inclusive.

187 *"She is able to have more control"*: Stephanie Sarkis, "Gender Inequality Led to the Rise of Women Entrepreneurs," *Forbes*, March 5, 2019, https://www.forbes.com/sites/stephaniesarkis/2019/03/05/gender-inequality-led-to-the-rise-of-women-entrepreneurs.

187 *less than 1 percent*: Ross Baird, "Concrete Steps You Can Take Today to

Respond to Charlottesville," Medium, August 14, 2017, https://medium.com
/village-capital/concrete-steps-you-can-take-today-to-respond-to-charlottes
ville-ff6f74545598.

187 *have raised .0006 percent*: "The State of Black Women Founders," Project Diane,
https://projectdiane.digitalundivided.com; Larry Jacob, "3 Trends That Prevent
Entrepreneurs from Accessing Capital," Kauffman, July 25, 2018, https://www
.kauffman.org/currents/2018/07/3-trends-that-prevent-entrepreneurs-from
-accessing-capital.

187 *"That is the incredibly limited"*: Panel, "Innovation and Entrepreneurship in an
Age of Concentrated Power," Open Markets Institute, Dec. 6, 2017, https://
www.youtube.com/watch?list=PL17VSnPfVKIjDjjK9yw6bQK4964lbJ
_Go&time_continue=8&v=bmYBv4Zbn2Y&feature=emb_logohttps://www
.youtube.com/watch?list=PL17VSnPfVKIjDjjK9yw6bQK4964lbJ_Go&time
_continue=8&v=bmYBv4Zbn2Y&feature=emb_logo.

188 *decreased by about 70 percent*: Raphael Bostic and Michael Johnson, "How to
Keep Community Banks Thriving," *American Banker*, January 15, 2020, https://
www.americanbanker.com/opinion/how-to-keep-community-banks-thriving.

188 *"you open up Inc."*: Hubbard, "Felecia Hatcher, Co-Founder of Code Fever and
BlackTech Week, Works To Make Startup Communities More Inclusive,"
Women Killing It, Feb. 28, 2017, https://womenkillingit.libsyn.com/ep-46
-felecia-hatcher-co-founder-of-code-fever-and-blacktech-week-works-to
-make-startup-communities-more-inclusive.

189 *"want to solve my world problems"*: Ross Baird, *The Innovation Blind Spot: Why We
Back the Wrong Ideas—and What to Do About It* (Dallas: BenBella Books, 2017), 8.

189 *sea of white men*: Janice Gassam, "Google's 2019 Diversity Report Reveals More
Progress Must Be Made," *Forbes*, April 7, 2019, https://www.forbes.com/sites
/janicegassam/2019/04/07/googles-2019-diversity-report-reveals-more-prog
ress-must-be-made/#4d28e4c83bef.

190 *so the techno-libertarian thinking goes*: see Adam Theirer, "Does 'Permissionless
Innovation' Even Mean Anything?" tech liberation, May 18, 2017, https://tech
liberation.com/2017/05/18/does-permissionless-innovation-even-mean-any
thing/.

190 *lead to women being raped and murdered*: Kate Conger, "Uber Says 3,045 Sexual
Assaults Were Reported in U.S. Rides Last Year," *New York Times*, Dec. 5, 2019,
https://www.nytimes.com/2019/12/05/technology/uber-sexual-assaults-mur
ders-deaths-safety.html.

190 *begin sending a push notification*: Cathy Bussewitz, "Uber Rolls Out Feature
Urging Riders to 'Check Your Ride,'" *Boston*, April 21, 2019, https://www.bos
ton.com/cars/car-news/2019/04/21/uber-rolls-out-feature-urging-riders-to
-check-your-ride.

190   *88.7 percent men*: Julia Carrie Wong, "Uber Diversity Report Paints Over-
       whelmingly White, Male Picture," *Guardian*, March 28, 2017, https://www
       .theguardian.com/technology/2017/mar/28/uber-diversity-report-white
       -male-women-minorities.

190   *a viral blog post*: Susan Fowler, "Reflecting on One Very Strange Year at Uber,"
       Susan Fowler, Feb 19, 2017, https://www.susanjfowler.com/blog/2017/2/19
       /reflecting-on-one-very-strange-year-at-uber.

191   *Uber is fighting it*: Catherine Shu, "Judge Rejects Uber and Postmates'
       Request for an Injunction Against California's Gig Worker Law," tech-
       crunch, Feb 10, 2020, https://techcrunch.com/2020/02/10/judge-rejects
       -uber-and-postmates-request-for-an-injunction-against-californias-gig
       -worker-law/.

191   *"tech fixes"*: Ibid., p. 160.

191   *"The New Jim Code"*: Ruha Benjamin, *Race After Technology: Abolitionist Tools for
       the New Jim Code* (Cambridge: Polity Press, 2019), 8.

191   *"people like to think of algorithms as outside"*: The Open Mind, "Death By Al-
       gorithm," PBS, September 10, 2016, https://www.pbs.org/video/open-mind
       -death-algorithm/, and see Cathy O'Neil, *Weapons of Math Destruction: How
       Big Data Increases Inequality and Threatens Democracy* (New York: Broadway
       Books, 2017).

191   *Each of the four tech giants*: Jamie Condliffe, "This Week In Tech: Algorithmic
       Bias Is Bad. Uncovering It Is Good," *New York Times*, November 15, 2019,
       https://www.nytimes.com/2019/11/15/technology/algorithmic-ai-bias.html,
       and Joy Buolamwini, "Artificial Intelligence Has a Problem With Gender
       and Racial Bias. Here's How to Solve It," *TIME*, Feb. 7, 2019, https://time
       .com/5520558/artificial-intelligence-racial-gender-bias/.

192   *discriminatory by age and gender*: Marie C. Baca, "Housing Companies Used
       Facebooks Ad System to Discriminate Against Older People, According to
       New Human Right Charges," *Washington Post*, Sept. 18, 2019, https://www
       .washingtonpost.com/technology/2019/09/18/housing-companies-used
       -facebooks-ad-system-discriminate-against-older-people-according-new
       -human-rights-charges/; Ava Kofman and Ariana Tobin, "Facebook Ads Can
       Still Discriminate Against Women and Older Workers, Despite a Civil Rights
       Settlement," ProPublica, Dec. 13, 2019, https://www.propublica.org/article
       /facebook-ads-can-still-discriminate-against-women-and-older-workers-de
       spite-a-civil-rights-settlement.

192   *"from policing"*: Benjamin, *Race After Technology*, p. 81.

192   *"the allure of accuracy"*: Ibid., pp. 82–83.

192   *"and the potential"*: About Queer in AI," Queer in AI, https://sites.google.com
       /view/queer-in-ai/about.

HOW TO STOP MONOPOLIES

Eight: How to Take Back Control

198   *the solution isn't antitrust, it's blockchain*: Don Tapscott, "We're Living in an Era of
      Digital Feudalism. Here's How to Take Your Data and Identity Back," Quartz,
      Sept. 11, 2019, https://qz.com/1706221/don-tapscott-on-using-blockchain-to
      -take-back-your-digital-identity/.

198   *cutting off competitors under the guise of protecting privacy*: House of Commons
      Digital, Culture, Media and Sport Committee, UK Parliament, "Disinforma-
      tion and 'Fake News': Final Report," Feb. 14, 2019, https://publications.parlia
      ment.uk/pa/cm201719/cmselect/cmcumeds/1791/1791.pdf.

199   *The gutting of anti-monopoly policy*: Sam Peltzman, "Industrial Concentration
      under the Rule of Reason," *Journal of Law & Economics* 57 (2014), S101–S120
      (increase in concentration in manufacturing); "Corporation Concentration: The
      Creep of Consolidation Across America's Corporate Landscape," https://www
      .economist.com/blogs/graphicdetail/2016/03/daily-chart-13, March 24, 2016.

199   *cartoon shows Standard Oil as an octopus*: Keppler, Udo, J. *Puck* (N.Y. J. Ottmann
      Lith. Co., Puck Bldg, September 7, 1904), Library of Congress, https://www.loc
      .gov/pictures/item/2001695241

200   *The 1889* Bosses of the Senate *cartoon*: Keppler, Udo, J. *Puck* (N.Y. J. Ottmann
      Lith. Co., Puck Bldg, 1889), Library of Congress, https://www.loc.gov/pictures/re
      source/cph.3b52004/.

201   *"The little boy [Common People] and the big boys [Trusts] prepare for the baseball sea-
      son"*: Opper, Frederick, 1901, Library of Congress, https://www.loc.gov/pictures
      /item/2005685051/.

202   *"The tournament of today—a set-to between labor and monopoly"*: Graetz, F. (N.Y. J.
      Ottmann Lith. Co., Puck Bldg, August, 1883), Library of Congress, https://www
      .loc.gov/pictures/item/2012645501/.

202   *"Our Uncrowned Kings"*: Ehrhard, Samuel D. (N.Y. J. Ottmann Lith. Co., Puck
      Bldg, September 7, 1904), Library of Congress, https://www.loc.gov/pictures
      /item/2011645513/.

205   *"politically-engaged trade associations"*: "Trade Associations and Membership
      Organizations," Google, https://services.google.com/fh/files/misc/trade_as
      sociation_and_third_party_groups.pdf; "Transparency," Google, https://www
      .google.com/publicpolicy/transparency/.

205   *"employed a Republican opposition-research firm"*: Sheera Frenkel, Nicholas Con-
      fessore, Cecilia Kang, Matthew Rosenberg, and Jack Nicas, "Delay, Deny and
      Deflect: How Facebook's Leaders Fought Through Crisis," *New York Times*,
      November 14, 2018, https://www.nytimes.com/2018/11/14/technology/face
      book-data-russia-election-racism.html.

206   *current understandings of corporate law*: See, e.g., Andrea M. Matwyshyn, "Imag-
      ining the Intangible," *Delaware Journal of Corporate Law* 34, no. 3 (2009), avail-
      able at https://ssrn.com/abstract=1503091.

207   *"I haven't heard from either"*: Nicholas Thompson, "Tim Wu Explains Why He
      Thinks Facebook Should Be Broken Up," *Wired,* July 4, 2019, https://www
      .wired.com/story/tim-wu-explains-why-facebook-broken-up/.

207   *"About 30%"*: Robert Reich, "American Firms Aren't Beholden to America—but
      That's News to Trump," *Guardian,* Jan. 11, 2020, https://www.theguardian.com
      /commentisfree/2020/jan/11/us-china-trump-agreement-tesla-investment.

208   *more than $9 billion*: Charles Riley and Ivana Kottasová, "Europe Hits Google
      with a Third, $1.7 Billion Antitrust Fine," CNN, March 3, 2019, https://www
      .cnn.com/2019/03/20/tech/google-eu-antitrust/index.html.

210   *filed sixty-two Sherman*: U.S. Department of Justice, "Antitrust Division
      Workload Statistics, FY 2008–2017," justice.gov, https://www.justice.gov/atr
      /file/788426/download; U.S. Department of Justice, "Antitrust Division Work-
      load Statistics, FY 1970–1979," justice.gov, 2015, https://www.justice.gov/atr
      /antitrust-division-workload-statistics-fy-1970-1979.

211   *"that contravene the spirit of the antitrust laws"*: Federal Trade Commission, "State-
      ment of Enforcement Principles Regarding 'Unfair Methods of Competition'
      Under Section 5 of the FTC Act," August 13, 2015, https://www.ftc.gov/system
      /files/documents/public_statements/735201/150813section5enforcement.pdf.

211   *fix bad court decisions*: see, e.g., *Brooke Group Ltd. v. Brown & Williamson To-
      bacco Corp.*, 509 U.S. 209 (1993); *Matsushita Electric Industrial Co. v. Zenith
      Radio Corp.*, 475 U.S. 574 (1986); *Weyerhaeuser Co. v. Ross-Simmons Hardwood
      Lumber Co.*, 549 U.S. 312 (2007); *Verizon Communications Inc. v. Law Offices of
      Curtis V. Trinko, LLP,* 540 U.S. 398 (2004); *Pacific Bell Telephone Co. v. LinkLine
      Communications, Inc.*, 555 U.S. 438 (2009); *Ohio v. American Express Co.*, 138 S.
      Ct. 2274 (2018); *Spectrum Sports, Inc. v. McQuillan*, 506 U.S. 447, 459 (1993);
      Associated Gen. Contractors v. California State Council of Carpenters, 459 U.S. 519
      (1983); *Comcast v. Behrend*, 569 U.S. 27 (2013); *Bell Atlantic Corp. v. Twombly*,
      550 U.S. 544 (2007).

212   *the FTC spent nearly $16 million*: "Oversight of the Enforcement of the Antitrust
      Laws: Before the Subcomm. on Antitrust, Competition Policy and Consumer
      Rights of the S. Comm. on the Judiciary, 116th Cong.," FTC, 2019, https://www
      .ftc.gov/system/files/documents/public_statements/1544480/senate_septem
      ber_competition_oversight_testimony.pdf. See also Bureau of Economics, "Fed.
      Trade Comm'n," FTC, last visited April 14, 2020, https://www.ftc.gov/about-ftc
      /bureaus-offices/bureau-economics. Note, the FTC does also enforce consumer
      protection law so some of these fees may not have been antitrust-related.

213   *prohibit platforms*: Elizabeth Warren, "It's Time to Break Up Amazon, Google,

and Facebook," Medium, March 8, 2019, https://medium.com/@teamwarren
/heres-how-we-can-break-up-big-tech-9ad9e0da324c; Lina Khan, "The Separation of Platforms and Commerce," *Columbia Law Review* 119, no. 973 (May
28, 2019), SSRN, https://ssrn.com/abstract=3180174.

213 *this structural solution has been done before*: Ibid.

214 *"it was the right decision to make"*: Sally Hubbard, "Serial Entrepreneur Jillian
Wright Lifts Up Other Women Entrepreneurs with the Indie Beauty Expo,"
Women Killing It, December 20, 2017, https://womenkillingit.libsyn.com
/ep-84-serial-entrepreneur-jillian-wright-lifts-up-other-women-entrepre
neurs-with-the-indie-beauty-expo.

214 *Facebook had identified WhatsApp*: "Note by Damian Collins, MP," UK Parliament, https://www.parliament.uk/documents/commons-committees/culture
-media-and-sport/Note-by-Chair-and-selected-documents-ordered-from
-Six4Three.pdf.

215 *drive up prices anywhere from 15 to 50 percent*: Bruce A. Blonigen and Justin R.
Pierce, "Mergers May Be Profitable, but Are They Good for the Economy?"
Harvard Business Review, Nov. 15, 2016, https://hbr.org/2016/11/mergers
-may-be-profitable-but-are-they-good-for-the-economy.

215 *that vertical mergers invariably promote*: Steven C. Salop, "Invigorating Vertical
Merger Enforcement," *Yale Law Journal 1962-1994* 127 (2018), https://schol
arship.law.georgetown.edu/facpub/2002

215 *"is likely to result in reduced"*: U.S. v. Google and ITA, Case 1:11-cv-00688, justice
.gov, https://www.justice.gov/atr/case-document/file/497686/download.

216 *Senator Amy Klobuchar has proposed a bill*: News release, "In Effort to Lower
Costs for Consumers, Help Even Playing Field for Business, and Encourage
Innovation—Klobuchar, Senators Introduce Legislation to Promote Competition," September 14, 2017, https://www.klobuchar.senate.gov/public/index
.cfm/2017/9/in-effort-to-lower-costs-for-consumers-help-even-playing-field
-for-business-and-encourage-innovation-klobuchar-senators-introduce-legis
lation-to-promote-competition.

216 *a major course correction is needed*: Robert H. Lande and Sandeep Vaheesan,
"Preventing the Curse of Bigness Through Conglomerate Merger Legislation," SSRN, Oct. 4, 2019, https://papers.ssrn.com/sol3/papers.cfm?abstract
_id=3463878; Sandeep Vaheesan, "Two-and-a-Half Cheers for 1960s Merger
Policy," *Harvard Law*, Dec. 12, 2019, https://orgs.law.harvard.edu/antitrust
/2019/12/12/two-and-a-half-cheers-for-1960s-merger-policy/; "1968 Merger
Guidelines." Justice.gov, https://www.justice.gov/archives/atr/1968-merger
-guidelines.

217 *"attention shares"*: Media Subcommittee, Digital Platforms Project, "How to
Protect the News Media in the Age of Digital Platforms," Pro Market, May

10, 2019, https://promarket.org/how-to-protect-the-news-media-in-the-age -of-digital-platforms/.

217   *$330 million on federal lobbying since 2008*: Frank Bass, "As U.S. Regulators Step Up Antitrust Scrutiny, Big Tech Has Increased Lobbying Bandwidth," MapLight, Sept. 5, 2019, https://maplight.org/story/as-u-s-regulators-step -up-antitrust-scrutiny-big-tech-has-increased-lobbying-bandwidth/.

218   *99 percent of the global market*: Kate Sprague, "Why the Airbus-Boeing Duopoly Dominate 99% of the Large Plane Market," CNBC, Jan. 26, 2019, https:// www.cnbc.com/2019/01/25/why-the-airbus-boeing-companies-dominate -99percent-of-the-large-plane-market.html.

218   *$285 million in lobbying since 1998*: "Top Spenders," OpenSecrets, https://www .opensecrets.org/federal-lobbying/top-spenders?cycle=a.

218   *Boeing used its political*: Kathryn A. Wolfe and Brianna Gurciullo, "How the FAA Delegated Oversight to Boeing," *Politico*, March 21, 2019, https://www .politico.com/story/2019/03/21/congress-faa-boeing-oversight-1287902.

218   *Boeing spent more than*: Philip van Doorn, "Opinion: Airlines and Boeing Want a Bailout—but Look How Much They've Spent on Stock Buybacks," *Market Watch*, March 22, 2020, https://www.marketwatch.com/story/airlines -and-boeing-want-a-bailout-but-look-how-much-theyve-spent-on-stock -buybacks-2020-03-18; Aaron Gregg, Jeff Stein, and Josh Dawsey, "Senate Aid Package Quietly Carves Out Billions Intended for Boeing, Officials Say," *Washington Post*, March 25, 2020, https://www.washingtonpost.com/business /2020/03/25/boeing-bailout-coronavirus/.

219   *"technological tools"*: News release, "A Letter from Alastair Mactaggart, Board Chair and Founder of Californians for Consumer Privacy," Californians for Consumer Privacy, September 25, 2019, https://www.caprivacy.org/a-letter-from-alastair -mactaggart-board-chair-and-founder-of-californians-for-consumer-privacy/.

219   *opting out takes seventeen clicks*: "Privolta Consent Study: Google," August 16, 2019, https://www.youtube.com/watch?v=y3xibDW-pVw.

219   *Forty percent of people abandon*: Neil Patel, "How Loading Time Affects Your Bottom Line," https://neilpatel.com/blog/loading-time/.

220   *"Data protection"*: Chris Wylie, "Written Statement to the United States Senate Committee on the Judiciary In the Matter of Cambridge Analytica and Other Related Issues," para. 67, https://www.judiciary.senate.gov/imo/media/doc/05 -16-18%20Wylie%20Testimony.pdf.

220   *"the U.S. can"*: David Dayen, "Ban Targeted Advertising," *New Republic*, April 10, 2018, https://newrepublic.com/article/147887/ban-targeted-advertising -facebook-google; see also Gilad Edelman, "Why Don't We Just Ban Targeted Advertising?" *Wired*, March 22, 2018, https://www.wired.com/story/why -dont-we-just-ban-targeted-advertising/; Ellen L. Weintraub, "Don't Abolish

Political Ads on Social Media. Stop Microtargeting," *Washington Post*, Nov. 1, 2019, https://www.washingtonpost.com/opinions/2019/11/01/dont-abolish -political-ads-social-media-stop-microtargeting/.

220 *"Yes, I give permission":* Written Testimony of David Heinemeier Hansson CTO & Cofounder, Basecamp," justice.gov, Jan. 17, 2020, https://docs.house.gov /meetings/JU/JU05/20200117/110386/HHRG-116-JU05-Wstate-Hansson D-20200117.pdf.

221 *"Anything made":* Shoshana Zuboff, "You Are Now Remotely Controlled," *New York Times*, Jan. 24, 2020, https://www.nytimes.com/2020/01/24/opinion/sun day/surveillance-capitalism.html.

222 *required nondiscrimination policies:* Open Markets Institute Discussion Paper, "America's Free Press and Monopoly: The Historical Role of Competition Policy in Protecting Independent Journalism in America," June 2018, https:// openmarketsinstitute.org/reports/americas-free-press-monopoly/.

223 *tech companies:* Oral testimony of Tristan Harris, House Committee on Energy and Commerce, Hearing on "Americans At Risk: Manipulation and Deception in the Digital Age," January 8, 2020, https://energycommerce.house.gov /committee-activity/hearings/hearing-on-americans-at-risk-manipulation -and-deception-in-the-digital.

223 *for a wide range of illegal behavior:* "Artist Rights Alliance Opposes Exporting Safe Harbors in Trade Deals," Medium, Oct. 29, 2019, https://medium .com/@artistrightsnow/artist-rights-alliance-opposes-exporting-safe-harbors -in-trade-deals-befc5fa3976d.

INDEX

Page numbers beginning with 231 refer to notes. Page numbers in *italics* refer to graphs and drawings.

ABOUT THE AUTHOR

SALLY HUBBARD is an antitrust expert and director of enforcement strategy at the Open Markets Institute, an organization developing solutions to America's monopoly crisis. She has served as an assistant attorney general in the Antitrust Bureau of the Office of the New York State Attorney General, and was previously an investigative journalist covering mergers, monopolies, and privacy. She has testified as a competition expert before the U.S. Senate, House of Representatives, and Federal Trade Commission. She appears and is cited regularly in a wide range of media, including the *New York Times*, CNN, BBC *World News*, *Vanity Fair*, *Washington Post*, *The Atlantic*, and *Wired*, and hosts the podcast *Women Killing It!* Hubbard lives in Brooklyn with her husband and two children.

F
Cad

44328

Cadell

Return match

JUN 14 '79	DATE DUE	
JUL 5 '79	NOV 2 6 '79	
JUL 2 6 '79	DEC 2 0 '79	
AUG 6 1979	FEB 1 4 '80	
AUG 1 6 1979	FEB 2 8 '80	
AUG 2 3 1979	MAY 1 '80	
SEP 6 '79	JUN 5 '80	
SEP 2 0 '79	AUG 1 4 '80	
OCT 4 '79	DEC 4 - '80	
OCT 1 8 '79	FEB 2 6 1981	
NOV 1 5 '79	JUN 1 8 1981	

RETURN
MATCH

By the same author

THE ROUND DOZEN
PARSON'S HOUSE
GAME IN DIAMONDS
THE FLEDGLING
DECK WITH FLOWERS
ROYAL SUMMONS
HOME FOR THE WEDDING
THE PAST TENSE OF LOVE
THE GOLDEN COLLAR
MRS. WESTERBY CHANGES COURSE
THE CORNER SHOP
THE FOX FROM HIS LAIR
CANARY YELLOW
COME BE MY GUEST
THE TOY SWORD
HONEY FOR TEA
SIX IMPOSSIBLE THINGS
THE YELLOW BRICK ROAD
SHADOWS ON THE WATER
I LOVE A LASS
THE LARK SHALL SING
MONEY TO BURN
THE CUCKOO IN SPRING
AROUND THE RUGGED ROCK
ENTER MRS. BELCHAMBER
SUN IN THE MORNING
IRIS IN WINTER
LAST STRAW FOR HARRIET

RETURN

MATCH

by

ELIZABETH CADELL

WILLIAM MORROW AND COMPANY, INC.

NEW YORK   1979

Library of Congress Cataloging in Publication Data

Cadell, Elizabeth.
  Return match.

  I. Title.
PZ3.C11427Re [PR6005.A225]   823'.9'12   78-27084
ISBN 0-688-03473-X

BOOK DESIGN   CARL WEISS

Printed in the United States of America.

First Edition

1   2   3   4   5   6   7   8   9   10

To my nephew,

Tony Coates,

with love

and thanks

CHAPTER

1

MRS. PRESSLEY ENTERED HER LIVING ROOM, WALKED TO THE glass-enclosed porch that adjoined it and, opening the front door, let in her two cats and a shaft of late spring sunshine. For some moments, she stood looking out at the new day. Her plum tree was in blossom; bluebells and daffodils were springing up where she could not remember having planted them. A privet hedge screened the garden from the narrow, tree-lined road, but through the low wrought-iron gateway in its center, she could see green fields and a glimpse of a slowly moving river. She gave a contented sigh.

"Lovely," she said.

It had been her daily salute to the scene for the past four months. How lucky—the thought was seldom far from her mind—how very lucky she was to have found this comfortable, inexpensive cottage set in a pretty garden in a pleasant English village.

The luck lay not in her circumstances but in her temperament, which disposed her to see blessings where most people saw drawbacks. The village, by name Longbrook, had long ago become a town and the town was being steadily sucked into the tentacles of Outer London. The cottage—two cottages made into one by a previous tenant—was ill-planned, damp and drafty. The garden was an untidy strip separating the building from the road.

She had noted these defects when the house agent had shown her over the property, but he had pointed out that they were offset by the remarkably low figure being asked by the vendors. He had advised her to snap it up and she had done so, though there had not seemed to be any other clients clamouring to outbid her. The reason for this had only become clear after she had moved in; but even this revelation, shattering though it had been, had not for long made her regret her decision to buy. One could, she reasoned, get used to anything.

She turned back to her living room. It was furnished with the large, upholstered chairs and sofa brought from her previous, far more spacious home, so that there was a general effect of overcrowding, but by using soft shades of green for covers and curtains, and painting all the woodwork white, she had achieved a kind of country charm and comfort.

She switched on the electric fire and went into the awkwardly shaped kitchen—made by removing the staircase of one of the cottages—to prepare coffee for herself and food for the cats. She carried their plates out to the porch and then, seating herself at the small gateleg table on which she had her meals, drank her coffee and listened idly to the song of the birds, the occasional sound of traffic passing along the road and the scraping of enamel plates on the stone floor of the porch as the cats licked up the last of their breakfast.

The gate opened with its usual shrill plea for oil. The milkman, grey-haired and portly, walked up the narrow path carrying a container full of dairy produce, and looked in at the door.

"Morning, love," he greeted her. "The usual?"

"Good morning, Mr. Gunter. No, not the usual. I want—"

"Thought so. That's why I come in, to ask. You'll be wanting extra from now on."

"Yes. If you'll leave two brown loaves and three—no, four pints of milk every day . . . Or perhaps three would do."

"Not for 'im, it wouldn't," Mr. Gunter said with confidence. "Not unless 'e's changed a lot. 'E used to get through quarts when 'e was 'ome last time. I'll make it four pints, and if there's any change you can leave a note in the bottles when you put 'em out. 'Ow about eggs?"

"I'd better take a dozen."

"Make it two dozen. You'll have forgotten 'ow much a grown man can get through. Cream?"

"No, no cream, Mr. Gunter. Everybody's so weight-conscious these days."

"I wouldn't cut down on 'is cream if I was you, love," Mr. Gunter advised. "I'll leave 'arf a pint. 'E'll be looking forward to some nice English cream after being in the jungle so long."

"Not the jungle, Mr. Gunter. He—"

"Well, jungle or not, 'e 'asn't been getting any milk from English cows, 'as 'e now? I daresay Brazil's got a lot of cows, but they won't 'ave been grazing on pastures like I've got up on my farm, will they?"

Mrs. Pressley said that she supposed not. It was not wise to argue with Mr. Gunter. He had a long and busy round, but he was always prepared to devote twenty minutes or more to filling in the gaps in his customers' knowledge on any one of a wide variety of subjects. To Mrs. Pressley's relief, he now showed signs of departing. He paused to ask a question.

" 'Ow is 'e?"

"He's fine, thank you."

"Been a long time since 'e was 'ome."

"Yes. Over three years."

"More like four. I don't suppose 'e'll be stopping 'ere all the time 'e's in England?"

"No, I shouldn't think so."

"I shouldn't think so, neither. 'E'll be off looking for all them girls 'e left behind. 'E needn't trouble 'imself; they'll soon be round after 'im. 'E ought to be a family man by now. What is 'e—thirty? Thirty-one?

"Thirty-one."

"And still single. Well, 'e won't be for long. One of them women'll get 'im." He took a step and then stopped. "Oh, nearly forgot. I've got the promise of some 'oney from Greaves upon the 'ill. 'Ow about me leaving a couple of pots tomorrow?"

"Well, I don't think—"

"I'd better leave 'em, just in case. You forgot butter. You'll need butter, won't you? I'll leave a pound to start off with."

He went away, leaving her conscious of the fact that she had once more been the victim of a stronger personality. It wasn't only Mr. Gunter, she admitted to herself; she had all her life tried and failed to make herself what her son called felt. Her husband, whose guidance after more than twenty years of widowhood she still missed, had said that she was born to be bullied, and perhaps it was true.

She finished her coffee and carried the tray to the kitchen. There were no sounds from her son's room; she concluded that he was still asleep, and thought it no wonder, considering the time he had gone to bed.

She opened the door of the refrigerator and took out the untouched food she had put in the night before. She had—very foolishly, she now thought—prepared a celebration dinner for two, but he had not arrived in time to eat it. While waiting for him, she had done her best to prevent the dishes from spoiling, but he had telephoned at half past ten from the airport to say that he had been held up and would not be home before midnight. She was not, he said, to wait up for him; he would not want anything to eat, and if he wanted a drink, he would look in the Chinese cupboard, which was where he supposed she still kept it. He was sorry not to have shown up earlier, he was longing to see her, it was nice to be in England again, and he must ring off because there was a long queue waiting for the phone.

She inspected the untasted dishes. The fish could be used for lunch in a salad. The steak, which she had intended to grill, would do for tonight's dinner. The sauce, the prepared soufflé, she would get rid of before Rona came home. She wouldn't like Rona to know that the celebration had not taken place.

Her chief feeling last night, when she had replaced the receiver after her son's telephone call, had been relief that her goddaughter was in London for the night. She had gone, Mrs. Pressley realized, with the object of leaving her alone with Nigel on his first night home. She would be back today and she would of course ask how the dinner went. Well, a lot of it was going into the garbage can.

There were sounds from above. A few minutes later, the door from the hall opened and her son, pajama-clad, appeared. He paused in the doorway to give a long, prolonged yawn.

"Morning, Mother."

"Hello, Nigel. I didn't think you'd be down so early."

He stretched, yawned again and bent to kiss her cheek.

"Old Gunter's chitchat woke me," he explained. "No, nothing to eat, thanks; just coffee."

"Did you bring some from Brazil?"

"Yes." He drew a stool forward and sat down. "I'm sorry about turning up so late last night."

"So you said—last night. That's about all you did say. Now you can start on all your news."

"Your news first. You've got some explaining to do, haven't you?" he asked her.

"Explaining?"

"That's right. Don't try to dodge, and don't put on that innocent air and don't look round for some sand to bury your head in. Just explain."

For some moments, she stood studying him. She was not a

tall woman, but her slenderness seemed to give her height. Her voice was quiet, and she spoke rather slowly. She was fifty-four, but her face was scarcely lined and her hair untouched by grey. She seemed to him to have changed little since their last meeting. She could not say the same of him: he looked taller, leaner, darker than she remembered. The image, she thought with pride, of his upstanding, handsome father. She thought it extraordinary that although he had been no more than eight or nine when his father died, he had many of his gestures, mannerisms, even his way of speaking. But he had not inherited his father's even temper; he was less patient, more critical, and like most of the young people she met, seemed to her to have a self-confidence bordering on the cynical.

"Go on—start talking," he prompted.

"I suppose you want to know why I bought this cottage?"

"I want to know why, when I sent you money to convert a well-built house into two flats—one for yourself, the other for letting at an exorbitant rent—you decided to sell it and transfer yourself to this two-into-one ruin."

"Oh, Nigel, it's a dear little—"

"—ruin. The staircase is about to collapse. The floors upstairs are about to give way—I thought my foot would go through at any moment. The windows don't fit the frames. There's damp in my room and—"

"I know you would have preferred the other idea, Nigel. I actually had the plans made; I wrote and told you. But when it came to the point, I couldn't bear the thought of living with other people so close. They would have had to use the same entrance hall, they would have left their cars in the drive outside my windows, they would have had to share the garden. I've got used to living without anybody round me, and I like it. I saw this cottage and I knew I could be happy here. When the house agent told me the price, I couldn't believe it was so cheap. I know it's rather near the road, but the road's just a nice country lane, and very little traffic goes by, so the cats won't get run over. There's the river just across the road, and those nice market gardens on one side, and all that open ground at the back, so it's almost like being in the country, and—"

"How many people live in that cottage next door?"

There was a brief pause before she answered.

"Only one," she said, and was relieved to find that he had not noticed her hesitation. It was the truth, she reassured herself. Not the whole truth, but true all the same.

"Did you take a good look round this place—inside—before closing the deal?" he asked.

She said that she had, but she knew that what she had closed had been her eyes, having decided that the ground floor would make a compact, self-contained home for herself, while the upper storey could be left for her son and her goddaughter whenever they came on visits. It was of course unfortunate that there was no proper entrance; the garden path led to the porch and the porch opened into the living room. And it was a pity that the living room had three doors, but they were all necessary: one opened to the porch, one to the kitchen, and the third to a confined space which she called the hall but which was no more than a small area round the foot of the stairs. Beyond this space were the small bedroom and bathroom she had appropriated for herself. Upstairs were three larger bedrooms and a second bathroom.

"Did Dagmar see it before you bought it?" Nigel asked.

"No. She was in London."

"Pity. She would have talked some sense into you." He shivered. "It's so damned cold—how can you stand it?"

"I don't go about in pajamas on a chilly morning, for one thing."

"How do you warm this kitchen?"

"I put the oven on and leave the door open."

"My God. I guessed there was something wrong when you

wrote me that description of the place: three pages about its advantages and not one line about snags. But if you like it, you like it."

"I like it very much. I've only been here four months, but it feels like home. I'm sorry you're disappointed, but I can honestly be very happy here."

This he believed. Her capacity for contentment had never ceased to surprise him. On his father's death, she had been left with a large house but a meager income. She had no skills, no training that would have enabled her to earn money, but she had the ability to make a little money go a very long way. She had sold the house, bought one in a cheaper district, and for years—until his father's brother came home from the Argentine, learned the state of affairs and came to their rescue —had managed to support herself—and him. He had a clear memory of those years, and he could not remember any shadows. He could recall austerities and economies, but none that had hurt. And then his uncle had arrived, had paid his school fees, given him a handsome allowance and on his death left him a considerable sum of money. The lean years were over.

"If you're happy," he told his mother, "I suppose that's all that matters. But there's not much point in sending you money if you won't use it. I sent you your fare to Brazil."

"I would have loved the trip, Nigel, but somehow I'd got involved with selling the other house and buying this one, and one way and another . . . But thanks all the same. Next time . . ."

He poured himself a cup of coffee, carried it into the living room and sank into one of the deep chairs.

"There won't be a next time," he said. "Not in Brazil."

She stood looking down at him with a frown.

"Aren't you going back?" she asked.

"No. They offered me the London office and I accepted."

"Oh, Nigel—you'll be in England!"

"For the next four years. After that, we'll see."

"But won't you miss Brazil? You liked living there."

"The London job's going to be interesting. I'm going to try and get the rooms I had before I went abroad."

She did not suggest commuting. He had joined a Brazilian textile firm when he was twenty-three and for the first few months had worked in the London office, but although he could have driven in and out daily, and although the trains were frequent, he had elected to live in rooms near Sloane Square. Some of his weekends had been spent at home, but the majority were passed in the homes of his numerous friends.

Sipping his coffee, he looked round the living room, noting the familiar objects which made up his mother's life: the sewing machine, the large workbasket on wheels, the desk, the rows of bookshelves, the easel on which stood her latest effort in oils. He had long ago accepted the fact that—with the sole exceptions of himself and her goddaughter—these made the frame within which all her interests lay. She had no intellectual bent. She had a certain civic sense, but was too shy and too self-effacing to sit on any of the town's major committees. She had one close friend and a few others she visited or invited to the house occasionally, but she had almost no interests outside the home. Within it, she pursued a leisurely routine, quiet, contented, never unoccupied.

"I suppose," he heard her say, "you think it's pokey?"

"It couldn't be called spacious, could it?"

"Perhaps not. But it's an easy house to run. That nice little kitchen, this room, the porch that gets the sun most of the day —and a bedroom and bathroom just the other side of the staircase. What more could I want?"

"Central heating. Room to move around. A few more items of modern equipment in the kitchen. A gardener to do something about that wilderness out there."

"I've got one. I couldn't find one when I first moved here, but last month I heard that one of Mrs. Montallen's old gardeners had decided to come out of retirement, and he's arranged to give me two hours twice a week." She hesitated. "I wrote and told you she died, didn't I?"

"Yes, you did. Which reminds me: I ran into her grand-daughter at the airport last night."

For some moments she was too surprised to speak. She walked to the sofa and sat down, staring at him.

"Maria Montallen? You—you saw her?"

"Yes. She'd just flown in from Zurich or Munich, I've forgotten which."

"But . . . you don't know her. You weren't in England when—"

"She knew one of the fellows I was with, and came over to speak to him. When she heard my name, she told me who she was."

"Did she—what did she call herself?"

"Montallen."

"I suppose you know she left Roger Underwood?"

"Yes. But I didn't hear it from you. That's something you didn't mention in your letters."

"I didn't want to be reminded of—of all that business."

"You didn't expect that marriage to last, did you?"

"Yes, I did."

"That's your incurable optimism. Maria Montallen filched him because he was the only man available at the time. I can't understand why nobody guessed what was going on."

"Do we have to talk about it?"

With her hands gripped tightly together on her lap, she realized that what she did not want to do was think about it. She had never been able to forget completely. She had never understood it, she would never understand it. But it was over.

"Is she staying in England?" she asked.

"No. She was meeting someone—some Austrian fellow— and they were going on to New York. Incidentally, there was someone else you know at the airport: Francis Latimer. He wasn't travelling; he was meeting someone. He filled in time by asking me to introduce him to Maria Montallen. I didn't realize they'd never met."

"He was in America when it—when she was here. Did she mention Roger?"

"Only to say that she left him two years ago and had no idea where he was, and didn't care." He got up and went to the kitchen for more coffee. "It was a pity," he said on his return, "that Rona brought him down here after they became engaged. She'd seen Maria Montallen. I would have said any woman in her senses would have backed away from competition of that kind."

"I'd rather you didn't say anything to Rona about your having seen her."

He looked at her speculatively.

"Why not? Forbidden topic?"

"I don't refer to it if I can avoid it, that's all."

"I see. Incidentally, how is Rona?"

Slow, unaccustomed anger at his casual tone rose in her.

"Incidentally, she's fine. Thank you for asking."

She heard the sharpness in her voice, and struggled for control. It had never been any use expecting him to see Rona through her eyes. She spoke in a quieter tone.

"I did tell you, didn't I, that she gave up her London job two months ago?"

"Yes. How does she like being back in Longbrook?"

"She's only going to be here for a year. I think she's enjoying herself."

"Why did you hand your car over to her?"

"Because I didn't need it. I never enjoyed driving, as you know, and it was silly to keep a car now that I can walk to the shops. And I'm near a bus stop, so old Mrs. Coles can still come twice a week to do some cleaning."

"What's Rona's job?"

"The same lawyers—the ones who gave her her first job. But now she's secretary to Bryan Hayling."

"Hayling, Harvard and Todd?"

"Yes."

"They used to be known as Wynken, Blynken and Nod."

"I know. But they're waking up. Mr. Harvard and Mr. Todd are both dead. Old Mr. Hayling retired last month. He and his wife have gone to live in—or is it on?—the Isle of Wight."

"Rona'll miss London, won't she?"

"I don't think so. She said almost four years of it was enough. And she seems to have a lot of friends here."

"Men?"

"Most of them, yes."

"Serious?"

"I don't know."

"Any hangover from the Underwood affair?"

"No." She repeated the word more firmly. "No."

"I just wondered. She's twenty-four; it's time she settled." He went into the kitchen and came back with a third cup of coffee. "But it's her life," he said, settling himself in his chair. "It's nothing to do with you or with me."

"Isn't it?" Once more, anger sounded in her voice. "Isn't it? Haven't we—you and I—anything to do with trying to make sure she doesn't make another mistake?"

He raised his eyebrows.

"I'd hardly call Roger a mistake. She decided to marry him and he skipped with Maria Montallen. That wasn't a mistake. That was misfortune. Or mismanagement."

"You never once said—wrote—that you were sorry about what happened."

"How could I? I wasn't sorry. I was relieved. I quite liked Roger—didn't we all?—but I never saw him as a steady."

"You could have shown some interest in what was happening to her. But that's something you've never done."

"Well, my God!" He sounded outraged. "All those years of helping her with her ruddy lessons, and putting her on her school train and taking her off it again at the end of term and putting up with her school chums and their pop records and their girlish giggles! That's probably what drove me to Brazil. Interest? She was round my neck for years and I hardly ever complained."

"You hardly ever did anything else. But you needn't worry; nobody's going to ask you to do anything now."

"If she decides to get married, I'll come down from London for the wedding and I'll give her away."

She said nothing. She had for years cherished a hope of seeing him at Rona's wedding—but not to give Rona away. Incurable optimism was right.

Perhaps, she thought, putting cups and saucers into the dishwasher, there had been some reason for her attitude. She had been a close friend of Rona's parents, a doctor and his wife living in Dover. She had been Rona's godmother; later, she had agreed to become her guardian. When Dr. and Mrs. Hume died, within a month of one another, there had been no relations able or willing to undertake the care of the ten-year-old Rosanna—so she had come to live at Longbrook with her godmother and Nigel. He was seventeen, and from the beginning she had grated on his nerves. She had been, at first, awkward and aggressive. At twelve she was boisterous, at fourteen given to giggling, at fifteen withdrawn and dreamy.

When he left to work in London, she had been sixteen and away at school. They had met on his return from Brazil—she had been nineteen, and already becoming a beauty, but he had too many women friends to occupy his attention; he had barely noticed her. When his next leave came, he had used it to tour the European offices and factories of his firm. He had visited Longbrook briefly before returning to Brazil, but she had been staying with friends in Scotland, and he had not seen her. When he left, she had become engaged to a man they had all known from his boyhood, a man they had imagined they knew well: Roger Underwood.

Nigel's voice brought her back to the present.

"How's the hot water supply?" he asked.

"It's all right if people don't have baths too soon after one another. I like my shower at seven and Rona likes hers at half past. After that, it's all yours."

He paused at the foot of the stairs.

"What's she like now?" he asked. "Still overweight?"

She gazed at him, wondering uneasily if she could be the type of mother who remained obstinately blind to her children's shortcomings.

"Rona? Overweight?" she said at last. "Rona was never overweight."

"Well, call it puppy fat if you like. She certainly went through a stage of avoir too many pois. So now what? Slender and willowy?"

"She's—" She made an impatient sound. "Oh, go and get dressed."

"I'm on my way."

"I won't be here when you come down. I'm going to see Sir James. The Charity Fund asked me to go and see if I could get some money out of him."

"You've been trying for years. He's never given them anything."

"And never will. But at the last meeting, I was deputed to go and have another try."

"Sheer waste of time. Well, I'll see you when you get back. Want me to drive you there?"

"No, thank you. Will you mind a cold lunch?"

"I'd prefer a cold lunch, today and whenever I'm here. Want me to take you shopping?"

"Not today. And not any other day, if Rona isn't working overtime. She brings home whatever we need."

"Any objection to my assembling my music-making apparatus in your living room? I've got some rather good Brazilian recordings, if you don't mind a little too much emphasis on percussion."

"There's no room in there," she objected.

"There will be, once I've disposed of some of the alien

items like the sewing machine and the workbasket. I won't touch the easel. I remember the uproar I caused once before when I suggested moving it."

"There was no uproar, and you didn't suggest moving it. You suggested doing away with it altogether. I know you don't like what I paint, but I like painting and I'm going to go on painting."

"Splendid. It's a shame to let an outstanding talent go to waste." He went to the door of the living room, put his head on one side and studied the canvas attentively. "I see a lot of improvement now that you're using the Florentine technique."

"The what?"

"Florentine technique. You know it, of course? A smooth impasto imposed on a monochrome underpainting in brown and white, with—"

"Very funny. Very, very funny. You haven't been so encouraging since I showed you my first effort and you told me I'd got to decide whether I was Monet or Grandma Moses. Go upstairs and have your shower."

Smiling, he went. She went through the porch into the garden—there was no back door—and walked round the house to the small square of ground she called the kitchen garden. Here there were a few rows of lettuces, a row of beans and some cabbages whose leaves had been worked by slugs into a lacy design. She picked lettuces and took them to the kitchen, pausing on the way to look with a mixture of apprehension and resignation at the roof of a barn next door, visible over the high fence. She hadn't said anything yet, she mused. It wasn't exactly cowardice; he was bound to find out, but there was no need to anticipate trouble.

She washed the lettuces, wrapped them in a cloth and put them into the refrigerator. She was about to go across the hall to her bedroom when she heard a car stop at the gate. The next moment she heard the gate squeak, and went into the porch to see a familiar figure hurrying along the path—a middle-aged woman, dark, with an eager, vivid face and clothes that sounded the latest note in casual elegance. She was calling as she approached, her voice high with excitement, her English fluent but foreign.

"Celia! I am back! I returned only late last night, but I came at once this morning to see Nigel. How is he? How are you? How is Rona?" She reached Celia and kissed her affectionately on both cheeks. "It's so nice to see you again. After all this time, you know, I feel like a stranger. I have been away so long, ages and ages."

"Two months," Celia corrected repressively. It was frequently necessary to damp down these conversational excesses. "It's nice to have you back. Come in, Dagmar. Did you have a good journey?"

"The sea was a little rough, but I didn't mind that. I couldn't come by air because I had so much baggage. I came by way of Paris because I had to buy new clothes: I had none, none at all, only old things out of fashion. Do you like my hair? It is the new man in Geneva, Myron Grunberg, a genius. I wish I could take you to him, he would take away that faded look your hair is beginning to have. You are not using that lotion I gave you to put on. Are you excited to have Nigel with you? Has he said that this house is not suitable for you? I have said so from the beginning. What did he say about it?"

"One thing at a time, Dagmar."

"Yes, yes, yes, you think me too excited. But to see Nigel, shall that not excite me after so long? And to see you too, naturally."

"Naturally."

"You are looking well—did Nigel say so? Celia, what dress did you wear to receive him? Not your blue?

"Yes."

"You are hopeless, hopeless, hopeless!" She sounded despairing. "You will never listen to me. Always, always the blue, so old, so unbecoming. What is the use of giving advice to you?"

"Come and give some to Nigel."

They turned towards the hall, the slender woman and the rounded one, the fair and the dark, a delicate pencil sketch and a bold crayon drawing.

Dagmar Renson was Swiss, the widow of Aubrey Renson, who before his marriage had been a shy, reserved schoolmaster living in a house he had inherited in Longbrook. They had met one long-ago summer in the Lake District, where Aubrey had been earning a little extra money by acting as courier to parties of tourists. Dagmar and her grandfather, Monsieur Chantard, had joined the last tour of the season.

She had been nineteen, plump and pretty, as she was to remain all her life. At the outset of the tour, he had an uneasy feeling that she was going to be more than he could handle; by the second day he was certain of it. She was still asleep when the bus arrived at the hotel for the scheduled morning departure. Once embarked, she was enthralled by the scenery —not so different, he would have said, from that of her native country—and disrupted the programme by pleading for halts unmarked on the itinerary, wandering away and failing to return, disregarding his lectures and bringing him bunches of wild flowers to identify. When, after sounding the horn of the bus in vain, he went to look for her, he came upon her clothes dropped in a heap by the lakeside, while an arm waved an invitation from the water.

When the tour ended, he returned to his house in Longbrook, and found that his mind remained full of his late passenger. She was spoilt, she was silly, she was probably selfish—but he loved her. She was twenty years younger than he was—but he could not live without her.

He knew nothing about her except her name and the fact that her grandfather owned a number of bookshops in Geneva. He obtained her address from the travel agency and sent her a letter in which he stated, simply and briefly, his feelings, his low financial bracket and his hopes for the future. The letter crossed a cryptic communication from her—an envelope containing a pressed edelweiss with her name, and his, entwined below it.

Their marriage in Geneva was attended by a sole Renson relation and innumerable Chantard cousins, uncles and aunts. Aubrey had by this time learned that under his bride's irrepressible spirits lay a foundation of solid Swiss business acumen. She had no domestic gifts, but she knew everything there was to know about bookshops. On her arrival in Longbrook, she had assessed shrewdly the business possibilities of the growing town, and with her *dot*, which was considerable, turned part of Aubrey's house into a bookshop. It prospered; when, in time, she inherited her grandfather's money, she enlarged the shop by buying two adjacent premises. Today, the business occupied an imposing frontage on the main street, while Dagmar and her family lived in comfort on the converted upper storey.

Accompanying the bride—to help her to settle in, it was said—came a distant cousin named Inga, and one even more distant named Claudine. After helping the bride to settle down, they settled down themselves. Plain, practical, tireless, they ran the house, cooking, washing, ironing, sewing and mending. Their English remained the smattering they had brought with them; Inga still spoke German-English and Claudine spoke French-English. In the house they spoke French or German, or both at once. Nigel, as he grew up, had during his visits acquired a working knowledge of both languages. He had sometimes wondered how Dagmar's husband had endured the loud voices and constant chatter of the cousins, but had come to the conclusion that he bore them because they solved the servant problem.

The friendship between Celia and Dagmar had begun when they came as brides to the town. They were almost the same age. Celia's son Nigel had been born in the same month as Dagmar's twin son and daughter, David and Monique. The two women, completely different in outlook and temperament, remained friends despite Dagmar's incurable habit of attempting to manage all those with whom she came in contact. Few people could endure for long her constant interfering, but Celia found her stimulating. There was more than a touch of missionary spirit in their association: Dagmar strove tirelessly to make Celia clothes-conscious, while Celia did her best to calm Dagmar's overexcitability.

She was now demanding to see Nigel.

"Where is he? That new car, that big one—it is his, no? Where is he?"

"He's having a shower."

"Then I go up."

"Just a minute, Dagmar." Celia put out a detaining hand. "Please don't say anything to him about—about next door."

Dagmar, on the bottom stair, turned in surprise.

"You didn't tell him?"

"No."

"Not when he came last night?"

"No. And not this morning."

"But that is so foolish. He must be told."

"I know. But—"

"If you are afraid, I will explain to him."

"No. Please don't say anything. He'll hear soon enough."

Dagmar gave one of her sudden, musical peals of laughter.

"Hear? Oh, yes, he will hear! How true!" She raised her voice and called up the stairs. "Nigel! I am here. It is your godmother, Dagmar. I come up. It is a long time since I see you having your bath. I come."

Nigel, draped in a towel, his hair dripping, appeared at the top of the stairs.

"No. I come," he told her.

They met halfway. Ignoring the dampness, she embraced him warmly.

"Now," she said, leading the way to the living room, "come and sit with me and your mother and tell us about all those Brazilian women that you have put into the family way. We sit here. Like you, I have only just come back from being away. I have been in Geneva, with Monique. You remember she married a Frenchman?"

"Of course I remember. Wasn't I at her wedding?"

"Oh, yes, yes, yes, so you were! Why did I forget such a thing? It was David's wedding that you missed. I went to Geneva because Monique has got a new little baby."

"How many does that make?"

"Three. All little boys."

"Congratulations."

"They are all very clever, but I do not think the new one will be as clever as the other two. It is too early to say. The one who is my favourite is little Pierre. Do you know what he said the first time he came in to see his mother after the new baby was born and she was feeding it? The natural way, of course." Her gesture sketched two full maternal breasts. "Pierre stood and looked while the baby sucked, and then he said, *'Qu'est-ce qu'il fait?'* So his mother told him that the new baby was having its breakfast. And do you know what little Pierre said, only four years old? He said: 'Why doesn't he have his breakfast off a plate, like me?' You must admit that this shows— But no more of my grandchildren. Celia, has the telephone started to ring and ring? You remember last time Nigel was here, you could never use the telephone because his friends were always telephoning to him?" She turned to Nigel. "You see how David has passed you by? Married already, and the father of a son, and in a few days the father of two sons."

"How's business?"

"The shop? It is doing well. David works very hard, but he is happy. Naturally, I advise him when it is necessary. After all, you must admit that nobody knows more about the business than I do. My grandfather used to say that I was born in a bookshop, and certainly it is in my blood. When I married, David's father knew nothing, absolutely nothing about a shop. He didn't have a business head, but that is what

I have—and David too. You will be surprised when you see him. He is not a boy any more. He is a husband and a father."

"Tell him I'll drop in this afternoon."

"You will like his wife very much. From the first, she and Rona have been friends. I will confess to you that I wished he had married a French or a German or a Swiss girl, but he chose Swedish and it is a great success. Not that she is a good housewife; nobody can say that. And with the baby, she has not of course got experience, but I have given her good advice and I will help her when the new baby comes. I hope you will be here to see it—but you will be going here, there, everywhere with your friends, as before."

"I'm going to devote my entire leave to my mother."

"This I don't believe. You have seen Rona?"

"No, he hasn't," Celia answered. "She spent the night in London. She'll be back for lunch. In fact, she ought to be back now." She rose. "And I ought to be on my way."

"Where are you going?" Dagmar asked.

"To try and get some money out of James, for the Charity Fund."

"Again? It will be the same as before: you will get nothing."

"That's what I told her," Nigel said. "He doesn't support small schemes; he's only concerned with large-scale handouts."

"Don't move, Dagmar." Celia was at the door. "Stay and talk to Nigel."

But Dagmar was on her feet.

"There will be many more talks with Nigel," she said. "I will drive you to James's house, and—" She stopped and gave a cry. "But wait! I have some news. I have forgotten to tell you. Now I will give you three, six, a hundred guesses to tell me who was in Geneva two days ago."

"Maria Montallen," said Nigel.

"You know already? But you do not even know her! You were not here when—"

"I met her at London airport last night. I'd just flown in from Brazil and she'd arrived from— I forget."

"I will tell you from where. She had come from Munich, and she had come to meet a young man, an Austrian, to go with him to New York. I talked with his mother; she was terribly upset. She told me that she and her husband were going to follow him and stop him."

"Stop him from what?" Nigel enquired.

"Stop him from running off with Maria."

"Why stop him?"

"Because you don't understand, he is their only son and he is heir to their beautiful estates and he is only twenty years old and Maria Montallen is nearly thirty years old and all it is, is kidnapping. She thinks that if this young man wants to go away with her, his parents will pay her not to take him. But she is going to be disappointed. His parents will stop him, but they will not pay her anything; they are not such fools as all that. How did you know who she was?"

"She knew one of the men I was with, and came over to speak to him. That was when she said she was going straight on to New York."

"She will not go. You will see." She walked to the door and then came back to kiss Nigel. "You will remember to come this afternoon to see David and Sigrid?"

"Yes."

"You promise?"

"I promise."

"Good. Come, Celia."

When they had gone, he went upstairs, finished drying and dressing, did some unpacking and carried downstairs the gifts he had brought back for his mother. There was also a small parcel for Rona. He put this on one side; she might bring herself to marry one of those men his mother had mentioned, in which case it would serve as an engagement present.

He was answering the telephone when he heard the sound of a car. When the call ended, he went to the window and saw on the drive the car that had been his mother's. He walked outside. Rona. So far, only a back view as she bent to get her suitcase out of the car. Nice legs.

He stopped beside her and spoke her name.

"Rona?"

She turned. And the words he had been about to utter, which had been to the effect that it was a long time since they had met, died on his lips.

Rona? Assuredly. But . . . did women change so much between nineteen and twenty-four? And was there, in fact, so much change? The wide mouth he remembered; the small, too-small nose. The eyes—he'd forgotten how large they were, or perhaps he had never really looked at them—wide-set, grey-green, candid, direct. It was all as it had been—but there was something that hadn't been there before. Poise? Yes; a quiet ease of manner, an attitude amounting almost to casualness, which he had never seen in her and had never expected to see.

She was about to put her suitcase on the ground; instead, she handed it to him. He had not yet greeted her.

"Go on—say something," she urged.

"I'm trying."

"I've never struck anybody dumb on first sight," she told him. "The effect has been gradual. Didn't you expect to see me grow?"

"Have you grown?"

"I used to come up to your tie. Now I'm up to your shoulder. Unless you've shrunk, that's growing."

She had begun to walk towards the house. He fell into step beside her and groped for his impressions. Had he asked his mother if she was overweight? This sensational figure? What had she done to all that hair she used to have? Bushes of it, there used to be, wild-looking. How had she achieved this smooth, softly falling effect? Well, there were good hairdressers in London.

He had not recovered before they entered the living room.

He carried her suitcase into the hall, put it down and then picked it up again and went upstairs.

"Which room?" he called.

"End of the corridor."

She had sunk into one of the chairs in the living room. Leaning back, eyes closed, arms hanging over the chair sides, she took in a long, deep breath, feeling a relief, a thankfulness so deep that she found herself trembling.

It was over. It had happened. And thank God, from whom all blessings were said to flow, here she was as she had hoped and prayed to be: unmoved, untouched. It was over: the words were a hymn of praise. He was here. She had met him, spoken to him—and felt nothing. She had, during the past two or three years, begun to believe that she might be cured, but she had never been sure. Not absolutely sure. She had needed proof—and here it was. She had met him, and for the first time since her sixteenth birthday, she had met him without emotion.

Wasted years? She supposed so. Or perhaps not. The pain, all the more poignant for being adolescent; the longing, the bitter frustrations had, she thought, done much to give her an inner strength that she had lacked. The unceasing struggle to hide her feelings from him, from Dagmar, from outsiders, above all from her godmother; the dread of giving herself away, the necessity of forcing herself to realize that she meant nothing to him, and never would; it had toughened her, strengthened her. And here he was, thinner, but in every other way the same, as good-looking, as charming—and all she felt was a mild pleasure at his return. Even the pleasure was less for herself than because she knew what he meant to his mother.

She was free. And perhaps, in a double sense, she owed her freedom to Roger Underwood. Or—curious thought—to Maria Montallen. Roger had been the means of removing her lingering feeling for Nigel. Maria Montallen had removed Roger . . .

Nigel joined her in the living room. She opened her eyes and closed them again.

"Where's your mother?" she asked.

"Gone to see Sir James, to try and get some money out of him."

"Waste of time. Why didn't you drive her there?"

"I was wearing a damp towel. Dagmar drove her."

She opened her eyes.

"Dagmar came?"

"Yes. More or less straight from Geneva. She doesn't change, does she? Still minding everybody's business."

"Not as much as she used to. She's concentrating on her grandchildren." She gave a sigh of satisfaction. "It's lovely to be home. Me, I mean. I can't bear London."

"Then why did you go there?"

"Better jobs. More money. More movement. More men. How do you like your mother's new cottage?"

"I've told her what I think."

"Did she mention any—any specific drawbacks?"

"Far from mentioning them, she didn't even notice them. But she seems to be happy."

She had closed her eyes again.

"Oh, she's happy. She'd be happy anywhere. Why can't we all have her nature?" She opened her eyes. "I'd like some coffee. How about you?"

"If you're going to make some—"

"Not me. You. I've been working hard this morning, clearing the last of my things out of my flat. You make the coffee."

He found himself, to his surprise, making it. Things had indeed changed, he thought with amazement and growing resentment. There was a time when he had only to express a wish, and she fell over herself: coffee, tea, pressing his jackets, tidying his cupboards, fetching and carrying, even at times giving a shine to his shoes. She had been in many ways a nuisance, but she had been useful. He had never imagined that she would sit dozing peacefully while he slaved for her.

The unnaturalness of it struck him with such force that he broke a cup.

"Tck, tck, tck," she said sleepily. "Clumsy." She got up and came to the kitchen door. "Not one of Celia's best set, was it?"

"Yes, it was. Don't you call her Aunt Celia any more?"

"No. We both thought it was silly. She won't be pleased about the cup. Would you like me to tell her I broke it?"

"Why the hell should you do that?"

"I often used to shield you thus in my extreme youth. I used to lie my head off telling her you were playing tennis when you were out with those predatory women. Do you know, we all expected you to bring back a Brazilian wife. Your mother even thought of starting to learn the language. They speak Portuguese, don't they?"

"They speak Brazilian. Where do you want your coffee?"

"Oh, in here." She was back in the living room, seated in her chair. He put the tray on the gateleg table, poured coffee and carried a cup to her. If she thanked him, he thought, his anger deepening, she must have swallowed the words with the first sip.

"That how you like it?" he enquired with exaggerated deference.

"Bit strong. But lovely flavour. Brazilian?"

"Yes." He carried his cup across the room and sat on the sofa. "My mother and I were talking about you. I was trying to catch up on everything that had been going on while I was away. We touched on the subject of your friends. Men friends. I asked whether you had any, so to speak, followers."

"You think I tell your mother about them?"

"I suppose not. I pointed out that it was time you settled down."

"Time I married?"

"Yes."

"But one doesn't have to, these days. Women have fought for and won the freedom to bestow their favours and withdraw them without notice, the way men used to. And women now command top jobs with top salaries, the way men used to. And women prefer dilly-dallying to marrying and settling down—the way men used to. Hadn't the news got as far as Brazil?"

He put down his cup. She had always, he knew, had a tendency to levity. Even his mother had sometimes found it excessive. Her teachers at school had complained. He himself had never had cause to complain, because never in all the years he had known her had the levity been directed at him. She had been, at times, what he considered pert, and he had then been at pains to emphasize the seven-year gap in their ages. Never had she looked at him, spoken to him, with this cool, amused tolerance.

Some of the pleasure of his homecoming seeped away. Something was wrong. Something had gone. It was not merely that he had come back to a house he considered built to the specifications of a family of field mice; he had not in recent years spent much time in the last house and was not planning to spend much time in this one. Perhaps he had been away too long. Perhaps it was too much to expect that after more than three years, he could return and slot in as though he had never been away.

For the first time, he regretted not having been in Longbrook during what he thought of as the Underwood affair. It was a pity he had decided to spend his last leave exploring the possibilities of European expansion for the firm. He had touched down briefly at Longbrook on his way back to Brazil, but Rona had been staying with friends in Scotland. It was Scotland that had started it all, he remembered. She had returned to London by train, and Roger Underwood had chanced to be on the train and that had been that. They had known one another in Longbrook, but they had been no more than friends. It had taken a trip on the Flying Scotsman to kindle a romance.

If he had spent that leave at home . . .

"Why aren't you talking?" she asked him.

"I was thinking."

"About?"

"You. You've changed."

She laughed.

"Oh, Nigel, of course I've changed! When we last met, I was just shedding school uniform. Not literally; just mentally. And I was living with your mother and going to old Mrs. Clancy down the road to learn shorthand and typing. That was rather different from going to live in London and getting a job and a flat and acquiring some degree of what's called sophistication. You've never changed because you were grown up when I first met you."

"What—at seventeen?"

"At seventeen. You were—the only word I can think of is worldly. I suppose it was because you'd been the man of the house for so long. You were formed. There was nothing for you to do but grow older. How long's your leave this time?"

"I'm not going back."

"Oh?" Her eyebrows went up. "Sacked? Sorry—redundant?"

"I'm going to do the next four years in the London office."

"Where you worked before?"

"Yes."

"Pity I gave up my flat. You would have liked it. Nice and central. Expensive, but worth it. I paid the rent with some totally unexpected money left me by a cousin I didn't know existed. I'm sorry in a way I didn't try to sublet. I'm only here for a year."

"You just said you hate London."

"So I do. But from a working point of view, it's the place to be." She held out her cup for more coffee. "When are you going to see David?"

"This afternoon. Dagmar said that you and his wife are friends."

"Yes, we are."

"What's she like?"

"She's—well, you'll see. She's absolutely right for David. You know how nervy he used to to be? He isn't any more. She's very calm and unfussy and down-to-earth. She's got a lot of sense."

"How does she get on with Dagmar?"

"She liked her at first, but it's wearing thin. She's getting pretty tired of all that interference."

"David learned how to handle Dagmar; perhaps he'll teach his wife."

"David's in the shop all day. Sigrid's stuck with Dagmar. She didn't mind so much before the baby arrived; she could ignore all the advice about her clothes and her cosmetics and her hairstyles, but she won't stand much more interference with the baby's routine. It'll be worse when this new baby arrives. Sometimes I get the idea that she's coming round to the idea of moving."

"Moving where?"

"Away from the shop. Away from Dagmar. There are quite a lot of houses for sale in and around the town."

"In that case, why did you let my mother buy this one?"

"You think I could have stopped her?"

"Did you try?"

"No. I was too late. By the time I came down for the weekend, it was all over. If you could spend some money doing it up, it might be worth it."

"It's not much bigger than a cupboard. And every room is damp."

"I know. But you could put in central heating and get an architect to redesign the kitchen and join the garage to the house and take away that awful staircase and put in a spiral one to give more room, and you could extend the living room into the hall."

"Nothing more?"

"If you don't do it now, you'll get married and then your

wife won't let you spend all that money. There's a very good architect here—Geoffry Steele. Remember him?"

"No. Unless he was that weedy chap who got kicked out of Harrow."

"He's not weedy, and he's very clever and nobody kicked him out. I'm having dinner with him one night; if you like, I'll ask him if he'll draw some plans for you. He charges a lot, but it would be worth it. Speaking of dinner, did you enjoy your mother's celebration dinner last night?"

He hesitated.

"Well, no," he said at last. "It was a pity, but I got held up. I didn't get here until after midnight."

A slight frown appeared on her forehead.

"Plane delayed?" she enquired.

He thought of lying, and decided against it.

"No. Not the plane. I fell in with friends at the airport. I couldn't phone because of the queues. I got through about half past ten and said I wouldn't be down."

She was silent for so long that he challenged her.

"Go on—say it," he urged.

"There's nothing to say. Your mother spent most of the day making preparations."

"How could I know that?"

"Only by using a little imagination. Did she wait up for you?"

"Yes and no. She went to bed and got up when she heard me drive in. Where are you going?"

"Upstairs to change." Her voice was cool. "I've got work to do."

He was between her and the door, and he did not move.

"It wasn't your dinner I didn't eat," he pointed out. "If my mother didn't mind, why should you?"

"You think she didn't mind?"

"All right; she minded. But she didn't make a fuss."

"She wouldn't. I hope your wife, when you eventually

choose one, will be harder on you than your mother has been."

"I'll be careful to pick out a big bully. Do we have to quarrel on my first day home?"

She seemed to consider the point.

"No, we don't," she said finally. "We've both got other things to think about."

"What work is this you have to do?"

"Lunch. Preparations for dinner. While I'm here, when I'm here, I take over the housekeeping. Which means that you show up for the dinners I cook, and show up in time."

"Can you work to music? I'm going to put some on."

"What sort of music?"

"Brazilian. Cha-cha-hoo-cha, that kind of thing. Like it?"

"Yes. Go ahead."

He had moved aside. She was on her way upstairs. He stood in the hall and looked up at her.

"You forgot something," he said. "We forgot something."

She paused.

"We did?"

"Yes. We forgot the correct greeting between brother and sister."

"Have we been doing it wrong all these years?" she asked in surprise. "I used to say 'Hello, Nigel,' and you used to say 'Oh, God, not you again?' That wasn't the right way?"

Her tone—impersonal, more than ever amused—made him want to walk back into the living room and crash the door behind him. But something stronger than anger kept him where he was. Something had gone wrong with his homecoming. A chill wind was blowing across his expectations, his plans. Something that had seldom deserted him—self-confidence—seemed to be slipping. He did not know what he was seeking from her, but he felt that he was reaching out for some kind of reassurance.

"That wasn't the right way," he managed to say in an

even tone. "What I should have had from you was a sisterly kiss."

"Oh, is that all?" She came down the stairs and faced him. "You shall have it. On the brow, in blessing—like this? Or on the cheek, the brush of a moth's wing—like this? Or—"

She was unable to go on because his lips were on hers. Gently, briefly.

His lips on hers. How often, she wondered, oh, dear God-from-whom, how often had she felt them in the past, sleeping or awake? How often? Never, if she ever had a teen-age daughter, never, never, never would she underrate the miseries, the agonies of girlhood.

His lips on hers. It had happened—and she was still standing upright. She hadn't sighed, she hadn't swooned, she hadn't been transfixed by bliss, she hadn't fallen down dead. She hadn't felt a sword going through her. She hadn't felt anything.

Nothing. This was the ultimate test—unexpected, final. She was cured. She was free.

She smiled—a smile of pure happiness—and spoke.

"Welcome home, brother Nigel."

CHAPTER

2

DRIVING WITH DAGMAR WAS ALWAYS A HAZARDOUS OPERA-
tion. Competent enough when alone in her large, powerful
car, she tended, when giving lifts to friends, to talk. As she
could not talk without using her hands to emphasize her
arguments, there were moments in which the wheel, to the
alarm of the passengers, remained unmanned.

Celia had no objection to her talking. She thought Dagmar's voice, with its throaty r's and eccentric stresses, was a
great part of her charm. But in the interests of self-preserva-
tion, she frequently guided the car round curves, relinquishing
the wheel when they were once more on the straight.

It was not more than four miles from the cottage to Sir
James Dartford's house.

"You don't have to take me all the way there," Celia said
as they turned out of the gateway of the cottage. "There's a
bus at the next corner."

"I know, I know. And if you had waited, Nigel would have

taken you in his car. But I have not seen you for so long, and I wanted to talk to you, and besides that, I have something special to tell you."

"What about?"

"First, you tell me: Why didn't you tell him about that noise from next door?"

"I thought I'd wait. He found plenty of other things to say against the cottage."

"I told you, didn't I? It was such a pity I was away when you bought it, Celia. I could have advised you. Why didn't you wear a new dress last night?"

"I put on one, but it was close-fitting and I couldn't bear it. So I took it off."

"And put on your blue. You are just like Monique: how many dresses have I bought her, beautiful dresses, expensive dresses, models—and what does she wear always? Her green suit, because once her husband said he liked to see her in it. Since then, he has not seen her in anything else. I am going to say something to you, and you won't like it, but it must be said. When did you last go to London to buy yourself new dresses?"

"I can't remember."

"So then where are you now buying them?"

"Well, I often see dresses in the windows of the shops here that—"

"Oh, my dear God! You call those dresses? This is what I was afraid of. Always, always, always, Celia, you will go the easy way if you can, if I allow you. You are in some ways so sensible, but then you show yourself otherwise. Those dresses, as you call them, that are in the windows here, are in the windows of drapers and not of dressmakers. They are not for you. You must go to London. I will go with you at any time for your fittings. In this matter, at least, you must let me advise you. If I know about anything, it is about clothes; you agree with this?"

"Yes."

"So you must let me go with you. When I buy anything, I do not allow people to persuade me to buy what I don't want. But you—you believe anything that people tell you."

Celia thought that perhaps there was some truth in this. She had certainly believed Dagmar when, on Aubrey's death, she had declared passionately that she would wear mourning for the rest of her life. Celia, visualizing a pathetic figure in perpetual, unrelieved black, had been surprised to learn that there were infinite variations on the mourning theme: black with white touches, white with black touches, misty greys, and a whole series of mauves, shading from purple to the palest lilac.

". . . so it is settled," she heard Dagmar saying.

"What's settled?"

"What we have just said: that I will go to London with you, to buy dresses. And now I want to talk about Nigel. He must marry, Celia. Look at David, married and so happy and such a good father. You and I—his mother and his god-mother—must put our heads together and find a wife for him. I don't mean any of those women who come running after him. I mean some nice girl who—"

"There wouldn't be time. He's not likely to be home long. He'll be in London, but—"

"London?"

"He's going to work in the London office."

"This must make you happy, no?"

"It'll be nice to have him so near, but I don't suppose I'll see much more of him than I did when he was in Brazil."

"The trouble is, he has too many friends, and though so many of them are women, they are not women of the kind that you and I would like to see him marry. And he is waiting too long. He must marry and give you grandchildren. Look how I enjoy mine! They are so sweet, so amusing! Only this morning I noticed David's little Arthur looking at me as if he wanted to tell me something—and I know what it was. He wanted to say that he doesn't like to have to feed himself. If he could have said this, I would have agreed with him, because it is much too early for him to do this. I told Sigrid this, but she said no, he must learn to feed himself. Why do mothers in these days push their children forward so quickly? Why can't the poor little things be babies for longer? Monique is the same, making the children do too much, too soon. I told her it was wrong. Babies will—" She threw up her hands in despair, and Celia took temporary charge. "Sigrid says that I talk too much about my grandchildren, so I must stop. You must stop me. We will make a plan: when I begin to talk about them too much, you must say a word, any word, a word that we will agree to say. Like amber."

"Why amber?"

"Because it is the colour that you see on the traffic lights and then you know the stop signal is coming. So you must say amber. You will remember?"

"I'll try. What were you going to tell me?"

"It is something interesting. When I was in Geneva, I heard— But I will tell you from the beginning. I have to begin with Maria Montallen's grandmother."

"Must we?"

"If you want to hear this, we do."

"Then go on."

"You know, I know, this whole town knows, that her house was full of treasures, beautiful things which she guarded and which she swore she would never part with. Isn't that so?"

"Yes."

"And up to the time when she died, nobody could ever make her sell anything. She refused fantastic prices. For as long as anybody knew her—and she lived here for how many? forty years—she kept, she cherished, she hoarded her things."

"Yes. So what?"

"I will go along step by step. We will now speak of Maria. Hasn't there been, for the last three years, a lot of puzzling in people's minds, one question which everybody asked but nobody could answer: Why did Maria Montallen go off with Roger Underwood? Why? Not for love; this she did not even pretend. What did she say many times for everybody to hear? She wanted a man with money. And when she said money, she meant millions. So nobody could understand when she went off with a man who had so little money to give. And now I come back to Geneva. I met a friend, and he asked me if I had heard of a lady called Montallen who had a private collection that included fabulous jewellery, and I said yes, she had lived in this town but she was dead. He told me that he had just come back from Casablanca, and he had seen there a necklace which had been in her collection and which she had sold. It was, he said, of very great beauty and very great value. I told him he must be mistaken, because she had never sold anything because these things were her inheritance and had been in her family for hundreds of years. He said no, he wasn't mistaken, he had seen the necklace. Then he described it to me, and I knew that I had seen it years ago, and so had you, when we paid our money and went to see the collection in Mrs. Montallen's house. It was in a showcase all by itself, lying on black velvet. It was a diamond bead necklace with gold bands to keep the strands together. You *must* remember it. It was—it was magnificent."

"Yes, I remember."

"And now she is dead and the collection belongs to the town, and we can still pay money to go and see it, but if we go, we can be sure that this necklace will no longer be there. Do you see why I am telling you this?"

"No."

"You should have guessed by now. *Think.* Who was Roger Underwood? I mean to say, what was his work?"

"He was the owner of— Oh."

"Oh. Now you are beginning to see. He began to be a portrait painter, and then his father died and left money to him, and with this money he bought a small picture gallery in London and began to sell not pictures only, but other things. But the gallery did not prosper, and instead of making money, he was losing it. We all knew that. So why would Maria Montallen marry a man who was losing money? But if her grandmother . . . you see what I am going to say?"

"Yes. But I don't believe it."

"Of course you don't. You will never believe that anybody can be wicked. You don't want to believe that old Mrs. Montallen hated her granddaughter so much that she gave Roger Underwood a valuable necklace so that he could sell it and get money and be rich enough for Maria to run away with."

"I still don't believe it. Mrs. Montallen would never have been able to bring herself to take anything out of that collection. She was fanatical about it."

"Then how would Roger get the necklace?"

"You don't know that it was Roger who sold it."

"Ah, but I do. You think I did not ask for proof? It was sold by the Underwood Gallery. Now do you believe it?"

"Maria could have taken it."

"With that collection guarded like the Crown jewels? No. The only way for her to get it was for her grandmother to give it. You have never believed, never admitted to yourself that Roger knew very well what he was doing. You always said he was weak, confused, that it was Maria who made him go away like that, only two weeks before his wedding to Rona. What I am telling you now is that Maria did not steal him before her grandmother gave him the necklace. She wouldn't give it to Maria, because she knew that Maria would sell it and come back for more. She gave it to Roger because she knew that he would know its value and he would not be able to resist something so rare. She gave it to him so that he could marry Maria and take her away. There was no love in it. The necklace explains everything. Do you see?"

She had slowed the car to walking pace. They were passing

a large house standing in spacious, well-kept grounds. A notice beside the gate read:

LONGBROOK TRUST.
THE BARVILLE COLLECTION
OPEN WEEKDAYS 10 A.M. TO 7 P.M.

Dagmar brought the car to a stop. Both women were silent for a time, gazing thoughtfully at the house.

"I suppose she was a wicked old woman," Celia said at last. "But she did something in the end to benefit the town. She left it this wonderful collection."

"Oh, poof!" Dagmar gave a contemptuous snort. "She was not thinking of the town. She was thinking only of those ancestors of hers, the Barvilles. She wanted to make sure they wouldn't be forgotten. What did she ever think about, talk about, but the ancient line of Barvilles?"

Celia said nothing. She was recalling the gaunt, witchlike old woman who had owned treasures but had nevertheless haggled with the town's tradesmen over petty items in their bills; a woman who had worn shabby suits and battered hats, and left a fortune to the town.

Mrs. Montallen had been born a Barville, a family which for centuries had fought wherever there were battles, seeking no renown, refusing honours and disdaining titles. A Barville who died in battle was accorded no respect by his family; their aim was to live to fight another day, leaving corners of foreign fields to the enemy.

Their disdain did not extend to the prizes of war. From every campaign, they returned laden with loot, and as they were as parsimonious as they were pugnacious, they clung closely to their gains. When time passed and opportunities for looting became fewer, they found themselves forced to retrench; they gave up land and houses, but did not part with a single item of what had come to be known as the Barville Collection.

Mrs. Montallen had been the last Barville. The house at Longbrook had been her husband's; on his death, she had continued to live there and in it had put the Barville Collection on view.

She had an only child—a son, who proved to have no Barville tendencies. He took after his peace-loving father, and relations between him and his mother became increasingly strained. On his coming of age, he announced his intention of leaving home forever, and demanded a share of the Barville heirlooms. This his mother absolutely refused to hand over.

After his departure, news items concerning him occasionally found their way to Longbrook: he was living in Canada, in Chile, in California; he had married an Argentinian; his wife was wildly extravagant; he had one child, a daughter named Maria; he was destitute, he was divorced, he was dead, his widow was dead, his daughter had disappeared.

When Maria Montallen reappeared, it was on her grandmother's doorstep. She drove up, unheralded, in a London taxi, unloaded from it several pieces of luggage and announced that she had come to stay.

The battle fought by her grandmother to dislodge her was as fierce as any that had been waged by the Barvilles of former days. Maria, tall, handsome, with the Barville curl of the lip, went on impassively with her unpacking, pointing out that she had nothing in the world but her clothes, and until she found a man with the means to provide replacements, she would remain in residence.

There were men enough in the town, but none of sufficient means to satisfy her. When at last she chose a husband, the fact that he was shortly to marry someone else had proved no hindrance. She left Longbrook as suddenly as she had come, taking her prize with her. On her departure, her grandmother took a step designed to protect herself from any return visit: she offered the collection to the town, together with her house and a substantial sum for its upkeep. On her death a few months later, she left everything she possessed to the Long-brook Trust.

Celia was letting her gaze roam over the beautifully kept grounds.

"The place didn't look like this in her day," she remarked.

"No, it didn't. It's a pity she didn't die sooner, because the town could have used some of her money to preserve land, instead of letting so much of it go to builders to put all those ugly apartment blocks everywhere."

She drove on, turning presently onto a narrow road that led to the crest of a low hill. From here it was possible to look down at the town and see clearly the uncontrolled building that had taken place in the early days of Longbrook's develop-ment—and to measure the generosity of the few public-spirited people, Sir James Dartford prominent among them, who by refusing to sell their land and by purchasing more whenever possible had preserved open spaces for the town.

Celia's gaze went to a small house at the foot of the hill.

"It must be lonely for her," she said, "living there all by herself."

"All by herself?" Dagmar echoed in surprise. "She's got a lame donkey, a one-legged seagull, I don't know how many geese, chickens, ducks, everything. How can she be lonely?"

"Nobody to talk to."

"She talks all the time to them. I've heard her. When I go there for eggs, she is having conversations with them."

They were speaking of Mrs. Todd, the widow of one of the partners in the firm of Hayling, Harvard and Todd.

"She should have moved when her husband died," Celia said.

"That is what I told her. But after all those years with that selfish old man, without any servants, cooking for him, washing and ironing for him, growing fresh vegetables for him, even walking about in wet fields to pick mushrooms for him, she was too tired. People said she was a martyr; what I say is that she was a doormat."

"He must have been a responsibility at the end," Celia said compassionately.

"Of course. Senile. How could they let him go on so long in the office?"

"Not senile. He just got more and more vague and absent-minded as he got older, that's all. He only went into the office two days a week. It was that accident—"

"—that finished him off. Yes, that is what everybody says, but he wasn't in it, he only saw it, so I don't understand why it should have made such an effect on him."

Celia did not reply. The car had stopped before a high, wrought-iron gate. From the nearby lodge a woman came to open it for the car to enter.

"Morning, Mrs. Pressley. Morning, Mrs. Renson. Nice day."

"Good morning, Mrs. Muir. Don't close the gate, please," Dagmar requested. "I shall be coming out in a few minutes."

"Right you are."

Mrs. Muir raised a hand in acknowledgment and went indoors. The incident typified the mixture of freedom and formality that characterized the members—five in number—of Sir James's staff. During the more than thirty years of his residence in Longbrook, the do-it-yourself age had caught up with and been accepted by most people in the town, but Sir James's servants were those he had engaged on his arrival, never changing and never, to the wonder of his acquaintances, showing any signs of wanting to change. There was envy mixed with the wonder, and disapproval that increased with the years: what did one man want with five servants? A man, moreover, who since the death of his wife had never invited anybody to his house to share a meal or even to drink a cup of tea. But Sir James, in this matter as in all others a man who went his own way, retained his staff and spent his days working in his beloved and justly famed garden.

Celia did not suggest Dagmar's staying to talk to him; she knew that they could not endure more than a few minutes of each other's society. She got out of the car and thanked her for the lift. Dagmar spoke in a tone of wonder.

"Do you realize, Celia, that it is fifteen years since his wife died? Fifteen years!"

"Nearly sixteen."

"Can you believe that? How old do you feel?"

"Nearly sixteen."

"Me, too."

She drove away, and Celia turned to look at the beautiful house which, when Sir James bought it, had been a crumbling farm dwelling. The garden he had created—lawns, flower beds, shady walks and shrubberies, fountains and lily ponds—had once been acres of scrub land.

She had seen all this beauty—house and garden—in the making. Sir James had come to Longbrook shortly after her own arrival in the town. He was a wealthy baronet who had sold his estate in Cheshire and had come to live nearer London. He had been forty, a bachelor, and from the first had shown no disposition to be social. He selected one or two friends from the neighborhood and kept everybody else at a distance, resisting all requests to join any local activities. But he had not been too detached to note the increasingly rapid rate at which multistorey buildings were springing up on once-open countryside. He had bought many of the remaining tracts of land; one was now a sports ground, another a park named after him. Yet another was the two-hundred-acre spread known as Mill Acres, which lay behind Celia's cottage. He had made this over by deed of gift to his wife, and on her death it had passed to her son, Francis Latimer.

The wedding had astonished everybody. Sir James, at fifty, had married a pretty widow named Mrs. Latimer, who had a son of ten. Wealthy, pleasure-loving, as social as Sir James was reserved, she had filled the house with her friends and the stables with her horses. He had looked on indulgently and gone on with his landscaping.

She had been killed in a car accident five years after the

marriage. She was at the wheel; he was seated beside her. She had died instantly, he had survived with injuries from which he took months to recover. It was said that his recovery had been a miracle, but Celia, who with her husband had been among his oldest friends, knew that he had never recovered his former clarity of mind. His memory of the past—especially the past immediately before and after the accident—remained hazy and confused.

There were no horses in the stables now, no riders, no grooms. And no guests.

The front door opened. Celia saw coming down the steps the small, neat figure of Joseph Brill, who with his wife was responsible for the running of the house.

"Good morning, Mrs. Pressley. It's nice to see you; you haven't been here for a long time."

"I know. I've been trying to get used to my new house. How is your wife?"

"She's fine, thanks. Twinges of rheumatics now and then, but that's about all. You'll find Sir James working down near the wood. He's still having trouble getting the water to go the way he wants it. Will you go down, or shall I ask him to come up?"

"Oh, I'll go down. How is he?"

"Well . . . he keeps active. He's getting on for seventy, you know; I think he's beginning to slow down a bit. It's only natural. He'll be glad to see you."

She went down the steps of the terrace and along a path that skirted the lawn. One of the gardeners was trimming a hedge; the other was with Sir James. They saw her as she came near, and for a few moments there was an unwelcoming frown on Sir James's forehead. It cleared as he recognized her. He came towards her, white-haired and weather-beaten, but straight-backed and soldierly, and spoke in his usual abrupt manner.

"Oh, it's you. That's all right. Thought it might be one

of those women who come asking for donations. What d'you think of my glen?"

"Is that what it is?"

"It's what it's going to be. When that path's finished, it'll be a more picturesque entrance to the wood. I'm trying to get the stream to make a slight curve, but I'm having difficulty."

"It's going to be lovely. How are you, James?"

"Older than when you last came to see me. Why have you stayed away so long?"

"Settling in. I wanted to have everything in place when Nigel arrived."

"He's here, is he? What did he say about that unfortunate purchase of yours?"

"Quite a lot. All uncomplimentary."

"What did he say about your neighbours?"

"I—he doesn't know anything about that yet."

"You didn't tell him?"

"No."

"So he'll get no warning. Poor fellow. I'm sorry you bought the place, Celia; I think you're going to regret it."

"I know. At least, I'm beginning to know. The saving is that wonderful piece of land at the back."

"Odd you should mention it. It's been in my mind lately. I've been wondering if Francis would consider a scheme to turn it into a golf course—nine holes. I'm going to discuss it with him while he's here."

"Is Francis here?"

"Yes. Didn't Nigel mention it?"

"He said they'd met at the airport, but he didn't say anything about Francis coming home."

"Home? He doesn't think of this place as home. I doubt if he ever did. But he's here. He arrived this morning: he rang Mrs. Brill just after breakfast and she got his rooms ready. I don't suppose he'll be staying long, but long enough for me to find out what he thinks of my idea. It's his land, and he's got the right to decide what he wants to do with it. He can't sell it; that was made clear in the deed of gift when I gave the land to his mother. And it can't be built on. But if he likes this scheme, I'll cover the expenses. As I said, he won't be here long."

Celia was surprised that he had come at all. Francis Latimer was not often seen in Longbrook. His rooms in the house were kept open, and after his mother's death he had spent part of his school holidays with his stepfather, but Sir James's sober company, and the limited entertainment to be had in Longbrook, had soon made him seek more sophisticated pleasures elsewhere. On his coming of age, he had shown little or no interest in the details of his mother's estate; he had given a power of attorney to the only surviving trustee—Mr. Todd —and now spent his time in London or at the stables his mother had owned near Newmarket, or in his villa in Italy. Sir James made no demands on him; he welcomed him when he came and—Celia thought—forgot him the moment he departed. There had been little sympathy between them in the past; there was even less today.

"Let's go up to the house," Sir James suggested.

She told him, as they went, that Nigel was not to return to Brazil.

"Where's he going to be?"

"London."

"Will he live there?"

"Yes."

He led her to his study and apologized for the litter of papers on his desk.

"Been trying to clear them up," he told her. "Years and years of accumulation. Not only here; boxes and boxes in the attics. I'll have to have a clear-out."

"I've heard you say that before."

"I daresay you have. How did you get here—walked?"

"No. Dagmar brought me."

"Glad you didn't bring her in. Five minutes of her is more than I can stand. How's Rosanna enjoying being back in Longbrook?"

"She seems to be enjoying herself."

He rang the bell and ordered coffee.

"I don't suppose she could spare me an hour or so of an evening to come here and tidy up some of these papers?" he asked. "Shouldn't take her more than a week or so. I'd pay whatever the rate is. She could make her own times—come when she liked and go when she liked. I'd leave her in here to work on her own. Ask her, will you, and see what she says."

"I will. James, I came—"

"Ha. Now it's coming. Not a friendly visit after all.—Pour out, will you?—You've come for money."

"I'm afraid so. The Charity Fund—"

"You're wasting your time. I've told you, my dear Celia, and I asked you to tell all those other women, that if I want to support a charity, I sit down and write a check. I can't and won't be bothered by every woman who's getting up a bridge drive or a concert or a whatever-it-is. I like to see you whenever you come, but I won't give you any money. I daresay you think I'm a mean old fellow."

She did not bother to contradict this. She gave him his coffee and spoke of other matters. When she rose to leave, he walked with her down the long drive to the gate.

"I could have sent you home with Brill in my car," he said.

"No, thank you. I want some exercise."

As they waited for Mrs. Muir to open the gate, he put a question.

"Heard anything about that women who made a lot of trouble here a few years ago? That woman who ran off with Rosanna's fiancé—Maria Something."

"Maria Montallen."

"That's it. My memory's shocking. I remember now. She was the granddaughter of that old woman who used to accuse all the tradespeople of cheating. Well, she's turned up again."

"Yes, I know."

"How do you know?"

"Nigel met her at the airport. As a matter of fact, he introduced Francis to her."

Sir James directed a puzzled glance at her.

"He introduced Francis to the Montallen woman?"

"Yes."

"Did he now? I wonder . . . Would you say that accounted for Francis's appearance this morning? I might have known he hadn't come to see me. He's come to see her."

"She wasn't staying in England. She was going on to New York."

"Then she must have cancelled her trip. She's here."

"She's—"

"She's here in Longbrook. She telephoned to Francis just before he got here, and left her name. She's at that flashy hotel they've built near the bookshop."

"Are you—are you sure?"

"Yes, I'm sure." He studied her stricken expression. "What's the matter? Haven't you got over that old business?"

"Yes. No."

"It's Francis she's after this time. Did you think she'd come after Nigel?"

She did not rely. She wanted, suddenly, to be at home. The thought of Maria Montallen in Longbrook, as she had been three years ago, coming and going in the streets and in the shops, to be met with at any moment, was making her feel sick with apprehension.

"Can't you forget it?" Sir James asked, his tone unusually gentle.

"I've tried."

"No, you haven't. You've hidden it under the carpet. Great mistake. Well, Francis can look after himself. I don't think she'll catch him, but if he's going to see much of her, he'll have to reach deep into his pocket. He won't bring her to this house; I'll see to that."

She said goodbye and nodded to Mrs. Muir and walked into the road. There would be a bus soon; but she did not want a bus. She wanted to walk. She wanted time to absorb the shock.

She turned in the direction of home.

CHAPTER

3

"AND THIS," NIGEL SAID, "IS MY FAVOURITE. IT'S THE SAME group as the last, but they've changed instruments. If you think that makes no difference to the sound, just listen."

Rona listened. They were listening in comfort. She had prepared a cold lunch, laid it out in buffet form on trays in the kitchen and come into the living room to join him. She was now seated on a rug, leaning against the sofa.

Sometime towards midday, he went to the Chinese cupboard in the corner and from it brought bottles and glasses. Unable to make himself heard above the music, he held up one of the bottles; she shook her head, but nodded as he held up a second. He poured a drink and brought it to her. Then he brought his own, flung another cushion down beside her and lowered himself onto it. He got up again to reduce the volume of sound.

"As you remarked earlier this morning," he said, "it's nice to be home."

"I thought you were going to say it was just like old times."

"And you were going to point out that it wasn't. You're right; I wouldn't have plied you with drink last time I was at home."

"And you wouldn't have played your records for me."

"Probably not. What made you decide to become a secretary? If I remember, it was the last profession on your list. The first was—"

"—to be a vet. Your mother sent me to the Gunter farm to let me take a close look. My enthusiasm waned."

"So you worked down the list?"

"No. I was offered a job here with Hayling, Harvard and Todd."

"Which of them did you work for?"

"Mr. Hayling. They didn't pay me much, but I was only a learner."

"Didn't you find working in a lawyer's office rather dull?"

"Dull? Divorces, embezzlements, last wills and testaments, leases and sales and mortgages and—"

"All right. Not dull. Who's your boss now?"

"Bryan Hayling. Old Mr. Hayling's son. He remembers you; he says you were always chasing after women. They were a mixed lot, weren't they? I used to award points—so many for looks, so many for charm if any, take off marks for trying too hard. What were we talking about? Oh, lawyers. Bryan wasn't in the office when I first worked there. When I'd been with the firm for about a year, I was offered—actually offered—a job in a lawyer's office in London, with three times the money. I leapt."

"Why did you come back to Longbrook?"

"I was getting rather tired of London, but I suppose I would have stayed there if I hadn't met poor Mr. Hayling one day, wandering along Fenchurch Street looking for the office I worked in. He'd come all the way from Longbrook to find me. He was desperate. He asked me to come back. His secretary, old Miss Corlett—remember her?"

58 /

"Yes. Dead?"

"No. Retired at seventy. Mr. Hayling was past seventy himself, but he was still pretty active. He'd tried one or two successors to Miss Corlett and they were no good, so he asked me to come back and work for him. I blackmailed him on the spot over the question of salary, and when he'd given in, I agreed to come back for a year. He retired a month later, and Bryan joined the firm and I began to work for him."

"Why aren't you at the office today?"

"No office on Saturdays. Bryan wants me to stay when the year's up, and I might. I like being back in the country, if you can still call this the country."

"I'd call it a flourishing town. My God, what a change since I was last here!"

"There are still some nice open spaces—thanks to Sir James and a few others."

"Who owns that land at the back of this cottage?"

"Francis Latimer. He inherited it from his mother. You can't buy any of it, if that's what you've got in mind."

"Why not?"

"Because he got it with a proviso that it can't be built on or sold."

"I see. If it had been for sale, I would have had to buy part of it, to stop some builder or other from putting up a block of apartments against our kitchen window."

The record ended, and he got up to change it.

"Don't put on another." She was getting to her feet. "I've got to take the car up to the garage at the top of the road."

"What for?"

"Servicing. If I let them have it now, they'll let me have it back this afternoon."

"I'll drive it up for you."

"Thanks, no. I'll go. I'd suggest your going to meet your mother, but she's probably left Sir James by now, and if she decided to walk, she could come three different ways, so you'd miss her. And if—"

She stopped. If she had gone on speaking, he would not have been able to hear her over the noise that was making the window rattle and shaking the crockery in the kitchen. The Brazilian music had been by contrast a mere whisper.

For some moments, he was too astounded to move. Then he strode across the room, banged the window shut and turned to face her.

"What the hell— My God, it sounds like a brass band."

She nodded.

"That's what it is," she said.

"Where the devil is the sound coming from? One would think it was next door."

Once more she nodded.

"That's where it is," she said.

"Next door?"

"Yes."

"Next *door*?"

"Yes."

"But my mother said there was only one person living there."

"That's right. Chan Fielder."

"Chan Fielder? Fatty Fielder?"

"Yes. He's the bandmaster. They practice next door."

"*Practice?* You mean this is just a—a practice?"

"Yes."

"You mean they keep doing it?"

"Twice a day."

"Fatty Fielder! That—that mountain? That overstuffed barrel whose father worked in the music shop?"

"The same. I didn't know him in those days, but he's certainly mountainous and he's certainly overstuffed."

"My God. I threw him in the river once. I'll do it again."

"I wouldn't advise it. He's a local hero. Besides which, you'd cause a tidal wave. He weighs about twenty stone."

The volume of sound had been rising and falling. There had been a brief intermission while a soloist practiced some difficult bars. Now the full band was playing a spirited march. Nigel waited until it ended. Then he drew a deep breath.

"My mother—" he began.

"She knew nothing whatever about it."

"I'll bet the house agent knew."

"Yes, he did. He's Chan's cousin, so naturally he didn't show her the cottage while the band was practicing."

"Naturally. Will you tell me how an entire brass band can fit into a cottage the size of this one?"

"They don't use the cottage. They've got a big barn: you can just see the roof over the hedge. The cottage is only half the size of this one. Chan lives in it. He—"

"Wait minute. Let's get this straight. His father went off with some woman or other, and his mother took Chan away."

"Yes. To her family in Yorkshire. When she died two years ago, he came back to Longbrook."

"Towing a brass band?"

"No. He got that together in the past two years. But nobody took any interest in it, or helped him, until they won the contest."

"Contest?"

"The band's called the Longbrook and District Brass Band, and it won the regional brass band contest and put Longbrook on the map. I told you that Chan was a local hero, and it's true. The winners of the regional contests have the right to compete in the national contest in London. Think of it: Longbrook represented at the Albert Hall. So the town adopted the band. The players get time off in the middle of the day to practice."

"My mother bought this place knowing nothing of all this?"

"Why would she know anything about brass bands? I knew nothing about them, either; I found all these facts out when I realized what she'd let herself in for. Your mother might have seen references to a band in the local paper, but they wouldn't have mentioned that it held its practices next door to the cottage she was proposing to buy—would they? It isn't too bad. They keep regular practice times. This is the twelve-to-one. Most evenings there's a seven-to-eight. They're good, they really are. I'm not a brass band addict, but this lot can really play. When you think of all the work and sweat and struggle Chan went through to get it to the pitch it's at now, you have to—"

"What happens when my mother has visitors?"

"Visitors? What visitors? You know very well that for years she's dodged out on going to see people, except Dagmar and Sir James, and she seldom invites anybody to the house. The Reverend drops in now and then, but that's all. I'm sorry if it's going to spoil your time at home, but your mother's got used to it and she honestly doesn't mind it now. Her big worry was what you'd say when she told you."

"So she didn't tell me. No wonder this place was so cheap."

She spoke in a reasonable tone.

"I know how you feel, but there's no point in showing your mother that you loathe it. Why don't you go next door and have a talk with Chan? He knows you're home. Is there anything more I can tell you about brass bands before I go?"

"No. But if I'm not looking too enchanted, add it up: My mother leaves a big, solid house and lands herself in this shack. She leaves a large garden—not that she's a gardener, or ever did much to it, but at least there was a lot of space. We could all spread out. We all had room to breathe. I can understand my mother buying a place like this when she's nearing the end of her seventies and is having trouble getting around, but this is too soon, and it's not going to be good enough once she stops telling herself how clever she was to find it. Wasn't there any other house in all this town that she could have been induced to buy?"

"I wasn't here. Dagmar wasn't here. Sir James didn't know about it until it was too late. If you're planning to get her out of it, you'll have to do it slowly. And tactfully. In her way, she's just as pigheaded as you are."

"Thank you."

He found himself alone. The band played, stopped, played again. He carried the empty glasses to the kitchen and stood staring unseeingly out of the window. Before the rival music from next door had begun, he had been enjoying himself. He had been enjoying his records, his drink—above all, enjoying her company. She had not, it seemed, shared his enjoyment. Her mind had been on car servicing and brass bands.

He had come and gone for years, but he had never before had this feeling of being left out of things. He had come home and taken what he considered his rightful place as the center of the household. When he had grown bored, he had removed himself. But now he felt excluded, a temporary member who would soon be on his way, leaving no perceptible gap.

Coming to a sudden decision, he walked out of the house and turned towards the cottage next door. If he was going to be compelled to listen to sounding brass, he thought, he might just as well take a look at it—and congratulate Chan Fielder on the convenience of having a cousin who was a house agent.

The small wooden gate giving entrance to the property was hanging on one hinge, propped open by a motorbike. A variety of other bikes, powered or pedalled, leaned against the fence. Cars of varying but inexpensive make lined the road. In the space which in his mother's garden was used for paths and flower beds stood a large Dutch barn, its sides hung with canvas to provide protection from the weather. Inside it were assembled the members of the Longbrook and District Brass Band. At their head, standing on an upturned crate, was the conductor, Chan Fielder.

Nigel walked slowly forward. Chan turned his head, recognized him and for a moment stood motionless. Then with an agile movement surprising in one of his immense bulk, he stepped to the ground and addressed the players.

"Intermission," he bawled. "Coffee in the kitchen, bread and ham, cut your own sandwiches, beer in the crate."

Then he went forward to meet Nigel, his arms upheld as though to shield himself from blows.

"All right, all right, all *right*," he said as he reached him.
"We'll skip the first few bars. You've come to make pork pies
out of me, and I don't blame you, but I'd like to inform you
that I'm not a cowardy-custard any more. I fight back."

Nigel looked at him in wonder. He had always been a
balloon, but now the balloon seemed to have been blown up
to double its former size. His fingers were so thick that they
could scarcely meet. Between auburn, upstanding hair and a
pendulous chin was a full-moon face with the narrow, slanting
eyes that had given him his nickname.

"I'd say it was nice to see you," he told Nigel, "only I
know this isn't a happy reunion. But before you say a word,
you're going to listen to me, see? When I'm through, you can
start. Come into the rehearsal room."

He led the way into the barn, kicked a soapbox towards
Nigel and then pushed two crates together to accommodate
his spreading posterior. The members of the band were on
their way out, and Nigel recognized many of them and greeted
them as they passed.

"You can talk to them later—if you want to," Chan told
him. "But first you can hear what I've got to say."

Hands outspread on his knees, he stared for a moment or
two at the row of instruments lining the bench that ran along
one side of the barn. Then he began his speech.

"You've come to ask me why your mother got landed next
door. Well, before we get to that, I'll tell you what me and
my boys went through in the early days of the band. I got
the boys together. That took time, but in the end we got to
be a team. We knew we were good—but who cared? Nobody.
All those louts on the council, the same ones who can't do
enough for us now—did they help us to find a place where
we could practice? Not them."

"But you—"

"Quiet. We tried all the halls—we even hired them, paid
good borrowed money for them—and got turned out because
they were too near this building or that building and the noise

was too much. My problem was that I had a band, and no-where to take it. And then what? I came across old Mansfield, that market gardener whose land's on the other side of your mother's house. He mentioned a barn he'd put up when he was living in this cottage. I came and took a look, and what did I see? The end of all our troubles. A place where we could practice for-tissimo and not in-commode a soul. This great barn, and the empty cottage for me to use as a home and give the boys a room they could eat and drink in. There was nothing at the back but open grassland. There was nothing in front except the road and the river, the river you once chucked me into, I've forgotten why."

"You—"

"Quiet, I said. Beyond the river, a long way beyond, there was that new primary school. I didn't want any trouble from them, so I went over to get the teachers' views on brass band practices. They told me there was such a dirty-word din going on in the classes all the time, a brass band wouldn't make a filthy-word bit of difference. So that only left the empty cottage next door."

"Which was for sale."

"Yeah, for sale. It—"

"And your cousin was the house agent."

"You've been out fact-finding, I can see that. Yes, Bert had got it on his books. He told me he didn't think anybody would buy the place: the word had got round that we'd got our headquarters here, and buyers shied off."

"My mother—"

"Yeah, I'm coming to her. Bert told me there was a lady after it. A lady. That didn't tell me much; I don't know any ladies. If he'd said her name, it might have got through two inches of lard and reached my brain, but all he said was this lady who he didn't think had ever heard of a brass band. Well, I thought it was tough on the lady, but by this time, we'd won the regional competition and there were notices, posters, hoardings twelve feet high all over the town, so if she could read, she'd know we existed, and if she was interested in what went on in the town, which she should've been, then she'd know where we practiced. But she didn't."

"Because your cousin took damned good care—"

"Ah-ah-ah. Watch your language. My mum made me watch mine. One dirty word, and she'd make me wash my mouth out with carbolic soap. But I'm grateful to her, all the same, because the way our native language is being mauled about these days makes me want to throw up. They—"

"Don't get off the point. Your cousin made sure you weren't practicing when he let my mother inspect that cottage next door."

"Cor-rect. Ab-so-lutely cor-rect. But there was a lot wrong with that place, you know, leaving out brass bands. I went over and looked. There was enough in the way of snags to put any canny buyer off. But your mum moved in. So there you are. There's the picture. On one side, me and the boys going in for the national contest. On the other side—"

"My mother."

Chan regarded him solemnly.

"Would you—now honestly, with your hand on the Good Book—would you have put up a notice warning people not to buy? Would you? Yes or no?"

"No. But—"

"But. Your mother bought cheap, but cheap or not, what Bert has to live on is his commission, and business is always business. But when I heard it was your mum, I was sorry, because she was sorry when you threw me in the river. I wanted to walk over, go and see her, to give her a list of practice times, so's she could go for a walk or visit her chums or stop them from coming to see her, or she could get out the cotton wool and plug her ears. Then I heard you were coming home, and I said to myself: You wait, he'll be round quick's a flash. And I was right, and here you are looking for someone to murder, but there's nothing you can do except join our fan club."

"I could chuck your cousin in the river."

"Those ducking days are over. What you've got to do, what your mum's got to do, is try to enjoy our music. We're good. We're going to be the best. I know, because I learnt everything there was to learn about brass while I was living up in Yorkshire. What those colliery boys don't know about the business isn't worth researching."

Nigel looked him over.

"How did you get into this?" he asked him.

"The hard way. The slow, hard way. If my dad had been around, it might have come easier—he knew a lot about music and he knew a lot about musicians—but he'd skipped. You remember him?"

"Fairly well."

"Bit of a Chinese look, like me. Don't know where it came from. He had a good job in that music shop, but he couldn't keep his eyes off women, poor chap. My mum used to pray for him. You didn't know her, but you might have seen her around. Scraggy, always down at the church helping out. She'd got religion on the brain, the kind of religion that had gone rancid, if you follow me. It was that that made my dad go off in the end. When he'd gone, she packed and went back to her family and took me with her. There were colliery bands all round the place, and I listened, and learnt a lot. Then I bought myself a cornet, and that was the real beginning. Soon's I came back here, I went round looking for chaps who might be interested in getting a band together. Anything else I can tell you?"

"Yes. You're amateurs?"

"Strictly. We get our expenses when we play here and there, but the unions keep a bright eye on us and so do the other bands; it's been known for one or two of them to smuggle in a well-disguised pro—no fee, but a nice addition to the performance."

"How many of you altogether?"

"Thirty. Thirty-one."

"Uniforms?"

"Kind of. We only use 'em for big occasions, or on marches. We don't march much; I'm not built for it."

"How do you manage two practices a day?"

"At the moment, the bosses are cooperating. But it's hard on some of the boys who live out of town. We're a mixed lot. I've got four bank clerks, five shop assistants, three blacks— one of them's a genius on the cornet—seven husbands and a couple of out-of-works. Most of them have got girl friends, and sometimes they make trouble and I have to go and talk to them."

"What's your job?"

"This one. If you mean how do I earn a living, I work as general fac-to-tum at that pub, the Three Feathers." He heaved himself to his feet. "Intermission's over. Tell your mum I'm sorry. How about taking a drink off me one evening?"

"Here?"

"No, not here. I live here, but I don't invite posh chaps like you. Make it the pub. Late evening, not early evening."

Nigel walked out into the road. Turning towards his mother's cottage, he saw her approaching. He waited; as they walked into the house together, the band began to play. She looked at him questioningly.

"I paid Fatty Fielder a visit," he told her. "They're there to stay. If you can't stand it, you'll have to move." He noticed her pallor, and frowned anxiously. "You look pale. Anything wrong?"

"Not really." She entered the living room and sank on to the sofa. "Could you give me a drink? Where's Rona?"

"She took the car to the garage." He brought her a drink and stood looking down at her. "Something happened?"

"No. I'm being silly."

"Did you walk all the way home?"

"Yes, but I'm not tired."

"Then—?"

"It was something James told me." She took a strengthening sip before proceeding. "Maria Montallen's here."

He stared at her.

"Here?"

"Here in Longbrook." She paused. "I know you wouldn't have asked her to come—anyway, you thought she was going to New York—but I was wondering whether perhaps you'd been—overfriendly."

"I swear to you that I said nothing, did nothing that she or anyone else could call friendly. If she's here, it's because Dagmar's story was true and she's lost her Austrian boy friend. If there were any friendly overtures at the airport, they came from Francis Latimer."

"He's here too."

"Then that explains Maria's appearance."

There was silence for a time. When he spoke, there was a puzzled note in his voice.

"Look," he said. "I don't quite get this. Maria Montallen's back, and of course you think she shouldn't have shown her face here again. But why should you mind so much?"

"Do you think I want to be reminded of—of all that again?"

"All what?" He pulled a chair close to the sofa, sat down and leaned forward with his elbows on his knees. "All what, exactly? Rona was going to marry Roger, and Maria snatched him. That was more than three years ago, and as far as I can see, it left no hangover as far as Rona's concerned. So what difference does it make if Maria's in town or not? Why can't the whole thing be buried and forgotten?"

"You weren't here. You don't know what it was like. And you don't know the whole of it. Neither did I, until Dagmar told me in the car today."

"What did she tell you that you didn't know before?"

"She spoke to someone in Geneva who told her he'd seen a necklace that was once part of the Montallen collection."

"Anything odd about that?"

"Yes. Mrs. Montallen never sold anything. And this was a—a fabulous necklace. You must have seen it when you went to see the collection—a diamond bead necklace with gold bands, in a case by itself. You must remember."

"Yes. Go on."

"Dagmar thinks that Mrs. Montallen gave it to Roger to induce him—bribe him—to take Maria away."

"And you think it's true?"

"Yes. It was sold by the Underwood Gallery. So Roger sold it, and they lived on the money, and when the money was spent, she left him. That necklace must have been worth a fortune. How could they have spent all that in a year?" She paused. "We don't have to tell Rona about this, do we?"

"Why not? It's all part of the story. She's entitled to know it all. Look, you're still pale; why don't you go and lie down?" As she hesitated, he added: "I'll break the news about Maria to Rona."

She looked relieved.

"Will you tell her I've got a headache and want to rest?"

"Yes. You think she'll be upset because Maria's turned up again?"

"No."

"You said that pretty confidently."

"Only because I know how wonderful she was when—when it happened."

"She was well out of it. I gave you my opinion: Roger was all right in some ways, but he didn't have what you could call staying power, physical or mental. Or, as it turned out, moral. Now go and lie down. Want me to tuck you in?"

She smiled.

"No, thank you."

He stayed in the living room, but he was not alone for long. He heard Rona's footsteps, and a few minutes later she was in the room.

"Your mother back?" she enquired.

"Yes. With a headache. She's lying down."

"Isn't she feeling well?"

"She's assimilating the shock of hearing that Maria Montallen's back in this town."

He watched her through the ensuing silence. Her eyes widened, but he saw no other sign that the news was of special interest to her. When she spoke, there was even a light note in her voice.

"Just dropped in, or staying?"

"I don't know. My mother thinks I had something to do with it."

"You? Why?"

"Because I met Maria at the airport last night. My mother didn't think it was a subject I ought to raise with you, so I didn't mention the meeting. I was given to understand that the topic isn't exactly forbidden, but—"

"As far as I was concerned, it could have been brought up and aired at any time. But your mother skates round it. How did you know who Maria was?"

"She came across and spoke to a man I was with. When she heard my name, she said it was time we met as we had so much in common. Or words to that effect. She said she left Roger two years ago and didn't know where he was, and didn't care."

"What was she doing at the airport? I mean, where had she come from?"

"Munich. She was to meet an Austrian boy friend and fly —in all senses—to New York. Apparently he was rescued in time."

"Rescued by whom?"

"His parent or parents. Dagmar told us about it. It was a baby-snatching act on Maria's part, I gather."

"Why did you say you'd got the blame for her being here?"

"My mother thinks I might have invited her. Which I didn't. The point is not what I said to Maria, but whether her turning up again will upset you."

"Oh, I see. That's what's worrying your mother?"

"Yes."

"Then I'll go and put her mind at rest."

"No, you won't. Not just yet. Now that this subject has been dragged into the open, you can sit down and furnish a few facts about what actually happened. Do you want a drink to fortify you?"

"No. I had one before I went out—and I don't need fortifying."

"Good. Take a seat and answer some questions. Then we'll have lunch and I'll take some in to my mother."

She seated herself on the sofa.

"This'll make her miserable," she said.

"It needn't. What seems to be worrying her is the thought of how you'll feel about it. So would you tell me how you do feel about it?"

"I don't feel anything. Should I?"

"Not unless you're the morbid type, which you're not. You should have outlived it by now. Will you please tell me exactly what happened?"

She did not reply at once. She had put her feet up, and her eyes were fixed absentmindedly on the cat, which had jumped on to her lap. She stroked it gently.

"I think that what gave the affair a slightly sensational touch," she said at last, "was the timing. There was only a fortnight to go before the wedding. The house was full of presents, packed and unpacked. The invitations—not many, but taking in most of the people we know in Longbrook—had been sent out and accepted. I hadn't bought a wedding dress, fortunately. I'd refused to have one made; I was going up to Harrods to buy one off the peg."

"Didn't anybody have the slightest idea of what was going on between Roger and Maria?"

"Not at first. I was the first one who heard the warning bell. I saw him lunching with her one day in Soho. I thought it odd, but not sinister—until he failed to mention it. After that, I—couldn't I strike a pose and say that the scales fell from my eyes?"

"Did you tackle him?"

There was a long pause.

"This cat's got such a lovely, soft velvety nose," she said.

"So has every cat. I asked you if you tackled Roger."

"Yes, I heard you. Well—no, I didn't tackle Roger."

"Why not?"

"Oh, several reasons, but the chief of them was that I didn't know how to do it. I rehearsed several openings: 'Here is your ring; take it back.' 'If you love her better than you love me . . .' You see what I mean?"

"You simply sat back and did nothing?"

"I did try to alert your mother, but she was pretty deep in wedding preparations."

"How did the thing break?"

"There was a prewedding dinner given by the Rensons— not at their house; at the Crown. Forty guests, mostly old friends. We all assembled—except Roger. That was the bad part. I guessed he'd gone, and gone with Maria, and it was hard to watch everybody gradually taking in the fact that I'd been left high and dry. Not dry; we all had drinks and we were beginning to need them. I would have liked to reassure everybody—I'd had a lot of time to adjust. But again, there seemed no adequate way of expressing what I wanted to say. 'Keep calm, folks, this is no surprise to me.' Or 'Don't worry about me, I'm fine.' I could see them gradually closing in, ready to catch me as I swooned. Women were shedding tears —for me. Your mother . . . she was just deathly white and stunned. So finally I got Dagmar to get the guests to table and start the dinner, and then she and I brought your mother home and put her to bed. Like now. It took weeks for her to believe that I'd survived and was likely to go on surviving. The town split on the issue of whether I was a brave little woman who had taken it on the chin, or whether I was tougher than any of them had realized." She paused. "I think I will have that drink."

He poured out two glasses and brought hers to the table beside the sofa.

"Have I given you the picture?" she asked.

"More or less."

"I suppose you think I should have kept Roger safely out of her reach?"

"After meeting her last night, I'd say she was pretty stiff competition."

"If I'd thought about it in that way, I would have taken the view that if a man's going to fall for every attractive woman he meets, you might as well find out before you marry him. And another thing—"

"Well?"

"It sounds a bit hard on Roger, but to be quite honest, I never thought she'd look at him. Not seriously. He wasn't in her league. He was good-looking and amusing up to a point, but she was so totally removed from our sphere that it never occurred to me that any of us could ever interest her. I've never understood what made her go off with him in the end. I'm certain it wasn't love."

"No. It was a necklace. Mrs. Montallen bribed him. That's something else my mother didn't want mentioned, but you're entitled to know. Dagmar learned about it recently in Geneva."

"A necklace?"

"Of very great value. Mrs. Montallen parted with it in order to get rid of her granddaughter. My bet is that the idea was originally Maria's. 'Make it worth my while,' she must have said, 'and I'll get out.'"

"She must also have said that she'd stay out. She sold the necklace?"

"Roger did."

She said nothing for a time. Then:

"It makes it sound even more sordid, doesn't it? At the

same time, it's reassuring to learn that it wasn't entirely Maria's magnetism that did it. She had to use money." Her voice became thoughtful, almost dreamy. "It's a pity you didn't spend that last leave of yours at home."

"I was going round factories, mills, offices all over Europe."

"I know. But it was a pity. We'd all looked forward to seeing you. Your mother, of course. Me, to be here for my twenty-first birthday. David, to be best man at his wedding."

"You were in Scotland."

"I wouldn't have been, if you hadn't written to your mother to tell her you weren't coming."

"You think I could have prevented what happened?"

She did not answer. She had displaced the cat gently and was getting to her feet. She went into the kitchen.

"Lunch," she said. "Fish salad and Camembert and biscuits and fruit. I'll take in your mother's; then she can see for herself that I'm still upstanding."

Celia, in a dressing gown, was seated on the bed, propped against pillows.

"Something to eat," Rona said, pulling up a small table and putting the tray on it. "And stop worrying. Maria can take up residence here for all I care. Nigel and I have been discussing my wrecked hopes. I must be the first woman who's been exchanged for a necklace."

"Don't joke about it, Rona."

"Why not? It has its funny side."

"Not for me. It's even worse now that I know that old Mrs. Montallen had a hand in it. I can't understand how people, people we know, people we've met and talked to, people who seem to be what I can only think of as normal, can behave in such a way. Deceit, faithlessness, callousness— and bribery. I feel lost when I try to understand it, understand them. I don't understand how such awful things can go on in the world as the things we hear about every day. I feel as though I grew up in a totally different world."

"The awful things were always going on," Rona pointed out gently. "It's just that your generation read a thing in the papers when it was all over and had lost its impact. You didn't see it all going on on television as it's happening. Nigel's generation, and mine—we've grown up with it."

"I know. I don't feel I belong any more. When I sit down and pick up my embroidery, I get an odd feeling that I'm a figure in an old portrait. A very old portrait."

Since this was exactly what Rona had often thought, she decided to make no comment.

"Any reaction from Nigel about the band practice?" she asked.

"He went next door and talked to Chan. He says there's nothing I can do, except move if I can't stand the noise. I've just remembered something, Rona. Sir James asked if you could give him an hour or two for a few evenings, to go through his papers and try to get them sorted out."

"It'll take more than a few evenings, from what I've seen in his study."

"Could you find the time?"

"I could fit it in after I come home from the office. It won't be much of a change; that's all we've been doing in the office for the past few weeks: clearing up years and years of mess and accumulations. And mismanagement. And muddle."

"It's a pity Bryan didn't join the firm earlier."

"It's more than a pity, it's a disaster. But he says if he'd come in while his father was still in charge, he wouldn't have stayed long."

"Was it his father who let things get into such a mess?"

"Partly. Old Mr. Harvard did his share, but it was mostly old Mr. Todd. Like Bryan's father, he couldn't bear the thought of retiring. He cut his visits to the office down to two a week. He used to take work home with him, so nobody in the office knew what was going on. A scandal, no less."

The door opened. Nigel entered with a bottle of wine.

"What's a scandal?" he asked.

"The way that trio of aged partners let the office run down. We have to deal with a succession of complaining clients. We're becoming expert at stalling."

The telephone was ringing.

"You go," Nigel said, busy with bottle and corkscrew.

Rona went into the hall.

"It'll be Dagmar," Celia said, "to remind you to go and see David and Sigrid this afternoon."

It was not Dagmar. Rona, returning, told Nigel that the call had been for him.

"A lady," she said. "Name of Maria Montallen."

"Tell her I'm not here."

"I did. I said you were at lunch, which was true. I would have called you, but I felt you'd need time to adjust."

"Quite right." He poured out wine and handed glasses to her and to his mother. "Expert at stalling is right." He raised his glass.

"A toast?" his mother asked with some surprise.

"Yes. The Longbrook and District Brass Band," he said.

CHAPTER

4

LUNCH OVER, CELIA DECIDED TO STAY IN HER ROOM AND read.

"Why don't you go with Nigel and see the Rensons?" she asked Rona.

"She's going," Nigel said. "We'll pick up her car and go straight on."

After a brief argument with the cats, who seemed disposed to accompany them, they walked to the garage at the end of the road to claim the car. Then they drove to the wide, shop-lined avenue which within living memory had been a narrow village street flanking a muddy stream and ending in a duck pond.

"When's the new baby due?" he asked on the way.

"Any minute."

"Bit soon after the other one, isn't it?"

"Not too soon for Sigrid. She wants a family, and not too spread out."

"Where did David meet her?"

"In Stockholm. She was born there but she was hardly ever there because she had a mother who liked to travel. Sometimes they stopped long enough for Sigrid to start school, but before the term ended, they were off again. So she likes being fixed in a home with a husband and baby, to say nothing of a mother-in-law and two Swiss appendages."

"She's happy?"

"Except for Dagmar, yes. She's never done any housework and doesn't particularly want to start, so she can leave it all to Inga and Claudine."

"What happened to her mother?"

"Remarried. So could Dagmar, if she wanted to, but she doesn't want anything but her children and grandchildren. Why is it that in some parts of the world the generations manage to live together and think it's right and natural, while—"

"—while in this country, it doesn't seem to work? I suppose the degrees of poverty or prosperity have something to do with it. In countries where people are really poor, the old get worn out with hard work and haven't the strength to tackle a new generation. So they sit in sunny doorways and smoke their pipes—or knit. I don't think you'll ever see Dagmar sitting down with her pipe and her knitting."

She glanced at him.

"You're fond of her, aren't you?"

"Yes. But I've never been around long enough for her to do much interfering."

"I feel the way Sigrid does: I can take so much of her, and no more."

They left the car in the car park and walked back towards the shop.

"Shop entrance, or house entrance?" she asked as they neared it.

"Shop."

He followed her inside; then he stood still and let the past come flooding back. From his earliest days, he had liked to stand gazing at the forest of books to be seen on every side. He had not for some time been aware that there was anything between the covers; all he knew, all he saw was the vivid colours of the jackets, lines and lines on shelves and in show-cases and on stands, an endless feast of pictures and lettering and design. He had watched the building and the stocking of the second shop, and then the third, until he could see, through the wide arches, from one end of the low-ceilinged, deep-carpeted expanse to the other. Books. Books beautifully arranged by Dagmar and now even more beautifully set out by David.

David, tall, thin, dark, was coming towards him.

"Hello, Nigel. It's been a long time."

"Too long. How are you, Dave?"

They had been through school together. They had spent their holidays together on beaches or on ski slopes. They had seldom been separated—until they were eighteen. Then Aubrey Renson died, and David sloughed off his English-schoolboy skin and overnight became a Chantard, no longer talking of bowling averages or boat race prospects, but only of books—buying them, selling them. When Nigel went up to Cambridge, David set out on a tour of Chantard relations in Geneva to learn, as his mother in her girlhood had learned, the business of bookselling.

He and Nigel and Rona walked up the wide staircase behind the shop.

"Husband and father," Nigel said. "You've left me behind."

David smiled.

"How long did you expect me to wait?" he asked. "You said we'd be married by the time we were thirty."

"How are Inga and Claudine?"

"Just the same—and looking forward to seeing you."

He had opened one of the doors at the end of a long corridor.

"Sigrid's in here," he said.

It was a sitting room overlooking the street. It bore no resemblance whatsoever to Celia's white-painted woodwork and pale curtains and pretty rugs. The furniture was dark, solid and enduring; much of it had been brought by Dagmar from Geneva on her marriage. The walls were panelled, the carpet a deep-piled, glowing crimson.

Sigrid was seated on a sofa, her feet on a footstool. She was very fair, her hair almost colourless, her eyes a vivid blue. Her manner free from any trace of self-consciousness, she waited for David's introduction and then held out a hand to Nigel.

"It's nice to see you at last." Her voice was clear, her English almost unaccented. "I've heard so much about you from David, I feel we're old friends. Come and sit here. I hope you're not going to rush away too soon, the way Dave says you usually do. You're not going back to Brazil, I hear."

"No."

"I suppose your mother will be glad. Or perhaps not. My grandmother used to say that after a week, she'd had enough of her children. Don't you think Dave's looking well?"

"Extremely well. Marriage suits him."

"It suits me, too."

"How about showing me the son and heir?"

"Would you like to see him? Dave, see where he is, will you?"

"I'll go," Nigel said. "I can see Inga and Claudine at the same time."

He made his way to the kitchen. Inga, on seeing him, gave a loud cry, dropped the rolling pin, shouted *geliebt knabe*, and fell on his neck. Freeing himself, he summoned his German, answered her questions about what he had been doing in Brazil and then told her he was looking for the baby. The *kleines kind*, he learned, had been with her, but was now with Claudine in the laundry room. Claudine, on his entrance, gave a shriek of joy, kissed him on both cheeks and said that she could almost imagine that it was his father who had come back to life. *Le petit Artur?* He had been with her, yes, but now he was with his *grand-mère* in her salon, having been transported thither after eating too much of a *gâteau* which could not have done him the least harm.

Dagmar relinquished her grandson with reluctance.

"It is always the same," she said. "If I do not watch, they spoil him. He has been eating cakes—imagine, when it is nearly time for his milk and cereal. I will go and bring him back soon, because you will all be having tea and of course he will want to have more to eat." She handed the baby to him and he took it with care. "Ah, I see you are accustomed to this, holding babies. It is what I have always suspected, that you did not waste your time with all those women in Brazil."

He made his way back to Sigrid's room. The baby, an engaging, pink-cheeked roly-poly, took a firm hold of his hair and leaned back to get a better view of his face. Approving of what he saw, he bent forward and pressed a series of moist kisses on his cheeks, uttering affectionate sounds in between.

"Now then, now then, let's take it as read," Nigel suggested. "You like me, I like you. Take it easy. Don't get mushy. Just relax."

He entered the sitting room, gave the baby to Sigrid, wiped the cake crumbs that had stuck to his cheeks, and smoothed his hair.

"Nice little chap," he said. "Congratulations."

"You could have waited a few days and congratulated me for two," Sigrid told him. "David thought it was too soon to have another, but I want a big family and I don't want to be in maternity clothes forever. Not that they hide much, as you see. I've bought some sensational dresses I'm going to get into as soon as I can fit into them. Tell me, are you going to do anything about finding your mother another house?"

"She's only just settled into this one."

"She should never have bought it. I find it extraordinary that for once, when Dagmar's interference would have been useful, she wasn't here to do something about it. But never mind that for now. I want to ask you something else. You met Maria Montallen at the airport, didn't you?"

Nigel, pleased with this direct approach to the subject, said that he had.

"Does she call herself Montallen, or something else now?"

"Montallen."

She turned to Rona.

"Did they tell you she was back here? Or didn't Celia want you to know? It's funny, Nigel, your mother always refused to talk about her."

"Any idea what brought Maria back?" David asked.

"Well, it might be pure coincidence—or anyway, coincidence," Nigel said, "but I introduced Francis Latimer to her at the airport, and he's turned up here too."

"I heard he was in town," David said, "but I didn't connect him with Maria. When you come to think of it, they make a good pair: she likes money, he's got money. If she's free, and if he can shake himself loose from his women, they might get together."

"One thing about this place," Sigrid remarked, "you don't have to wait long to hear any gossip that's going. That's why I'm surprised that none of us knew about the brass band before your mother went to live next door to it."

"Have you seen Chan?" David asked Nigel.

"Yes. They were having a practice. I don't know what I was planning to say to him, but I didn't get a chance to say it; he did most of the talking."

Sigrid was leaning against the cushions, quiet, relaxed, the baby on her lap. Nigel felt that she was the right kind of wife for David; she would act as a tranquillizer on his highly strung temperament. A similar happy state, he knew from his mother, had existed between Aubrey Renson and Dagmar, though in their case it had been the husband who had exerted a calming influence.

The door opened. Claudine came in pushing a laden tea trolley. The men rose to help her. Dagmar came in and claimed the baby; Sigrid gave him up and poured out tea.

When Rona and Nigel took their leave, it was generally agreed that there was no point in making plans for future meetings; they would have to wait and see when the new baby arrived.

"Well?" Rona asked as they walked to the car. "Like her?"

"Yes. Nice and matter-of-fact. They're a good pair. And a nice baby. I hope I'll turn out to be as good a father as David is."

"You won't."

"Why won't I?"

"Don't you remember what you said when I asked you why hens made such a noise when they laid an egg?"

"No, I don't."

"I was ten, and I'd just come to live in your house, and you were loathing it—and me. I said *Why* do hens make such a noise when they've laid an egg, and you said they did it to make sure that someone would take their children away and boil them for breakfast."

"Can't you," he asked irritably, "let bygones be bygones?"

"I'll try. I've got quite a forgiving nature, on the whole."

"You'll need it, with Maria Montallen floating round town. You could prove you've got a forgiving nature by letting me take you out to dinner tonight."

She shook her head.

"You can't, and I can't," she said. "You've got to eat the celebration steak, and I'm dining with Bryan Hayling."

"You shouldn't mix pleasure with business."

"Do you remember him?"

"Vaguely. Mad on sailing. Can't picture him in an office. Wasn't he the great-outdoors type?"

"He stays out-of-doors when he's not in the office. He grows vegetables."

He was driving out of the car park.

"Where to?" he asked.

"Home. Let's play some more music."

The gate of the cottage was open. Driving through, they saw standing before the porch an ancient motor bicycle with an open sidecar. Nigel looked at it apprehensively.

"I've seen that before," he said. "But without the sidecar. Why the sidecar?"

"He takes his sister around with him nowadays. Remember her?"

"Yes. Name of Monica. Why does he have to take her around?"

"Because she's getting lame and can't go for walks any more, so this is the only outing she gets."

"Does he often come here?"

"Fairly often. Your mother feels sorry for him. So do I, but I try to keep out of his way, or I get caught up and made to help in his schemes for getting money."

"Church still falling down?"

"Yes."

"What does—"

He stopped. A figure in clerical garb was following Celia out of the house. Beside him was a thin, elderly woman in a shabby black coat. Rona and Nigel got out of the car and went to meet them.

"My dear fellow!" The clergyman took Nigel's hand and shook it vigorously. "How fortunate, how very fortunate to catch you before we left. You remember my sister, of course?"

"Of course. It's nice to see you," Nigel told her with as much sincerity as he could summon. He helped her to settle herself in the sidecar and wrapped the threadbare rug round her. Then he fastened the string that held the door shut.

"Comfortable?" he asked.

"Oh, thank you, thank you, yes. I do hope you'll come and see us soon. Goodbye."

Her brother was shaking hands again.

"You must certainly come to see us. Your mother tells me you're not going back to India."

"Brazil," Nigel corrected.

"Brazil, was it? Do you know, I was certain you were in India. But Brazil, you say?"

"Yes."

"Then I must make a note. Coffee. Nuts. That kind of thing. Goodbye, dear Mrs. Pressley. Goodbye, Rona, my dear. Goodbye, goodbye."

They stood watching the pair as they drove away.

"They haven't changed," Nigel commented compassionately. "Poor devils."

The Reverend Morton Vale, known simply as the Reverend, was tall, cadaverous, in his middle sixties, and had for more than forty years been vicar of Longbrook. For most of this time, he had conducted a lonely, unceasing and unavailing campaign to direct his parishioners' attention to the needs of the church—by which he meant the building itself. This, once beautiful, historic, had during the last war been extensively damaged. It had been patched up by the church authorities to await further repairs, and had then been to all appearances forgotten. To the signs of dilapidation the sparse number of worshippers remained indifferent.

The Reverend's life was an unending plea for donations, large or small, for the building fund. But his flock was not numerous, and belonged to the less affluent sections of the community. Sunday collections had fallen to a derisory sum. The Easter offering, in days past a welcome addition to his stipend, was now a sprinkling of coins on the bottom of the collection plate.

His lack of success in filling his church was in a great measure due to his chronic inability to remember faces. He would pass even his most loyal helpers without recognition, and newcomers felt at first disconcerted and then resentful at being treated on each successive meeting as total strangers.

Rona had always liked him. Accompanying Celia to church during her early days in Longbrook, she had been struck by the difference between his irritating, ingratiating manner on social occasions and the dignity and authority with which he conducted the services.

"Did they drop in for tea?" she asked as they went into the house.

Celia nodded.

"Yes."

"You didn't offer them the cake I made for Nigel, did you?"

"Well, I—"

There was no need to continue. The cake plate was empty.

"And the cucumber sandwiches I made for your tea? And the oatmeal biscuits, and the almond crunch?"

"They always seem so hungry," Celia said apologetically.

"Well, don't let them depress you," Nigel said. "Sit down and we'll play you some nice cheerful records."

"Not yet. I'd like to go and change. And I'm not depressed. It's just that whenever I see them, I remember how much money people have poured into this town—for everything except the church. It's falling down, and nobody cares, and fewer and fewer people go to the services. I don't understand it. When I was young, did we go to chuch regularly just because we were unenlightened and superstitious? Or was it just the fashion? Or what?"

"Or what," Nigel diagnosed. "The Reverend's trouble is that he doesn't make his appeals in a popular form. For example, he hasn't got a decent choir because the one he had evaporated and he couldn't get another one going. He should have done what they did at my school: call in a big name known in choir circles, institute auditions and make it hard to get in. To be in the choir at my school was a status symbol; but who wants to join a choir with poor old Monica wheezing at the organ, and Mrs. Gunter singing half a tone out of tune?"

"Nobody. But he organized a food fund," Rona told him, "and that was a popular appeal: everybody who had a spare jar or packet or can of any food was asked to leave it at the church, and there was to be a big sale with the money going to the building fund. Big sale? Nobody left anything—except us and Mrs. Gunter and one or two others."

"The trouble is that the leading citizens won't help," Celia summed up. "Like Sir James. He's never been inside the church." She went towards the door. "Oh, Nigel, I left another list of phone calls on the table. They all asked if you'd call back."

He picked up the paper. Two calls from the London office; no hurry about those. The house agent about accommodation in London; that could wait. The girl he'd written to once or twice, the one up in Darlington. The woman who'd been touring Brazil. The girl he'd sat next to on the plane—fast worker, she. And Dorothy Kestrel, the actress: a London phone number, which meant that the play she had been in in Manchester must have come off.

He crumpled the paper and dropped it into the wastepaper basket. Rona passed him on her way upstairs.

"Put on some music," she said. "I'm going up to change, but I won't be long. Bryan ought to be here soon. Oh, about dinner: the steak's ready to be put on the grill. The vegetables are in the casserole; I cooked them a bit this morning, but they want finishing off. Would you put them in the oven later, gas number four?"

Her tone, to his amazement and growing fury, held nothing of apology or regret at having to leave him to cook the meal. He had returned from thousands of miles away, home is the sailor, and she was going out to enjoy herself, leaving him with his mother and some half-cooked vegetables. If he put anything into the oven at gas number four, it would be Bryan Hayling.

"Nothing else?" he enquired sarcastically. "Shall I whip up a soufflé?"

"No. There's cheese and wine. Could you put the drinks out?"

He put them out. Then he selected a record. Before he could

put it on, the brass band began its evening practice. He closed the window with a bang and stood fighting his feeling of frustration.

She had said that she would not be long, but she came down only a few moments before Bryan Hayling came in. Her greeting seemed to Nigel unnecessarily warm.

He looked the visitor over. Heavier, he noted critically; you could see he'd be piling it on in a few years. Clothes—he must have spent a lot of time deciding on that tie. And he was certainly at home; no need for her to ask what he was going to drink; she knew.

"Nice time of the year to come back to England," Bryan remarked after testing his gin and lime and pronouncing it just right. "I understand you're not going back to Brazil."

"No."

"Settled where you're going to live?"

Nigel said that he had decided to live in London.

"It's a pity he couldn't have taken over my apartment," Rona said. "But I've given it up and they've re-let it."

"It was a nice place," Bryan said. "I looked for something like it when I was working up in London, but there was nothing that I liked—at my price, that is. I settled for— Oh, good evening, Mrs. Pressley. I think I've got your favourite chair."

He vacated it, went into the porch and returned with a small parcel which he presented to her.

"Something I know you enjoy," he said. "I picked them an hour ago."

"Oh, delicious new peas! Thank you, Bryan." She turned to Nigel. "Bryan grows the most beautiful vegetables, and he knows I love new little baby peas. Would you put them in the kitchen?"

He took the parcel and laid it on the kitchen table. Note that, Pressley, he told himself savagely. When you go wooing, don't arrive holding a posy for your girl friend. Make a dent where it'll be most effective: in the good graces of her godparent. If it's spring, come with peas, but it would better to wait until autumn, when you could walk in disguised as a harvest festival, weighed down with the fruits of the earth.

It struck him for the first time, as he went back to the living room, that his mother was no matchmaker. Any other woman, in these circumstances—that was to say, with a girl of twenty-four to be joined in matrimony—would have been busy hustling up the local talent. But his mother seemed to have given no thought to the matter. She would eat the peas and enjoy them but she would do nothing to further the grower's cause. And he, N. Pressley, would do nothing to further it, either.

"I thought," Bryan was saying, "that Rona and I might try this new restaurant—the Chinese one. I haven't been there yet, but I'm told it's good."

"I like Chinese cooking," Celia said. "They use a lot of vegetables."

"That's true," Bryan agreed. "They eat about the same amount of meat as the Italians, which is a long way short of the amount the Americans and the English and the Argentinians get through."

"I remember eating something they told me was a mixture of chicken and bamboo shoots and ham and mushrooms and minced pork," Rona said. "I don't know whether it was good, or whether I only thought so because it was the favourite dish of a gentleman of the Ch'ing Dynasty called— Can't remember."

"Li Hung-chang," Bryan supplied. "He was a famous minister." He finished his drink and shook his head when Nigel got up to refill his glass. "No, thanks." He looked at Rona. "I don't want to hurry you, but I think we ought to be going."

Nigel walked with them to the door of the porch and stood watching as they drove away. A fine homecoming, he thought bitterly. A wonderful reception. This is my new little cottage, brass band laid on next door, hello, brother Nigel, make the coffee, grill the steak, put the cassarole in the oven and don't lay a place for me, I'm going to dine with the Chinese minister.

He made an effort to throw off his depression. What was the

matter with him? he wondered. What was he complaining about? He was free to make his own plans. He could pack a suitcase and go and see his friends and come back when it was time to move to London. There was nothing to stop him.

He went back to the living room. His mother had moved to a straight-backed chair and was unfolding a piece of embroidery. He switched on the lamp beside her.

"No, don't do that," she said. "I can't settle. I must do something about our dinner."

"You needn't. Rona's told me what to do. It's all more or less ready."

She looked at him in surprise. No wonder, he thought; it hadn't sounded like his voice and it must be the first time in his life that he had volunteered to cook anything more than the breakfast toast. Well, not exactly volunteered.

He poured himself out a drink.

"Rona been seeing much of this fellow?" he asked.

"Seeing much of Bryan?" She considered. "Well, yes, I suppose she has. I think he relies on her a good deal in the office; in fact, Dagmar thinks it was Bryan who induced his father to bring her back to Longbrook and give her this job."

"What do you think of him?"

"Of Bryan?" Once again she had to think it over. "Well, he's got very nice manners. He always had, even as a boy. And money didn't spoil him."

"I didn't know the Haylings had money."

"Not his father; his mother. She was related in some way to Sir James's wife and I think their money came from the same source, whatever that was. You ought to go and see him before you go away, Nigel."

"I will." He paused at the kitchen door. "How about soup?"

"Soup? Well, we don't, as a rule. But if you want some, there are some cans in—"

"No, not for me. I thought you might like some."

He went into the kitchen. Light the oven, put in the casserole.

He was obliged to concentrate on the grilling, if only for the reason that he did not want to burn himself or the meat. His mother opened the gateleg table and laid it for two. She came in to remind him to heat the plates for the steak.

"The vegetables," she said, opening the oven to inspect them, "don't look as though they're ready."

"They've got to be," he said. "The steak is. Sit down, will you, and I'll serve it."

It was almost black outside, blood-red inside; just as he liked it. His mother, who preferred it well cooked, asked apologetically if her piece could be replaced on the grill.

"If you like," he said, "but there's no sense in overdoing it."

He took it away and relit the grill. Then he opened the door of the oven and looked for a cloth to protect his fingers. The nearest was the towel; he folded it, took hold of the casserole and drew it toward him. Then he lifted it—but the fold of the towel did not reach far enough, and two of his fingers encountered the side of the dish. With a yell of pain, he let go. The dish, more than halfway off the bars of the oven, slid the rest of the way and crashed to the floor. The next ten seconds were occupied by him in dredging up from the dark places of his mind all the suitable words he could think of.

"Darling." His mother had come in and was dealing efficiently with the pieces of glass and the heap of mixed vegetables. "Don't use that awful language. It's absolutely all right; I wasn't keen on vegetables anyway."

"Leave that," he said. "I'll clean it up."

"It's done." She pressed the pedal of the garbage bin and dropped in the mess. "Now come and— Oh dear!"

The steak which he had replaced on the grill was now alight. He drew it away, blew furiously and stood looking at it.

"I'm not a meat-lover, as you know." His mother spoke consolingly. "I just bought the steak for your dinner last night. Now come and eat yours, and I'll have cheese and biscuits, which is all I really need at night."

He did not move.

"Look, let's leave this," he said, "and go and dine out. That's what I would have suggested before, but I knew you wanted to use the damned steak. Come on—let's go. We'll dodge the Chinese place."

"It's nice of you, Nigel, but honestly, I think that by the time we get somewhere and order, and they've served it, it'll be too late for me to enjoy it. Sit down and eat your steak before it gets any colder."

It was not hot, but it was good. Finishing it, he joined his mother over the cheese board. He was beginning to feel more like himself; his lack of spirits, he decided, must have been due to hunger.

They cleared away and put the plates into the dishwasher. Celia made coffee and he laced his liberally with cognac. She took up her embroidery again, but he did not sit down.

"Would you mind if I went along and dropped in on David?" he asked.

She looked relieved.

"Of course not. But you saw him this afternoon."

"Not by himself."

"Will you walk or drive?"

"Walk. I need exercise."

He also, he thought, needed a change of scene. Perhaps David would welcome a change, too. If Sigrid was in bed, perhaps he could be induced to go out, and they could go along to their old haunt, the Three Feathers.

Later, walking with David past the still brightly lit shops, he could say with truth that this was like old times. He could not recall how often they had sought out one another, as he now sought David, when in need of company or advice or solace.

The Three Feathers, down a narrow side street, was almost full. There was a good deal of noise, with voices raised, some in argument, others in song. The smell of beer was almost thick enough to be felt. The cigarette smoke was a fog through which they made their way, drinks and sandwiches in hand, to the last vacant table.

"Why sandwiches?" David asked. "Didn't you have enough dinner?"

"I made a hash of it. Rona was out. Hayling took her to that new Chinese restaurant."

"I took Sigrid there when it opened. She wouldn't go again."

"Food no good?"

"Service too slow. She said she thought they had to go to China to fetch the stuff."

"Do you know him well?"

"Know who well? Oh, Hayling. Fairly. He's got a good brain. He's going to pull that office together. My mother has an idea that it was his suggestion to get Rona back into it. But strictly between you and me, the idea was Sigrid's."

"What did Sigrid have to do with it?"

"She's got what you might call a Noah complex: she likes to see the species in pairs. She guessed Bryan wanted to get Rona here, and she wanted to get her here too, because she wasn't seeing enough of her. So Sigrid and Bryan got together, and old Hayling was persuaded to put the proposition to Rona. So Rona came back. Mark you, Bryan isn't having it all his own way. That architect chap is giving him trouble."

"Architect?"

"Geoffry Steele. He didn't get into the act as early as Hayling, but he's a faster mover. Hayling likes to take one step at a time, and that's dangerous when you're trying to outdistance rivals."

"Rivals?"

"You don't imagine Rona spent her free time in London watching the telly, do you? Sigrid knows more than I do about what she did when she was working there, but even Sigrid thinks she's cagey. Wide open on most subjects, but inclined to clam up about her affairs."

"Affairs?"

"Well, women have them. You ought to know. Funny thing: when Sigrid met Rona, she thought it odd that neither of us— you or I—had fallen for her. For Rona, I mean. I pointed out that we grew up with her and certainly in my own case, it's not so long ago that I stopped thinking of her as a kid in a gym tunic. You, of course, always found her a pain in the neck. Who'd have thought that she would have turned out such a beauty?"

There was no reply from Nigel. David peered at him across the table.

"Something on your mind?" he asked.

"No. Why?"

"You look low. Woman trouble?"

"No. My God, does everybody in this place put me down as a woman-chaser?"

"Yes. So what's the trouble?"

"None. It's just that I don't seem to belong at home any more."

"Why should you? You only drop in every three years or so."

"I used to feel I'd still got a home here. I think perhaps I'm feeling cramped. I miss the space we had in our other house. It wasn't a mansion, exactly, but it had big rooms and a lot of them. Coming to this—well, as I said, I feel cramped."

"Maybe your mother and Rona feel cramped too, with you in residence. But I agree it's too small. When Dagmar saw it, her blood pressure went up. She thinks you ought to get your mother out of it, and as soon as possible. But you can't blame her for getting caught with Chan's band. But for that row, you might have put some money into the cottage and improved it."

"Not unless one could have bought some of the land behind it."

"That?" David shook his head. "Nobody'll be able to get hold of any of that. People have been after it for years, offering big money. You know it belongs to Latimer?"

"Yes."

"He couldn't sell it even if he wanted to. But he doesn't need the money. He—" He broke off. "Talk of the devil."

A broad-shouldered, good-looking man had entered and was elbowing his way to the bar. Catching sight of Nigel and David, he changed direction and came across the room to speak to them.

"Did he say anything at the airport," David asked as he approached, "about turning up in Longbrook?"

"No."

"Was he with Maria when you left?"

"Yes."

"Then they must have worked fast."

Francis Latimer reached their table, and Nigel experienced once more the feeling of mingled dislike and suspicion which the man had always roused in him. It was a dislike he thought was mutual, and it dated from the time of Sir James's marriage and the arrival of Francis Latimer in Longbrook. The three boys—Nigel, David and Francis—had been almost the same age, but the newcomer had never shown the slightest disposition towards friendliness.

The people of the town for the most part shared Nigel's dislike. Francis Latimer's manner had an underlying arrogance, a scarcely concealed contempt for local pursuits and activities, and he had from the beginning made it clear that his interests lay elsewhere.

Studying him now, Nigel wondered why he remained unimpressed by a man so friendly, so amusing, so well informed and so urbane. His hair, he saw, was already beginning to recede; it seemed to give him an additional air of authority. He moved with a kind of loping grace. His voice was loud, firm and pleasant.

He addressed the two men with friendly warmth.

"Haven't seen you for years, David. I hear you're a family man."

"Yes." David indicated a chair. "Join us?"

"I'd like to. Wait till I get a drink."

He returned holding three tankards.

"Refills," he explained, handing two to the others. He sat down and sent a disparaging glance round the room. "Same old faces," he observed. "Nothing changes here, does it?"

"It changes all the time," David told him. "You ought to come down more often; you're out of touch. As a matter of fact, we were just talking about you."

"Scandal?"

"No. Nigel's mother bought a cottage on the edge of that land you own. That big spread."

"Mill Acres?"

"Yes."

"It's a big spread, as you say."

"I understand," Nigel said, "that it can't be built on."

"No." He seemed uninterested in the topic. "We ought to be drinking champagne instead of beer," he told Nigel. "You did me a good turn."

"I did?"

"Yes. You introduced me to Maria Montallen. She's here, did you know?"

"Yes."

"At my invitation. I decided it was time I came down to visit my stepfather, so I suggested her coming to keep me company. I've put her in the new hotel—the Brook. Next door to your shop, David. She says she knows you."

"Yes. She met my wife, too. I was married just before she married Roger Underwood." He hesitated. "She's not exactly a favourite here."

"Nor am I." Francis laughed. "I suppose you're talking about her breaking up the engagement between Underwood and"—he turned to Nigel—"Rosanna Hume." He waved a careless hand. "It was a long time ago. The dust has settled, and Maria won't raise any more; I'll see to that. How about—"

He stopped abruptly. Then, with a quick movement, he got to his feet.

"Got to go," he said. "I'll see you around."

He was gone. Nigel stared after him with a puzzled glance.

"Am I imagining it," he asked David, "or did he have a scared look?"

"Kind of. He turned round, saw something or somebody—and went."

"Probably remembered Maria was expecting him. He didn't even finish his drink. Did you notice how lightly he brushed aside the Underwood episode?"

"Why not brush it aside? He wasn't here, and Maria has probably forgotten all about it. Pity you weren't here. Not that you could have done anything."

"I might have been able to talk some sense into Rona. Underwood wasn't the kind of man who could have made her happy."

"So Sigrid always said. She—"

He stopped. An outsize hand had descended on his shoulder. He did not need to look up to know that it belonged to Chan Fielder.

"Sit down," Nigel invited. "Drink?"

"Thanks. Same as you're drinking." He waited until Nigel returned with a full tankard, then drank and wiped foam from his lips. "I would've joined you earlier, but I didn't like the company you were keeping."

"Latimer?" David asked in surprise.

"The same." Chan pulled his chair closer to the table. "I didn't like him when I was a boy in this town, and I don't like him any better now. So I waited till he went. And he went with pre-cip-i-tation, did you notice?"

"Yes. Why did he?" Nigel asked.

"It was her." Chan jerked his head in the direction of a group standing by the bar. "That girl's Maureen Yates, daughter of Yates the builder, and when I say builder, you've got to remember that a builder in this town isn't an ordinary builder. He's a chap who's made it in the building boom and tucked a big fortune down his sock and turned into a gent and sent his children to posh schools like the one you two went to.

That's Yates and his buddies with her. Builders all, rich men all and if you ask me, crooks all. I watched them as they came in just now—swaggering, you'd call it. But what I was going to say was that Maureen Yates had been the dolly-girl of our nonfriend Latimer, and he didn't want to risk what's called an en-counter. So he skipped."

Nigel said nothing, but he did not believe that Francis Latimer would have been disturbed by the presence of Miss Yates. It was a situation, he felt, that had been dealt with many times before by Latimer, and not by a policy of avoidance.

"Are you going to win the championship?" he asked Chan.

"Depends. Sometimes I think yes, sometimes I think no. Sometimes I wish I was playing instead of conducting. My father would've made a first-rate conductor."

"Do you ever hear from him?" David asked.

"He keeps in touch. Touch is the word. He never could keep money. His lady friends keep him supplied when he's got lady friends, but when they walk out, he looks me up. I feel sorry for the old six-letter word. My mother should've stuck to him. She was always talking about doing your duty, but she didn't do hers when she left him all by himself. Funny how her religion made her so miserable. Wouldn't you think that with a reserved seat waiting for her in heaven, she would have felt nice and happy? But no. She shouldn't have left Longbrook. She missed the Reverend and the church. She kind of pined away. But it wasn't that that finished her off in the end. It was those astronauts."

"Astronauts?" echoed David in bewilderment.

"That's right. Remember when that Russian chap, Yuri or Guri, did the first package tour into space? Remember how he looked out of his little window and saw the earth? Well, after that there were pictures. Photographs. There was the earth, round like they'd said. And spinning. My mum had never believed all that about us revolving in space. You could offer her proofs, but all she said was that it was against nature. But when she saw that chap on the telly going down his little ladder and stepping onto the moon and digging great holes in it, that was the end. She couldn't take it. She wouldn't go out of the house for months, and when she did, she clung to things—the gate, the postman, the bus conductor, anything. She'd got used to thinking her feet were on a nice solid floor, and spinning didn't suit her. And another thing, it got her all confused about where heaven was. If it wasn't up in the clear blue sky, like the hymn said, then where was it? It was a relief, really, when she took to her bed and died."

A respectful pause followed this speech. Presently Chan rose.

"Got to go," he said. "Any time you want to come to a band practice, just walk in. Ta for the drink. My turn next time."

"We'd better go too," David said when he had left. "There's a baby due any minute and they'll want to know where I am."

They walked slowly back to the shop; then Nigel went on alone to the cottage.

When he reached it, he saw no sign of Bryan Hayling's car. The porch light was still burning. So she was not back. Well, David had said that the service was slow; and dinner could be merely the beginning of an evening, a prelude.

He stood irresolutely in the living room, and then decided to go up to bed. Staying up might look as though he was waiting for their return. He wasn't ready for bed, but he'd better get out of the way.

He undressed and lay in bed reading. Midnight came and went. One o'clock. Two. She's grown up, that was clear. She was on her own, independent, out with a man who was in love with her.

It was half past two when he heard the car stop outside the gate. There were footsteps, two pairs to the house and one pair back to the car. No prolonged farewells. They'd probably got them over—where? Did Hayling have a place of his own?

He had left his door open. When she went past on her way to her room, he assumed the posture of a man falling asleep over a book. She stopped, and he gave a prolonged yawn.

"Nice evening?" he enquired.

"Yes, thank you."

"Dinner good?"

"Yes."

"David said the service was a bit slow."

"So it was. You've seen him?"

"He and I went along to the Three Feathers. Francis Latimer came and joined us. He suggested champagne, to celebrate his introduction to Maria Montallen. He's brought her down here and installed her in the Brook Hotel."

"For long?"

"He didn't say."

"You never used to read in bed. Are those pajamas real silk?"

"Of course. They're a bit warm for this weather, so don't close the door. What do you sleep in nowadays? It used to be that stuff you didn't need to iron."

"It still is."

"Will you be free for dinner tomorrow night? That's to say, tonight?"

"Sunday. The places that aren't closed will be overcrowded. We can dine at home and I'll make you a chop suey. Good night."

"You could come in and make that more, or less, fraternal, if you cared to."

She smiled.

"Wouldn't be safe," she said. "You're the susceptible type."

He heard her door close. It had a depressingly final sound.

CHAPTER

5

THE NEXT DAY OPENED WITH A STRUGGLE BETWEEN THE sun and some clouds that seemed to be gathering in preparation for a downpour. By nine o'clock, when Nigel decided to get up, the sun had won and the weather was set fair.

He had wakened early and before getting up had given his attention to a list of current London entertainments. He marked two plays, two concerts and a performance by a Spanish dance company. He passed over the two musicals advertised as sexual sagas; anything they could do, he felt, Brazil had already done better.

When he went downstairs, his mother was in her room. Rona, in the living room, had rolled back the rugs and was kneeling before a spread of material and a paper pattern, cutting round its edges. She greeted him without looking up.

"Morning. There's coffee keeping hot for you on the stove."

"Thanks." He leaned against the door, watching her. "What's this garment going to be?"

"Beach dress. Would you take your mother to church?"

"Church?"

"Yes. She's getting ready."

"But—"

"It isn't a long service. You'll be back before twelve."

"Is this a weekly performance?"

"No. Don't you remember? Every first Sunday. Don't go in at the main door, or the Reverend will catch you and make you take round the plate."

She had not so much as glanced at him. He walked into the kitchen and poured himself out some coffee. Yesterday's feelings of dissatisfaction were beginning to creep back. He had no objection to taking his mother to church, or helping in any other way he could, but he would like to be consulted first.

Cup in hand, he went back to the living room. Her hair had fallen over her cheeks. She raised her head and he saw that her mouth was full of pins.

"Take those out," he ordered sharply.

"Um?"

"Take those pins out of your mouth. It's damn dangerous." He had given the cup a jerk and some coffee had spilled on the floor. "You might swallow the lot. Your stomach isn't a pincushion. Take them out."

She removed them and dropped them into a box beside her. He stood in silence, ruminating. Ridiculous thing, fashion, he told himself sourly. A coutourier created a dress, suited to a particular type of woman, and then ten million other women copied it, tall women, short women, thin and fat women, young women, old women. Which was why only one woman in ten million looked well dressed.

She looked at the clock.

"If you don't hurry, you'll have to leave before you finish your second cup."

"I've been marking one or two shows I'd like to see." His tone was chilly. "If you've got any free evenings, perhaps you'd come with me."

She stopped work to give the matter her consideration.

"I'm free on Thursday. Would Thursday suit you?" she asked at last.

"Yes. Musical or straight play?"

"Play."

"Dinner before, or supper after?"

"Supper. We'd have to rush dinner, which would be a pity. Thank you for asking me."

When he had driven away with his mother, she sat for a time brooding, her hands idle. He wasn't enjoying his leave, and she wasn't exactly helping him. But he was acting out of character; why hadn't he gone off to visit his friends, as he had always done before? Why had he done nothing about that growing pile of telephone messages? How long was he going to hang about here looking gloomy?

In love? She doubted it. He had been in and out of love as long as she had known him, and the state had never made him depressed. It had made him happy—happy when the affair began and happier when it ended and left him free. She had in the past been able to chart his amorous progress, but she could not do so now. He seemed to be marking time. Perhaps he had said something to David at the Three Feathers last night; if so, David would tell Sigrid and Sigrid would tell her. She had only to wait.

She brought her mind back to the work in hand. Finishing the cutting-out, she gathered the sections of the garment, folded them neatly and laid them along the back of the nearest chair.

She did not hear the gate open because it had already been opened for the car. She was too absorbed to hear footsteps on the path. It was only when a shadow fell across the porch that she realized that somebody was standing at the outer door. Looking up, she saw a figure that for some moments made her doubt the evidence of her eyes.

Maria Montallen.

She was still kneeling, too astounded to move. Only when the visitor, after waiting in vain for an invitation, entered the room, did she realize that this was no trick of vision or memory.

The silence was prolonged, but there was nothing awkward about it. Maria stood giving the room a careless survey that reduced Celia's decorations to homecraft level. Rona was taking a long, frank look at the visitor and seeing much that she had not seen, or not noted, three years earlier.

Beautiful? No. Better than beautiful. Striking. Arresting. Tall, thin, dark skin, heavy features, a full-lipped, petulant mouth. Black hair smoothed back into a knot on the neck. Narrow dark eyes, wonderful complexion. And those clothes . . .

Assessing their cost, she felt she could understand some of the problems that must bedevil women of this kind, whose prime need was money. This one looked—and was—a being from another world, where beautiful clothes, expensive jewels, luxury suites and oceangoing yachts were taken for granted. Her outfit was the current casual amalgam—skirt, shirt, wide leather belt, scarf tied with studied carelessness —but the garments were of a cut and quality that marked them the product of the great designers. In a few months, Rona told herself, she would be kneeling on the floor cutting out replicas. But she would have to do without that handbag: very large, of soft leather with gold clasps. One look at the Maria Montallens, she acknowledged to herself, and you could forget those illusions you'd harboured about your own appearance. It was all very well to say that if you caught the latest craze as it came, you could get by; but the Marias wore clothes that were creations and not crazes. Dagmar was beautifully dressed, but her clothes were today's. Maria's were tomorrow's.

She heard her speaking.

"I think you should ask me to sit down."

She spoke very slowly, the words not so much drawled as dragging, as though speech were an effort. Her English was perfect, with only the slightest foreign intonation.

"Sit down if you want to," Rona said.

Maria sat on the sofa, tried and rejected the cushions and leaned back.

"I suppose you're surprised to see me?"

"Yes."

"Did you know I was in Longbrook?"

"Yes."

"I rang Nigel—more than once. Did he get my messages?"

"Yes."

"Then he should have answered them. I can understand his mother nursing a grievance, but what happened was nothing to do with him. He wasn't even here." She groped in her bag and extracted a cigarette case and a lighter—both gold, Rona saw without surprise. "Why don't you sit down too?"

Rona sat down.

"I suppose," Maria continued calmly, "you hate me?"

Rona hesitated.

"I hate what you did," she said at last. "But that's rather different."

"What I did? Shall I tell you what I did, if you don't know already? What I did was save you from dying a slow, a lingering death from boredom. That was what I did. It was a long time ago and thank God, I've forgotten most of it, but one thing I haven't forgotten, and that's what I've come to talk about. I was going to ask Nigel to bring you to the hotel —if you would come—but he didn't ring. This morning, I saw him from the window of the hotel, driving with his mother towards the church. I knew that would keep them out of the way for a time, and so I came here to see you. I wanted to have a talk with you. I wanted to—how shall I put it?—to draw a line under all that old business."

"I could make you some coffee, if you'd like some."

"No, thank you." She lit a cigarette and dropped case and lighter back into her bag. "You know, when I was here before, when it was all going on and my hell-hag of a grandmother was still alive, I didn't give you credit for much intelligence. You seemed to me uninteresting, of not much account. And then—afterwards—I began to think that I had been wrong. When I had made the mistake of marrying Roger Underwood, I began to wonder if perhaps you had been so unintelligent after all. I was puzzled."

"Why?"

"Because I began to feel more and more sure, to feel at last certain that you must have known what he was really like. You had known him for years, known his parents, known all about him. Hadn't you?"

"Yes."

"After thinking about it, after thinking about you, I was more and more sure that you knew there was nothing he could offer except his looks. Inside, nothing. No ideas, no opinions, no information, not even any conversation that was not about himself. Dull, dull, dull. Deadly, deadly dull."

"I'm sorry you were disappointed."

"Oh, don't make any mistake. I wasn't disappointed." She ground out her half-smoked cigarette. "I didn't expect him to amuse me. But I began to ask myself why you had let him go so easily. Why, having become engaged to him, when you were so soon going to marry him, why didn't you make any effort, any struggle, to keep him away from me, or later on to take him away from me? You must have known what was going on. You may not have liked what I did, but you will admit that I did it in the open. He may have tried to hide the situation from you, but everything I did, I did without concealment. You must have known that I was going to break up his engagement with you. Didn't you?"

There was silence.

"Well, didn't you?" Maria asked again.

"Yes. I guessed."

"And having guessed, you decided to wait and see what happened. You did nothing to keep him. You let him go. So there was only one conclusion I could come to: that you had used me. I didn't like the idea, but I could understand it. I use people. I use people all the time. How can one go through the world without using people? You used me to get rid of him. I told him so, but he wouldn't believe it. He could bear the thought that he'd ruined your life, but he couldn't face the possibility that perhaps he hadn't, after all."

For Rona, listening, reality had receded. The tall, languorous form, the low, unhurried voice were re-creating the past. Roger Underwood, so handsome without, so hollow within, was taking shape in the room. She remembered their meeting in the train. She remembered their engagement, and her almost immediate conviction that she had made a mistake. Who had used whom? With Nigel totally uninterested in her, making no attempt to get in touch with her on his last leave, returning to Brazil without a word—hadn't she used Roger Underwood as a means of curing herself of her infatuation? Could she have kept Roger if she had wanted to? She had certainly made no attempt to keep him. When he had gone away with Maria, all she had felt was deep thankfulness.

She came back slowly to the present.

"How long were you together?" she asked.

"Until the money ran out. A year. Less." She lit another cigarette. "You know, in those old fairy tales, it was always the men, the young princes, who had to go and seek their fortunes. In my experience, it has always been the women who have had to do the seeking. My mother and I had some money while my father was alive, but it was never enough, and what there was, we spent. When he died, my mother taught me how to use people, and when she died, I perfected the technique. The only person she didn't use was my grandmother, because she believed what my father told her: that we would never get anything out of her. He had asked her for some of the Barville things before he left her house—

after all, he was entitled to something; he had Barville blood. But he got nothing and he warned us that we would get nothing." She paused. "It's strange how crazed she was about that collection. It was stolen, all of it. Loot."

"The spoils of war."

"If you like. She said it had been paid for in blood—the blood left by the Barvilles on the battlefields. That sounds stirring, doesn't it? But my father told me that there were things in the collection that weren't paid for in blood or in anything else, for instance the pearls and diamonds that he believed were part of the royal jewels that vanished from Greenwich in sixteen nineteen and are still unaccounted for. So you see?" Once again, she leaned forward to crush out her cigarette. "I did get something in the end, by using blackmail. I told my grandmother I would go away with Roger Underwood if she made it worth my while. She made marriage a condition. Then, to get rid of me, she dipped into her collection."

There was silence. Rona, feeling that no comment was called for, made none.

"Yes, I got something," Maria repeated reminiscently. "I got something because her love for her loot wasn't as great as her hatred of me. I didn't get anything until she was sure I would marry Roger Underwood. While I was unmarried, she thought that people would feel that I had some claim on her. If I married and went away, she could shake loose. She gave me a necklace. With the necklace, which I wanted, and the man I didn't want, I went away. And you must have been very relieved. I took him off your hands. That's true, isn't it?"

"That was a conclusion you came to later," Rona pointed out. "When you left, you believed that I was in love with him. That's the real issue, isn't it?"

"You mean that's the score. Yes, I suppose it is. But as I relieved you of a man you didn't want, why not acknowledge the debt? What I did suited you, so you did nothing to stop me. You won't mind my saying that even if you had tried, it wouldn't have made any difference? When I go after something, I usually get it."

Again, Rona felt comment to be unnecessary. And when Maria next spoke, it was clear that her interest in that past episode, briefly revived, was over. She had satisfied her curiosity and she had closed the book.

"Now I'll go." She rose. "I don't want to be here when Mrs. Pressley comes back. Isn't it extraordinary how people like her cling to their prejudices? I'm sorry I didn't meet Nigel earlier. If he had been in Longbrook, you would have had to keep your Underwood."

They walked together to the gate. Outside was standing a very large car.

"This belongs to Francis," Maria said, settling herself in the driving seat. "Will you tell Nigel I'd like to see him if he can come any time for a drink? And you can thank him for introducing Francis Latimer to me; in other words, for providing me with a man just when I needed one. You don't know him well, do you?"

"Francis Latimer? Nobody here knows him well. He doesn't spend much time here."

"He doesn't belong to a place like this. I hear Nigel doesn't spend much time here either. You can't blame them; what is there to keep them here? Francis only comes because he has to visit his stepfather now and then; he's his heir, so it wouldn't do to give him cause to complain. But he came this time because he had some business to do down here. When it's done, we shall go away. I suppose it's no use asking you to come one evening to have a drink?"

"Thank you. But I don't see much point; do you?"

"I suppose not. Goodbye."

"Goodbye."

Rona went back to the living room. Absently, she replaced the rugs and cleared away her dress pattern. The cut-out material now looked to her like something out of a ragbag. She went into the kitchen and prepared a cold lunch; then she went up to her room. Seated on her bed, she reviewed Maria Montallen's visit and felt again the sense of reliving the past. Would she, if Maria had not freed her, have freed herself? Would she have had the courage to acknowledge that she had made a mistake? She did not know. She would never know.

Brief though the visit had been, she found that it had had at least one interesting result: it had shown her that she had developed enough, matured enough to meet Maria Montallen on equal terms. She was no longer unsure of herself, no longer disposed to be unduly disturbed by values or outlooks different from her own. She was aware, now, of her own qualities—good and bad.

She heard Nigel coming into the house, but she did not move. After a time, he came upstairs and addressed her from the doorway.

"Anything wrong?"

"No."

"Brooding?"

"No. Just thinking."

He came in and sat beside her on the bed.

"Any thinks in particular?" he asked.

"Only one. Do you know anything about some jewels that disappeared from Greenwich in sixteen nineteen and were never heard of again?"

"Greenwich? Sixteen nineteen?"

"Yes."

"It connects, but with what?"

"Take your time."

"Sixteen nineteen. Let me see. James the First, right?"

"You're doing the research."

"He married Anne of Denmark. Ah."

"Ah what?"

"Ah I've remembered. When she died, James sent to Greenwich for her coffers. Empty. The jeweller Herrick—Herrick? Yes—Herrick had supplied her with jewels to the value of thirty-six thousand pounds. Where were they? Nobody knew. Where had they vanished to? Nobody ever found out. What made you dig up that old puzzle?

"I didn't. Maria Montallen mentioned it."

He turned to stare at her.

"Mentioned it when?"

"This morning."

"She rang?"

"No. She came."

"Came? Came here?"

"In person. And not to see you. She saw you and your mother going past the hotel on your way to church, so she came to see me."

"I'm damned. To talk about Roger?"

She hesitated. Truth was truth, she reflected, but you didn't have to tell it all. It wasn't likely that Maria would broadcast the fact that she got Roger Underwood because his fiancée hadn't wanted him. That secret was undoubtedly safe.

"She came to tell me what she'd saved me from," she said.

"I could have told you. How did she get here?"

"In Francis Latimer's car. She's at the Brook Hotel and she'd like you to drop in for a drink."

"She's in the bridal suite and Latimer's paying for it and I don't think he'd like me to drop in. Did her visit upset you?"

"No. It tied up some loose ends. I enjoyed looking at her —and she cleared up a point that had always puzzled me: why she had actually married Roger, instead of going away and living with him. I would have said she wasn't the marrying type. But it was her grandmother who made the condition: no marriage, no necklace."

"I doubt whether it was entirely her grandmother. My guess is that Maria's one of those women who believe they can get more out of a man by marrying him than by living with him. A mistress can grab all she can while she can, but his wife gets his name and his home and the confidence of the tradespeople. Maria's been on the loose since she left Roger two years ago. Husbands in the bracket she needs don't stroll by every day. I think the Austrian she was meeting at the airport was tagged for her next husband; why else would his parents have panicked? They wouldn't have worried about a mere affair."

"You think she wants to marry Francis Latimer?"

"I'd say so. I'm pretty sure he'd like to marry her. She's quite a prize for anybody who can afford it. If they stay long, we might see some interesting developments."

There was silence. She was still thinking of Maria Montallen's visit. He was feeling happier than he had done since his arrival, for it had come home to him that he need not, after all, worry too much about those other men she knew. This was where he scored over them, here with her in the house, in the home, intimate in a way they could not rival, bound to her by the past. It had taken him fifteen years to realize that he could claim a brother's privileges, but from now on, he was going to make the most of them.

Brother? One of her hands was between them. It touched his own, and the question was settled. No. Not brother.

She was speaking.

"Where's your mother?"

"At Dagmar's. I forgot to tell you. Dagmar flagged us down as we drove past the shop. She wanted company—my mother's. Dave and Sigrid had taken a picnic lunch and were planning to drive over rough country, to give the baby a hint."

She rose.

"How about asking Chan to come over and eat her share of our lunch?" she suggested.

"Doesn't his band practice on Sundays?"

"No. He's alone."

"Then let's go over and invite him."

The gate next door, having come off its remaining hinge, was leaning against the fence. The barn was empty. The cottage, in strong sunlight, looked a ruin. Nigel knocked on the door.

"Chan! Chan, are you in?"

An answer came from behind the house.

"Round here, friend."

They walked round to the back. Chan, stripped to the waist, revealing an incredible breadth of torso, was bent over a basin of water placed on an upturned box. He looked up, blinked away the water dripping from his hair, saw Rona and gave a loud and joyful exclamation.

"A lady! Why didn't you say you'd brought female company? Rona, love, avert your eyes from this exposed mountain of flesh."

"It doesn't get enough exposure," she told him. "You're all white. Don't put that shirt on; let the sun get at you."

"Never." Chan had put aside the towel and was struggling into his shirt. "No sun for me, I thank you. I've got a couple of ep-i-dermises missing; ten minutes in the sun and I come out in blisters as big as beetroots. I turn into two hundred and twenty pounds of raw beef." He shuddered. "Horrible." He picked up a soiled shirt and a pair of socks from the ground. "Wait a minute while I do my laundry, and then you can tell me to what I owe the honour of this visit."

He plunged the shirt and the socks into the basin, lifted them out, squeezed the water from them, spread them on the kitchen windowsill and put a large stone on them to keep them in place.

"No soap?" Rona enquired in surprise. "No scrubbing? Just that rinse?"

"Just that rinse, Rona love." Chan emptied the contents of the basin over the surrounding weeds. "I don't get dirty, I just get sweaty, if you'll excuse my language. That rinse makes all the difference between sweet and sour. Have you two had breakfast?"

"Ages ago."

"Me, too. I get up with the early bird and take coffee back

to bed and enjoy it in warmth and comfort. I can offer you beer, if you'd like some. No? Then come inside and see my little nest."

He preceded them down a narrow passage and held open a door at the end for them to enter.

"My parlour," he said. "On your left is the kitchen, but I handed it over to the boys so's they could do their cook-ups. I live here, in the parlour. Come on in. Not only parlour, as you see, but kitchen and workroom too. The bedroom's through there, but I wouldn't like you to see that. Sit down."

"Sit down where?" Nigel asked.

"Oh, sorry." Chan removed a cornet from a wooden chair and transferred a pile of sheet music from a stool to the littered table. "There you are. I'll stand; good exercise. I daresay you find these rather cramped quarters, but I fit in all right."

So, Rona saw, did everything else. On the table was a selection of unwashed crockery, the remains of a loaf, an opened packet of butter, a half-empty tin of sardines and a can of baked beans. In a corner stood a small electric stove. From an inadequate cupboard protruded some roughly folded sheets and towels. Stores—cans of soups and peas and vegetables, a bottle of milk, paper bags full of oranges—were stacked beside the stove. Several pairs of old shoes, a pair of espadrilles, a large plastic water container, a pile of paperback books and a selection of saucepans shared the uncarpeted floor. Chan had not used a duster, she guessed, since he moved in.

"Not very tidy," he admitted, following her glance, "but I'll tell you something: when I want a thing, I can lay my hands right on it."

"Why were you performing your ablutions outside?" Nigel asked him.

"Performing my— Oh, I see what you mean. That's right —ablutions. I like words, you know. They didn't teach us enough of them at the old Longbrook School. Remember what it looked like, Nigel boy? Converted cowshed, my dad called it—and look at it now! Rows and rows of lovely big windows so the boys and girls can look out and see the world. Cor! things have changed since those days, haven't they? Take one example: My mum was a cook before she got married. She cooked in a basement and used Stone Age implements and got to know all the beetles by their first names. But when cooks went out and the ladies had to do the cooking, they had to have formica and frills on the windows and gas and electricity and washing-up machines and ex-traction fans and double sinks and eye-level grills. Marvellous. What were we saying?"

"Ablutions. Why outside?"

"Because unlike those posh people living in the cottage next door, I don't have any water laid on. Electricity, yes. Water, no. Gas, no. When I say not water laid on, I'm misleading you. I fixed up a barrel as rain-catcher, and that gives me enough for my ab-lutions, and I get a lot extra through the holes in the roof. You wouldn't call it ideal, but it's the first time I've ever had a home of my own, and I have to keep scratching myself to see if I'm really here. Think of it: a nice little parlour, water to wash in and electricity to cook on if I ever decide to cook, a band that's going to be the best in the country—and speaking of country, you can add that lovely bit of land we've got at the back. That's like having my own private park, that is."

"Did you say you don't cook?" Rona asked.

"I could if I ever got round to it," Chan claimed. "I could toss a nice fluffy pancake once upon a time, and I could cook eggs a different way every day in the year, but what I do now is open cans. I can always get a decent dinner at the pub: the Three Feathers serves some first-class cold beef, and their meat pies are almost as good as my mum's used to be, and just the job for a chap like me who doesn't have to watch his weight. Look, I'm talking too much. What can I do for you two?"

"My mother went out and left her lunch. We wondered whether you'd care to come and eat it."

"You're inviting me to lunch, sorry, luncheon?"

"We are. Will you come?" Rona asked.

"That's a silly question, Rona love. Consider the al-ternative: a hunk of bread with a couple of sardines spread on it, with a can of pineapple to follow. Do you want me to put on my bandmaster's uniform?"

"No. You can come as you are. It's a cold lunch; do you mind?"

"Did you say it was what Mrs. Pressley was going to have?"

"Yes."

"Then I'm honoured. Let's go."

When Rona served the meal, he ate with frank enjoyment and without any sign that he had ever heard the word diet. He spread bread with an inch of butter, helped himself liberally to potato salad, had several more slices of bread and butter with his cheese, and poured cream and sugar into his coffee.

"Best grub I've had since I was weaned," he said, helping to carry plates to the dishwasher. "Hey, Nigel, don't take that coffee away; I'd like some more."

Cup in hand, he walked to a small table to study a photograph in a leather frame.

"That's your dad as was, isn't it?" he asked Nigel.

"Yes."

"My mum said he was a good doctor. She went to his funeral, along with a few other hundreds of patients or admirers. You were living in one of those big houses in Regent Crescent, and then you moved to Beech Grove, near us. That's where I remember you. First time I knew you, you were watching the builders working on the extension to the Renson bookshop. I was watching too. And Dave."

"And one of your gang heaved a brick at us."

"He missed. But that set the tone, as you might say, for

future relations. Wish I could remember why you pushed me in the river. That was when I first saw your mother. She stopped me on the street and spoke to me and said she was sorry and she hoped I hadn't caught cold. She said you were sorry too, but I didn't swallow that one. I was really upset when Bert told me she'd bought this place. Is she getting used to the band?"

"She won't have to get used to it," Nigel said. "I'm going to find her a drier house to live in."

"I'm glad. All the same, some people enjoy listening to us." He took his empty cup to the kitchen. "It's a funny thing," he said, returning, "what a lot of people there are who know nothing about brass. Even that poet, Keats. You know what he called trumpets? He called them silver, snarling trumpets. Put me off, that did, because they're not silver and they don't snarl. I told the teacher so."

"The teacher should have switched you to Dryden," Nigel told him. "He talked about the trumpets' loud clangour, and he was right. You ought to come over here and listen to the row you make."

"If I was over here, I wouldn't be making it. There was something in the Psalms I couldn't figure out once, something about showing yourselves joyful before the Lord with trumpets and shawms. I asked our teacher what a shawm was, and he didn't know, so he pretended there was a draft and told me to shut the window. I looked it up later and found it was a kind of oboe—double-reed—and I told him the next day and got sent out of the class for trying to show off."

"How many players are there in your band?" Rona asked.

"I'll tell you. In fact, I'll show you. But you don't want to get me going on brass bands, do you, love?"

"Yes. Just numbers."

"Well, you've asked for it. First, the bandmaster. I'm him, over by the door, see? Over there's the percussion, and there you've got the tubas and—"

"Numbers."

"Four tubas. Do you want to know about B flat and E flat?"

"Not if it's complicated. Next?"

"In front here, the horns, solo, first, second, third. Then on my left you've got the cornets. The cornet's the main solo instrument in a band, I mean it's the chief brass instrument of *soprano* pitch. You've—"

"How many cornets?"

"I'm trying to tell you. But you'd have to know about repiano and flugel and—"

"No. Just how many, that's all."

"Call it seven. Euphonium, which is the solo instrument of the bass section; first baritone, second baritone. Trombones, solo, first, second, bass or G. And—"

"What sort of percussion?"

"Full drums for concerts, that's to say side drum, bass drum, triangle, cymbals, gong, tambourines. Why don't you just say thirty, thirty-one and have done with it? The conductor ought to be a bit further up and further back." He stepped onto Celia's embroidered footstool and came heavily down as it split under his weight. "Oh, Father in heaven, look what I've done! No, don't touch it; leave it to me. One of my boys has got a job in an upholsterer's and he'll make it look as good as new. No damage to the flowers, I'm glad to say. You wouldn't get a man doing that, would you?"

"Doing what?" Rona asked.

"Em-broidering flowers and then putting his dirty great boots on them." He put the footstool under his arm. "Look, I don't want to go, but I've got a date with the Reverend."

"The Reverend?" Nigel echoed in surprise. "I didn't know you—"

"Just personal. He came to the Three Feathers and asked if I'd give a band concert for his building fund, and like the fat fool I am, I said I would. Why is it," he asked, "that more people here don't take an interest in putting the church to rights? I mean it isn't as though we could offer much in the way of local interest, is it? That church is what my history teacher called Our Heritage, in capitals. He made us do a couple of walks to look over it, and anything you want to know about it, I can tell you: twelfth century, Norman tower, sixteenth-century retable, choir stalls carved by—by—doesn't matter. What I'm saying is that we're short of anti-quity here, so why don't we preserve the church? I don't go to it, but that's beside the point. I was baptized in it and believe it or not, I was confirmed in it too. I'd have been married in it if I'd been a marrying man."

"If you're late, I can give you a lift," Nigel offered.

"Lift? Man, when I travel, I travel in the band's bus for all to see. Thanks all the same."

"Where's this concert going to be held?" Nigel asked as they walked to the gate.

"That's the difficulty. I don't want to have it too near the building, or we'll have it collapsing on the band as soon as they start blowing. It might be the vicarage garden, but that's next door to the churchyard, so what if the corpses think we're sounding the last trump? And if it rains, then what? So long. Thanks for the feast."

The bus went by some moments later. Rona looked out at the sunny garden.

"I'd like a walk," she told Nigel. "Wouldn't you?"

"I wouldn't mind driving to those woods at the back of Sir James's house. There are some nice walks from there."

"Then let's go. Geoff Steele rang this morning to say he might be able to get to Longbrook in time to take me out to dinner, so I can't be out too long. He's just finished a job down in Cornwall and he's coming back to finish off one he's done in the High Street here."

He said nothing. The future was the future; for the moment, she was with him.

They drove to the edge of the woods and set out for a walk. It was close on five o'clock when they returned to the place at which they had left the car.

"We're not more than a mile from the Gunters' farm," Nigel pointed out. "Mrs. Gunter would give us tea."

"Later. I'd like to sit in the sun first."

He chose a sheltered spot and carried the car cushions to it and laid them on the ground. She sat on one, propped another against a tree, leaned against it and closed her eyes.

"Isn't this heaven?" she murmured. "After all that awful rain."

"Don't go to sleep yet." He was beside her, leaning on an elbow. "I want to do some filling-in."

She opened her eyes reluctantly.

"Won't it do when I wake up?"

"Yes, but perhaps I could get some of the information before you drop off."

"Information on—?"

"On how you got involved with Underwood."

She was adjusting the cushions; then she lay back, staring up at the cloudless sky.

"I told you," she said. "I met him in the train."

"Did you recognize him and decide that he'd improved so much that you'd like to marry him?"

"No. He spoke to me first. It was a night train. He had a sleeper but I'd run out of money and I was going to sit up all night. We had dinner together in the dining car and—I suppose it was the two bottles of wine that did it—he offered to change places."

"At the table?"

"Don't be silly. Are you a genuine seeker after facts, or are you merely trying to be funny?"

"Genuine seeker. He offered you his sleeping berth?"

"Yes. It would have meant fixing the car attendant, but he said he could do that."

"So you slept in comfort?"

"No. I sat up."

"Why?"

"Several reasons. The visit to Scotland hadn't been much of a success. My fault. Everyone was very kind, but somehow I wasn't in the mood. Meeting Roger was fun, but I got the idea that he was going to bribe the car attendant to let him in as well as myself. So I sat up. The carriage was full, but I slept. Next morning, I woke up just as the train was pulling into King's Cross, and Roger took me to his hotel and gave me a wonderful breakfast."

"Hotel?"

"He'd been living at his gallery, but he'd decided to use the rooms to enlarge it. So he moved into this hotel nearby till he could find somewhere to live. He wasn't looking very hard; he liked hotel life. I'd just settled into my job in London—and there we were."

"And so you fell in love?"

She did not answer for a time, and when she spoke, her tone was thoughtful.

"At certain stages in people's lives," she said, "I think they talk themselves into doing things. They put the situation to themselves and they decide that this is the thing to do and this is the time to do it. So they do it."

"Now I know what they mean when they say that words are what we use to hide our thoughts. What were you really trying to say: that you talked yourself into falling in love with him? Or did he do the talking?"

"I said to myself: 'I am twenty-one, I have been leading a free life for some time, I've known a number of men who've put forward a number of interesting propositions, including marriage, and I don't seem to be getting anywhere, so what do I want? A home and children.' If you remember, I never had a home. Your mother was wonderful and I love her and I'm everlastingly grateful, but it was her home, and yours. The one I had before my mother and father died . . . Well, you know about that. If my mother wasn't ill, my father was. From eight onwards, I spent almost all my school holidays at school. So there you are. I wanted a home and children, and that was what Roger said he wanted. Is that enough filling-in? Can I go to sleep now?"

"Yes."

"Wake me up if you want to know anything more, won't you?"

She drifted into sleep, and he sat lost in thought. It hadn't been her home, and when she left it, there had not been anything or anybody for her to lean on. He had been out of touch. His mother was hardly a prop for a girl trying to find her way through the sex jungle. Underwood must have looked like a fortress of security. She had known him before, known his family; he looked the right husband material. So she had talked herself into it, and by the grace of God, with considerable assistance from Maria Montallen, the thing had come apart. Now she was free, and she would not talk herself into anything again. She had both feet firmly on the ground. If she still wanted marriage and children it would be . . .

He woke her. She sat up and yawned.

"Time to go?" she asked.

"Not yet. I wanted to do a bit more filling-in."

"And you woke me just for that?"

"You said I could. What I want to know is whether that Underwood episode changed your attitude towards a husband and children."

"Of course it didn't. The only difference is that the children won't be Roger Underwood's, that's all. I was having a lovely sleep. What's the time?"

"Teatime. Want to go to the Gunters'?"

"No. Let's go home and you can make some tea when we get there."

"Why me? You're the housewife. You used to do the work, instead of relegating it."

"You used to sit and give orders, like a caliph. What's a caliph, exactly?"

"I'm glad you asked. The name means successor. It's the

title given to the official head of Islam. Successor to the Prophet. But sometime in the early twenties, the National Assembly at Ankara abolished the caliphate and threw out the Caliph. No more caliphs, so I couldn't have sat round looking like one. I know about emirs and shahs and rajahs too, if you're hungry for information."

"Thank you. Some other time. Let's go home the long way round—a nice drive round the countryside. May I drive?"

"If you want to."

He helped her to her feet and replaced the cushions in the car. They drove for an hour, along routes they both knew well and lanes along which they had sometimes ridden on hired horses, over fields in which she had gathered mushrooms. He had not seen this part of the country for many years, and many of the old landmarks had gone.

They reached the cottage to find it empty.

"Dagmar said lunch, not tea and dinner too," Nigel remarked. "Where do you think my mother has got to?"

"Ring and find out."

He went to the telephone and dialled the Rensons' number. She heard him give an exclamation, paused on her way to the kitchen and turned to find him helpless with laughter.

"Well?" she asked, when he put down the receiver.

"Good thing we didn't go to Gunters'. They'd had enough for one afternoon. Dave and Sigrid were there."

"Having tea?"

"No. They went on their picnic and then they went for a drive—and the baby took the hint. Dave turned for home, but Sigrid told him they wouldn't make it, so he panicked and drove to the first building in sight—Gunters' farmhouse."

"The baby was born there?"

"No. Mrs. Gunter rang for an ambulance. The baby was born on the way to hospital. It was Inga on the phone. Half of it was in German, but I think I got it right. Dagmar's at the hospital. So's my mother."

"Girl or boy?"

"Girl. Want to go to the hospital and find out any more?"

"No. Tomorrow. Did you gather whether your mother's coming back for dinner?"

"She isn't."

He was about to suggest dining out, and decided against it. They could be alone here, talking, listening to music. He could watch her, listen to her . . .

The telephone rang. The call was for Rona. He handed her the receiver and went to get drinks, but her side of the conversation told him what was coming.

"Geoff," she said. "He'll be here soon. No, not a drink for me, thanks; I'll wait till he comes. I'll go up and change. Don't worry about dinner for yourself; it's all fixed. I took a goulash out of the deep freeze this morning and all it needs is heating."

"Thank you."

"I hope you won't be lonely," she said as she went out of the door.

"Oh, no, no. No fear of that. I've got the cats."

Standing in the middle of the room, he reviewed home life as he had once known it. He remembered his mother preparing well-cooked meals and Rona, an eager, too-eager assistant laying the table in the big dining room. Tall candles flickering in silver stands, wine cooling, napkins folded into water-lily shapes, a summons when all was ready. It was he himself, he admitted, who had broken the pattern. He had made it only too clear that he was using the house as a brief halting-place on his way to the houses of his friends.

But now he had no desire to leave. His only hope, he felt, lay in staying here, being near her, doing his best to nourish the new relationship that was growing up between them. His excuse for staying—the excuse he would give if asked why he was staying so long—was sound enough: he meant to find his mother another, a more suitable house.

He heard Rona coming downstairs. She looked so lovely

that he felt weak with longing and a new emotion which he feared might be jealousy.

His misery was not lightened by discovering that Geoffry Steele proved to be a good deal less impressive than his reputation as an architect had led him to expect. Studying him, he found it impossible to understand why a girl who had a full-sized man at her disposal could go out to dinner with one who looked as though he would have to clamber onto a table before he could be glimpsed by a head waiter. A man, moreover, who persisted in talking shop.

"I'm sorry to be back here, in a way," he confided to Nigel, after giving a nod in acknowledgment of Rona's introduction. "I don't care for the clients I'm dealing with."

"Who are they?" Rona asked.

"Name of Wallace. The father owns that big chemist's at the end of the High Street. He bought this house I've been working on for his daughter. The upper storey's going to be for living in and the ground floor's going to be a shop. Beauty parlour."

"Who's going to run it?" Rona asked.

"The daughter. Shirley. Know her?"

"Everybody knows her. She's twenty-one and she's been married twice. There are two beauty parlours here already."

"This is going to be something special. One of those exclusive setups. I was given a free hand. Did you see the way I did those windows looking onto the street?"

"Yes. Nice. I like arches."

"They look even better from inside. I lowered the ceiling and put in some pillars. I don't know which I'm more pleased with: upper storey, or ground floor.—No, not another," he told Nigel, who was offering to refill his glass. "I've got a table booked for eight fifteen."

They drove away. Nigel stood weighing goulash against meat pies at the Three Feathers, and decided that going out was better than staying in.

He was home by ten o'clock. His mother came in shortly afterwards and gave him a detailed account of the dramatic events attending the arrival of the new baby. When she went to bed, he stayed in the living room, reading.

Rona came in at midnight.

"Hello. How was the dinner?" he asked.

"Not bad. Sundays are always too crowded. Did you like Geoff?"

"What there was of him."

"What's that supposed to mean?"

"Well, there's not much of him you could cling to in an emergency, is there?"

"Everybody can't be ten feet tall."

"True. You mustn't let him talk shop."

"Why not?"

"Unless it's more interesting than his conversation when he's not talking shop. Everybody can't be eager to hear about the Shirley Wallaces. Any light in Dave's windows as you went by?"

"I didn't notice. You've forgotten to put the cats out."

"They were keeping me company."

She stood frowning at him.

"Look, is there anything the matter with you?" she asked.

"I don't think so. Do I look as though I'm running a temperature?"

"No, you don't. You've got your faults, but I never thought sulking was one of them. You hate this cottage, don't you?"

"Yes."

"Then why don't you go away?"

"Because I've decided to stay until I've found another house for my mother."

"If she likes it—"

"If she likes it, she shouldn't. God knows we never lived what they call graciously, but we had standards. All she saw when she bought this place was those damned diamond-paned windows and the Goldilocks look. I'm going to find her a house which might be less picturesque but which will be a good deal more practical. It ought to be possible in the two months I'm free."

"You're going to stay here for the whole of your leave?"

"Yes. I'm going house-hunting, and this time, I'm going to do the buying. If you're not too tied up, perhaps you'd help me. Or are you against the whole idea?"

"No. I suppose I'm in favour. We all thought she'd made a bad mistake. But until you find something else, could you try not to let her see how much you loathe this cottage? If you're going to stay—"

"If I'm going to stay, smile. Is that what you were going to say?"

"Yes. Good night."

He did not reply. He watched her go, and put out the cats and switched off the lights and went upstairs wishing he were thousands of miles away, in Brazil.

With her.

CHAPTER

6

RONA, PAYING A VISIT TO THE HOSPITAL AT LUNCHTIME ON the following day, found that Sigrid had allowed very little time to elapse before putting on what she explained was a postmaternity model: a dress of pure silk, with a foam of lace at the neck.

"I thought I'd find you lying against the pillows, looking wan," Rona told her. "Congratulations on your beautiful daughter. They've just shown her to me. I think she looks a bit like Dagmar." She put her tribute to the newly-born on the table by the door. "How did it go?"

"Well, you heard. I shouldn't have gone for that drive. I wasn't feeling too safe before we started. I suppose it was lucky that we got as far as the Gunters' farm, but I couldn't help feeling sorry for them. I was all right; after all, I'd been through it before, but David thought the baby wouldn't survive and it would be his fault. So he needed more attention than I did. I thought the ambulance would never get there.

I got into it exactly eight minutes before the baby did. I knew it was going to be a race; the first baby didn't linger on the way, so it wasn't likely the second was going to."

"Are you going to feed her yourself?"

"Oh, heavens, yes. I'm overflowing, like last time. I don't know why I don't produce quadruplets: there's enough for them all. I think I must be like those women who used to wet-nurse the chatelaine's babies, leaving her free to watch the jousting."

"What does David think of her?"

"He said she looked like a rosebud. Imagine!"

"And Dagmar?"

"Dagmar was in this building twenty minutes after I was carried into it. Now she's taken over. She was here most of the morning, telling the staff how to look after babies. Rona, I've got to do something about her."

"Not yet. You don't want to turn all that lovely milk sour. Put it out of your mind for a few weeks and then tackle it."

"Few weeks! It's impossible. The situation's impossible. Dagmar's impossible." She waved a hand towards the bed-side table. "There's a letter there from Monique. After less than two months of Dagmar, her husband's having to take her to Biarritz to recuperate. So what do you think I feel like with her on my neck for the rest of my life?"

"Is it really so bad, Sigrid? I know she's—"

"She's impossible. She always has been, but it didn't matter so much when she was helping to run the shop. When David took over, he didn't expect her to drop everything at once and leave him to it. But as time went on, he realized that she'd never stop interfering, only she switched from the shop to her grandchildren. She got on his nerves, and now she's getting on mine. She practically took over Arthur from the day he was born. I didn't mind at first; I thought it would wear off. But it didn't. Now she's giving orders about the new baby. We've already had an argument about the name. I won."

"What's she going to be called?"

"Karen Sigrid. Do you know what Dagmar wanted? Davina Dagmar Claudine. I told you I won, but it was a real fight. She doesn't give up until you make yourself unpleasantly clear. When I get out of this place, which will be in three days, I'm going to have a—what's that word?"

"Showdown?"

"A showdown, yes. I'm going to tell her that David and I are going to look for a house of our own."

"Don't do that, Sigrid. Please. Not yet."

"David and I have talked it over, and over, and over. He doesn't want to move, naturally. Where will he find room for all the things he's clung to all these years? He even kept his schoolbooks, and those things he made in the school workshop, and his skis and his water skis and his camping equipment and his thousands of records—where is it all to go? We'll need a warehouse. I know it won't be easy, but we'll find something."

"It would upset Celia terribly."

"I know. Whatever upsets Dagmar, upsets her. I wouldn't mind if Dagmar had any modern ideas on the subject of child-rearing, but she hasn't. She was brought up by grandparents in a nineteenth-century Swiss tradition, and that's all she knows, and it was fine in the nineteenth century but it isn't what I want for Arthur and Karen."

A nurse entered, placed two vases of flowers on the table and went out again.

"But I don't want to talk about Dagmar," Sigrid went on as the door closed. "I want to ask you about Nigel. David's worried about him. He says he's different. Have you noticed?"

"Well, yes."

"It can't be his job that's on his mind. Dave says he's looking forward to working in London. So if it isn't the job, it must be a woman. And if it's a woman, then something's wrong. The affair isn't what Claudine calls marching. So why isn't it?"

"I don't think it's a woman."

"Then what? Dave always told me that as soon as he arrived here, he was ready to go away again. Has he lost all his old friends?"

"No. They still ring. The messages pile up and he does nothing about them."

"There's your proof. He's lost interest because he's dreaming about some woman or other in Brazil. He's in love, but she's probably married already and she won't divorce her husband because she's a devout Catholic."

"No. I've seen him in love. It's never affected him like this."

"Can't you ask him straight out, for goodness' sake? You've known him since you were—what? ten, eleven. Surely you could ask a simple question like are you having an unhappy love affair and if so, where is she?"

"Dave could ask him; I couldn't. He and I were never on—well, I suppose you could call it equal terms. There was too much difference in our ages."

"What do you think he's suffering from?"

"He wants to find another house for his mother. He feels she's got herself into a mean sort of house."

"Mean? Humble?"

"No. Humility's a virtue. Meanness is a vice, and the work that was done on the cottage was done in the cheapest possible way. Nigel says it'll need constant repair, and he thinks the damp will affect his mother's health."

"So he's going to look for another house?"

"Yes."

"Then when he looks, I'll look with him. He can say he's looking for a house for his mother, and I will say I'm helping him, but what I'll really be looking for will be a house for David and myself. It will have to be close to the shop, because David won't go far away; he's got this I-am-the-only-son-of-a-widowed-mother complex, like Nigel. It's ridiculous, because both their mothers are perfectly able to look after themselves. Are you having lunch with Celia?"

"Yes. I ought to hurry; I'm late."

"Look, Nigel's lunching with David and they're both coming on here afterwards. So you and Celia will be alone. Couldn't you say something to her about Dagmar? Couldn't you ask her to make Dagmar see that I won't stand any more interference? Will you make her do something, anything to put a stop to it?"

"I'll do what I can."

But on her way to the cottage, she felt there was little that could be done by anybody. Celia felt free to criticize Dagmar, but she did not like to hear her criticized by others. Nor did she have the least idea how long Sigrid had been working herself up to the point of rebellion.

Over lunch, she felt her way cautiously. She was turning over in her mind various ways of leading up to the subject, when Celia introduced it.

"Didn't you think the baby was lovely?"

"Yes. She'll look like Dagmar when she grows up, won't she?"

"Perhaps. But Monique started off looking just like her mother, but she doesn't look like her now. I like the names Sigrid chose. The baby was only four hours old when I saw her. It's the sixtieth baby born in the James Dartford Hospital; did Sigrid tell you?"

"No. Let's hope it's a lucky number."

"How did you think Sigrid was looking?"

"Well . . . a bit depressed."

"That's only natural. I remember feeling awful after Nigel was born."

"It's not the baby, exactly. We talked about Dagmar." She summoned her courage. "Sigrid wondered whether you could do anything."

Celia finished an apple and pushed her plate away.

"Do anything about what?"

"Sigrid's getting a bit restless. As a matter of fact, she feels that Dagmar—"

"You needn't go on." Celia spoke coldly. "I'm not blind. I've been watching Sigrid for some time. I suppose she's working herself up to quarrel with Dagmar?"

"Worse than a quarrel. She's talking of getting out."

"Getting out? Getting out of what? I don't understand."

"Out of the house."

"You mean she's talking of—"

"Yes. Of getting a home of their own."

Celia made no reply. She sat staring at the table. Rona got up and fetched coffee from the kitchen.

"She couldn't," Celia said as she returned. "It would be utter madness. I'm quite certain she's not serious. You said Sigrid was depressed. When she gets over the—"

"Three and a half years," Rona broke in, "is a long time to have one's life run by Dagmar."

Celia stared at her.

"You're on Sigrid's side? Yes, I suppose you would be."

"I'm not taking sides. But facts are facts, and you can't ignore the fact that Dagmar bosses everybody all the time. Some people can dodge; Sigrid can't. She says it was bad enough when there was only Arthur; now that there's another baby, it'll be twice as bad."

Celia spoke with certainty.

"She couldn't do it. David wouldn't do it."

"Yes he would. I don't think he wants to, but it must be awful for him to be caught between the two of them."

"Dagmar would never get over it. Never. She wouldn't understand it. People like her don't realize what effect they have on other people. She thinks she's only doing her duty and helping an inexperienced daughter-in-law. If she ever guessed, ever knew they thought of leaving the house, she— They mustn't do it."

"They—"

"I'm not saying it's easy for Sigrid. But can you mention one daughter-in-law, apart from that one in the Bible, who ever found her mother-in-law easy to get on with? Mention just one."

"Perhaps they weren't all shut up in the same house, like Sigrid and Dagmar."

Arguing with Celia, she reflected, was difficult. Most people grew angry or excited. If Celia did, neither of these emotions showed on her face or in her voice. She had grown pale, but she spoke calmly.

"You just mentioned facts," she said. "The fact is that although they live together, they live in a place large enough to give them complete privacy and seclusion—if they want it. Sigrid and David have their rooms; Dagmar has hers. By the time Arthur was born, Sigrid knew that Dagmar was inclined to interfere, but when I advised her to use the room near hers as a nursery, she refused; so he was next door to Dagmar, and of course she was always going in to see him. Next time Sigrid talks to you about Dagmar's bossiness, you could point out that she hasn't done so badly since she married David: a beautiful place to live in, people to wait on her, kindness and consideration, comfort, leisure, a devoted husband and a successful business."

"Yes. But—"

"Why don't young people *try* any more? A marriage isn't a marriage until it's been through quarrels and maladjustments and stresses and strains, and stood up to them. The only word you hear nowdays is incompatibility."

"It's easier for young couples if they can live on their own."

"This case is different. David wouldn't have had a shop at all if it hadn't been for Dagmar's initiative and hard work. Isn't that something that Sigrid ought to remember?"

"Your coffee's cold. I'll get you a fresh cup."

"Thank you. Do you know what I really think?" she asked when Rona returned.

"No. What?"

"I think it isn't fair."

"What isn't?"

"The position that so many grandparents get pushed into. What Dagmar's being asked to do, what most grandparents are asked to do, is cut themselves adrift from habits they've had for the past thirty or forty years of their lives. When a man retires, he can usually find something to interest him; but his wife's interests have probably been centered on her grandchildren, and it's hard to be told she's not needed any more. Dagmar has always been the driving force. Where is all her energy to go to? She can't stop generating it, can she? So she has to find outlets. She's not needed in the shop. She hasn't a husband to look after. Her two children are grown up and married; so what can she do but transfer her attention to her grandchildren?"

"I don't know. All I know is that Sigrid's going to start looking for a house of their own."

"How can she do that without Dagmar knowing?"

Rona hesitated.

"She planned to go with Nigel. He's going to try and find a house for you."

Silence. Another cup of coffee grew cold and was replaced.

"Are you angry?" Rona asked.

"No. And I'm not surprised. I think that's been in his mind ever since he set foot inside this cottage."

"Why don't you go with him and help him?"

"No. Let him learn what an exhausting job it is. When he's inspected the first fifty or so, I might try to help."

"Will you talk to Dagmar?"

"I'll think about it. Hadn't you better hurry back to the office? It's getting late."

Celia was still sitting at the table when Nigel returned. He looked from the uncleared plates to his mother, elbows on the table, chin on her hands, lost in meditation. After waiting in vain for a word from her, he pulled up a chair and sat down.

"If it's a problem," he said, "I could probably solve it."

She stirred, sighed and laid her hands on her lap.

"This is Sigrid's problem. And Dagmar's," she said.

"Oh, that one? I'm well up on that. I had it all through lunch with Dave. I had some more of it when we dropped into the hospital after lunch. The baby didn't say much, but Sigrid gave me a rundown on her mother-in-law's failings."

"Do you think they'll move?"

"What you mean is: will Dagmar discover that they're planning to move? That's what's worrying you, isn't it?"

"Yes."

"People differ a lot," he pointed out gently. "Finding out, for Dagmar, wouldn't be the thunderbolt it would be for you, if you found yourself in the same circumstances. You wouldn't claim, would you, that she's unduly sensitive?"

"She'd never get over it. Sensitive or not, she'd never get over it. But perhaps"—she pushed back her chair and rose —"it won't happen. Where could Sigrid find the same accommodation? Where could they find servants? Inga and Claudine would certainly stay with Dagmar. Do you know something? If anybody has had reason to complain of Dagmar, it's been myself. True, I haven't lived in the same house, but we meet almost every day, and there isn't a single thing in my life, and in your father's life when he was alive, that she didn't interfere in. We stood it because we were fond of her. Rona asked me to talk to Dagmar, and I will, because if things have got as bad as this, she ought to be given some warning. But the person I'd like to speak to is Sigrid. She owes Dagmar something. I'd like to tell her so. And another thing: if you're embarking on house-hunting for me, I hope you'll enjoy it. I'm glad I'm not going to have to go through it all over again."

He went up to her, took her chin in his hand and tilted her head to look up at him.

"If you were anybody else," he said, "I'd hesitate about

pulling you out of a place you'd only just settled down in. But I know you, and I know that once you've got over lamenting the loss of the damp and the drafts, you'll be contented in any house I find for you." He pressed a forefinger affectionately on her nose. "You're the contented kind."

Bringing up the dreaded subject with Dagmar, Celia thought, was one of the most difficult things she had ever been called upon to do. She spent an almost sleepless night rehearsing and rejecting ways of approaching the matter. She must be gentle, but at the same time she must make the situation quite clear. Whether Sigrid was right or wrong, her decision seemed to be made, and she was not likely to go back on it. She was a woman who knew what she wanted, and Celia thought her basically hard enough to make certain that she got it.

She had intended seeing Dagmar on the following day, but Dagmar had a number of engagements, and it was not until Wednesday morning that they could meet. Their talk, Celia felt, would be easier if it was held at the cottage; she asked Nigel to take Rona out to lunch, and invited Dagmar to a cold lunch at the cottage.

It was not a success. Dagmar, on arrival, proved to be in high spirits, which meant, Celia knew, that she would behave like a car with a powerful engine and inadequate brakes.

"I have just come from the hospital," she announced on her arrival. "Sigrid is going to leave in two more days; can you imagine how silly, so soon? It is the modern way, which most of the time means that it is not so good as the old way. You and I stayed for ten days, and not in such a beautiful hospital as this new one. But she is fixed to go, she says. Do you know what I took for her? Not for her; I bought a little toy for Arthur, because when she goes home and shows him the new baby, she must give him a toy and tell him that the baby brought it for him. In this way, there is no jealousy." She groped in a vast handbag. "Look what I have brought for us—a bottle of this delicious white wine you liked at my house the other day. Will you get out some ice? And also that nice silver bucket Nigel gave you. We will put it to get cool. And now if you will give me a little sherry, or some Dubonnet, we can talk till the wine is ready."

"How was the baby?"

"Beautiful. But before we talk of babies, Celia, I want to say something about Nigel. I am worried about him. He is not himself, you must have seen? Sigrid agrees with me that he is in love."

"If he had been, he would have told David."

"But he has not said a word. So there is a difficulty. Perhaps she is black. In Brazil, this is a possibility."

"It's a possibility anywhere."

"That is true. You would not object to a black daughter-in-law? The children would be enchanting. I know from Inga's brother—four children, all café au lait, with lovely little curls, and they are nearly grown up and the marriage has been a great success, so you see it is as I have always said, in a hundred years we shall all be café au lait and there will be no more stupid fuss about who is black or white or spotted or striped. If this woman is Brazilian, you will have to throw away all the dresses you bought from the drapers' windows, because if you will believe me, the only women in the world who look better in their clothes than Brazilian women are women from Argentina. You can see well-dressed women in London or Paris—look at me, I am beautifully dressed—but those women are part of their clothes. Like Maria Montallen, if you will excuse me for mentioning her."

Certainly Dagmar looked part of her clothes, Celia thought. She was in a new outfit, close-fitting, elegant. One plump, pretty hand with outsize rings held her glass while the other waved in emphasis, making her heavy bracelet swing and clash. Her eyes, large and beautiful, velvety, were full of light and life.

"Nigel isn't worrying about a woman, Dagmar. He's been

worrying about this cottage. He's going to look for another house."

"And Sigrid is going to help him. She told me when I saw her just now. She will be useful; the Swedish people know all about modern houses, big windows, light and air, good equipment, good living."

Celia spoke in what she hoped was a casual tone.

"Do you think Sigrid will ever decide to have a home of her own?"

Dagmar looked astonished. Then she looked at her glass, found it empty and handed it to Celia to be refilled.

"Why," she asked, "should Sigrid want a home of her own? She is in a home of her own already."

"She's very independent. She might prefer to—"

"I don't know what you mean by independent. She is very happy to be waited on by Inga and Claudine. She is not a housewife, you know. She knows nothing about keeping a house because she has always been in hotels, travelling about with her mother, never stopping anywhere for long, can you imagine such a sad way to live? It is good that she is settled at last. But how is she independent? She has, of course, ideas about babies, but the ideas are all out of books, and when you take them out of the books and try them, they won't work. She doesn't know how to cook, and doesn't want to learn. She doesn't like to order the meals or to talk over the dishes with Inga or with Claudine, and she doesn't like to make the beds or to arrange the house. She likes to sew, but only embroidery, like you. I would pity David if she had to look after him without somebody to do everything for her. I don't call this independent."

"But young couples do like to live by themselves."

"Some young couples have to. Some young couples have no opportunity to live in a beautiful house that one of them has grown up in. It is very silly, I think, the way that old people are left in a house which is useless for them, while the young couples squeeze themselves into a small house and can't find servants to work for them. Look at Monique: she refused to live with her parents-in-law, and what is the result? She has this too-small house, and not enough help, and she gets too tired and then her husband has to take her away, to Biarritz where his parents have a summer house, and the parents look after the babies in Geneva while she is away. And such lovely babies, they are of course glad to have them. They love them all, just as I do. Do you know, I am going to teach little Arthur to read with cards. Already he knows the kings and the queens and the knaves. He is not more clever than his cousins, but I think he is more quick to catch what you say to him. He—"

"Amber," said Celia in desperation.

"—is really a highly strung child, as David was. He—"

"Amber."

"What did you say?"

"I said amber."

"Why should you say amber? We are not talking about amber."

"You were talking about your grandchildren."

"Yes. I was saying about little Arthur— Oh, I see. You said amber to stop me."

"You asked me to."

"I didn't ask you to—"

"Dagmar, you did. You even chose the word I had to say. Don't you remember?"

"Naturally I remember. But I did not mean that you should stop me when I was talking about my grandchildren to you. I thought that you liked to hear about them."

"I do. But—"

"But you stopped me."

"Because we agreed—"

"Yes, I know. We agreed that if I talk about them too much with strangers, they may not be so interested. But with you, I thought I could talk about them. But if every time I speak of Arthur or the baby or Pierre, you are to stop me, I think that is showing yourself not to be interested."

"I am. I told you I am."

"But still, you stopped me. I am not blaming you. Even David says that I talk too much about them, think too much about them. But I am their grandmother. You have no grandchildren as yet. You also have no daughter-in-law who lives with you. Rona is here, but she will go away again. I am glad that in France, in Switzerland, we still believe in the whole family. You remember what Aubrey used to call it? The round family: from the old grandparents down to the newest little baby, happy together, helping each other. What is better than that?"

"Only one thing: letting the young people find their own feet and stand on them."

"That is another idea." Dagmar nodded in agreement. "But it is better when it is an idea than when it is really so. With the round family, there is what Aubrey said: continuity. All are linked. If the grandparents are sick, the parents can help. If the babies are sick, the grandparents can help. There will be disagreements, naturally, sometimes; these are natural. You don't know how many times I find Sigrid stupid, so full of ideas that won't work. But I am patient. I try to help her. I even try to hide from David that in some ways she is not competent. Celia, I think the wine is cool enough. I think we should have lunch."

They had lunch.

CHAPTER

7

THURSDAY EVENING SEEMED TO NIGEL A LONG TIME IN coming, but he found himself at last at the wheel of his car, Rona beside him, driving in the direction of London.

He enjoyed theater-going, but he was not thinking of the play as he drove; he was savouring the thought that tonight he would have her to himself. They were together; for the next few hours he would not have to share her company with his mother or with Sigrid or David or Bryan Hayling. This would be an evening for two.

"Got the tickets?" she asked as they set out.

"Yes."

"Did you have trouble getting them?"

"No. I know a man who knows a man."

"I see. When did you last go to a London theater?"

"Just before I went back to Brazil. Do you often go?"

"No. This play we're going to see—they were going to take it off, did you know that?"

"No. It recovered?"

"Yes. Don't you check before you book seats? There was that Australian actress in the lead, but she went back to the bush, and now it's another one. Name of Dorothy Kestrel."

"Dot Kestrel—playing the lead?"

"You know her?"

"I used to take her out once. Intermittently. She used to vanish into the provinces to say a couple of lines in some play or other, and then she'd be back, out of a job. I thought it a hell of a profession, but she must have stuck to it. She phoned, but I didn't remember to ring back."

"You'll have to get into the queue. Her picture's in every paper I pick up. Could we go backstage and see her? I've never been in an actress's dressing room. Have you?"

"Off and on."

"Do they really have screens and go behind them and throw their clothes over the top?"

"I didn't see any screens."

"One of the girls at school wanted to go on the stage. You ought to remember her; her name was Bevis and she was deeply in love with you at the beginning of the holidays."

"Not at the end?"

"No. You'd gone by the end, but she was cured because you didn't come up to her intellectual standards. We had holiday tasks to do and we wanted help from you, but didn't get it. She said it was a pity you looked so much cleverer than you really were."

"What did she want to know?"

"We both wanted to know. About pragmatic sanctions, for a start. We had to name four. You could only tell us the name of one, and we knew that one already, the one about Maria Theresa and the Austrian succession."

"Blame my father. He always said that one needn't store up miscellaneous facts. If you needed them, you could look them up."

"That's what we did—in the town library."

"Find anything?"

"Yes. We found the pragmatic sanction of St. Louis, about limiting the power of the Pope in France. I've forgotten the other two. But I can remember something else you didn't know. We were asked to name four famous columns, and the only one you knew was Nelson's. Bevis asked you for a list of the popes; you didn't know that, either. I asked the history mistress what good it did to learn it all, and she said something about training the mind. I think there was too much mind-training and not enough hand-training. Not once were we shown how to paper a wall or mend an electric switch or put a new washer on a tap or fix hinges or put in a pane of glass. My children are all going to be apprenticed to carpenters and plumbers and electricians. It wasn't until I came back and found your mother settling into the cottage that I realized how little I could do to help. It was a pity you weren't there; you're not a bad handyman. You did some good repairs over the years."

"Over the years . . . Ten to twenty-four."

"Half my childhood and all my girlhood. And your early youth—all gone. Hadn't we better hurry? We're going to be late for the show."

Reluctantly, he put on speed. He had no great desire to reach the theater. He would have liked to turn the car and head for open country, nosing down unlit lanes, stopping to peer at crossroad signs, alone with her, enclosed by the night. He wished he had suggested dinner without the theater; a leisurely dinner, long-drawn-out, intimate. He thought that intimacy would be difficult to establish; he did not think that when she went out with other men, she talked about her schooldays and her holiday tasks. But he was handicapped; he was part of her past, and fixed firmly in her mind as an inmate of the house, coming and going, interested not in her and her friends but in a succession of women.

He drove fast for the last few miles; in spite of having to park the car some distance from the theater, they reached it in good time. Groups of people were still standing in the foyer.

Prominently displayed on an easel was a photograph of the leading lady, Dorothy Kestrel.

"Pretty," Rona commented, studying it. "How long have you known her?"

"Can't remember exactly. She—"

He stopped. A large, square-shouldered man with greying hair and a florid face had stopped beside them and spoken his name.

"Nigel. Glad you could make it." He put the two large baskets of flowers he was carrying on either side of the photograph. "This is going to make Dot's evening complete, knowing you're here. She wanted to get in touch with you, but you weren't anywhere she tried. See you later."

With a half bow to Rona, he went round to the back of the box office.

"Who?" Rona asked.

"Fellow named Frosting. Mike Frosting. Last time I saw him, he was calling himself Dorothy Kestrel's manager and trying to convince anybody who'd listen that she was a great actress. Well, we'll soon know."

The theater was not full.

"You should have seen it a couple of weeks ago." Mike Frosting, reappearing as they were entering the auditorium, spoke in a confidential whisper. "All but closing. Then they put Dot in the part, and before the end of the week, business began to pick up and is going to go on picking up. I've told her you're here. Don't go round in the interval, there's a good chap; she's excited enough as it is. I tried to make her put off the shenanigans until Sunday, but no, they had to be on the right day, so now we're up to our ears. I'll take you round after the last curtain."

"Look, Mike, I'm afraid—"

"Where are you sitting?"

"Fourth row."

"I'll tell her."

"I'd rather see her some other time. I'm going on to—"

"What other time? This is the big day. She's calling it her twenty-fifth; nobody's going to argue about that. She doesn't look any more."

He was gone. They took their seats; the curtain rose, and halfway through the first act, Miss Kestrel entered to a storm of applause. The part—that of a stockbroker's dimwitted mistress—was not demanding, but it suited her.

When the act ended and the lights went up, a fair-haired young man in the row behind leaned forward.

"Coming round to see Dot, Nigel?"

"No."

"Oh, come on! There'll be all the old crowd there."

"Sorry."

The man glanced at Rona, nodded as though understanding the situation, and made his way out of the auditorium.

"I could drive your car home," Rona suggested drily. "You could get back by train."

"Nice of you to suggest it. Would you like to go out for a drink, or would you rather stay here?"

"I'd rather stay here."

He looked relieved. She guessed that the bar would be filled with more friends of his or the leading lady's.

"Why don't you join the celebrations?" she asked him.

"I don't want to. I was never interested in Dot Kestrel, and apart from being glad she's got to the top, I'm not interested now. Why the hell did I choose this show, anyway?"

"I'm enjoying it. So's everybody else."

As the final act opened, he sat making plans. There would, he knew, be a gathering of friends and admirers and well-wishers immediately the last curtain fell; he resolved to get Rona away before anybody tried to draw him in.

But she had meant it when she said she was enjoying the show. She remained deaf to his suggestions that they should leave before the end. All he could do was persuade her to come away before the audience began to stream out.

They had reached the foyer and were going down the steps to the street when his arm was firmly grasped.

"Oh, no, you don't." Mike Frosting's voice was grim. "Oh, no, you don't. Just got you in time." Still holding Nigel's arm, he turn to Rona. "Look, this isn't going to spoil your evening," he pleaded. "We're all going on to a nightclub to give Dot a slap-up birthday party. And you two have got to be there. You're Nigel's date, I know, and I shouldn't be butting in, but this party is for a girl who rates one; she's had a long wait before getting where she's got. If you don't want Nigel to join in, of course he can't. But if you'll come along too, we'd love to have you, and . . . Will you?"

Rona looked at him speculatively.

"Let me see," she said slowly. "You said a nightclub?"

"Yes. The—"

"A really expensive, exclusive nightclub?"

A glimmer of appreciation began to show in his eyes.

"Italian. Members only."

"And, of course, champagne?"

"French. The best."

"Caviar?"

He was smiling.

"Russian."

"Then it's a deal."

"Splendid. Come with me."

Before Nigel could prevent him, he had swept her down the steps and joined a group waiting for cars. One drew up and carried some away; Mike Frosting, with Rona, was among those in the next. Nigel was hemmed in by the fair-haired young man and his companions.

So much, he thought bitterly, for his evening-for-two.

Seated some time later on Dorothy Kestrel's right at the largest of the three tables booked for the birthday celebrations, he found that it would not be possible to show any lack of enthusiasm for the party. It was, he knew, an occasion for genuine rejoicing; Dot had worked and waited a long time for this entry into stardom. She was surrounded by old friends, and she was generous enough to cede the limelight now and then. All the members of the cast were given a share of the congratulations, and friends were not forgotten. Nigel was toasted as Our Guest from Brazil, and loudly cheered when Dot pressed a lingering kiss on his lips.

Rona, at a smaller table, found that, as Mike had promised, there was champagne. But there was no caviar, since there appeared to be a shortage on the other two tables, and hands reached out and whisked away her share.

Mike Frosting, seated beside her, showed frankly that she interested him. From time to time he paid a brief visit to the largest table to see that Dot had everything she wanted.

"Who," Nigel seized him to ask, "is that fellow sitting next to Rona?"

"Him? He's the famous playwright, Pershore."

"Who?"

"Haven't you heard of Graham Pershore?"

"No."

"My God. Well, don't tell anybody; they'll think you've fallen out of a tree. If you're worried, relax. He's not absolutely sober, but he's absolutely safe—Enjoying yourself, Dot darling?"

Reassured on this point, he returned to Rona. Mr. Pershore had in the meantime swivelled slowly in his chair to address her. He was very thin, very dark, somewhat dishevelled, and was beginning to have difficulty in articulating. Leaning towards her, he addressed her gravely.

"As I was telling you," he said, "you mustn't waste your time trying to write a play. Just write a *part*, that's all. Sit down and write one, big, juicy *part*. Somebody—Shakespeare, I fancy—said that the play's the thing, but believe me, my dear girl, he was wrong. The play isn't the thing. The *part* is the thing. No actor cares two h-h-hoots about being in a good play. What he wants, what in fact he needs if he's to stay in business, is a good *part*. Write him one, and you're made. I speak from experience. I wrote good plays, but nobody would touch them. Nobody. Then I said to myself: If you were an actor, my dear Graham, what would you be after? A *part*, I answered. So I wrote one. I knew it was a part that would make any actor, and it did, and I became rich and you, too, can succeed. You have it in you. I've always thought so."

"You have?"

"Always." He leaned back in order to study her. "Do you know, you grow prettier every time I see you."

"Thank you."

"You've put on a little weight. I'm so glad. I told you that the scraggy look would soon go out, and I was right: it did. Women were made with curves. No man likes to have bones sticking into him. Delicious curves. The very words present their differing pictures. Bony: you note the hard sound? Now take curvacious. It's like champagne on the tongue. It's— What became of the champagne?"

"Mike took it to the other table."

"The hell he did. Mike!" He stood up and roared. "Mike! No, no, no, not *that* mike. No, I refuse to say anything. I'm merely a guest. Will you please go away?"

The reporters went away. Why, Mr. Pershore asked fretfully, wasn't anybody dancing?

Everybody danced. The dimensions of the dance floor precluded any but the most restricted movements, but this did not lessen Rona's enjoyment. When at last the party showed signs of breaking up and Nigel made his way to her, she followed him reluctantly to the car.

He was silent for a time. He could not express his intense disappointment at the way the evening had turned out, and he did not want to hear her telling him how much she had enjoyed herself.

"You're not a party man, are you?" she remarked after a time.

"No. I never was."

"Im sorry you got dragged into this one."

"You seemed to enjoy it."

"I did. They were nice not to leave me out. I've never met stage people before. They seem to go on acting off the stage. And they've got a kind of club language. You get the feeling they don't say things they really mean."

"Who does, at parties? That's why I loathe them. If you want to enjoy someone's company, you can enjoy it without jostle and din and clatter."

"Dot enjoyed it all."

"Dot? Oh, yes, Dot enjoyed it. Success, celebration and herself dead center. You got on very well with Mike, I noticed."

"His wife doesn't understand him."

"She understands him well enough to keep away from him. Where," he asked with real curiosity, "did you learn to deal with these Mike characters?"

"You learn as you go along. I don't drink much when I'm out; that helps."

"Helps what?"

"Helps me to see trouble coming. I noticed that when girls drank too much, they got to a swimmy stage and lost their initiative, among other things. I like to keep track of what's going on. The kind of men who give you the most trouble are the overconfident ones; you have to try and block them before they reach the aggressive stage. I don't like being mauled."

The faint air of fastidiousness in her tone made him smile. Now that they had touched on sex, he would have liked to ask for her views on certain aspects of it. That they would be downright, he had no doubt.

"I'm terribly hungry," she said suddenly. "Aren't you? No, you can't be; there were lashings of food at your table. I'm going to make sandwiches when we get home."

"You could eat before you got home."

"Isn't everywhere closed at this time of night, morning?"

"Not everywhere. Ever heard of a place called the May-day?"

"Yes. Nobody's ever taken me there. You have to pay in gold bars."

"We'll go now."

It took them fifteen minutes to reach it: a long, low building round three sides of a courtyard. A number of cars, very large and sleek, were ranged outside. Inside were low ceilings, low lights, low voices and a very large room filled with tables at which people were eating.

"Full," Rona said resignedly.

"Almost. There used to be a head waiter here by the name of Leandro. If he's still— Ah."

Leandro led them to a table that looked out onto the court-yard. Nigel ate little; Rona proved that her claim to hunger had been well founded.

"It can't be much fun for you, just watching me eat," she told him halfway through.

"You'd be surprised."

Dawn was breaking as they drank their coffee. The bill was discreetly presented and paid by check. Rona, with an apologetic sigh, watched it being borne away.

"Your year's bonus?" she asked.

"Practically. How do you feel?"

"Wonderful." Another sigh, this time blissful. "I don't think I've ever enjoyed an evening as much as I've enjoyed this one. Thank you."

"You're welcome."

She was asleep, her head on his shoulder, when they reached the cottage. He roused her gently. Still half asleep, she went upstairs, her coat dragging behind her. He walked with her to her door.

"Want any help undressing?" he asked.

She spoke through a long yawn.

"No, thanks. Good night."

He bent and kissed her.

"Good night. Sleep well."

In his room, he undressed slowly, thinking over the evening. He felt strangely content. He did not think he had made much progress, but he was sure that they were not on the footing they had been when they set out for the theater.

Soon, he thought, she would perhaps begin to think of him as a man, and not as someone who had helped her with her homework.

CHAPTER

8

NIGEL SPENT THE NEXT TWO DAYS IN LONDON. HE OFFERED to take his mother up with him, but she refused, for which, later, he felt glad, for the business he had to get through took a great deal longer than he had anticipated.

He began by driving to his old rooms to seé whether they were available. They were not, but the flat above was to let and he could have it if it suited him—and if he could afford the price of the lease.

He went up to inspect it. It had a very large, sunny room overlooking the street, two bedrooms, a bathroom, a small shower room and a well-fitted kitchen. It was what he wanted; there was a long lease, and the rooms needed no redecoration.

On the following day, when the formalities had been completed, he drove to the warehouse in which his furniture was stored, and arranged to have it removed at the end of the month. His lunch was sandwiches and beer in a pub; after this he went to his former daily help to report his reappearance in England and to find out whether her services would be available. Reassured on this score, he drove back to Longbrook. He passed on the way a large car going in the direction of London, and recognized it as Francis Latimer's. He was at the wheel, with Maria Montallen beside him. Off for the weekend, Nigel guessed; nothing to amuse them in Longbrook.

He reached the cottage to find his mother finishing tea. Rona, he learned, had answered an appeal from an old school friend to help with the move to a new house.

"When'll she be back?"

"She'll go straight to the office on Monday. Oh, Nigel, I nearly forgot. David rang about an hour ago. Your old headmaster is driving through Longbrook this evening and asked him if he was free to meet him for dinner. When David told him you were in England, he was delighted and asked you too."

"Damn. Is the headmaster's wife with him?"

"Yes, but she isn't the one you knew when you were at school. Will you go?"

"I suppose so."

"If you get a chance, could you try to find out how David feels about Sigrid's idea of moving?"

There was no chance before dinner, since the headmaster and his wife arrived early at the restaurant and were already talking to David in the bar when Nigel arrived. Dinner was an exhausting meal, for the headmaster's conversation skimmed lightly over his somewhat arid present and dwelt exclusively on his busy and authoritative past. Reminiscences of his days at the school issued in serial form between bites and in an increasing stream between courses. His wife, in the mistaken view that the two younger men wanted nothing more than to recall their feats on the games field, interpolated eager questions about sport. When the evening came at last to an end, David and Nigel, without a word said, turned in the direction of the Three Feathers.

"Brandy," Nigel said when they arrived. "Poor old devil, what a wreck."

"Was he always a windbag?" David asked.

"I suppose so. Seems fantastic to think that we ever took him seriously. Remember those sermons of his?"

"My God, yes. I heard someone say recently that he got his headship because he was a famous scholar—not because he knew the first thing about boys and their needs."

"Next time he appears in this town, don't drag me in." He drew his chair closer to the table. "My mother wants me to find out what you think about this idea of moving to a house of your own."

"I was just about to bring up the topic. Did you ever hear about the fellow who was caught between the devil and the deep sea? I feel like him."

"You're against moving?"

"I hate the whole idea. I hate it like hell. Every time I go into a room, I see the accumulation of stuff I've got in it. My entire life."

"You were always a great one for hanging on to things."

"Why not?"

"I've never cured you, have I? Material possessions, chains round your neck—"

"Not neck. Ankles. It was the millstone you said was round my neck. And don't leave out the bit about clipped wings. So all right; I hoard. So every time Sigrid talks about moving, I think of the vans and pantechnicons lining up and all my possesions being loaded into them—and you do realize, don't you, that a good part of the furniture is mine, left to me by old Grandpa Chantard?"

"Yes."

"So there you are. Getting it out's easy, but where's it all going to be unloaded?"

"Apart from that, would you go?"

David hesitated.

"Not if it only concerned me, no," he said at last. "I've

learned to live with my mother. When she gets into one of her bossy sessions, I can cut out; I don't hear half she says. But with Sigrid, it's different. She's got a case. Dagmar dishes out advice about how, when and where to feed, clothe or bring up babies. Another thing: if you remember, there used to be a rule that nobody went into anybody else's sitting room without being invited. Until I married and for a time after I married, Dagmar observed the rule. Now she thinks she does. She'd be amazed if you told her that she's more in our rooms than out of them—but that's the way it is. And still another thing: housework. Sigrid's never in her life handled a kitchen knife or a duster. She's convinced she could whisk round the work in a couple of hours and then sit down to play with the children. If you subtract Inga and Claudine, what are you left with?"

"You."

"That's what I'm afraid of. One thing, I've got Arthur on my side."

"He doesn't want to move, either?"

"How could you move him? Every morning, he counts. He wants to see: one, his mother; two, his father; three, his grandmother; four, Inga; five, Claudine. All of them, every morning without fail, and in that order. Once, he used to have to be carried round; now he makes the rounds himself. He staggers down the corridors yelling the appropriate name as he goes. If anybody's missing, if anybody's late in showing up, there's hell to pay. I'm waiting to see how long he takes to get the idea that there's one more on the list: his new sister. No, I can't see Arthur moving. All I can see is that once, we all lived in that house without friction. I think we could do it again, but I don't see how. Maybe there's some peasant in me; I like the whole family setup, from toothless old Granddad down to toothless little Karen. Think, will you, and tell me how it can be done?"

"I suppose your mother and mine would never consider living together?"

"No. Your mother's a loner. And there's no hope of getting Dagmar to go back to Geneva. Monique's going to sit hard on that plan. To turn from my problems to yours: you're not keeping any secrets from me, are you?"

"Could I ever?"

"Not in the past. You came home in a peculiar mood—any particular reason?"

"No."

"No entanglements?"

"Not a single one."

"I'll believe you. I don't think Sigrid will."

They drove away in Nigel's car. He stopped at Renson's and David got out.

"I'm short of exercise," he said. "How about some tennis tomorrow?"

"Good idea."

Tennis helped to make Sunday pass. Monday came. Rona came to the cottage for lunch, unpacked, changed and went back to the office.

"Oh, about the work at Sir James's house," she said on her way out. "Bryan says it would be better if I left the office at four every day and gave Sir James an hour and a half."

When she returned, Bryan was with her.

"You were kind enough," he told Celia, "to tell me I could drop in for tea anytime. So I've dropped."

"You're welcome, Bryan. Sit over there. I'm the only one who's really interested in having tea. Rona never wants any, and Nigel just keeps me company."

He took his cup from her, refused her offer of something to eat and spoke dejectedly.

"I keep wishing," he said, "that I'd joined the office years ago. I suppose you could say that the mess we're clearing up now is partly my fault."

"What I don't understand," Nigel said, "is how old Todd got so much into his own hands."

"I can answer that," Celia said. "He and Sir James were

great friends. I don't think there was a day when Mr. Todd didn't walk up the hill and drop in for a game of chess, or a chat, or to listen to records of those symphonies they both liked so much. Sir James never liked what he called paper work; he wanted to be free to spend his days in his garden, so he left everything to Mr. Todd."

"With the result," Bryan said, "that the office didn't have the faintest idea of what was going on. You're Sir James's friend and you won't like to hear him criticized, but I'd like to say that he's the worst type of client, the kind that asks you to draw up a deed or a document, gives you a rough idea of what he wants and then forgets about it and goes back to planting seeds. If you ask him to clear up a detail here or there, he intimates you're not up to your job."

"He wasn't always like that," Celia said. "It was only after his wife's accident that he became so forgetful. He was seriously injured, you must remember, and although the doctors said there was no brain damage, I don't think he ever got back to normal. I find, talking to him, that there's a good deal about those days that he can't recall."

"It doesn't make it any easier to clear up his papers." He looked at Rona. "I can run you to Sir James's if you like."

"Nigel's providing a two-way transport service, thanks all the same," Rona told him.

"No chance of seeing you this evening for a drink?"

"None, I'm afraid. I'm standing in for David and having dinner with Sigrid."

"No free evening this week?"

"If there is, I'll call you."

He went away, and Nigel felt sorry for him. The office in a mess, and his love affair dragging.

When he returned to Sir James's house to fetch Rona, Sir James was working on the terrace below the drive. He beckoned Nigel.

"Tell your mother, will you, that I spoke to Francis about

a scheme I had in mind, a scheme for making a golf course out of land at the back of her cottage. He wasn't interested. He didn't even trouble to hear me out. I thought she'd like to know."

"I'll tell her."

In the car, Rona spoke thoughtfully.

"Funny he should mention that land. One of the men in the office said he'd heard that Francis Latimer was selling it."

"He can't."

"I know he can't. It's odd, all the same."

"Mere rumor. But you'd better not mention it to my mother."

"It wouldn't worry her, if she's moving. But Chan's there to stay. You had dinner with your old headmaster, didn't you?"

"Dave and I, yes."

"Enjoy it?"

"No."

"Did you say anything to Dave about the move?"

"Yes. He's dead against it. I asked him if his mother and mine could ever live together, and he said no. But I don't see why they shouldn't. They've been friends for years."

"If they couldn't get away from one another, they'd soon stop being friends."

He had nothing to say to this. When they arrived at the cottage, he went into the kitchen to inspect the preparations for dinner. All he saw was a packet of defrosted fish.

"You and I," he told his mother on his return to the living room, "are dining out."

"But, Nigel, I've got some nice—"

"A nice, quiet, not-late dinner at a nice, quiet, not-full restaurant. I'll book a table."

"Would you mind very much if we asked Dagmar to join us?"

"Do we have to?"

"Rona's going there to have dinner with Sigrid. Inga and Claudine are going to the International Club. It would be nice if—"

"—if Dagmar made a third with us rather than a third with Rona and Sigrid. All right; ask her. But my God, if she gets onto the subject of her grandchildren, I—"

"She won't."

It was a more enjoyable evening than he had anticipated. It could not be said that Dagmar was less exuberant than usual, but there was no talk of babies. He said little, being content to listen and to note the contrast between the two women. They were both, he thought, wearing well; his mother's looks were perhaps beginning to fade, but Dagmar still had a kind of dark beauty. Or perhaps, he thought, her gestures and vivacity and rapid changes of expression kept people's attention off any signs of aging.

His mother, content but tired, went straight to bed on their return. He decided to wait up for Rona. When she arrived, she went into the kitchen and began to cut sandwiches.

"Didn't you eat any dinner?" he asked in surprise.

"Not much. I could have asked for more, but Sigrid's slimming and I thought it was mean to gorge while she was pecking. You can't be hungry," she protested, as he helped himself to a sandwich. "You dined out."

"I'm just filling a corner. I wouldn't mind a nice cup of cocoa if you could make it with milk."

She cut more bread; he buttered it and laid slices of ham on top. Then they made cocoa and carried the tray into the living room.

"Nice peaceful interlude," she remarked, sinking into a chair.

"Between—?"

"Between Sigrid's troubles—and Bryan's. He thinks this clearing-up is going to be easy. Well, fairly easy. Any papers of Sir James's that aren't among those I'm dealing with in his house must be—Bryan says—in the office. Well, perhaps.

But thirty years is a long time for papers to pile up. That's the last sandwich you've eaten."

"I thought you'd had enough."

"Are you going to clear away these things, or are you going to watch me doing it?"

"We'll do it together. Then I'll kiss you good night."

"It's becoming a habit."

A habit, he noted with the first real hope he had allowed himself to entertain, that she was making no effort to break. He had always thought patience one of the least rewarding virtues. Perhaps he had been wrong.

CHAPTER

THERE WAS A GOOD DEAL OF HOUSE-HUNTING THROUGHOUT the week, but there was also some confusion as to who was hunting for what for whom. Nigel and Sigrid claimed that they were looking for a small house that would suit Celia. Dagmar and Rona were also looking for a small house that would suit Celia. David and Sigrid were seeking, surreptitiously, a house that would accommodate them, their children present and to come, and their possessions, without being too far from the bookshop. The common factor in these activities was that nobody saw anything they liked.

Rona's time was limited. She was going regularly to Sir James's house, driven there and back by Nigel. She had agreed to the transport arrangement only after some argument, but she was beginning to realize how much she enjoyed his company. She was not clear as to which of them had changed so much that pleasant companionship was now possible between them; whichever it was, it made the years of disagreement seem a great waste. She knew that she was now completely at ease, completely happy when she was with him. She knew him in a way she knew no other man. She could now smile at her girlish passion for him; their present calm relationship seemed to her infinitely preferable.

She worked methodically and patiently at sorting Sir James's papers. He had told her that he would leave her to herself, but she was nevertheless surprised that he had never looked in to ask how she was getting on. He stayed down in the garden, and the only visitor she had was Francis Latimer, who came into the study when she had been at work for a few days.

"Hello. I heard you'd been given this job," he said. "I don't envy you. How's it going?"

"Slowly."

"You can blame some of the mess on my stepfather." He sat on one of the leather-covered chairs and lit a cigarette. "But most of it's the late lamented Todd's. I suppose you never knew him?"

"No. He died soon after I came to Longbrook."

"He was one of the trustees for my mother's estate. The only time I ever had anything to do with him was when he handed me over a list of what I'd inherited. I thought him pretty inefficient, but I didn't give it much thought at the time. I felt the office must be behind him, keeping a check on what he was doing, so I let things slide."

"I was told that he was—"

"—a semi-invalid. Yes, I know. They all said it was because he witnessed the accident that killed my mother and sent my stepfather to hospital for six months, but I think he was dim-witted long before that. I've just begun to look into things—a bit late, I admit—but it seems to me that things in that office are only one degree less chaotic than they are here. Hayling's digging at that end; he told me you were working from this end of the tunnel."

She nodded. She had sometimes seen him on his fleeting

visits to Sir James, but she had never before talked to him for so long, or seen him alone. She had not been interested enough to form any opinion of him, but studying him now, she could agree that he and Maria Montallen made an impressive-looking pair.

"Pity you and Maria tangled at the crossroads," he said, as though he had read her thoughts. "She told me she'd held out what we might call the hand of friendship, but you wouldn't grasp it. Pity. She's bored here. We spend most of our time in London, but I've got to put in a bit of time here; I've got some business to see to."

She smiled.

"If you'll go and see to it," she said lightly, "I can get on with this job."

"All right." He rose and stood looking down at her. "Do you hear much of the town's gossip?" he asked. "I mean about Maria and myself."

"No. I don't think there's much gossip. There's some speculation."

He frowned.

"About my business here?"

"I don't know anything about the business angle."

"If all they want to know is whether Maria and I are going to be married, the answer is yes, we are."

"Congratulations."

"That's more than I got from my stepfather."

"You told him?"

"Yes. I wanted to save it until we were leaving, but he cornered me and asked me about it. He's not pleased. He doesn't like her. Nobody here does, of course; this is a small town full of small people with long memories. How long d'you think you're going to be at this job?"

"A week. Two weeks. Three."

"What I came in to ask was whether you'd come across any documents with my name on them."

"Not so far."

"I had a look through the files Hayling has at his office. The document I'm looking for wasn't there. Which means that it's here. When you get through, perhaps you'd let me know." He was at the door. "If you ever feel friendly, drop in and see Maria. For some reason she's never explained, she feels you've got talents that are wasted in Longbrook."

Nigel was waiting for her when she left the house. On the way to the cottage, she told him of Francis Latimer's visit.

"Do you think Sir James will mind much if he marries Maria?" she asked.

"I don't suppose so. She's more or less the type of woman he must have expected him to marry. The fact that she went off with Roger Underwood will count against her, of course. Not on moral grounds; simply because it upset my mother. He'll probably be along tomorrow to see her."

Sir James came the next day. He walked from his house, and met Rona at the gate as she came home from the office.

"I hope to get a lift back with you and Nigel," he told her. "But give me half an hour here, will you?"

He refused tea. Seating himself on a chair by the window, he plunged straight into the reason for his visit.

"I suppose you've heard about Francis and that woman?"

"Yes. Rona told me," Celia answered.

"I came to find out what you thought about it. For myself, I don't care much. The only way it affects me is in the matter of the house. It'll be his when I'm gone, and I had a faint hope he might marry a woman who'd want to live in it and look after it. This one won't. He'll put the house on the market and some stranger will buy it."

"You're not going to worry about it, are you, James?"

"Worry? No. Gave up worrying when he came of age and didn't even trouble to pay me a visit. He celebrated elsewhere, then he dropped in, had a brief session with Todd, showed no interest in his mother's estate and was off again. No, I'm not going to worry. Regret, yes; that's another matter. She'll cost him plenty, that woman, but that's his lookout. He'll need all his mother left him, and anything he's made since, to keep her supplied with all she'll need. All the same, he—"

He stopped. A motorbike had come puttering through the gate and had stopped outside the window. Sir James glanced out, and his face darkened with annoyance.

"That Reverend, confound him," he said. "Not often I come in for a chat."

He rose to take his leave, but the Reverend was already ushering his sister into the room.

"We're not going to stop a moment, not a moment," he said. "We wouldn't dream of disturbing you. We just dropped in as we were passing."

"Come in and sit down." Celia spoke with warmth, in an attempt to make up for Sir James's scowl. "You know Sir James, of course?"

But the Reverend's memory did not stretch to the last time he had encountered Sir James. After peering at him, he said that he had not had the pleasure.

"Are you making a long stay?" he asked him.

"Eh?"

"You should. Longbrook is delightful this time of the year. The town has grown, but we still have some beautiful country round us. And some delightful walks. I'm writing a little booklet on our local walks; I hope to get somebody to publish it, and I shall then sell copies for our building fund."

"Sir James lives here, Morton," his sister told him.

"He does?'

"Yes. On the hill, in that house that was rebuilt."

"Really? Such a good view from up there," he said to Sir James. "I knew that house when it was a farmhouse. Derelict, it was. Then somebody bought it and as I believe they say in America, made it over. Rona, my dear girl, you mustn't bring out more scones for us. We want nothing, nothing. A sip of tea—oh thank you, Mrs. Pressley." Seated beside his sister, he took one of the scones Rona had placed between them. "Delicious, delicious. Monica, you must ask for the recipe."

"It was your sister who gave it to me," said Rona.

"Really? Have you heard any rumours, Mrs. Pressley, about this land behind your cottage—Mill Acres—being sold?"

"If there are rumours," growled Sir James, "you can scotch them. It can't be sold."

"I'm so glad to hear it. We have far too many multilevel blocks in this town. Have you been over our little church?"

"No."

"You should try to find time to go, while you're here. It's in bad repair, very bad repair, but there are certain features that I'm sure would interest you. You must ask Miss Hume to take you round. She's a good guide. This tea"—he held out his cup to be refilled—"is Darjeeling, is it not?"

"A mixture of Darjeeling and China," Celia answered.

"We go in for tea bags," he told Sir James. "Then my sister puts the leaves on her pot plants. She's an indefatigable worker, and always full of new ideas for getting money to rebuild the church. It won't be done in my time, I'm afraid. But someone will come when I am gone, and the good work will go on."

"You've done wonders," Celia said with feeling.

"Wonders? No, dear Mrs. Pressley, not wonders. But we have done something. Nobody would believe that the small sums we are able to collect could add up to so much over the years."

He put out his hand for another scone. The plate was empty. Rona replaced it by one on which was a large walnut cake.

"Oh, thank you, thank you. I'm afraid you spoil us. We mustn't stay long, you know."

"The concert," his sister reminded him.

"Dear me, fancy my forgetting to tell you about that," he said to Celia. "There is to be a band concert in aid of the building fund. Mr. Fielder has arranged it. There was some slight difficulty about where it should be held, but I'm glad to say that we've been given permission to hold it in the park. The park," he explained to Sir James, "was given to the town by a generous benefactor, but unfortunately he didn't think of building a bandstand. A great pity, especially as we now have a band. I have asked the Scouts to take a collection. I hope we shall get a good response. And now, Monica my dear, we must really be on our way. Thank you for inviting us to tea, Mrs. Pressley; so kind. Goodbye." He bowed to Sir James. "I hope we shall have the pleasure of seeing you on some future visit."

Rona went out and helped to tuck the rug round Monica. Nigel, who throughout the visit had remained outside in an attempt to cure the motor bike of its cough, noted with satisfaction that he had effected a great improvement and went to his car to find a rag on which he could wipe his hands. Sir James came to the door with Celia and stood staring at the gate through which the Reverend had just vanished.

"That fellow," he said, "is losing his mind."

"Yes," Celia agreed, "I think he is. But in a very good cause."

"Don't know about good cause," growled Sir James, "but you can hear his brains rattle. Pity they ever put an oddity like him in this town."

"He's not an oddity in church," Celia said. "You don't go, so you don't see the difference between what he's like when you meet him, as you did just now, socially, and when he comes into church to take a service. He's two men, and only one of them is odd."

"I'll take your word for it. Well, I suppose I'd better go, or Rona won't have any time to give to that clearing-up job."

He got into Nigel's car. Rona, already in, leaned out to call to Celia."

"You know I'm dining out?"

"Yes." Celia came nearer. "So am I. It's Inga's birthday

and Dagmar's taking her out to dinner. Claudine and I are invited too. Nigel, your dinner's in the oven; all you have to do is warm it up."

"Thanks."

He drove to Sir James's house, left his passengers there and drove back feeling depressed. Her escort tonight, Rona had told him, was a man named Bayard Dutton. She had not needed to add details; they were available in the sports pages of every newspaper. A world-class skiing champion, Mr. Dutton had lately taken to performing spectacular somersaults above the ski slopes, a battery of cameras levelled at him from the village below.

In an attempt to fill in time, he went upstairs and unpacked two small trunks in which his mother had put the things he had left behind when he went to Brazil. There was little space for them here, and his irritation at these cramped quarters revived. He selected certain items, ranged them on the available shelves and packed the rest back into one of the trunks. He pushed this into a corner and carried the empty one down to the garage.

On the way back to the porch he glanced at his watch. Fifteen more minutes to put in before he had to fetch Rona.

He went into the house, tripped over both the cats and almost fell headlong. Steadying himself against the doorway of the porch, he heard a car drawing up at the gate. It was a very long-nosed, low-slung sports model; getting out of it was a tall man dressed in a dark suit.

She certainly liked variety, he told himself grimly. The athletic Hayling, the pint-sized Steele, and now this over-publicized aerial acrobat.

He waited. A good deal too much self-confidence, he noted sourly. And that smile ought to be saved for his fans.

"Good evening." The visitor's eyes made a rapid top-to-toe survey that made Nigel conscious of the dusty state of his garments and the grime on his hands. "I'm a bit early, I'm afraid. My name's Dutton—Bay Dutton. You must be Pressley.

From Brazil, aren't you? When do you go back?"

Nigel told him that he was here to stay. He had not moved from the doorway. Mr. Dutton, after a slight hesitation, took a step nearer to the house and then paused to inspect it.

"Funny coincidence," he remarked. "An aunt of mine was looking at houses in this part of the world, and a house agent showed her this, but she didn't think much of it."

"Too large?" Nigel enquired politely.

"She didn't go inside. I suppose your mother's going to do it up in time? One can make quite a success of these little properties, if one's prepared to throw a bit of money around. Bit close to the road, though."

"Do you think so?"

"And not much garden. Saves paying gardeners, I suppose. Rona in?"

There was a pause, which Nigel was aware should be filled by an invitation to enter and have a drink while waiting. But his impressions of the visitor had added up with electronic speed to a total that made him stand more squarely in the doorway.

"Rona," he heard himself saying, "isn't here."

"Not here?"

"No."

Mr. Dutton frowned in displeasure.

"I hope she's not going to be long. I came early on purpose: I thought I could hurry her up a bit. Perhaps I could come in and wait? If she doesn't show up soon, I'll give her a ring and tell her I'm in a hurry."

The tone in which the words were spoken sealed his fate.

"As a matter of fact," Nigel said, "she went up to London."

"Went— You must have got it wrong. I've just driven down from London. We're meeting here. I told her I'd pick her up here."

"She couldn't have been listening."

"You mean she's actually gone up to town to meet me?"

"She didn't tell me what she was going for. She just went."

"When did she go?"

"Let me see . . . I suppose she could have caught the six twenty. That would have got her up there in time to meet you."

"But I don't understand. We usually meet at my place in Chelsea, but I made it quite clear that this time, we were to meet here."

"If she missed the six twenty, she might still be at the station. You could pick her up there."

Mr. Dutton said several words that Chan Fielder would have been unable to utter. He turned and walked rapidly to the gate and then paused to ask a question.

"Do you think she'd come back if she missed the train?"

"No. Your best move is to get back to town and pick her up on her way to your place in Chelsea."

The car disappeared with a roar, and with it went Nigel's ill humour and depression. He brushed the dust and the incident from his hands. There would be repercussions, of course, but they would not come until later. For the moment, she was without an escort, free to spend a whole evening in his company. That would fortify him, recompense him for the recriminations to come. Take what you want, and pay for it, said the Lord. Splendid advice.

He went upstairs at high speed, undressed and stood under the shower, singing loudly. From next door came the sound of the band. Rehearsal time. He chose a dark suit which he felt compared favourably in cut and style with the one now speeding back to London.

There was no sign of Sir James when he reached the house. In the study he found Rona putting away sheaves of papers.

"How did it go?" he asked.

"Not too well. But I think I'm beginning to see a bit of daylight. You're looking very smart."

"I did some unpacking and got dirty and changed. Am I late?"

"No, but we'd better hurry. Bay Dutton will be doing a war dance on the porch step."

Nigel did not think that he would, but he said nothing.

"What time's your date?" he asked when they were in the car.

"Six thirty. And when Bay says six thirty, he means six thirty and not six thirty-one."

"What happens if his girl friends don't own stopwatches?"

"He tries to train them. He's having trouble training me."

When they reached the cottage, there was no sign of a car at the gate.

"Time for a drink?" Nigel asked.

"Yes. And time to go upstairs and do my hair."

She was downstairs again before he had poured out the drinks.

"Nice and quiet," she said, sitting down and taking her glass from him. "What's happened to the band?"

"They were going full blast when I left to pick you up. You've had a long day. Tired?"

"No. But I don't like this extra job. I can't find any of the papers Bryan's asking for." She glanced at the clock. "It's not like Bay to be late.

"Puncture?" he suggested.

"Maybe. I'm sorry you're going to be alone. Why didn't you arrange to go and have dinner with Dave and Sigrid?"

"My dinner's in the oven. I'll manage. Where are you dining?"

"I don't know. Bay likes going to new places. His friends think he's a kind of authority on good eating; they ring him and ask him where to go, and he tells them."

"Some people make a profession of it. Very profitable. But perhaps he doesn't need the money. Is he far up on your list, or low down?"

"You think I keep a list?"

"A mental one. Doesn't everyone? Some friends give you

more pleasure than others. When you go out with this Dutton, do the autograph-hunters come crowding round?"

"No. People stare and point him out. It's going to his head a bit. Perhaps you'll notice, when you meet him tonight."

Nigel, on the point of saying that he had already noticed, pulled himself up in time.

"Aren't you getting hungry?" he asked.

"Not hungry. Angry."

"How long are you going to give him?"

"Ten more minutes. Then I'll share your dinner."

"In ten more minutes, we'll be on our way out to dinner. You can leave a note saying he's crossed off the list and needn't bother you again."

They waited until half past seven. The band played, and in between musical items they talked, at ease, relaxed, content. They drove away finally without leaving a note, and Nigel began to speculate on the possible consequences of his evening's work. They would be hearing from Mr. Dutton, that much was certain. And unsatisfactory as he might seem as an escort, she wouldn't be pleased when she discovered the reason for his non-appearance. She had very little tendency to bad temper; it had taken real effort on his part, in the past, to irritate her to the point at which she fought back. But when that point had been reached, the sequel had been rewarding. The storm didn't last, but while it lasted, it was spectacular. It would be worth while, he thought, to shake her out of this friendly, sisterly attitude he was beginning to find frustrating. To arouse any emotion would be a nice change.

"If there isn't anywhere special you want to go," she suggested, "let's go to Scarlatti's."

"Scarlatti's?"

"You've forgotten it?"

"Almost. Didn't we go there once on my mother's birthday?"

"She got a migraine at the last moment, so you had to take me, and you weren't too pleased, but when we got there, it was wonderful."

"You enjoyed it because they made a fuss of you."

"It was the first time anybody had ever treated me like a grown up, over the girl border and into the young woman. I chose the wine."

"With my assistance."

"And the food. And we had champagne at the end because it was your mother's birthday."

"How old were you?"

"Seventeen. And desperately, deeply, dangerously in love."

He half turned to give her a look of surprise.

"In love? With—?"

"With you, of course."

He did not know that he had put on the brakes, but the car was stationary.

"You needn't feel embarrassed," she said. "I got over it."

"You—got over it?"

"Yes. I know that music is said to be the food of love, but I don't agree. Love has eyes which need to gaze on the loved object. Love has ears which need to hear soft speeches now and then. You weren't there most of the time. The big crash came when you went back to Brazil without seeing me, without even leaving a message with your mother for me. I faced the terrible truth: my love was unrequited. Could we continue this conversation while driving? I'm starving."

He drove on, his thoughts spinning. Desperately, deeply and dangerously in love. And not a schoolgirl passion. Over the girl border and into the young woman. In one sentence she had shattered one image of the past and substituted another.

He found something to say at last.

"You're exaggerating."

"No, I'm not. Sometimes I think it would have been a lot easier if I'd been one of today's uninhibited teen-agers. I could have burst into your bedroom and offered myself to you, free of tax. But as I said, you were never there, and when you came home, I was given the job of sorting out your women and saving you from getting too entangled. There's no food for love in that, is there? Oh, look, horrors! No dinner."

He had stopped the car on the edge of the wood that bordered Sir James's property. Before them was a small restaurant with a painted sign: Scarlatti's. And on the door, a notice: CLOSED UNTIL 1ST JULY.

"Now what?" she asked. "Home?"

"No." He was turning the car. "Mrs. Gunter used to cook us eggs and bacon whenever we wanted them. And we want them now. It's only a mile and a half and we won't have to wait while they unfreeze the food."

When they arrived at the rambling old farmhouse, Mrs. Gunter came to the door, as buxom and pink-cheeked and as voluble as Nigel had always known her.

"Well, look who's 'ere!" she exclaimed in surprise. "The Nabob come 'ome from foreign parts. Come on in, both of you. 'Ave you come to see me and the old man, or is this one of your egg-and-bacon visits?"

"We're both hungry, Mrs. Gunter," he told her. "We went to Scarlatti's but it was closed."

"I could've told you. On 'oliday, they are. When they've got over the Easter rush, they pack up and 'ave a rest till the summer rush starts. Wish I could do the same, but you can't shut up a farm the way you can a resterong." She was setting two places at the long trestle table in the kitchen, and putting plates to warm. "I won't call the old man. 'E's got 'is nose glued to the telly. Funny 'ow I never took to it. Wicked waste of time, I call it, sittin' hour after hour looking at a lotta monkey-faced shaggies banging drums and twanging them gi-tars. No tune, nothing. I'm not going to give you bacon. I've got some beautiful 'am I'd like you to try. Now let's see: you both like tomatoes with it, don't you?"

"Yes, please," said Rona.

"And chips," said Nigel.

"Tomatoes and chips it is, then. And I 'ope you're not going to frighten me out of me life like those two did, telling me the baby was coming. I don't want no more of that caper, thank you. I will say that Sigrid kept 'er 'ead, but David! You should've seen 'im! 'Ow's the baby, by the way?"

"She's fine," Rona answered. "They should have named her after you."

"Not much chance of that. I'm called Euphemia. Now wait while I serve your grub."

The plates came laden with golden eggs, pale pink slices of ham, halved tomatoes, fried potatoes and a layer of Mrs. Gunter's home-made tomato ketchup. While they ate, she sat opposite to them and talked—a monologue that left them free to enjoy the food.

"Long time since you done this," she told Nigel as he was scraping up the last of his second helping. "Rona, now, she keeps coming with 'er friends, but you only came along in between popping off to 'ere and there. The old man tells me you're going to work in London now. I never understood why a strong young fellow like you stuck 'imself in an office. I said to your mother at the time: look at all that lovely land Sir James 'as got, why can't a young man buy a bit and take to growing things to eat. There's too many people in offices and not enough people planting potatoes, that's my opinion. There's more beer if you'd like it, son."

"No, thanks, Mrs. Gunter." He wiped his mouth on one of the kitchen towels she had provided. "I can't tell you how much I enjoyed that."

"You're welcome—any time, like I told you all those years ago. I don't get much change, what with being busy on the farm all day long and nothing to do when I come in of a night, except put my feet up. If the old man 'ud let me, I'd run a little supper place 'ere in this kitchen. Just three or four couples, and just bacon and eggs, or 'am and eggs, same's you've just 'ad."

"You couldn't dish it out free, as you've so often done to us," Nigel said.

"That's true; I couldn't. But I'd enjoy doing it. If the old man ever turned up 'is toes, that's what I'd do."

They took their leave and drove away. Nigel stopped the car at the foot of the hill they had always called Sir James's Rise.

"Too dark to see the view," she commented.

"I'm not interested in the view. I've been thinking."

"About?"

"About something that's always puzzled me. Your engagement. My mother's letters telling me about it weren't very informative. What I'm trying to work out is the timing."

"You think I recovered from my passion for you and rebounded on to Roger?"

"Is it so unlikely? Let's take for granted that you really had that schoolgirl—"

"Schoolgirl! Well, all right. Perhaps that's what it was at the start."

"I went back to Brazil. You got over your schoolgirl passion, met Roger Underwood—and got engaged. Couldn't that be called on the rebound?"

"Perhaps."

"Don't you know? There's been time enough for you to have made some kind of assessment. Did you love him?"

"I must have done. I can't imagine getting engaged to someone I didn't love."

"Can't you remember, for God's sake?"

"What does it matter? It's all over."

"If it weren't all over, we wouldn't be discussing it. What I'm trying to do is find an explanation for something I never understood: why you decided to marry Underwood. You didn't like him much when he was in Longbrook; you didn't like his tendency to tell what he called white lies, and you thought he was snobbish and conceited. Which he was; but as most people liked him, I thought it showed good judgment on your part to be able to size him up on your own. He couldn't have outgrown all those defects when you met him again. But it was just after you claim to have recovered from an adolescent affair—and that, as far as I'm concerned, explains it. And if I can figure it out, you must have figured it out too—long ago. Did you?"

"Well, I—"

"Did you or didn't you?"

"I'm just—"

"'Yes or no?"

"If you mean did I realize I'd rushed into it, then—yes."

"When did you come to that conclusion—when it was all over, or while you were still engaged to him?"

"What is this—an inquisition?"

"Yes. My God," he said wonderingly, "I would have said that I knew you pretty well, but I'm discovering that I knew nothing whatsoever about you. And in the process, discovering new facts, such as that you're either secretive by nature, or you're a first-class liar."

"Can I choose which?"

"Later. For the moment, we come to Maria Montallen. She paid you a visit. You said she had come expressly to tell you what she'd save you from. Is that all she wanted to say?"

"Do you want me to be secretive by nature, or would you like a first-class lie?"

"I'd like the truth. But perhaps I know the truth already. Maria Montallen, being no fool, must have done some thinking and she must have wondered, as I wondered, why you took so few steps, in fact no steps at all, to try to stop her from snatching Roger Underwood. You saw it coming; you told me so. So what Maria Montallen wanted to ask you was the question I'm asking you now: did you sit back and do nothing because you saw a splendid way of freeing yourself from an unfortunate entanglement?"

"You really want an answer to that?"

"No. I don't need one. Maria didn't need one either. Did she hold it against you?"

"No. She said she uses people all the time."

There was a long silence. Nigel broke it at last.

"So now we have the real you," he said. "A girl with a secret, kept for years—how in God's name did you keep it from my mother and Dagmar? And rushing into an engagement, realizing it was a mistake and off-loading the man onto that seasoned campaigner, Montallen. And coming out of it with the reputation of being a brave little thing who took it on the chin. Rosanna Hume."

"The secret life of. But I didn't plan anything. It just happened."

"How many times have I heard you say those words: it just happened. When you broke anything—it just happened. When you put up the wrong hymns in church and got the poor Reverend into a hell of a stew—it just happened. When you made a slide on the ice outside the house so that everybody entering the gate tobogganed spectacularly to the front door—it just happened. When the fiancé you didn't want went off with the woman who didn't really want him—it just happened."

"Now that you've summed up the situation, couldn't we go home?"

"You want to?"

"I don't want to sit near a damp hillside being driven into a corner by you."

"You loved me once. You said so."

"Once."

"I'm free of all entanglements. If I devoted myself to you, if I breathed on the ashes, couldn't I revive some small spark?"

"I'm not free of all entanglements."

"If you were, and if I told you that I loved you—deeply,

dangerously and desperately, would you believe me?"

"When I'd stopped laughing, I'd tell you that you'd missed that particular bus. It passed you years ago—and you stood and watched it go."

"I've never kissed you properly, have I?"

"Not in so many words."

"Could I kiss you now?"

"I don't see why not. If I wanted to screech for help, there's nobody closer than old Mrs. Todd across the valley."

It was some time before he released her. She took a deep breath.

"Expertise born of experience," she said. "The perfection that comes after long practice."

"No spark revived?"

"Is that what you were doing—blowing on the ashes?"

"Breathing. Not blowing."

"Sorry. Well, breathing or blowing, no spark revived."

"Have you got a waiting list you could put me on?"

Her answer came after a pause.

"It's funny, isn't it? You can live with someone for ten or more years, and you don't know the first thing about them. You about me; me about you. Not the first thing."

"It's a matter of stages, or phases. It's like two trains approaching a station. Haven't you ever sat in one, going into Waterloo or Charing Cross, watching the other one getting ahead and then falling back and then getting ahead again? But they usually reach the terminus neck-and-neck."

"That's supposed to be a poetic image—two trains?"

"No. It's meant to illustrate the varying rates of progress. In the end—"

"—the trains reach the terminus neck-and-neck. And you don't blow on ashes; you breathe on them. When you take me home, if you ever do, I'll write all that down in my Gems of Literature notebook."

"You really want to go home? Home to your lonely bed?"

"That's the first attractive word-picture you've painted this evening. Home to my lonely bed."

"Rona—"

"Well?"

"I love you."

There was a silence that he thought interminable. Then her voice came through the darkness.

"Do you think Mrs. Gunter has any idea what effect her ham and eggs can have on a man? If she ever opens that little supper spot, there ought to be some interesting developments."

Without speaking, he started the car. They drove in silence. When they reached the cottage, she got out of the car, thanked him and went indoors. When he had put the car in the garage, he went into the house and locked the doors of the porch and living room. Then he heard the telephone.

If his mind had been clearer, he would have remembered Bayard Dutton and he would have got to it first. But he did not hurry, and only when he heard Rona's first words did he realize that judgment was at hand. He waited beside her.

"But Bay . . . no, of course not. No, I didn't. I was . . . well, no. Who? But that's impossible. He wouldn't . . . He said *what*? I see. Well yes, it was very hard on you but . . . no, I don't see any reason to make such a fuss . . . Yes, I do understand, but . . . Look, if that's all you have to say, I'm ringing off. Good night."

She put down the receiver.

"You—you sent Bay back to London. You told him I wasn't here."

"You weren't, at the time."

"You said— Are you *crazy*? What makes you think you have any right to—"

"No right whatsoever."

"Then why did you do it? It was a cheap trick, the kind I wouldn't have thought you'd play on anyone. You lied to him and made him drive all the way back to London be-cause— *Why*?"

"I didn't like him. If you want fun, go out and have it. I don't mind Bryan Hayling, and I don't really mind Steele, what there is of him. But that prancing Narcissus—no."

"He drove all the way from London—"

"So he said. In a car like his, it wouldn't take long."

"The point is that you lied to him and made him go away and—"

The door of Celia's room opened. Holding a dressing gown round her, she stood regarding them in amazement.

"You're *quarrelling*?"

"No," said Nigel.

"Yes," said Rona. "He's gone off his head and he's interfering in my business. I'm sorry we disturbed you. Good night."

She went upstairs. Then she came down a few stairs to address him.

"You didn't even say you were sorry."

"I'm not sorry. I stole his evening and I'm sorry for him, but that's all."

"But I don't understand why! Why did you do it?"

"It just happened," he said.

They heard the door of her room close. Celia, after waiting for him to say something, gave a shrug and went back to her room. Nigel walked into the living room, stood at the window and stared out at the darkness.

Lying fully dressed on her bed, Rona reviewed the evening's events and found only one thought emerging from the confusion: that her hard-won emotional freedom had not, after all, been final. It had been an intermission. He had come back and she had been sure that he could not disturb her life.

She was back where she had been. And he? She could not believe that he loved her. He had said so, and if he had been any other man, she would have known how much to trust to his words; but however well she had thought she knew him, this was a side of him that was new to her.

For a few moments she put aside doubts and hesitations

and allowed herself to dream. It would not be the first time she had stared at the ceiling and seen there their two figures, his and hers, united and happy. But it was the first time she had entertained the smallest hope that it might be more than a dream.

CHAPTER

10

THERE HAD BEEN WIDESPREAD INTEREST IN THE FIRST LOCAL
concert to be given by the Longbrook and District Brass
Band. There had also been widespread dissatisfaction at the
decision to hold it in the open. This month, the pessimists
pointed out, had been for the most part wet and was showing
no signs of becoming drier.

But when the first notes sounded on a sunny Wednesday
afternoon, the park was even more crowded than it had been
on the day Sir James had declared it open.

Chan had chosen a varied and popular programme, the
highlight of which was his own setting of "Annie Laurie,"
with a cornet solo so movingly played that the crowd clapped
and cheered until an encore was given. Among the crowd,
the Reverend and his sister beamed, delighted at the record
turnout. A splendid attendance, he told Celia, meeting her
as he threaded his way through the throng.

Notices had been placed at intervals along the paths, stating
that the concert was being given in aid of the church building

fund. Confident that the crowd's pleasure would be reflected in the collection, the Reverend went in search of the Scouts who were to take round the collection boxes. And at this point, the crowd began to melt slowly, inexplicably away. By the time the concert ended, only a sprinkle of listeners remained. The coins in the boxes, when counted, added up to a sum so paltry that the enraged Chan felt it to be an insult to church and performers alike.

"Dirty lot of cheese-parers," he ground out to Celia, who on leaving the park had met Nigel and Sir James and was walking back with them to the cottage for tea. "Mean lot of misers. Piddling lot of close-fists, excuse me, Sir James. They took one look at those collection boxes and made for the gates, pretending they'd lost their eyesight or they'd got to get home in a hurry. Never again. Never, so help me, never another concert for this town while I'm alive and conducting. I'm not a churchgoer, and most of that crowd isn't either, but it's their church and they ought to keep it going. Do you know how much we took, how much the poor old Reverend took?"

"Yes. He told me," Nigel said. "Six pounds and thirty pence."

"Right. Six mouldy pounds and thirty miserable pence, which works out at about one pence per person. I told him I thought open plates would be better—you can shame people into putting in something better than buttons—but he said no, boxes would be better because the banknotes would be blown off the plates. Banknotes!"

"Is he very disappointed?" Celia asked.

"Disappointed? Yes, he's disappointed. But he's used to being disappointed. They both are, him and that skinny sister of his. They'll call it God's will. You'd think they'd be fed up with God, wouldn't you, the way He's treated them all these years? It's a million to one he'll die and be buried before he can fix up that church he's so crazy on. He'll die and then all those six-letter so-and-sos on the council will open their ears to all the citizens who'll say they don't want a church, don't need a church, they need the ground it's on or the room it takes up, and then there'll be greased palms and the Reverend will have lived for nothing, and I don't know why I'm sorry, but I am. I know what it is to go after something and wonder if you'll ever get it. I was lucky. I wanted a band and I got it, but I didn't have to starve myself to get it, like the Reverend, and I didn't have to wear my knees out praying and I didn't have to watch people in this town spending hundreds on package tours and drinks in pubs and cars and tellies, and then slinking through the park gates without leaving so much as a fifty-p coin in the box. I'm sorry I've kept you on the road, but a chap of my build has to let off steam. I could let off steam better if I could use some dirty words. Maybe they'll come out one day, and then my mum'll turn in her grave. So long. So long, sir."

He sketched a salute in Sir James's direction, and went angrily on his way.

Rona was not at the cottage on their return. She telephoned to say that she was staying on at the office to do some extra work, and would be bringing Bryan back for a drink before dinner.

Bryan's first remark, when he had taken a seat and accepted a drink, was that if anybody wanted him to state that the late Mr. Todd had been dead a good many years before he was laid in his grave, he would be prepared to agree.

"We're in trouble," he said frankly. "Latimer's been in more than once, asking for papers. So far, he's accepted my explanation—that there's a mix-up between the stuff in the office and what's in Sir James's house—but he's getting impatient."

"Is it possible," Celia asked, "that Mrs. Todd could have overlooked some of the deeds he kept in his house?"

"No. No chance," Bryan said dejectedly. "My father did the clearing-up after Todd died. He went through everything. If Mrs. Todd had come across anything later, she would have brought it to the office."

"Was he ill for long before he died?" Rona asked.

"No, he wasn't actually ill," Celia answered. "But he wasn't himself. He'd given up almost everything but the trusteeship; after he'd handed over to Francis Latimer on his coming of age, he seemed to lose interest in life."

"How long after the accident was that?" Rona asked.

"About three years," Bryan said. "Latimer was fifteen when his mother died; he was eighteen when Mr. Todd died. The accident happened the day after Sir James had made over Mill Acres to his wife by deed of gift—which was fortunate for Latimer, since he inherited it. Todd took the deed to Sir James's house to be signed. We haven't come across it yet. All we've got is Todd's letter—that's to say, a copy of Todd's letter to Sir James, telling him he'd call at the house at midday on Tuesday the fifth of April."

"Fifteen years ago," Celia said reminiscently. "Poor Sir James."

"What exactly happened?" Rona asked.

"Sir James and his wife were coming back in their car from London," Celia told her. "They'd taken Francis up to put him on his school train. James needn't have gone, but he liked to give Francis the feeling that he was interested in his affairs. So they put him on the school train at ten o'clock, and drove back to Longbrook. She was driving; James was beside her. She was a fast driver, but a good one. She overshot the gate—which Mrs. Muir had opened for them—and swerved at speed to try and get the car through the gateway. She missed. It hit one of the stone pillars and ended upside down on the drive. She was killed outright. He was terribly badly injured. The only eyewitnesses were Mrs. Muir and Mr. Todd—he'd walked up the hill on one of his visits and was right on the spot when it happened. You can imagine the awful scene—and the state poor Mr. Todd was in. Mrs. Muir said she had to see to him before anything else. She got him into the lodge and then she rang Brill, who phoned the police." She paused, staring into the past. "I used to go and see him

188 /

afterwards. At first he just had a sense that something awful had happened; later, things became clearer, but—like Sir James—he could never remember any clear details."

"What I'd be glad to know," Bryan said, "is whether Sir James knew what a muddler he was, and put up with him because they were such great friends, or whether he was as great a muddler as Todd. Between them, they've landed us in trouble. If we can't produce all the papers we're supposed to have in our safekeeping, Latimer's going to stir up a lot of mud."

There was the sound of a car outside. The door of the porch was pushed open, and David and Sigrid came in. Sigrid was carrying several small parcels; she walked with Rona into the kitchen and laid them one by one on the table.

"Ham," she said. "Eggs. We've come to dinner. A pizza with Claudine's love. Apple strudel with Inga's love. Cold scrambled eggs with asparagus, David's favourite. Chocolates with a brandy filling made by Claudine for Nigel, his favourite. That's all. David's got the wine." She followed Rona back to the living room. "This was my idea. I remembered that there wouldn't be any band practice this evening, and I was in the mood for a party. Are you staying for dinner too?" she asked Bryan.

"He is now that you've brought all that food," Celia said.

Nigel put on records and poured out drinks. Rona and Sigrid set out food and plates and knives and forks. They were ready to eat when there was a knock on the porch door. Nigel opened it and saw Chan.

"Come in," he invited.

"I know you've got company," Chan said, stepping inside, "but they're my friends too and I'd like them to listen to what I've come to say. Have you all got five minutes to spare from making merry?"

"Yes. Drink?" Nigel asked.

"No drink, thanks." It was clear that he was not in a social frame of mind. His face, which usually radiated cheerfulness, was sagging with worry. "Just wanted to ask you something. Yes, I'll have that drink. Got something strong?"

"Whisky?" Nigel offered.

"Yes. Don't overdo the watering-down." Chan took the glass. "I can't say cheers. I don't feel like cheering."

"What's wrong?" Bryan asked.

"I don't know. I'm trying to find out." He drank, wiped his lips with the back of his hand, put down his glass and brushed aside Nigel's offer of a chair. "Look, have any of you heard any rumours lately about that land at the back of these cottages?"

"There's been a whisper or two," Bryan answered. "You don't have to worry. It can't be sold."

"That's what you say. That's what you think. That's what my cousin Bert, the house agent, always understood. But this rumour's got roots, and they're growing. They say that Latimer's selling—and you know who to? To Sugden. If you don't know who Sugden is, I'll tell you. He's the dirty shark who bought that stretch of land this side of the Gunters' and put up four blocks of the ugliest apartments that ever got past a planning committee. He put up that lot of so-called villas that look as though they're going to fall in a heap any minute. He's been handing out bribes, big money, for years, Bert says. He got that land that the other builder, Yates, was after—snitched it from under Yates's nose and put up a factory that'd be in full view if Sir James's trees didn't happen to hide it. He did the school out of that extra plot that was scheduled for a playground. That's Sugden. He doesn't belong here—or he didn't. He used to operate in London, but he got the smell of big deals here in Longbrook, and came running. He's a crook, but he's clever. So why would he be going round telling people, in strictest confidence, of course, that Latimer's going to do a deal and sell him this land at the back of us?"

"He can't," Bryan repeated.

Chan looked at him for a few moments and then spoke slowly.

"Look," he said, "I know the people in this town better than you do or ever will do—because I belong to them. So do my boys in the band. I hear, and they hear a lot more than you do about what's cooking. I've been listening, and they've been listening, and we don't like what we've heard. Because if that land sprouts apartment blocks, where do I go? Where does the band go?"

"The reason Latimer can't sell," Bryan told him, "is because he inherited the land with the proviso that—"

"Ah! Proviso. I like words, but sometimes they don't mean anything. What's a proviso to a chap like Latimer? What does a crook like Sugden care about provisos? Latimer sells, somebody objects, and Sugden starts shelling out hush money, and they hush. Do you think Sugden's got where he's got without knowing how to find his way round a proviso or two?"

"Then take it this way," Nigel suggested. "If Latimer sells, if the sale actually goes through, the person who'll do the most objecting will be Sir James, because it was Sir James who put in that proviso. If Latimer does a deal with Sugden, it's quite certain that he'll lose the inheritance that's coming to him from his stepfather. Sir James has never made any secret of the fact that Latimer's his heir. If the land is sold, he'll cut Latimer out of his will. Is Latimer likely to risk that?"

"Risk what?" Chan spread out his hands. "What's he risking? Who knows how much the old chap's worth today? He was a rich man when he came to Longbrook; all the dough in the world, my Dad told me. But that was thirty and more years ago, and since then, he's been spending like flood water: land here, land there, the hospital—what d'you think that cost to build and equip?—and Dartford Park. And look at the way he lives, no entertaining, that's true, but servants— add up what those have been costing him for over thirty years. So who knows whether he could compete with the six-figure trade that Latimer could do with Sugden? Could he? If I'm asking you, you can bet that Latimer's asking himself."

"Latimer inherited a fortune from his mother," Bryan pointed out.

"Ah now, so he did. And that was a long time ago, too. And about *that*, every citizen can tell a tale. Disguise yourself as an innocent bystander and go out there and listen. Race-horses? He's been pouring money down the drain for years, and nothing coming back. Those plays he backed—winners? No. And years of keeping those fancy women, and sailing round the Greek islands on his yacht—how much do you suppose that's set him back? Rumour says he's near the rocks, and rumour's right. That's why I'm here—to tell you that you're not going to be able to believe in provisos much longer. You're in this, same as I am," he told Celia. "You're lucky; you're moving, but soon I'm going to have a Sugden apartment block staring me right in the face, close enough to touch."

"If Sugden's talking about it," David said, "surely Sir James must have heard something?"

"I've just told you: you have to be one of the crowd to hear what the crowd's saying. Nobody spreads rumours round that garden of his." He turned to Celia. "You're a friend of his. Go and talk to him," he pleaded. "Tell him what you've heard and ask him how much underpinning that proviso has got. Ask him to ask his slippery stepson what's going on. Let's get the thing out in the open, where we can take a look at it and see if it bites. Will you talk to him?"

"Yes. I'll go and see him tomorrow. And please don't worry —and sit down. There's a lot of food, and you're going to stay and help to eat it."

"Unless you've got a date," Sigrid said.

"Date? The only date I ever have's with the band, and the boys are off tonight."

Rona and Sigrid went to the kitchen. David addressed Nigel.

"I've just thought of something," he said. "Remember the night you and I were at the Three Feathers and Latimer joined us? Remember how fast he went out? Chan said he'd seen his ex-girl friend, name of Yates. But—"

"My God yes! Yates was standing at the bar," Chan broke in, "but so was Sugden. And Latimer saw him—and didn't want anybody to know they knew each other. So he bolted. So you can bet there's more than rumour in this, and if those two are planning a deal, then you can roll up that proviso and chuck it in the river, the way Nigel chucked me."

He left soon after dinner; if he was not his serene self, he was considerably happier than he had been on his arrival. Sigrid and David left shortly afterwards; Bryan went with them.

"That's two worries," Celia said despondently. "Sigrid's still determined to move—and now this business of Francis Latimer."

"Neither of which," Nigel pointed out, "is your problem."

"I suppose not," she admitted. "But how can one help worrying?"

She said good night and went to her room. There was not much clearing-up to be done; Rona and Sigrid had put most of the things into the dishwasher.

"No ashtrays to empty, thank goodness," said Rona. "I hate emptying ashtrays. Sigrid said she tried taking up smoking again after the baby was born, and didn't like it. What are you doing?"

"Going to make myself a cup of cocoa. You?"

"All right."

They drank it in the kitchen. Since the night they had been to supper at the Gunters' farm, they had slipped back into the easy friendship that had preceded the outing. Both knew that this was an interval; both were grateful for it. The future might not be clear, but they were both enjoying the present.

And when he said good night, there was nothing brotherly about his attitude.

Sigrid was in bed, sitting up in the vast one which Dagmar had once shared with David's father, and which now belonged to David and herself. She was feeding the baby. David, in pajamas, was seated in an armchair giving part of his attention to the book he was reading, and the rest to the meal that was in progress. The adjacent room, once his dressing room, had now been taken over by Sigrid as a night nursery, to keep her son and daughter within reach—and out of Dagmar's reach.

After a time, David put aside his book, rose and went to stand by the bed, looking down at his infant daughter.

"She's had enough, surely?" he asked, anxiety in his voice.

"When she's had enough, she'll stop."

"She's been at it an awfully long time."

"She doesn't know yet about times; she only knows about getting enough to drink. There, look."

The baby, satisfied, had fallen asleep, her head against her mother's arm.

"You can take her now." Sigrid lifted her and David took the small bundle into his arms. "On her side, not on her back."

He stood gazing at the tiny features.

"Marvellous, aren't they?" he said wonderingly. "Look at that beautiful little button; that's going to be a nose one day."

"I'll look when you've winded her."

He put the baby gently against his shoulder, and was rewarded by a loud belch close to his ear.

"Arthur never made a noise like that," he complained.

"Arthur was a gentleman. Don't put the shawl over her; it's a warm night. And don't stand riveted beside her cot; I want to talk."

He came back yawning. Standing beside the bed, he ruffled

his hair in the gesture she knew so well. The sight of him as he was now—sleepy, pajama-clad, with his hair standing on end—was one that appealed most strongly to her maternal sense. People would be surprised, she thought, to learn that this tenderness, far more than the sexual urge, was the reason for the swift appearance of her first two children.

"What did you want to talk about?" he asked.

"Nigel. I've discovered what's the matter with him."

He had seated himself on his side of the bed; he swivelled round to face her.

"Well, what?"

"You're the one who ought to do the talking. You and he were David and Jonathan—you said. You had no secrets from one another—you said. And you couldn't see at a glance tonight that he was in love. So who does this lifelong friend of yours love? Rona."

"Rona?"

"So you see, I was right. I said he was in love. Everybody said, Oh no, no, when he's in love he's happy, not sad. That was because when he was in love before, he was getting some response. This time, he isn't getting any."

"How do you know?"

"By observation."

"In love with Rona? I don't believe it."

"I suppose he can hardly believe it, either. Didn't you tell me they never used to get on?"

"They didn't. You've got this wrong. Even if you were right, and he was in love with her, why wouldn't she respond? He's far and away more—more worth responding to than any of the other men she goes around with. So why wouldn't she respond?"

"Work it out. For the first time in his life, he's up against a woman who sees him as he really is. She knows all about those other women he used to chase after. She knows he was spoilt by his mother and never raised a finger to do anything in the house, and that he used his home as a place where he could unpack and repack for the next trip. That's how she thinks of him, and that's why she isn't responding. I'm glad he's suffering at last."

"You're sure, you're absolutely sure he feels that way about her?"

She gave an impatient sigh.

"Tell me something," she requested. "When it's Arthur's dinner time and you go up to him and say, 'Arthur, din-dins,' how does he look?"

"Hungry."

"Say 'Rona,' and you'll see that look on your old friend's face."

"What about Bryan? I thought you were backing Bryan."

"I was. He's not in the running any more."

"But if she doesn't want Nigel, then—"

"Did I say she didn't want him?"

"No, but—"

"What we don't know is whether he's said anything to her."

"What the hell can he say? Can he tell her he's sorry he didn't like her when she was young, and he's sorry he didn't behave nicely to her, but he's suddenly realized he loves her, so please will she forget the past? Is that what he'd have to say?"

"It would be a pity if they didn't get together. If Celia had had any guts, she'd have fixed it long ago. She's wanted it for years. Now will you stop talking and put out that light?"

"Haven't you got any plans for getting them together?"

"No. They've got to work it out for themselves. Put the light out."

"I've still got something to say."

"Save it. I don't want to talk any more."

"Then what do you want?"

"My marital rights."

CHAPTER

11

AT TEN O'CLOCK ON THE FOLLOWING MORNING, SIR JAMES
arrived at the cottage.

It was what Celia thought of as one of his state visits. He
came in his ancient, hearselike car, driven by Brill at twenty
miles an hour.

He refused to sit down. He had come, he said, merely to
put her in possession of certain facts.

"The land," she said. "It's more than rumours?"

"A great deal more." His tone was grim. "A plain intention
to sell. And to sell to that swine Sugden. He told me so an
hour ago. He said he's in debt. If he acknowledges that, it
means that he's in up to his eyes. He needs money, he says.
I told him that the deed of gift makes it clear that the land
can't be sold. He said nothing to that, which left me to conclude that he and that builder have found a way of getting
round any restricting clauses. He's going to marry that
woman. He's gone up to London with her; I don't suppose I

shall ever set eyes on him again. I'm sorry, for his mother's sake. They're going to be married at three o'clock tomorrow afternoon and then going straight to one of those Caribbean resorts. Something he didn't tell me until he was leaving: Sugden's presenting him with a check after the wedding. That shows you how confident they are, the damned crooks." He turned to stare out of the window. "I didn't get that land cheaply. With this spread behind these cottages, and the continuation on the other side of the London road, there's over two hundred acres. Land values have trebled since I bought it, so he tells me he's getting a six-figure sum from Sugden. How he managed to get through the fortune his mother left him, I shall never be able to understand. That's all I came to say. I wanted you to know. Incidentally, he said he's never seen that deed of gift. I'm going to the office to see young Hayling about it. Then I'm going up to London to see my lawyers. God knows what they can do. Well, that's all."

"James, don't let this worry you too much."

He shook his head. She thought that he had aged several years since she had last seen him. He refused her offer of coffee, said goodbye and walked to his car. Nigel went with him. Brill put a hand under the old man's elbow to assist him, and Sir James, for once, did not shake it off.

Returning to the living room, Nigel found his mother gazing listlessly at the cat seated on her lap.

"Cheer up," he said gently. "The old boy's a lot tougher than he looks."

"I know. But he's been so generous, and . . . What's the use of talking? You're lunching with David, aren't you?"

"Yes." He glanced at his watch. "Time enough."

When he joined David at the restaurant at which they had arranged to meet, he found that there was no need to give him Sir James's news.

"It's all over town." David signalled the barman and ordered drinks. "I'd like to report that everybody's on the old boy's side, but it wouldn't be true; a lot of people wouldn't mind seeing a few more batches of apartment blocks going up, and to hell with open spaces. But I didn't bring you here to talk about Sir James."

Nigel was looking round the comfortable bar and the restaurant—new and expensive—adjoining it.

"I thought you had something in mind," he said, "when you invited me here, instead of suggesting sandwiches at a pub. What's on your mind?"

David did not tell him until they had claimed their table and ordered lunch.

"Well?" Nigel asked as the waiter bore away the menus.

"I want to ask you a question, but I've got qualms."

"How would you define qualms?"

"They're what you get when somebody you expect to confide in you doesn't confide in you, so that you have to bring yourself to ask them what you want to know. We're not as close as we used to be in the old days, otherwise I wouldn't have any qualms; I'd just ask you straight out."

"Fine. Ask me straight out." He helped himself to a bread roll and buttered it briskly. "You're paying a lot for the information. Did you note those prices on the menu?"

"I did."

"So what do you want to know?"

"If you're in love with Rona."

Nigel hesitated for only a moment.

"Yes," he said.

"Then Sigrid was right."

The wine was brought, tested and approved. Nigel put a question.

"How did she guess?"

"She claims that she watched you and saw signs. Have you said anything to Rona?"

"Nothing she took seriously. God knows I'm not superstitious, but I find myself wondering if I'm not due for some kind of nemesis."

"You mean you've had it easy with women all these years,

and now you've come against one you can't impress?"

"Something like that."

"I wish I could listen to you telling her you didn't mean all those things you said to her in the past. Is there anything Sigrid and I can do to help you out?"

"No, thanks. I'll work it out myself."

"I wouldn't hang it out too long, if I were you. She's a honeypot, and bears come after honey. The only one I think you need worry about is him."

He jerked his head in the direction of a table in the corner. There were four men seated at it; one of them was Bryan Hayling.

"He's a nice chap," David went on. "He was Sigrid's choice, but she'd rather see you going up to get the prize. Nice neat finish it would be."

"Too neat."

"Any idea how you stand with her?"

"We're friends."

"That's no good. Well, I wish you luck."

Nigel was watching Bryan Hayling and his companions leaving their table. They walked to the exit, but instead of going out with the others, Bryan turned and came back, threading his way among the tables until he stopped beside Nigel and David.

"Sit down," David said.

"Thanks. Could you order me a brandy? I need it."

David gave the order and then studied him.

"Trouble?" he asked.

"Yes. I've had Sir James in the office. He's gone up to London to see the lawyers who used to act for his wife. He's also going to see Sugden's lawyers. That won't get him any-where. He wanted to see that damned deed of gift. Rona had told him that it wasn't among the papers at his house, which meant that it must be in the office. Well, it isn't. I don't know quite how I managed to put him off, but he wants the thing by tomorrow at the latest." He sipped his brandy. "My God, this is good. I've been losing sleep over this business."

"What you've got to do, I take it," David said, "is find out what Todd did with the papers when he'd got them signed?"

"Yes. He never came back to the office after the accident. He still looked after Sir James's affairs, such as they were. In other words, they met almost every day and played chess and listened to symphonies and dealt with business papers by shoving them into pigeonholes to be attended to later." He finished the brandy and rose. "Thanks. I'll do the same for you one day. I'm going back to the office to look under the floorboards."

The result of his search, Rona told Nigel that evening, was negative.

"I've looked everywhere and he's looked everywhere, and it isn't anywhere. If we don't find it, it'll mean that Francis Latimer can go ahead without being faced by any provisos. I wish poor old Sir James hadn't had this to cope with. I'm sorry for Bryan, too. Did you enjoy your lunch with David?"

"Yes. He hesitated, and then came to a decision. "Are you in a hurry?"

"No."

"Then can we make a detour and find a place free from petrol fumes?"

"If you like."

He turned the car off the main road and drove until they were within sight of the Gunters' farm. Then he stopped the car and turned to face her.

"This won't take long," he said. "I should have said it all before, but when you want something very badly, you're sometimes afraid to put it to the test. So here it is: I've loved you since the first morning I saw you, when you came back from London and I walked out onto the drive to meet you. You've known me long enough to know what sort of man I am. I don't suppose I'll be any worse as a husband than I was as a brother, but all I want you to know now is that I love you. That's all. Thanks for listening."

For some time, there was no sound that he wanted to hear. The birds sang; the wind sighed—but there was no human voice.

"No more?" she asked at last.

"For the moment, no. I'd like to know what my chances are."

She spoke almost absently.

"Remember what you said about those two trains passing and repassing on the way to Waterloo, or it may have been Charing Cross?"

"Yes. I'm sorry I couldn't put it more poetically."

"It wasn't a bad way of putting it. First me in love. Then you in love. But being in love used to make you happy. Why did falling in love with me make you miserable?"

"Not miserable. Frightened. I've never been afraid when I thought of the future, but I am now, because I can't imagine a future without you."

"Shall I tell you what I want?"

"Yes."

"What I'd like," she said dreamily, "is to know that you love me, and let things stay that way for a little while. Not for long. But you don't know, you'll never know about those day-dreams I used to have about the two of us. I loved you, and—in the daydreams—you loved me, and it was such bliss, such heaven. I want to live that again, knowing that this time, there's no waking up to face. I don't want to think about plans and engagements and the future. I want to drift, as I drifted all those years ago, just the two of us, in love. Nothing intruding from the real world; just happiness together, the way I used to imagine it."

"Do you love me?"

"Haven't I just said so? I got over it once—I thought. I'm glad you breathed on those ashes. Now I'd like to drift for a while, and when I've stopped drifting, I'd like to spend the rest of my life making you pay for all the misery you caused me in the past. Sweet, unending revenge. Is that a prospect you can face?"

"Yes. Can we tell my mother?"

"Later. I said nothing intruding from the real world, didn't you listen?" She paused and then spoke despondently. "But we can't dodge the real world. Sir James in London, Bryan searching for vital papers, that beast Sugden preparing to put up dozens of apartment blocks and Francis Latimer keeping Maria Montallen on the proceeds. Suppose those papers don't turn up?"

"Stop worrying. I want to demonstrate something."

"Demonstrate what?"

"Expertise born of experience."

CHAPTER

12

BEFORE BREAKFAST WAS OVER THE NEXT MORNING, BRYAN arrived at the cottage. His face was white and drawn.

"Disaster," he said as he entered. "A letter from Sugden's lawyers asking to see the papers relevant to the sale of the land. They speak of the sale as through; asking for documents is their way of rubbing in salt."

"Has Sir James been in touch with you?" Rona asked.

"No. Thank God he's out of the way for today at least. I rang Yates; he claims to be Sugden's business partner. He was crowing. He told me that the wedding's at three o'clock and after the ceremony Sugden's going to hand over a check to Latimer. It's their confidence that frightens me. We've got to find that deed of gift. Whether we find it or not, the sale will go through, but without it, there's no hope of getting Sugden to court. So what in God's name do we do now?"

He had addressed the question to Nigel.

"Since you've asked me," Nigel answered, "the first thing is to coopt my services. Looking for papers isn't a highly skilled job; I can do my share. The next thing we do is follow the advice of the French master I used to have at school. When we'd searched unsuccessfully for anything we'd lost, he made us stop searching and sit down and—as he expressed it—'look inside our 'eads.' It was a good system and it nearly always worked. So let's try it now, and let's start by laying all the facts on the line."

"All right, here they are," said Bryan. "We know by the copy of the letter sent from the office by Mr. Todd to Sir James, that he was going to the house on Tuesday the fifth of April and taking with him the deed of gift, which was to be signed by Sir James and his wife. Sir James remembers nothing of the visit. And that's where we stick."

"Brill would remember, wouldn't he?" Nigel asked.

"And Mrs. Todd." Celia spoke for the first time. "Surely she'd remember?"

Bryan rose.

"There's only one way to find out," he said. "Let's go."

Nigel and Rona went with him in his car. Their first stop was at Sir James's house. Brill listened attentively to their question: Had Mr. Todd come to the house on the day before the accident, with documents for signing? After long consideration, he shook his head.

"I really couldn't tell you, Mr. Hayling, sir. We all got left with a bit of fog in our brains after that time. What happened just before, what happened just after . . . I couldn't tell you for sure. Nor could my wife. Her memory's even more confused than mine is about that awful time. We remember what happened on the day; we'll never forget that. You'll never know what it was like that morning, Mr. Hayling. From living so peacefully here, to find ourselves suddenly in the middle of that terrible tragedy. It put years on us all. But you could ask Mrs. Muir if she remembers seeing Mr. Todd the day before. She would have let him in."

Mrs. Muir remembered nothing definite.

"I can only tell you," she said, "that Mr. Todd walked up most days to see Sir James. He used to come to play chess, or to borrow a book, or a record of one of those symphonies, they called them. If I could answer your question, I'd like to, but I'd only be guessing. If you wanted to know about the day of the accident, then yes, I could give you every detail. But the day before, no."

They drove to the small house of the foot of the hill to see Mrs. Todd.

This was a painful visit. Mrs. Todd had throughout her married life deferred in all things to her husband. Her days had been spent in preparing the special diet he insisted on, and in running the house unaided, for no servants could put up for long with Mr. Todd. On her husband's death, she had planned to move to a more labour-saving house, but the effort of clearing up the accumulation of years had kept her where she was. She had few friends. Her only regular visitor was the Reverend, for whom she had deep respect and affection.

She ushered her vistors into an untidy drawing room. No, she told them, she couldn't remember whether her husband had gone up to see Sir James on the day before the accident. She had known nothing of his work; he did not tell her anything about it; he worked in his study and never mentioned office matters. All she could say—and she said it at considerable length—was that he had been Sir James's best friend and had let scarcely a day pass without walking up the hill to pay him a visit.

"Are you absolutely sure, Mrs. Todd," Bryan asked her, "that your husband kept all his papers in his study?"

She said that she was absolutely sure.

"He kept all his things in there—his papers, his gramophone records, the books Sir James lent him, the orchestral scores he liked to borrow—I never touched anything in that room. He dusted it and tidied it himself. I knew he'd want Sir James to have all his records when he died, so I sent them up to the house and Sir James was very grateful. I gave the books to the library and I gave his clothes to the Reverend to be sold for the building fund. He was very good to me when my husband died. In fact, I don't know what I would have done without him on the day of the accident. He was here when they telephoned to tell me what had happened, and that they were going to take my husband to the hospital to be treated for shock. It was a miracle that he was here that day, though you'll probably say it was just coincidence. He and I happen to have birthdays on the same day, and he never once missed coming to wish me a happy birthday."

That was all. They had to wait through more repetitions, and then they took their leave.

"What now?" Bryan asked as they got into the car.

"Home for coffee," Nigel said. "To think things over."

"I've got to go back to the office," Bryan said. "I've had the entire staff searching; perhaps they'll have found something."

He left Rona and Nigel at the cottage and drove away. They entered the house to find Celia waiting anxiously in the living room.

"Any result?" she asked.

"None. Bryan's gone back to the office," Rona said.

A tray with coffee cups was on the table. Celia brought in coffee.

"I thought you'd need this," she said. "Sit down and try to forget this business for a little while. I'm sorry Bryan didn't come back with you; he was looking terribly tired."

"I suppose, when you come to think of it," Rona said, "it's hard for anyone to turn their minds back fifteen years and try to recall details. Brill didn't remember anything about the day before the accident. Neither did Mrs. Muir. All Mrs. Todd supplied was the news that the Reverend had been with her on the day of the accident, wishing her a happy birthday. Never missed. Why? Because their birthdays were on the same day."

"He called in to see me on the way home that day," Celia said. "It was from him that I learned about the accident. I'd just come in from the Charity Fund committee meeting, which was on the first Wednesday of the month, and he came in and said he had something to say that would be a shock. He—"

"Tuesday," Rona said. "It was a Tuesday."

"No, Rona. The Charity Fund has never held committee meetings on any day but Wednesday, because that's the only day that—"

"It must have been a Tuesday. Tuesday the fifth of April. It was in Mr. Todd's letter. I saw the copy in the office. Tuesday the fifth."

"I can assure you that—"

"My God." Nigel was staring across the room at Rona. "Do you see what this means?"

"I don't . . . Yes, perhaps I'm beginning to. He said Tuesday, April the fifth. He got the day wrong, and nobody bothered to check."

"So the question we now have to ask," Nigel said, "is whether the mistake was ever discovered. Did Mr. Todd, armed with a deed of gift, walk up to Sir James's house on the Tuesday, or—having, with the approach of his wife's birthday, realized he'd got his days mixed—did he tell Sir James he'd go on Wednesday instead?"

"Sir James might have discovered the mistake," Rona said. "We'll never know. So how can we discover when they arranged to meet?"

"All we can discover," Nigel told her, "is whether Mr. Todd went up to the house carrying documents on the day of the accident. He certainly arrived on time: midday. Had he gone to get the signatures?"

"Do we go round again, asking them—"

"No. We can confine this to one person: Mrs. Muir. She was the person who was first on the scene—after Mr. Todd." He looked at Celia. "Can you remember what Mrs. Muir said about that morning?"

"Yes. She went out and saw Mr. Todd and realized he was on the point of collapse. She could see that Sir James's wife was dead; she thought Sir James was, too. She managed to help

Mr. Todd into the lodge, and made him lie on the sofa, and then she rang Brill. She waited beside Mr. Todd until the doctor had finished outside and came in to see him. He sent Mr. Todd to the hospital to be treated for shock."

"So now we go and see her and ask if he was carrying any papers?" Rona asked.

"Yes."

Mrs. Muir, glad to be able to supply more definite information than she had done on their previous visit, gave them a crisp and matter-of-fact account of the accident that did not differ very much from Celia's version.

"The ambulance men came in and carried Mr. Todd out," she ended. "And that was the last I saw of him for a long time. And when Sir James came back from the hospital, and Mr. Todd started to come and see him again, he wasn't the same man. They were both changed men."

"Can you remember," Rona asked, "whether Mr. Todd was carrying any papers that day—perhaps in a briefcase? He often came to see Sir James on business, didn't he?"

"That's right; he did. But he didn't have his briefcase on the day of the accident. I'm certain about that."

"No papers, no files?"

"Nothing of that kind, no. He didn't have anything of his own, because if he had, I would have sent it to the hospital with him. I looked round when they were taking him out to the ambulance, but there was nothing he'd left behind. I would have seen."

There seemed nothing more to say, nothing to stay for. Mr. Todd had come, had witnessed the accident and had been carried off to hospital. He had brought no briefcase and no papers.

They walked out to the car.

"If I'd had a pound for every time I opened this gate and closed it again after poor Mr. Todd," Mrs. Muir said solemnly, "I'd be a rich woman. Almost every day, it used to be. If it wasn't books, it was gramophone records, and if it wasn't them, it was those big flat books he called scores—those music books where you can follow what the orchestra's doing."

Nigel had opened the car door. He closed it again.

"Do you happen to remember, Mrs. Muir," he asked, "whether Mr. Todd was carrying a musical score on the day of the accident?"

"Yes, he was," she answered unhesitatingly. "Did you want to know about that? I didn't put it in the ambulance with him because it wasn't his. It was Sir James's."

"Can you tell me what you did with it?"

"Yes, I can. I took it up to the house and left it with Mr. Brill, to be put with all the others of the same in the study."

"Thank you, Mrs. Muir." He took Rona's arm and led her back to the drive. "I think we'll go up to the house."

They walked to it in silence. It was a long way, but they were glad of the interval between hope and certainty—success or failure.

Brill took them to Sir James's study and left them, having indicated the stand on which Sir James kept all his musical scores. They were, he said, welcome to look through them.

Nigel allocated half to Rona and went to work on the rest.

"They're open scores, thank God," he said. "If they'd been miniature or pocket scores, we needn't have bothered to go through them."

"You think he put that deed of gift into the score he was carrying?"

"I think it's possible. Probable. He would have borrowed another one to take the deed away in."

They worked in silence. It was Rona who, twelve minutes later, found the documents between the middle pages of Beethoven's Sixth Symphony.

Wordlessly, she handed them to Nigel. He spread them on the desk and they stood looking down at them.

"Poor devil," he said at last.

He might, Rona thought, have meant Sir James, who had been injured in the accident. Or his wife, who had lost her life. Or old, muddle-headed Mr. Todd, walking slowly up the hill carrying under his arm a musical score, to keep a midday appointment . . .

"Do you suppose," she asked slowly, "they saw him just as they got near the house, and had forgotten the appointment, and she— No, it would have been Sir James who had forgotten, and perhaps he gave a sudden exclamation, or something, and she lost her concentration just for a second or two and—"

"We shall never know," he said. "It isn't any use trying to reconstruct what happened that morning. If it's as you say—if Sir James remembered and said something to startle her—it's a mercy he can't remember."

"Yes." She stood lost in thought and then roused herself. "We've got to tell them."

"Them?"

"We've got to let them know about the deed. Sir James, and Bryan. And that builder. Sugden. I can ring them from here. Sir James will probably be lunching at his club, so he might be there now."

She went towards the telephone. Nigel took her arm in a firm grasp and brought her to a halt.

"It's only twenty past one," he said. "You can ring later."

"Why later?"

"In the first place, I'm hungry. You'll feel hungry too, when this excitement has worn off. We're going to lunch at that restaurant David and I went to yesterday. It's expensive, but we'll send the bill to the office."

"What's the point of not ringing now? There's a phone here. Why wait till later?"

"I'll tell you why. Francis Latimer was on the point of bringing off a very dirty deal, yes?"

"Yes."

"And Sugden is confident that he's pulled off another of his crooked transactions; so confident that he's parting with a fat check which he's going to hand to Latimer after the wedding. Yes?"

"Yes. So I've got to—"

"That check was to provide Latimer with a downy cushion on which to recline with his bride, well known to us as Miss Maria Montallen. The wedding is at three o'clock. If you break your news now, what will happen?"

"That's easy. No check."

"Precisely. So the downy cushion will be whisked away, and Miss Montallen will—"

"Well, naturally. She's not going to marry him if he's got no money, is she?"

"Certainly not. And I think it would be a pity to spoil so unmercenary a romance. Therefore you will ring later."

She stared at him.

"You mean you—you want the wedding to take place?"

"Yes. I do."

She said nothing for a time. Then:

"This is nothing to do with you," she told him.

"Oh yes, it is. It's a great deal to do with me. Maria Montallen made my mother extremely unhappy. She also stole a fiancé from our family. I wasn't here at the time, so she had it all her own way. She won the first leg; but she has to play a return match, and this is it. Now she's playing against me. If you want to forgive and forget, nobody's going to stop you. But even if I had nothing to forgive, I can't forget that Maria Montallen and Francis Latimer, separate and apart, can do a lot of damage. Tied together, for however short a time, they'll be out of circulation. He betrayed an old man who trusted him. He'll do very well as a husband for Maria. So I'm going to make sure that no call is put through before three o'clock. You can then ring Bryan, who will then ring Sugden to inform him that the land is the property of Sir James Dartford. I don't think he'll hand over the check, after all. Do you understand?"

"Yes. But I don't think it's right to do it."

"I didn't think you would. So between now and three, or three fifteen, I'm going to keep you in sight."

"Can't I just tell Bryan?"

"No. Bryan is a nice fellow, so much nicer than I am, that I suspect he might have more regard for Francis Latimer and Maria Montallen than I have. I doubt it, but I'm not going to take the risk. As the office is paying for this lunch, would you like to ask him and my mother to join us, or would you rather keep it to just us two?"

"Just us two," she said without hesitation.

CHAPTER

13

ON SIR JAMES'S RETURN FROM LONDON, BRYAN, IN THE course of a formal call, handed him the unsigned deed of gift. Sir James sat looking at it for some time, and then came out of a melancholy silence to speak with less gruffness than usual.

"People have always said hard things about Todd," he said, "but he didn't deserve all of them. I was the one who was to blame for the mess we got into. We can thank Todd for getting us out of it. He kept at the job too long, but that's a fault most old men have. I miss him. He was never a good lawyer, and he was a poor chess player and he wasn't much of a husband, but he was a good friend. Yes, I miss him." He paused, squared his shoulders and spoke in his usual tones. "You driving straight back to the town?"

"Yes."

"I'd like you to drop me at Mrs. Pressley's, if you would.

But not yet. There are one or two matters I want you to arrange for me."

When Bryan left him at Celia's he found her alone. Rona was at the office and Nigel was out with Sigrid, looking at houses.

"Glad you're by yourself," he said. "Want to tell you something. When I realized I couldn't remember anything about a matter as important as that deed of gift, I told myself I was finished. Failing. Now that I know that Todd brought it to the house on the very day, it's no wonder I couldn't—"

"Don't dwell on it, James."

"I've come to the conclusion that it's a kind of protection, not being able to remember. If the mind could recall all the details, one would be living under a perpetual cloud."

"I know. Things are better this way. I'm glad the land is still yours."

"Yes, the land's mine. I've been thinking a lot about it— and about other matters. The truth is, Celia, I've had a jolt. I've been through a bad time since I knew that Francis . . ."

He stopped. She said nothing. She was opening the door of the Chinese cupboard. She took out a bottle of Madeira and two glasses.

"This is for extra-special occasions," she said. "I think we should have some now. You'll join me?"

"Thanks." He took the glass, sipped and nodded with approval. "Good. Very good. Where did you buy it?"

"I didn't. It was a present from Dagmar."

He sat in silence for a time, his gnarled hand on the stem of the delicate glass. Then he spoke.

"I'm going to see young Hayling at his office. I've asked him to attend to some matters for me. I didn't go with him because I wanted to tell you what I was going to do. Don't make the mistake of thinking that I'm doing it because this business with Francis unsettled me. It did, but I've had these matters turning over in my mind for some time. I hope I'll live a good many years yet; my father and my grandfather went on until they were in their nineties, and I don't see why I shouldn't. All the same, I'm going to put my house in order."

She got up to refill his glass.

"Thank you. I'm going," he said, "to live in the lodge."

"To . . . But your lovely house?"

"It's going to be a horticultural college. The gardens will be opened to the public. Brill and his wife are going to look after me at the lodge; the others are going to be given pensions. Except the two gardeners; they'll stay on, but their wages will be paid from the trust I'm creating. I shall go on directing their work as long as I'm able. The land behind this cottage is going to be turned into a nine-hole golf course. The rest . . ." He got stiffly to his feet. "You'll hear about it soon."

"You're not acting—"

"—hastily? No. I know what I'm doing. Would you mind phoning for a taxi?"

She did so.

"I feel better for that Madeira," he told her. "I'll tell Brill to order some and bring me a glass every morning at about this time. Did me good. I'll order a few cases and I'll see you get a bottle or two."

"Thank you, James."

"Why don't you come into town with me? Bryan Hayling said that Rosanna was taking an hour off to go and look at a house for you. Surely you're going with her?"

"Four of us are going—Dagmar, Sigrid, Rona and myself. But it's too early for me to go yet."

"Then I'll leave you. There's the taxi. I'll need you to help me with my move to the lodge. It'll mean selling off a good deal of my furniture. Perhaps there are one or two pieces you'd like to have. Think it over."

She saw him off and walked thoughtfully indoors. It was

sad, she thought, to have money and no children to leave it to. He had no close relations. He would provide for his old age and for his servants, and the rest, she guessed, would go to the trust he was setting up.

She knew that she ought to be feeling pleased by the happy turn that events had taken, but there was still a shadow on her mind: she dreaded the moment when Dagmar would learn that David and Sigrid were planning to leave her.

The house she was going to see this morning was the one which had been converted by Geoffry Steele. Shirley Wallace, for whom the conversion had been done, was going to Canada with her third husband. The ground floor was to be let or sold as business premises; the upper storey was for sale as a private apartment. It was this that she was going to inspect.

When she arrived at the house, Rona and Sigrid and Dagmar were waiting for her.

"I have been inside," Dagmar told her. "I came early on purpose to see it and make my own opinion. It is just what you need. Come and see. Not downstairs; that is of no interest. Upstairs."

The architect had provided access to the upper storey by adding a little round tower and putting into it a circular stone staircase. The four women went up and found themselves in a small hall with doors opening to a large living room, a kitchen and—cleverly set between tower and hall—a miniature cloakroom. Along the south side, the side opposite to the street, ran a balcony which overlooked the park created by Sir James.

"You see how well it is done?" Dagmar pointed out. "A quite separate entrance for you, up the tower staircase. You see there is also this little spiral staircase beside the hall; this was put because Shirley Wallace was going to live above her shop, but if someone wishes only the downstairs, the connecting staircase will of course be taken away. This the house agent told me. You see, Celia, how you could live here and be very comfortable and happy, and you would be near to me, just across the street, and I could come and see you just by coming over. It's all perfect, isn't it?"

Celia found herself agreeing. As could have been expected from the doting Wallace parents, no expense had been spared on fitments. The drawing room had walls with recessed shelves on which she was already picturing her ornaments. The kitchen was fully equipped, a model of careful planning. The two bedrooms had capacious cupboards; the bathroom and the cloakroom were tiled in a cool shade of lemon.

"It's beautifully done." Sigrid spoke with approval. "Celia, you can't let it go. It's exactly what you want, isn't it?"

Celia, who had arranged all her furniture, hung curtains and laid down carpets, returned with a sigh to reality.

"It's lovely," she agreed, "and I'm grateful to you for finding it, but . . . no."

"Why 'no'? Rona asked. "Name one single snag."

"Price. I'm not saying the price is too high. I'm just saying it's too high for me."

"But you like it? You could live here?" Dagmar asked.

"I think it's perfect. But I can't afford it."

"Afford? Afford? You will simply say to Nigel: 'Here is something that you have wanted me to do, to move from that cottage to something more suitable like this, so you must help me to pay for it.' "

"No."

Against the tone of resolute refusal, even Dagmar felt it useless to argue. It was Sigrid who broke the silence.

"We've all seen it; we all like it. Now we can go away and think about it."

"It would be madness to let it go to somebody else," Dagmar declared. "At least let us tell the house agent that we are probably going to take it. Then I shall bring Nigel here. So now let us go. But not that way; let's go down this little curly staircase and go out through downstairs."

They followed one another down the spiral staircase and stood in the room—occupying most of the space on the ground floor—that was to have been the Shirley Wallace Beauty Parlour.

"It's strange," Sigrid observed, "how most artists can't help playing their own signature tune all the time. Painters, composers, writers, you can nearly always recognize the style. But I didn't realize that it went for architects, too. Every building in this town that Geoffry Steele has had anything to do with, whether he designed it or only changed it, has this look: arched windows, low ceilings, pillars. I think it's an almost over-decorated look."

"It is a feminine look," Dagmar said. "That is why I like his work. It is never too plain, never uninteresting."

"I agree with Sigrid about the pillars and the arches," said Celia. "Reminds me of the mosque at Cordoba. On a baby scale, of course."

"But you can see all the same how pretty all the cosmetics would have looked in this setting," Dagmar pointed out. "It is— what word do I want?"

"Sophisticated?" Rona suggested.

"Yes. This"—Dagmar waved a hand at the pillars—"this is a salon. A boutique. You can see at once, when you come in, that it would be a good class of boutique. The dresses— you would put them there and there, to make a good show. There is, if you will come and look, this little room which of course is an office, and over there you have space for the fitting rooms, and there is this lavatory for the customers and another one for the office. Those two big windows looking out into the street are show windows, very pretty with those arches. It is exactly what I said about it: it has got this feminine touch which is so unusual. In this case, he has created a perfect boutique; don't you agree?"

She was standing at one of the windows, and threw the question over her shoulder. After some moments, it was borne upon her that nobody had agreed. Nobody had in fact said anything.

She turned. The silence and the stillness were total. Three

pairs of eyes were fixed on her. On Celia's face there was speculation, on Rona's resolution and on Sigrid's the dawn of hope.

"What are you all staring at?" she demanded.

"We're not staring. We're thinking," Rona answered.

"Dagmar—" Celia began, and stopped.

"Who but you?" Sigrid addressed her mother-in-law. "Who else in all this town but you? You were born to open a boutique. You could—"

"This is nonsense, Sigrid," Dagmar broke in firmly. "Why should we waste any more time here? We shall tell the house agent that—"

"Who else in this town knows what you know about clothes?" Celia was proceeding. "Sigrid's quite right; it's what you were meant to do. You've just shown us how you'd do it. You made us picture it. And you saw it as it could be, you can't deny that. You've laughed at me, very often, because I can see the end when I'm only at the beginning, but you've just seen your boutique."

Rona spoke with a wave of her hand, sketching a shop sign.

"Lovely name for it: *Dagmar's*," she said.

"And not only dresses. Please, Dagmar," Celia pleaded, "not only dresses. Matching accessories too. When I've bought a dress, the hard part begins. Where can I find this to match, that to match? Hours and hours of searching, and in the end giving up. That's why I've never looked finished, like you. I give up half way, and then I look wrong. Please, matching accessories."

"You are all going out of your minds," Dagmar said in disgust. "Do you imagine for one minute that I—"

"No rival establishments," Sigrid pointed out. "Other dresses in other shop windows, yes, but not one shop which stocks the kind of clothes you wear. Where in Longbrook could you find a cute suit like the one you're wearing?"

"At *Dagmar's*," said Rona. "You know *Dagmar's*? You

can't miss it. You just go past Renson's book shop and cross the road, and there it is." Once more she made a flourish. *"Dagmar's!"*

"Very well, enjoy yourselves," Dagmar told them. "Be as silly as you like. And now it is time to go."

"Why should people have to go up to London to buy dresses like yours?" Celia asked. "Why? This isn't a poor town. This is a town full of people with money, a lot of money. And not much taste, because they've got used to dragging up to the London shops, like me, and being so tired when they got there that they bought the first thing they tried on. You could open a boutique—this one—and you could still be near your home and—"

"Ah. My home! I am glad that you have remembered that I have a home. So I am to open this boutique, I am to ruin myself and my son by stocking it with beautiful clothes, for which naturally I would go to Paris, and I am to give up my leisure, I am to leave my home every day and my family, my little grandchildren, to come out every morning, spring and summer, autumn and winter, out into the street and across the road, rain, snow, to open this boutique each day, to stand all the time on my feet with customers, to think all the time of advertisement, accounts, profit, no profit? I am to give up the rest of my life to this?"

"You'll have Saturdays and Sundays free," Rona pointed out.

"At my age, I am to begin a new business, put all my time into it, even Saturdays and Sundays because you do not stop working when your customers have gone; I am to build up another Renson business? I am to do this? It is absurd, fantastic, a silly joke. That I am a person who knows about clothes—this it would be silly to deny. That I could educate these women in this town, who do not know how to make themselves look *chic*, this also is true. But I have to think of my health, my duties to my family."

"You're as strong as a horse, and you've done your duty to

your family," said Celia. "Could matching accessories include shoes? Hours and hours I've spent, trying to get shoes to match a new coat. Think of—"

"You are crazy. All of you, crazy," said Dagmar passionately. What do any of you know about what would be necessary, what I would have to do? I would have to make the fitting rooms. I would have to put furniture into the office. I would have to arrange showcases for your matching accessories, as well as curtains, carpets, good carpets because that is what makes the style, the tone of a good shop. There would be decorations, and naturally I would have to have perfumery on glass shelves over there, and dresses—casual, formal, this season, next season, coats, suits, hanging behind glass doors— do you know what all that would cost? A fortune. Do you realize that I would have to work just like a slave, planning, preparing, engaging people to make alterations, trying to be in Paris and in the boutique at the same time, killing myself with work in the office and then coming out with a smile to receive customers? Do you understand that to do this, I would have to leave Inga and Claudine to manage alone, I would have to leave Sigrid without my help with the children, only two now but certainly more to come? It is impossible, quite impossible, as well as silly. To speak like this about it, all right. But to carry out this, I tell you it is impossible. Quite impossible. Impossible, impossible, absolutely impossible."

She stopped to take breath. Nobody moved. Nobody spoke.

"Impossible," she repeated. "But naturally, I am going to do it."

CHAPTER

14

IT WAS NIGEL WHO BOUGHT THE HOUSE, OVERRIDING FIERCE protest from Dagmar and milder opposition from David.

"It is for me to buy it," Dagmar told him. "Then I will ask your mother for rent for upstairs."

"I'm going to buy it," he answered, "and I'm going to ask you for rent for downstairs."

"But you have ordered that the little inside staircase shall be taken away. Why? How shall I get up quickly to your mother when I wish to talk to her?"

"You can't talk to her, or you shouldn't be able to talk to her, during shop hours. After shop hours, you'll have to use the entrance that all her other visitors use. Any other objections?"

"Yes. You have told the builders that I cannot have a big light over my name in the front of the shop. Why is this?"

"Because it would shine just under my mother's bedroom window and keep her awake at night. The Dagmar sign will look far more effective done in subdued lighting."

"And you have also said that my customers may not park their cars in the side entrance. So where shall they park?"

"The side entrance belongs to the upper storey, and therefore to my mother. It's going to be made beautiful with a long wall with roses growing up it. Your customers will leave their cars where everybody else has to leave their cars: in the municipal car park."

"And if it is raining, snowing, they must walk back to my shop?"

"The whole six hundred yards; yes. Anything else?"

"No. But you are behaving very strangely."

"I'm behaving like a landlord. All landlords make conditions, and all tenants have to stick to the conditions. Incidentally, I met the editor of our esteemed local paper. He wants to know if you'll take a whole page to advertise the opening of the shop."

"Of course, a full page. What does he think? Two lines where nobody will think to look? This shop, which you think is only for this town, will soon be known to everybody, people far from here. It is going to be a big success. I am going to make a lot of money with it."

"I'm glad. You'll need it. The rent's going to be quite steep."

With his mother, who shared Dagmar's unwillingness to have the spiral staircase connecting the upper and lower storeys removed, he was as firm as he had been with Dagmar.

"No. No connecting staircase," he said over tea the next day. "She'll be too busy to use it for the first two months, but once the shop gets going, she'll be skipping up half a dozen times a day."

"Well, why not? If she wants to see me, and she hasn't a short cut, she'll have to go outside and use the other entrance."

"So she won't use it when it's raining or snowing or when it's cold and windy. I'm trying to protect you."

"I know. From her. You've never understood that I don't

find her as irritating or as domineering as you do. I can deal with her."

"You could deal with her by going into your own little hole when she drove you too far. You could leave her, come home and haul up the drawbridge. If you were living over her shop and she could get at you every time she wanted to, she'd drive you crazy. So no spiral staircase."

"No spiral staircase. Now that you've got that settled, why don't you attend to your own affairs? You haven't got the furniture arranged in that flat of yours yet."

"No hurry. Rona and I will do it this weekend. Or next. There's still one more thing to settle."

"Yes. Putting up this cottage for sale. The house agent was asking me about it."

"Chan's cousin?"

"Yes. He thinks he's got a possible buyer.

"Someone who's keen on brass bands, I hope. I'll go and see him tomorrow and talk about the sale price. He ought to— Damn."

They had heard the sound of the Reverend's motorbike. Nigel went reluctantly to the door, and his mother set about making fresh tea. She set out two cups, but she found that the Reverend had not brought his sister on this occasion.

"Do come in and sit down," she invited. "You haven't brought Monica?"

"No. No, no." The words were spoken breathlessly. "She's —she isn't very well."

They looked at him anxiously. His face was flushed. He seemed to have difficulty in enunciating. Nigel pushed a chair close to him.

"Sit down, Reverend."

"Thank you, thank you." He sat down and immediately stood up again. "I mustn't stay. I really mustn't stay."

"Is your sister ill?" Celia asked.

"Oh, yes. Well, no. Not as you might say ill. But upset. Very. She's praying."

"Praying?"

"Yes. You see, that was the first thing we knew we had to do: pray. Though to tell you the truth—I do hope you won't think this odd—what I really wanted to do was sing. The spoken prayer didn't seem to me to be enough. 'Oh come let us sing unto the Lord'—yes, that was how I felt, how I feel. 'Sing to the Lord with cheerful voice.' I wanted my prayers, her prayers, to go aloft on wings of song. Prayer and praise." He caught one of Celia's hands in his own. "Do you know what I said when they told me? I said, '*Auditis an me ludit amabilis insania.*' "

"Who told you what?" Celia asked.

"The lawyers. They told me. Told us. It would have been better if they had told me alone; I could have broken the news more gently to my dear sister. It was too much for her. But she will recover and she will come to believe it fully, as I have done, as I am doing."

Celia had poured out a cup of tea for him. He lifted the cup, drained it and resumed.

"Thank you, no tea. I only came to tell you the glorious news. I wanted you to be among the first to know. Do you remember the lines I quoted to you once in this room? Those beautiful lines:

> But if He bless and keep you He will bring
> Gifts that shall beggar all our reckoning.

Ah, how true!"

"You haven't explained," Celia began gently, "why—"

"I cannot explain. I am overwhelmed by this gift, Mrs. Pressley. You will know what it is. He is your friend, he will have told you. I am not to thank him personally, the lawyers said; he wants no thanks from me. He is right to refuse them, because this gift is not given to me, but to God's house, to the glory of God. We shall live, I pray God, to see our beautiful church in all its former beauty. People will come from far and near to see it and seeing it, they will stay to pray.

And now I must go back to my sister."

He was hurrying to the door. It opened from outside, and Rona stepped aside to allow him to pass. He paused to press her hands, but tears were pouring down his cheeks, and he could say nothing.

Nigel saw him off and returned to the living room.

"It's money from Sir James. It must be," Celia said.

"But didn't he tell you? Isn't that what he came for?" Rona asked in surprise.

"I think so. But it was all terribly muddled. And Latin. What was that Latin bit, Nigel?"

" 'Or is it a delightful madness that makes sport of me.' He's got his money for the church?" he asked Rona.

"Yes. From Sir James. It's part of a trust which is to be administered by three trustees. Bryan's one of them. Nigel's going to be asked to be the second, and the third isn't chosen yet but might possibly be David. I suppose you already know that this land's going to be a nine-hole golf course?"

"Yes. I wonder if Sugden plays golf?" Nigel mused. "I'd like to—"

He stopped. Someone was tapping on the window. When Celia, who was nearest, opened it, she saw Chan, and was struck by the fact that he looked even more enormous with only his upper half framed in the opening than he did when the whole of him was visible.

"Why don't you come in?" she asked him.

"Been hanging round waiting for the Reverend to push off," he said. "He came to tell you the glad tidings, didn't he?"

"Yes. Come in and sit down," Nigel invited.

"No. Got to go. They're saying the Reverend won't live to see the beginning of this restoration, let alone the end—unless he simmers down."

"You look as though you could do some simmering-down yourself," Nigel commented. "What's exciting you?"

"This and that. You've heard what's going to be done with this land?"

"Yes. I wish I knew how news gets round so fast," Rona said. "It was only released an hour or so ago."

"Bush telegraph. Nine-hole golf course, yes?"

"Yes."

"Good. That'll dish Sugden and his brother crooks for all time. What I'm excited about is this proposition Seth Daly's just made."

"Who's Seth Daly?" Nigel asked.

"You ought to know who he is. Solo trombonist. Black chap; one of the three black chaps in the band. He's the little thin one, looks nothing till he starts blowing, and then you realize how big he is. He heard this cottage was up for sale and—"

"Second sight?" Nigel enquired.

"Well, Bert's been putting two and two together, and he said this place would be coming on the market. So Seth told his mum and dad. You know them?"

"No."

"I know them," Rona said. "They run a snack bar behind the cinema."

"That's right. Well, they want somewhere to live. At least, Mrs. Daly does. She says she's never had a real home, only a back room. They think they can get a mortgage and buy this place and live in it and keep on the snack bar until they find out whether they could run one here. They'd have the band to feed, for a start, and then maybe they'd get some tired golfers coming in, and that way they'd get known. Seth and I were talking, and we thought one day we might knock down the fence in between the two cottages, and have the barn made into a proper concert room. We need a base, and we wouldn't have to ask Sugden to help us with the building; me and the boys could make a good job of it. The only snag's the mortgage, but if the band's as popular as I think it is, we ought to be able to pull a few strings. So if I'm excited, that's why. I'm going to get the boys together and tell them. If you thought we made too much noise blowing before, just think what we'll sound like from now on. 'Bye. Thought you'd like to know about it."

He went away—skipped away, Celia thought, wondering if so huge a bulk could be said to skip. She closed the window.

"I feel like celebrating," Nigel said. "How about a nice, quiet, simple, astronomically expensive dinner somewhere?"

"I can't," Celia said. "I'm going to dine with Dagmar. Why don't you ask David and Sigrid? They probably feel like celebrating, too. Dagmar forgot to supervise Arthur's dinner today."

"The shape of things to come," Nigel said. "But Rona and I will keep this outing a twosome, I think."

Something in his tone brought his mother's eyes to rest on him in surprise. The surprise turned to speculation. But she made no comment.

"Go ahead and tell her," Rona said. "But as a dead secret."

"Tell me what?" Celia asked.

"Don't ask him. Ask me," Rona said. "You see, there were these two trains coming into Waterloo, or Charing Cross, and one got in front of the other, and then— Well, to cut a long journey short, we're in love."

"You're—you're what?"

"You heard," Nigel said. "But perhaps you ought to sit down and take it in slowly. Here."

Celia ignored the chair.

"You wouldn't," she asked slowly, "be so cruel as to—to joke about a thing like this?"

"She would. I wouldn't. I give you my solemn assurance that I'm going to make her your daughter-in-law."

"You mean you—"

"Now you've made her howl," Rona said. "What with the Reverend and his money, and us and—"

"I'm not howling. I just—"

"I know how you feel," Rona told her sympathetically. "You saw what a brute he was to me when I was younger, and you're worried on my account. But you needn't be. I can fix him."

"When?" Celia asked shakily. "I mean when—how—"

"It just happened," said Nigel.